WHITE LIES

WHITE LIES

The true story of Clarence Brandley, presumed guilty in the American South.

NICK DAVIES

Chatto & Windus
LONDON

Published in 1991 by
Chatto & Windus Ltd
20 Vauxhall Bridge Road
London SW1V 2SA

A CIP catalogue record for this book is
available from the British Library

ISBN 0 7011 3724 X

The lines from 'Strange Fruit', by Lewis Allan, are
reprinted by permission of Carlin Music.

Photoset by
Input Typesetting Ltd
Wimbledon
Printed in Great Britain by
Mackays of Chatham plc
Chatham, Kent

For Sheridan

Prologue

This is a true story. When I started work on it in the autumn of 1987, I intended to write a short feature for a magazine in London and assumed I would be finished within a week. Instead, the story took over my life for the next two-and-a-half years. One of the reasons for this was that by the time I arrived on the scene, many of the details of the story had already been exposed in extraordinary detail by the efforts of attorneys and private investigators who had invested thousands of man-hours in attempting to discover the truth. While I had imagined that I was working on a simple story about one man's fight for justice, their work showed that this was really the story of a whole community and of the survival of a way of life which I, at least, had been happy to assume was dead. The more I looked the more I found, and so I became embroiled.

The hard work which had been invested by the attorneys and the investigators had a more fundamental importance. Even though some of the central characters were still trying to smother the truth in lies and confusion, the facts which they had uncovered now emerged with such force that even the courts of Texas, which had resisted them in the past, were compelled to accept them. This, in turn, gave me the chance to reconstruct the whole story with unusual accuracy and confidence. The times, dates, places and events were all now matters of record. Where I wanted to reproduce dialogue, I was often able to work from sound or video recordings made by the attorneys and their investigators, or from the transcripts of court hearings. Many of the people in the story were inspiringly generous with their time (the first time I sat down to talk with Don Brown, it was 11 hours before we got up) and these interviews gave me the raw material for the thoughts of characters and occasionally also for their dialogue. With all this support, I was able to set out to produce a narrative which would be accurate in all its detail. If I have succeeded, it is largely due to the hard work of these people.

Clarence Brandley, who has through his unusual experiences become an unusually philosophical man, urged me to see that the people of Montgomery County are not all bad. He is, of course, right and, while working in the county, I was treated with great courtesy and kindness even, oddly, by those who have at other times been willing to behave with terrible cruelty. Brandley also wanted me to thank the people of the county who have fought so courageously for him against such awesome opposition and I, too, in my less significant role, would like to add my gratitude to all those who were brave enough to tell the truth.

N.D.
London

Part One
Strange Fruit

Southern trees bear a strange fruit
Blood on the leaf and blood at the root
Black bodies swinging in the southern breeze
Strange fruit hanging in the poplar trees

First sung in 1939 by Billie Holiday

I

Conroe is the kind of town that strangers never notice. From a distance it is no different to the last town they passed, just the usual muddle of power lines and road signs, a glimpse of rooftops and railway tracks. Conroe squats on the edge of the Sam Houston National Forest about 40 miles north of Houston City just after Interstate 45 crosses the San Jacinto River on its way up to Dallas, but to a stranger's eye it could be any town on the edge of any freeway. Even those who, for some reason, leave I-45 where it bends to the west, and take the northward fork up Frazier Street and into the centre of Conroe, find little to distinguish it: gas stations, shopping malls, billboards lining the road like beggars in a bazaar – 'Krispy Chicken – eight pieces for $3.89 . . . A bigger deal at the new Burger King . . . Feed and Farm Supplies . . . Beer and Bar BQ and Bait . . .'.

Half-way through the town, Frazier Street is crossed by Route 105 which runs from east to west so that the two roads form a crucifix, dividing Conroe into four quarters. The crucifix is shadowed by railways, the Missouri Pacific running north and the old Santa Fe Railway cutting across it. At the centre of the crucifix is the courthouse square, the town's heart, where the scene is just as familiar. There is Scotts Pharmacy with the chipped and fading sign outside; the Casey Jones Bar BQ with its rows of empty seats; Nita's Beauty Shop ('walk-ins welcome'); the Capitol Drug Store with a handwritten sign offering 'Valentine Candy, 60% off'; a restaurant where the grubby window bristles with credit card signs – Visa, Amex, Texas Restaurant Association, Carte Blanche – and a notice which says it is closed for good. There are usually a few pick-up trucks with men in baseball caps sprawling spread-legged in the back, and a couple of old Fords with rusting

3

dents sitting soaking up the heat outside Montgomery County courthouse.

The courthouse is the only building that might catch a stranger's eye: a squat, square, five-storied block of brickwork with flags flying on its roof and janitors spiking scraps of trash from its grass. Its featureless walls shine as bright as a whited sepulchre. It is not only the self-evident pride of the building which marks it out from its humbler neighbours but also the air of business which surrounds it. The rest of the courthouse square – the old Crighton Theater as well as the restaurants and stores – have been more or less deserted in favour of brash new shopping malls with names like U Save and Crossroads which were built out by I–45 in the 1970s, but the courthouse is still a thriving place. White men in shirtsleeves talk earnestly on the steps; deputy sheriffs with holsters jiggling on their hips keep pushing through the double doors. On the top floor, the holding cells are usually packed with prisoners from all over Montgomery County. On the lower floors, five district judges dispense justice. Yet this, too, is really nothing special, just another courthouse in a small town.

There was a brief period in the 1930s when Conroe was raised from normality after a geologist named George Strake struck oil just outside the town and Montgomery County was suddenly the biggest oil-producing area in Texas. They called Conroe 'The Miracle City'. It had more millionaires per head than any other town in the United States. Families who had been land poor, who had been scratching 25 or 50 cents out of an acre and bartering bushels of peas for a pair of shoes, suddenly found that their barren land was floating on liquid money. Thousands of itinerant workers, pushed south by the depression, descended on the town to share the spoils. Oil-rich families tried to polish up the town to match their new status. That was when they built the gleaming white courthouse so they no longer needed to hold prisoners on a chain strung between two trees, and when they put up the theatre which they decked out like a Venetian garden, with an Italian ceramic tile floor and Grecian garden scenes on the ceiling. They also started a country club with a golf course. But the boom faded, pigeons infested the new theatre, wild hogs got through the fence on to the golf course and Conroe subsided into peaceful indifference again.

There, as far as a stranger can tell, the town still rests. Its couple of thousand old-time residents keep cattle and horses, and sell timber and creosote. They have been slowly outnumbered over the years by newcomers from Houston and the north, who have built high-priced new satellite communities with names like Village Hill and Willow Ridge out on the edge of town. There is a bottling plant for Pepsi-cola and a factory where they make reinforced elevators to move nuclear warheads about in submarines. There are new roads and a small airport, two new fire stations and a new sewage plant. It is, in all appearances, a peaceful, plump little town, just like a thousand others, entirely devoted to its own obscurity.

The events which finally betrayed the truth about Conroe began one hot, sticky Saturday in the summer of 1980 when the lives of two people who had never even heard of each other crossed and became ruined.

One of them was Clarence Lee Brandley, then aged 28, a stocky, round-faced black man with a cheerful, easygoing disposition. He liked to wear his hair a little too long and when he shaved he carefully preserved a thin black moustache running down either side of his chin. In August 1980, Brandley was living in a small apartment in a housing project in the south-east quadrant of Conroe and working as a janitor in the high school on the other side of town. He had been married, but had separated from his wife and left her and his five children in Houston. He lived alone unless his girlfriend Beverley was visiting.

This particular morning, Brandley was not feeling too good. He was tired, his head hurt and he needed a smoke. The last thing he wanted was to go up to the high school and spend the day working, moving chairs and picking up other people's rubbish, especially on a Saturday. All he really wanted to do was to fall back into bed with Beverley. She was lying there now, all warm and soft, telling him not to go to work today and just stay in bed with her. But he had to go.

School was starting in ten days' time. There was a lot of work to be done and he was determined to do it. This job meant a lot to him; not that it was the best job in the world. He had had better down in Houston, working for the light company and driving the Metro buses. But it was a steady job and a steady life and he had made up his mind that if he was ever going to settle down, he had to keep this damned job. That was why he had left Houston – to get out of the fast lane and get away from the fast life he had been living there. The money here was OK, better since he had been promoted a few weeks back to be supervisor of the other janitors at the school. It was the best he was going to get, in a town like Conroe. He stripped off and headed for the shower, calling back: 'Beverley, you gonna have to give me a ride.'

Under the spray of water, he rubbed the tiredness out of his eyes. It had been a rough night. He knew he should have stayed in with Beverley, but he had gone out drinking in one of the juke joints and started playing dice and, before he had known it, the whole night was gone and most of his week's money, too. He was not going to do that again. He had had enough of spinning his wheels, living for just one day at a time and burning up his money. And there was something else – his eldest son, Clarence jr.

He had talked to his wife and she had agreed that if he could settle down and earn enough money, Clarence jr. could come and live with him. He wanted that badly. So apart from working up at the high school he was putting in part-time work at a gas station as well as down the road at Oscar Johnson's funeral parlour looking after the mourners, who seemed to like him. People had always said he had a friendly way with him.

Brandley reckoned he had been doing OK since he came back to Conroe. He had been going to work every day, he hadn't had any trouble with anyone and he had already put aside some money. And he had been looking for a school for the boy. It was plain dumb to go and blow a whole week's money on dice like that. This was a new life he was making here. In this town. In his part of this town.

Ten minutes later, Brandley was in his worn blue jeans and white T-shirt, sitting next to Beverley while she headed her old Mercury out of the shade of the housing project and bounced over the pot-holes into the sun on South Seventh Street. None of the

6

roads in this part of town had regular names. It was different on the other side of Conroe, where they had Shady Oaks Drive and Cochran Street and all sorts of names which referred to people who had lived there or places they wanted to remember. Not here. They did not even call this place Conroe: they called it Dugan. On the maps, it was part of Conroe. For the postman it was part of Conroe. But for everybody who lived in Conroe it was Dugan. Nobody even remembered where the name came from, but everybody knew what it meant if a person came from Dugan.

Brandley looked out of the window and wished he had a cigarette. He looked at the wooden houses with their peeling paint, the windows patched with plastic sheets, the roofs of rusting corrugated iron, the old people sitting silent in the shade, the dogs and children playing in the dirt. Beverley turned right into Avenue E, past the shack where he and most of his brothers and sisters had been born in the front room and where his mother, Minnie Ola, still lived, past the rotting brown shed where his aunt lived in a single room with the clothes drying on a line over the bed and the rain always finding its way through the roof. She kept a magazine page pinned to the bare wooden wall, at the head of the bed where a crucifix might have hung, with the face of Martin Luther King gazing down from it.

Then the shacks thinned out until there were only a few hiding behind the trees, as if they were not quite sure whether they should show themselves at the main road. The last one was a battered yellow cabin with a rain-stained roof and a sign tacked on the front that said Jeanne's Beauty Salon. They had come to the railway track.

Beverley slowed down and the old Mercury tripped over the lines. The sign said: 'State Law – Observe Warning Signs'. Beverley turned left and drove down Route 105 towards the centre of town. She drove carefully. She didn't want any trouble. It was 7.15 a.m. on 23 August, 1980.

The stranger whose life was to cross that of Clarence Brandley was a 16-year-old schoolgirl with blonde hair and blue eyes named Cheryl Fergeson. She was tall and slim, and people always said she was pretty. She lived with her father. Her mother had died of cancer a year earlier. Her brothers had grown up and found their own homes in Houston. Apart from her Siamese cat Crook, with the bent tail, she lived alone with her father and looked after him on the ranch at Kenney, ten miles outside Bellville.

Cheryl was always busy with one thing or another. She liked drawing and painting and she had just finished designing a large mural at Bellville High School all about sport, with pictures of different team mascots and a slogan which said in big letters: 'Get with the spirit'. She worked on the school paper taking photographs, and she had been to a seminar at the University of Texas about journalism and photography. But more than anything, she liked roller skating – she spent every spare minute at the Rolling Oaks rink in Bellville. She even had a part-time job there so that she could earn some pocket-money and skate with her girlfriends and with Frank, too. She was going to marry Frank when they had finished school.

Cheryl liked to wear western-style clothes like her father, who used to ride the rodeos. She often wore boots of cowhide or suede, blue jeans slung low at the waist and a heavy leather belt with an ornate iron buckle. Across the back, her name was stamped into the leather in big letters, CHERYL. Around her neck she always wore a delicate gold chain with a crucifix.

Right now, Cheryl Fergeson was in a hurry. She had got up early, eaten breakfast on the run and left home without having a chance to say goodbye to her father so that she could be at the high school on the edge of Bellville by 7.15 a.m., in time to catch the bus for the volleyball tournament. She had only been manager of the volleyball team for two weeks and she was keen to do well, so she was right on time.

Cheryl parked the big blue and white Chevy Blazer round the back of the school, grabbed her purse, her pillow, her scorebook and her red bag full of volleyballs, and ran across to where half-a-dozen other girls were standing round in their grey tracksuits waiting for Susan Norris, the volleyball coach, to arrive with the big yellow school bus. But Mrs Norris was late. When she finally turned up, apologizing and explaining that she had had trouble getting the engine started, they realized that there was still one girl missing from the team – Dierdra. She had overslept and, by the time she arrived, they were even later leaving. It was 8.10 a.m. when Mrs Norris finally started up the bus and set off with a plume of black smoke in her wake, for the tournament, 60 miles to the north-east at a high school where they had not played before, in a town called Conroe.

Beverley pushed the old Mercury along Route 105, past the railway intersection where the freight trains crooned, past the pawn shop ('We pay cash for almost anything'), past the white slab outline of the county courthouse in the centre of town, across Frazier Street – driving slowly near the pick-up trucks with the bumper stickers which said 'I'm OK. You're the shithead' and 'Don't Mess with Texas' – through the shopping malls and out to the western edge of town where the high school lay, Conroe's most precious jewel.

With the long, low redbrick high school on her right, Beverley slowed down and turned into the side road at the far end of the main building. She stopped between the end of the school and the new vocational building, in the area where the students waited for their buses every afternoon. The other four janitors had already arrived.

Brandley could see Icky Peace perched behind the wheel of his battered green Chevrolet, like a pudding on a plate. Icky was very short, about 4' 10", and very fat, probably 12 stone, and he had a voice like a little girl, pure and high-pitched. He wore thick glasses, he could neither read nor write, he had false teeth which he pulled out when he ate, and he claimed to have diabetes. He was in his late 30s, still unmarried and, so far as Brandley knew, he had never even had a girlfriend. He had lived with his mother until she died and now he lived with his sister in Cleveland, 30 miles east of Conroe. It was his sister who had nicknamed him Icky, after the noise he made when he was a baby. His real name was Henry Martin Peace jr., but that never suited him. So he was Icky. Brandley had never met anyone quite so strange as Icky Peace, but he liked him.

When he had first become supervisor a few weeks earlier, Brandley had had a little trouble with some of the other janitors who were not too happy to work for him. But Peace had never given him any problems. He just got on and did as he was told, and when he did well he was proud of himself, like a child. But Brandley had discovered that, in spite of some strange habits, Peace was not nearly as dumb or as innocent as he made himself out to be.

As Beverley drove off, Brandley waved to the little fat janitor. 'All right, Icky?'

Peace bounced out of the Chevrolet, rubbing his hands and ready for work. 'Mornin', Clarence,' he piped.

Brandley nodded towards the other three, who were sitting together in the shade of the bus shelter. They didn't bother to reply, but got up, flipped their cigarette ends into the road and started strolling slowly over to the school doors.

Gary Acreman was the last to move, his hands jammed into his pockets as he walked, sneering as usual. He was tall and thin, like a slice of a normal man, just turned 21, with reddish brown hair and a face like a fox – long, thin snout and small, dark eyes. Acreman had only been at the high school for two months, but Brandley had already learned to beware of him. Brandley had tried to treat him right, had even bought him food when he turned up without money one day, but there was something sly about the man that he didn't trust. He was always wise-cracking and mouthing off about something. Brandley knew his type.

Brandley stood with his back to the vocational building, fished the fat bunch of keys out of his back pocket and unlocked the door at the end of the main school building.

'OK,' he said. 'Let's get to work.'

'Man, this had better be worth it.' It was Acreman. 'I ain't coming in on no Saturday just for some one hour's pay.'

'Y'all can leave it to me,' said Brandley. 'We'll take it easy. There ain't so much to do. We'll work till round noon and I'll put y'all down for a full day. Just take it nice and easy.'

As he opened the door, Brandley could smell the drink on John Sessum's breath. Sessum had been drinking for years and he carried a thick scar across his right temple as a reminder of some long-forgotten bar where a fight had got out of hand. He was always dirty and dishevelled and usually quiet, sunk in some private misery, or just plain drunk. He was originally from Mississippi

but he had been in East Texas for years now, drinking and dragging himself from one dumb job to another. Brandley did not
know him very well. He did not normally work at the high school
but he had been called in for this Saturday job because the other
regular high school janitors were not interested in working over-
time. He lived to the east of town, in a little bunch of shacks and
trailers called Cut and Shoot. Brandley had never been out there:
he knew he would not be welcome.

Icky Peace and Gary Acreman followed with Sam Martinez, a
young Mexican with bushy black mutton-chop sideboards and a
frizz of curly dark hair. Martinez had also been called in from
another school to help out. He was married to a woman who lived
in Dugan and seemed like a straight guy to Brandley. He was
pretty quiet. He came to work, he did his job, he took his pay
and went home.

The five men set off down the main hallway which ran like a
spine through the school, with different rooms on each side like
ribs. First on the right was the teachers' lounge. That was going
to have to be cleaned up. Opposite, on the left, was the little
janitor's office. That was where Brandley was headed the first
chance he got: he was going to buy some cigarettes and take some
time out in there to try and wake himself up.

Some 20 feet further on, Brandley stopped at the edge of the
main lobby, which opened up to his right and led to the big
parking lot on Route 105. The lobby was dominated by a large
glass case containing a stuffed tiger, the high school mascot. Right
now, the lobby was also cluttered with folded tables and orange
plastic chairs, all stacked in piles.

The hallway stretched on in front of him, right through the
school, with the cafeteria on the left and the big auditorium
opposite it. In the distance, at the end of the auditorium, he could
see the characters from Sesame Street painted on the wall next to
the restrooms and beyond that the sports area, where the gymnasiums and dressing-rooms were.

There was work to be done with all these tables and chairs lying
around in the lobby. Brandley reached for his bundle of keys,
walked down a short flight of steps to his left and let the others
in at the end of the cafeteria. He told them how he wanted the

tables and chairs to be laid out in rows. There was to be a big
meeting on Monday, all the teachers in the Conroe School District
getting together to prepare for the new term. Everything had to
be set up ready for them. Brandley started moving some chairs
himself so that they would understand what he was talking about.
He went off and found a two-wheeled trolley to help them.

Acreman shook his head and leaned against the back wall of the
cafeteria with his arms folded, while drunken John Sessum and
Sam Martinez started to walk laboriously to the lobby to get some
chairs for themselves. Brandley told Peace to come with him and
he and the little pear-shaped janitor returned through the lobby
toward the teachers' lounge; but they were still within earshot
when one of the others spoke.

'Goddam nigger. He can kiss my ass.'

The yellow school bus ploughed along the backroads, through
Hempstead and Magnolia and on to Interstate 45. Mrs Norris did
not want to be late. She pushed northwards as fast as she dared.

A few seats behind her Cheryl Fergeson sat quietly reading,
curled up on the pillow she had brought with her. Bright sun beat
on the windows. Endless days of heat had laid waste to the land.
Fruit withered on the vines, lawns lay like brown blankets, wood-
land was burnt black, fields were scorched from fires kindled by
sparks from passing trains. Everything was brittle and dead.

Cheryl read her book. The bus pressed on into Conroe, past
new stores and supermarkets and hypermarkets, past Tudor-style
homes with central air-conditioning and private swimming pools,
past the Safeway where members of the Republican's Women's
Club were holding their white elephant garage sale, past the aud-
itions for the Conroe Chorale and the Conroe ballroom where
the Southbound Country and Western Band were rehearsing for
the evening's entertainment, and past the Lincoln Continentals
and the Buick station wagons with their bumper stickers – 'Jesus
is my special friend' and 'Christians for Ronald Reagan'.

The yellow bus swung off I-45, mounted the slope of Route
105, and travelled west towards the high school. Susan Norris saw
other buses lined up in the big car park in front of the school and

she joined them. As soon as she stopped she checked her watch. She had wanted to be there by nine.

'We're late,' she told the girls. 'Nearly ten minutes. Still, I guess it could have been worse. Let's hurry on now.'

The seven volleyball players climbed out of the bus and into the sticky heat. Cheryl came last, carrying the big red bag full of balls, the scorebook and her purse. She made sure the bus door was shut. They headed off to their right and found a gym door open. Inside, the room was filled with the sound of shouts and gym shoes squeaking on the polished floor. The tournament had started. They hurried to find a dressing-room.

Brandley started to work slowly through his routine. Rubbish bins; toilet rolls; locks and keys. He felt dog-tired and was more or less sleep-walking, but he was determined to do this damned job the way it should be done.

He took Icky Peace back down to the beginning of the hallway to the teachers' lounge and showed him how he wanted the floor cleaned up: how to stack all the furniture by the walls and mop the wooden floor with soap and water, then how to mix wax with water and spray that on; finally, how to use the big electric buffer to polish it all until it shone. He helped Peace to haul the buffer out of the closet and into the lounge. He told him: 'I know you going to make a real good job of this, Icky.'

The little janitor rolled up his sleeves and got down to work. Brandley set off to get his cigarettes. It must have been about 8.30. There was not too much to do and there was plenty of time to get round to it. It was just another day; it was no big deal.

Brandley walked down between the cafeteria on the left, where he could see Acreman and Sessum and Martinez slowly laying out the chairs, and the auditorium on the right, which was all locked up, then past the Sesame Street mural where the restrooms were up on a landing. He climbed the steps, checked the boys' restroom and made a mental note to bring some toilet paper later. He would have to find someone to check the girls' room for him.

He walked on towards the gymnasiums and was surprised to find some white woman trying to prop open the big swing doors at the end of the hallway with a rubbish bin. That was the first time he found out that there was supposed to be a volleyball tournament in the school that day. The white woman turned out to be one of the volleyball coaches from Conroe High and she told him there were eight teams going to be playing here today, but she had to get these doors to stay open. He lent her his wrench and showed her how to fasten it to the crash bar so that the door no longer automatically locked itself. This end of the school turned out to be full of people. A girl in a tracksuit came past and he asked her to go down and look in the girls' restrooms there by Sesame Street to see if they needed paper. He never liked to go in the girls' rooms himself. By the time he had finished putting his wrench on the door, she was back to tell him he didn't have to worry about the paper down there.

It was 8.45 a.m. He was desperate for a cigarette, but if there was going to be a tournament he had to get busy. He would have to unlock all the doors to the gymnasiums – they were using the boys' gym as well as the girls' – and make sure the right restrooms were open, as well as doing all his regular duties. The cigarettes were going to have to wait for a while.

He shuffled quietly from one job to the next, wondering how Beverley was, worrying about Clarence jr., fixing rubbish bins and toilet rolls. He unlocked the restrooms in the dressing-room, where he guessed these volleyball teams would be changing. He locked the restrooms by the public gallery in the gym. The white lady had opened them with her own key but he didn't want them all messed up. There were already some girls going inside when he got up there. He grinned at them. 'You better be out quick, or I'll lock you in.'

It was ten past nine before he finally finished and walked out of the building towards town and down to the Shamrock gas station on Route 105 to buy a pack of Kools.

Cheryl Fergeson hurried through the gym, following the seven team players in their grey tracksuits which said Bellville Girls Athletics in bright red letters. As manager, she did not have to wear a tracksuit. She could wear a shirt and her regular Western-style blue jeans and cowboy belt, though she was wearing sneakers instead of her normal boots. They were late. All the space in the dressing-room was taken so they had to leave their belongings in the corner of a little warm-up gym where there was no restroom.

Mrs Norris told the girls to loosen up, start doing some stretching exercises and throwing a ball around. It was going to be at least thirty minutes before they played their first game. Mrs Norris went off to find the Conroe High coach, to check on the playing schedule.

Cheryl dropped her red bag full of volleyballs and her score-book and her purse on the floor of the warm-up gym. There was just time to find a restroom before she got busy, setting up the game with Mrs Norris and then keeping the score.

She walked out into the hallway. First, she turned towards the dressing-room, where the other teams had changed, but the door was closed and there was no sign to tell her that there was a restroom in there. If Cheryl Fergeson and her team had not arrived late, she would have been inside that dressing-room and she would have seen that there was a restroom there, but as it was, she turned and walked away, away from the gyms and away from her friends, down the long, empty hallway.

A minute later, Mrs Norris was back in the warm-up gym. She needed her team manager.

'Where's Cheryl?' she asked. 'Anyone seen Cheryl?'

Nobody had.

It was 9.15 a.m. on 23 August 1980.

Clarence Brandley wandered slowly down to the Shamrock Station, feeling the heat of the day warming his shoulders. He never felt good in this part of town. Ever since he could remember, it had been like that. When he was a little boy, his grandma used to bring him across the railway tracks to go shopping downtown near the courthouse. She always told him he had to be on his best behaviour so as not to antagonize any of the white people who lived there.

So he had learned how to address white people – respectfully, standing a yard or two back so they didn't think he was trying to touch them – with his head bowed and his hand raised, waiting for permission to speak.

It was nothing he had ever felt mad about; it was just a fact of life. Like when he used to go downtown to see movies at the Crighton Theater, he would always go straight upstairs to the black seats and he never hung around downstairs where the white kids were. Or when they used to go to the old McGee Hotel to get a hamburger, they had to enter by the side door right next to the kitchen, while the white kids went in the front and sat down.

It was just a fact of life, though sometimes it hurt. His brother, O.T., had got into trouble once when he had gone to a white lady's house where their mother, Minnie Ola, was working as a maid. O.T. hadn't known any better so he went right up and knocked on the front door. That white lady looked at him with her eyes so hard, and their mother had warned them they must never go to the front door again or she could lose her job.

Another time, Minnie Ola was working in one of the restaurants downtown, near the courthouse. It was at the time of integration, and when some black people came to eat in the restaurant Minnie Ola felt proud, but it hurt her heart when they smashed the plates the black people had eaten off so white people would never have to share them.

It was a fact of life for anyone who lived in Dugan. It had always been that way, as long as anyone there could remember. They all knew the stories, the bad things that happened to people who got out of line. And often enough they happened to people even if they did not step out of line. Like the black man who had lived in Montgomery, the old county capital 15 miles north-west of Conroe. He was well known in the town and everyone called him by his nickname, 'Putt'.

Putt worked on the Santa Fe railway fixing the track, but he was also a gardener and a handyman and, by simple hard work, he managed to save enough money to buy 40 acres of his own land. That was no easy thing round here in the 1940s. Very few black people owned land; those who tried were often laughed at or threatened, and no white bank would lend them money. Often, they could only do it if some sympathetic white person agreed to front for them. But Putt did it and he planted his land with cotton and corn and sugar-cane, and in his own small way he began to prosper.

One Saturday morning Putt rode into Montgomery on his

horse, and he was just walking down the main street through the middle of town when a white man walked up to him and shot him. Then, in front of all the people who came running out of the stores to see what all the noise was about, the white man walked over to Putt where he lay moaning on the ground and put two more bullets in his black body.

Everyone knew who the white man was. He was the town bully. He had a job at the First State Bank but he spent most of his time frightening people. No one really knew why he had done it – if he had had some argument with Putt or if he just did not like the sight of a prosperous nigger. But Putt was dead and the white man was never even arrested.

Brandley often heard that story at home, because Putt's real name was Dennis Brandley and he was Clarence's grandfather.

These were just facts of life. It made no difference what laws came and what laws went. Brandley never felt good in this part of town: he bought his pack of Kools and trudged back to the high school. It was now nearly 9.25.

On the way back down the hallway, he saw the white lady from Conroe high school again, took the rubbish bin out of her office and asked her if she was sure there were enough toilet rolls in the girls' room in the dressing-room. It was hot. He was worried about the volleyball teams, so he went into the gym and opened the windows and switched on the big electric fans.

Then he stopped by one of the janitor's closets near the gyms and picked up some toilet rolls. He would just drop them off in the boys' restroom by Sesame Street and then finally get into that nice quiet little office at the end of the hallway opposite the teachers' lounge and have a peaceful smoke.

He was half-way to Sesame Street before he realized that the other janitors were all standing around there. Gary Acreman was hanging about at the top of the staircase that led up to the restrooms and John Sessum and Sam Martinez were lurking around by the water fountain at the bottom of the stairs.

Acreman looked at the toilet rolls in Brandley's arms and said: 'Don't go in the girls' restroom, Clarence. There's a girl in there.'

Brandley reckoned this was Acreman's idea of a wisecrack, just trying to stop him from doing his job. Since he didn't want to go in there anyway, he paid no attention. 'I ain't going in there,' he said. 'Y'all finished in the cafeteria?'

They nodded.

'What you want us to do now?' asked Martinez.

'Well, we gotta fix some stuff in the vocational building. You go back across the street and wait for me. I'll be on over soon enough, let y'all in.'

It must have been 9.30 by now. Brandley was beginning to think he was never going to get this smoke, but what the hell? They could wait for him, it would do them no harm and it would help to kill some time so they could claim a full day's money.

He put the toilet rolls in the boys' restroom and headed down the hallway to his office, where finally he managed to sit down, switch on his little black radio, put his feet on the desk and light up his cigarette. He would go across and see to them soon enough and check in on Icky, too, see how he was getting on with buffing the floor in the teachers' lounge.

He began to feel a little better. The cigarette was real good. Brandley sat quietly in the warm air, resting his eyes. He might even have dropped off for a moment. He thought he might take Beverley out partying that night. If he could get away around noon and catch up on some sleep in the afternoon, he would be all right for the night.

Eventually he heaved himself up from his chair. He had better let those guys into the vocational building. He had no idea how long he had left them waiting; he had no watch on. But it must be after ten o'clock now, and there were some 85 chairs that had to be laid out in there for Monday morning. There was going to be a meeting of all the janitors in the Conroe School District. While the teachers were over in the main building discussing the new term, the janitors would be in the vocational building with their boss, Mallie Davis, talking about their work.

As Brandley came out of his office he saw that the outside door at the end of the hallway had been propped open with a rubbish bin. That was not right. It was his job to make sure all external doors were closed and locked. He slid the rubbish bin out of the way, stepped out into the bright sun and almost collided with Icky Peace.

'Clarence,' chirruped the baby-faced janitor. 'When you gonna let us in?'

'You finished in the teachers' lounge already?'

'Sure I am. I done a real good job. You wanna see?'

'I'll check it later, Icky. Here, take the key.'

Brandley lobbed him the key to the vocational building. Across the road, Brandley could see Gary Acreman, sitting sullen on the steps of the vocational building with a cigarette in his mouth, and John Sessum lying flat out on the top step, apparently fast asleep. By the side of the building, Sam Martinez seemed to be checking out the pay phone. Brandley explained to Peace about the chairs that had to be laid out and left it to him to get the other janitors working. He watched Peace waddle back across the road.

Back in his office, Brandley lit up another Kool. That Icky Peace truly was a strange person. He might look like a big baby, but he had some grown-up thoughts in his head. Several times now when they had been working together on their own, Peace had got on at him about women, complaining that he couldn't get one because he was short and ugly, and asking Brandley to get one for him. Brandley just used to smile at him and shake his head.

Peace might seem dumb, but in his own way he was pretty smart. He had been kicked around all his life and had learned to spot trouble coming and talk his way out of it. Brandley had seen him tell tales – just like that, off the top of his head, and you would never know he was making it up. Icky Peace knew how to look after himself. He had a gun, too. He had been showing it off one day in school. And there was talk about how he did some kind of work for the police. He even had his own identity card with his picture on it and everything that was something to do with the police. He was a strange one.

Brandley sighed and smoked and listened to the radio and let the time roll by. It was after eleven by the time he pulled himself together and wandered back out of his office and over to the vocational building. He checked the work there and decided to call it a day. They had done four hours since 7.30.

'Y'all can go on home, now,' he told them.

'What about our money?' It was Acreman's familiar whine. 'You said we'd get a full day.'

'I'll put y'all down for a full day. Eight hours.'

As the four white janitors turned to leave the vocational building, Brandley caught Peace's eye. 'Hey, Icky, can you give me a ride? I just gotta lock up and we can go.'

'OK, Clarence.'

With the egg-shaped janitor at his side, Brandley started to cross the road to the main building when something caught his eye. It was a police car, a Conroe Police Department car, sitting by the bus ramp with a cop at the wheel.

Brandley was curious. 'What's the problem?' he asked.

'They're looking for a girl,' said the cop, who was young and white. 'She's been reported missing.'

The policeman didn't seem too worried. Brandley led Peace inside, praised him to the skies for his work on the floor of the teachers' lounge, checked the cafeteria and found the other three had not finished the job. He and Peace were just laying out the last remaining chairs when they heard voices. It was girls shouting.

'Cheryl! Cheryl!'

Brandley and Peace went out to the hallway to take a look. There were three girls there in tracksuits. 'Is that you hollerin'?' asked Brandley.

The girls seemed worried. They had lost their friend; she had been missing for two hours now. She was blonde, and wearing blue jeans and a shirt, they weren't too sure what colour. But she was missing. She had even left her purse behind. Nobody had been too worried to start with, but now they had stopped the tournament and one of the coaches had called the police. They were all looking.

'I guess we better look, too,' said Brandley. 'C'mon, Icky.'

While Brandley locked the cafeteria, Icky Peace drifted over to the main lobby by the stuffed tiger. His voice sang out. 'Hey, Clarence, this door's open.'

He was right. One of the swing doors that led from the lobby into the parking lot on Route 105 was unlocked. That was not right. Brandley was just about to lock it when he noticed that one of the doors that led from the lobby into the auditorium was also open. 'We better go take a look, Icky. Could be somebody in there vandalizing things.'

They pushed through the door. Inside the auditorium it was dark. Icky shot a nervous glance towards Brandley and hesitated, but Brandley was determined to go in. He had cleaned this whole place up during the week, ready for the new term. Then he had locked it and left it so it would stay clean. If there was anyone skulking around in there in the dark, he wanted them out before they messed the whole place up again.

'Anyone there?' he shouted and started walking along the dark aisle between the seats. 'Anyone there?'

Twisting his fingers into a knot, Peace shuffled in the dark behind him, his head sunk down between his shoulders, round eyes switching from side to side, feeling his way to his left, to the side wall that ran alongside the main hallway. Finally, he found the light switch and flicked it on.

Now they could see the whole auditorium, the rows of seats running down to the stage, a door to the left in front of the stage that led to the restrooms at Sesame Street, a door on the other side that led to the parking lot and Route 105. Brandley had already reached this door. 'Icky,' he shouted. 'Look here. This one's open too.'

Brandley was now very suspicious. Someone had been playing around with these doors. He had heard about all this from some of the old janitors – kids hiding in the auditorium and missing class, or boys and girls going in there to make out. 'We better check this out, Icky. Take a look up on the stage there. I'll check round these seats.'

Brandley walked back up the aisle, away from the stage, checking each row of seats to see if anyone was crouching down and hiding. He climbed up to the little spotlight booths at the far end of the auditorium. There were couches in the booths. Some of the janitors had found incense sticks and cigarette ends up there. But Brandley found no one and nothing.

He headed back to the stage where Peace was still shuffling around, avoiding dark corners and gawping at the shadows as if he expected to see a ghost. 'Icky, I'm gonna check behind the stage here. You go up them stairs there. See what's up there.'

Peace started to walk very slowly up a winding metal staircase. 'Go on, Icky. There's nothing to be scared of. I'm right here, man.'

Brandley could see the little janitor was getting nowhere. 'OK, man. I'll come with you.'

Their feet rang dull chimes on the metal steps. The stairs wound upwards past ropes and pulleys to a small loft, which was dimly lit and cluttered. There was a sledge and a big yellow mat and a bunch of wooden sheets with different scenes painted on them. It was some kind of props loft. The only light came from a row of coloured bulbs along one side. It was hot and dusty. They started feeling their way about. Peace turned over one of the wooden sheets and the body of a blonde girl with blue eyes rolled away from the wall and lay back on the floor, her eyes staring upwards, her mouth frozen open, the tip of her tongue lying on her bottom teeth. Her hands were wide open, the palms pressing upwards. She was naked except for her socks. Peace screamed.

'Oh, my god,' said Brandley. 'I'll go get help. Stay here.'

'Clarence, couldn't I go get help? I don't wanna stay here.'

'Just stay there, Icky.' Brandley was already clambering down the metal steps. 'Don't do nothing. Just stay there.'

Peace pulled his work knife out of his back pocket and clasped it to his breast. His mouth was trembling.

Brandley raced along the aisle, burst out of the open door at the end of the auditorium, round the corner and out into the open air by the bus ramp where he and Peace had seen the policeman in the car. He was gone. There was another policeman driving past. Brandley waved him over.

'Come with me. We found something. Come with me.'

Events started to race. Brandley became a spectator.

The policeman looked at the body and called another cop on his radio. Then they called more cops, who called the detectives and the Justice of the Peace and the funeral home and the school officials and the press. Soon there were white men in big boots swarming all over the props loft and the auditorium and up and down the hallway, opening doors and asking questions, herding schoolgirls into different rooms and asking questions, while

Brandley and Peace sat in the front seats of the auditorium trying to figure out what was happening.

Peace was almost in tears. Brandley tried to comfort him. He had been in the army for a couple of years after school and he had seen dead people before, but the truth was it had shaken him up, too. He could still see it in his mind's eye. She had seemed so young, but she was surely dead: her lips had been blue and all around the front of her neck there had been an ugly red, raw stripe. Brandley had been there when one of the cops checked underneath her body. He had seen the mark in the middle of her back, right between her shoulder blades, where the weight of her killer, pressing her down against the floor, had printed the shape of her crucifix in the flesh.

After an hour or two, the cops seemed to run out of things to do. Two of them came up to Brandley and Peace and asked them if they would come downtown to make a statement. They agreed. The cops drove them away. On the side of the car it said, 'Conroe Police Department. We Care.'

Brandley felt strange sitting in that car. He had never had too much to do with cops. There was no reason. It was just another of those facts of life you learned when you grew up in Dugan. No one there had forgotten what happened to Greg Steele a few years back.

Greg Steele was only a kid, 18 years old, just out of school and about to join the army. He was a big, soft kind of guy, like Yogi Bear, with a permanent grin across his face. He spent his time playing football and basketball in Dugan, listening to loud music and hanging about with his girlfriend. And that was where the trouble started, because the girl was white.

At first it was nothing too heavy. People in Dugan warned Greg that there had been some white man driving round looking for him, making threats about the girl. Greg just shrugged and said there wasn't much he could do about that. Then one Saturday night – just before Christmas 1973 – Greg got into some kind of trouble in a juke joint in Dugan called the Blue Jacket. It seemed he had been in there drinking beer and shooting pool and some drinks got spilled and the people who had lost their drinks turned ugly. The owner called the police who came and arrested several of them, including Greg. The next thing that anyone in Dugan heard was four or five hours later, when Greg's mother and step-father went up to the police station to get him bail and they were told their son was dead.

The police said Greg had pulled a knife on an officer who had had to shoot him in self-defence. No one in Dugan believed it. The others who had been arrested with Greg said they had all been searched and Greg never had a knife. They said they had heard Greg being beaten. The police could not explain why, if Greg was attacking the officer, all three bullets which had hit him had gone into his back. Nor could they explain why the knife which he was supposed to have been holding was never splashed with any of his blood. Everyone in Dugan knew that Greg's white girlfriend had an uncle who was a policeman. They had no doubt about what had happened, but all the same the officer who killed him was cleared of committing any crime and allowed to stay in the police force.

Brandley stared out of the window of the police car and tried to relax. Downtown, he and Peace were led to a portable cabin behind the old city jail. Peace was taken to one room, Brandley to another. Two white men asked him what happened. He told them. They wrote some of it down; he signed it. The two white men took his work knife from his pocket. They took his finger-prints. Then they asked if he would mind coming down to Medical Center Hospital to give them some samples of blood and hair. He said OK.

They put Icky Peace in the back of a police car with him. Brandley could see he was frightened. His eyes were as round as an owl at night and he was gaping about him as if he had just woken up on another planet.

'You OK, Icky?'

Peace nodded.

At the hospital, a police officer took Brandley to a room. He sat and waited. A nurse and a doctor came in. They took samples of his saliva and blood. Then the nurse used a pair of tweezers to pull some hairs from his head and a couple more from his pubic area. The white doctor looked at him hard.

'You know what you're doing?' he asked.

Brandley shrugged. He didn't know what he meant. 'I guess,' he said.

Two policemen drove Brandley and Peace back to the high school. Peace had had samples taken from him, too. He was worried. He started saying that he needed his sister and that he couldn't read or write and that he didn't know what was going on here. Brandley told him it would be OK.

At the school, the cops told Brandley to sit down by the bus ramp and then took Peace across to his '72 Chevrolet Impala, which was still parked where the little janitor had left it that morning. The officers started searching it. Brandley watched. He saw an officer pull out a little knife from the front of the car and then a bigger knife and then some kind of billy club, and then the hand-gun that Peace had been showing off at school. Peace looked uncomfortable. The cops told him it was an offence to carry weapons in a car. Peace was wide-eyed.

Then one of the cops walked back to the bus ramp with Peace. Brandley stood up. The cop paused and stared at the two of them, the black man in his white T-shirt and shabby jeans, the little white man with the thick glasses and the ballooning belly.

'One of you two is gonna hang for this,' said the cop. Then he turned to Brandley. 'Since you're the nigger, you're elected.'

James Harold Keeshan jr. was nobody's fool. He had sailed through law school at the University of Texas in Austin, built himself a career in the Air Force as a Judge Advocate, and then arrived in Conroe and become District Attorney of the Ninth Judicial District of the state of Texas when he was still only 35. Everyone in the courthouse said how smart he was and how he could dance his way past any defence attorney who tried to take him on. And how charming, too. That was Jim Keeshan – with his dapper suits and way with words and sharp blue eyes. If he couldn't win a case with the evidence, he could win it with his smile.

For a District Attorney in Montgomery County, winning was not always easy. Some of the people he had to work with were not as highly trained and sharp as he was. Only two months earlier, in June, there had been a bad fire at the county library in

Conroe. Two days later the fire department announced that they had investigated the incident and ruled out the possibility of arson. Three days later, they announced that they had investigated it again and it was arson after all. The county sheriff's department was no better. The previous month, a patrol car had seen a motor-cyclist speeding down I-45 and set off in pursuit, calling for back-up as he went. A couple of miles down the road, the patrol car had lost the motor-cyclist and stopped, at which point a back-up patrol car which had responded to his call for help had run straight into the back of him, 'totalling' both cars. And in the gaol house Keeshan had just had to deal with a whole lot of fuss about a man who had been charged with killing a 12-year-old girl. In court, the man claimed that he had been abused and threatened by his gaolers, who tried to make him eat maggots from the dead girl's corpse. That was bad enough, but then the gaol supervisor got up in court and confirmed the man's story. Keeshan had sorted things out and the gaol supervisor had left to take up another job, but it all made winning more difficult.

Still, Jim Keeshan's record spoke for itself. In five years as District Attorney he had never lost a single jury trial. There were people outside the courthouse who said Jim Keeshan was too damn smart for his own good and that he cared more about his career than he did about justice. There were even some defence attorneys who went so far as to say that he did not play fair. But they all agreed that he was nobody's fool.

That Saturday evening when Jim Keeshan switched on the television in his comfortable, detached home on the edge of Conroe and saw the news of the murder at the high school, he watched very carefully. The news bulletin caught all the commotion at the high school – the shocked students and the detectives pointing to the spot where the body was found – and it closed in on Monty Koerner, the pot-bellied captain of detectives.

When he was cornered by the reporters, Captain Koerner seemed lost for a moment. Then he started stammering, as he often did, and finally told them: 'We've got an investigation going. There's nothing staring at us in the face, but we're running down several possible leads.'

Keeshan watched carefully and did nothing. He would just wait a while, and see what old Monty Koerner came up with. The murder of Cheryl Fergeson would come his way soon enough.

It was hot again that Sunday, the kind of heavy humid day when young kids and old men like to take their fishing lines out to the nearest water and swat the flies and talk a bit. That is what John Henry Faulk was doing that day, just a little to the north of Conroe.

Faulk was a household name in Texas, famous as a folklorist and stand-up comic who took his one-man show from town to town, playing out the parts of dozens of different Texans he had met over the years, satirizing them and teasing their weaknesses, especially their racism. Many of the characters he played on stage were modelled on people he had met in Montgomery County.

This particular Sunday afternoon, Faulk was down by the river with an old friend of his who had lived all his life in that part of Texas and who had become the raw material for one of Faulk's most popular characters. Faulk looked on him as a living symbol of a certain kind of white Texan. Soon enough, the conversation turned to this dreadful killing at the high school. It had been all over the front page of the Conroe *Courier* that morning: 'Girl found slain at Conroe High. Police say teenager strangled.' Faulk's fishing partner explained that there was one thing for sure.

'When they catch him,' he said in his slow drawl, 'when they catch the man who did that thing, it'll be a nigger.'

Faulk looked at him and sighed.

'Sure as you're born,' continued his friend, 'that's a typical damn nigger crime.'

John Henry Faulk nodded slowly, not because he agreed with one word of it, but because he knew that was the kind of thing that his friend was bound to say. Faulk had been listening to it all his life. On stage, he would often launch into a monologue that was entirely based on the words of his friends in Montgomery County. It was all about good niggers and bad niggers.

'You gotta unnershtan',' he would start with his voice creaking out of the side of his mouth in a parody of an east Texas accent. 'There's good niggers and there's bad niggers. You gotta know how to treat 'em right. Take for example, if you got a good nigger and you gotta whup him, don't go haulin' him out in front a his wife and children and humiliatin' him 'cos that's how you turn a nigger bad, see? You can run a nigger off doin' a thing like that. No. You gotta treat a good nigger with respect – take him down the woods and give him a whuppin' there where no one can see!'

Then he would laugh, and even in a place like Montgomery County he would get his audience laughing with him, teasing them with the truth about themselves, and he would speak a few more of their hidden thoughts. 'Y'see, if a nigger keeps his place, he'll get no trouble. No trouble at all. He can sit there in his little ole shack and eat his corn and play with his old nigger woman and no one's gonna pay him any mind. But, you know, once a nigger's gone bad, there's no helpin' him and he'll cause nothing but trouble till you get shot of him. And nothing makes a nigger go bad quicker than thinkin' 'bout white pussy.'

If they were still laughing with him at this point Faulk would go deeper, right into the heart of their prejudice. He would talk about his old aunt, Ole Miss Waters, who reckoned little black boys tried to spy on her in the toilet 'because they develop their sexual urges young, the little stinkpots' and who would never let her children go swimming down by Grogan's Mill because of the black men who worked there. 'They got the biggest ole organs you ever seen and they just love to catch a little white girl and the first thing they'd do is just rape you, just get you and there'd be an orgy of violence right there.' Then he would talk about one of his earliest confidants, old Mr Brodie, who explained the other side of the story in his parched voice. 'You know one of the greatest wonders in the world? Is why God put all the best pussy on the nigger woman. You ever think of that? 'Cos it's the truth. You tried any yet?'

If his audience was really good Faulk could spell it out, how he discovered as a boy that as a white man he was allowed to take any black woman he saw. Just like the old slave masters who had had their way with the slave women and who offered a little black girl to any white man who came to stay as a house guest. It was not so different today, he would say. No white man was ever going to get into trouble for raping a nigger woman. No white woman could sue for adultery if her husband was playin' round with a nigger woman. Everyone knew that. A white man could do what he liked with a black woman. But a black man had better not even look at a white woman – not even look – or he would touch a nerve so bare, so vital, that every white man in the area would only be doing his manly duty if he helped to hunt that black-assed nigger boy down and taught him a lesson once and for all.

As he watched his fishing line trailing through the water that Sunday afternoon, John Henry Faulk's heart was heavy.

By Monday morning no one in Conroe felt safe, on either side of the railway tracks. The *Courier* said that the dead girl had been raped as well as strangled. The Justice of the Peace who had been called to the scene of the crime, J. P. Bailey, warned parents and teachers not to let any child go off anywhere alone. 'They should go in numbers,' he said. 'Never go alone, and this goes for boys as well as girls. It isn't safe. If it can happen in Conroe, it can happen anywhere.'

And it had happened in the high school – of all places! That building was Conroe's pride, a shining symbol of the town's stability, a corner-stone of its future. It was supposed to be safe. Everybody had always trusted the school. But now the school's head of security Calvin Blake was taking calls from 30 different parents a day, trying to reassure them that they could trust his security arrangements. At the school board the superintendent, Chuck York, was beginning to feel the heat. Parents were threatening to keep their children away from the start of term next week unless the killer was caught. Some were even buying mace gas for their children to carry in their lunch boxes.

Then there was talk that the dead girl's family or school might sue Chuck York and the school board for failing to protect the volleyball tournament. York pleaded that he had done all he could. 'We can't put a person in every hallway every hour of the day,' he said.

He promised he would try to be more vigilant, but there was not much time. The new term was due to start the following week: Monday was Labor Day and on Tuesday the school doors opened. At least, Chuck York hoped that they would. He kept calling the police and begging them to get a break in the case. He went to see the security director for all the schools in the Conroe area, Lonnie Williams, and told him they were going to have a problem if they could not calm down this panic among the parents. But what could they do? They fixed it so that someone stood guard while the Golden Girls practised their cheer-leading routine in the high school auditorium. They told the school nightwatchman that he should look out for people as well as property. But what else could they do? They just hoped for a break.

Chuck York was not the only person calling the police. Half the town seemed to be on the phone to the Police Department, demanding action, demanding that their school be made safe again. But the police did not have much to say. Captain Monty Koerner tried to be reassuring. 'It's priority number one,' he said. 'We hope to have this thing wrapped up before school starts.'

In Dugan, the grape-vine was twitching with talk about the murder: a strange man had been seen up at the school dressed as a woman; the dead girl had been killed because she had stumbled on a drug ring using the school laboratories to make speed; the killer was a Mexican who had followed her from Bellville; another girl had been raped but they were trying to keep it quiet. The gossip was a veil for fear – for the old fear that anyone who had ever lived in Dugan had felt at some time.

Minnie Ola Brandley felt it badly now. She had gone to her son when she heard about the murder and she had told him: 'Clarence, don't you go back there. Don't you go back to that school.'

He had smiled and shrugged like he often did. 'Momma, I ain't done nothing.'

'I know. All the same, why don't you leave off working up there?'

'It's my job, momma. I ain't done nothing.'

So Brandley went to the school again on Monday morning, determined that he would not be afraid, and did some of his regular duties, checking the restrooms and throwing rubbish out in the dumpsters, or skips, before going over to the vocational building to sit with all the other janitors from all the schools in Conroe and listen to their boss, Mallie Davis, talk about rubbish bins and toilet rolls.

Afterwards, they all hung around talking. Icky Peace told Brandley something that made no sense at all. According to the little janitor, while they had all been sitting outside the vocational building on the Saturday morning waiting for Brandley to unlock the door, Gary Acreman had gone back into the main building. When he came back, he had told Peace he had seen some girl's clothes scattered around in there. Brandley didn't know whether this was just Icky making up stories again or whether this was somehow important. Since he was the supervisor, he decided he should try and find out. He found Acreman in the crowd and asked him about it.

Acreman twisted his mouth and shook his head. 'Oh, man, I was just bullshitting Icky,' he said. 'I never saw no clothes.'

Brandley guessed Acreman had just been mouthing off as usual. It made no sense to him. Just then Mallie Davis came over. He had heard from Conroe police. They wanted to see Brandley and all four white janitors who had been at the school on Saturday. They were all to go downtown right now to the Police Department.

Brandley wished he could just get on with his work. He had helped them all he could. He had told them everything he knew and even given them his hair and blood. Still, he had better go.

When they got down to the old city jail, Acreman and Sessum and Martinez were taken away to give statements about what they had seen on the day of the crime. Then a policeman came up to Brandley and Peace and asked them if they would mind going down to Houston to take a lie test.

Brandley couldn't see what they wanted with a lie test; he had already told them the truth. But he guessed he might as well do it. He had nothing to hide. The way he saw it, as long as he co-operated he couldn't go wrong.

But Peace was worried. 'I need to talk to my sister,' he pleaded. 'I don't know about lie tests. I can't read nor write. I need my sister.' The police persuaded a minister to come down to Houston with them to hold Peace's hand.

The lie test was simple enough. Brandley sat in a chair. The cop ran a bunch of wires all round his arm and chest and asked him a lot of questions about himself. Then he looked at the machine and asked him some more questions about the crime. Had he killed the girl? Had he raped the girl? Had he ever raped anyone?

Brandley just answered the questions and told his story, the same as he had on Saturday. Then the cop looked at his machine again. 'OK,' he said. 'You passed. You don't got nothing to worry about.'

Brandley felt relieved, which was strange. Until that moment, he had not admitted to himself that he had ever been worried.

The murder of Cheryl Fergeson was finally brought to the District Attorney's office on Tuesday morning, when Captain Monty Koerner stumped over to the courthouse to brief Jim Keeshan on the investigation so far. The captain of detectives tried to be upbeat about it. He told Jim Keeshan that he was doing everything he could. They had collected a whole bunch of stuff at the scene. There were these hairs that one of his men had seen on the dead girl's thigh and he had saved them – put them straight into his cigarette pack so they wouldn't get lost. They had found a bit of her bra in the loft: it looked like it had been cut off her. There was a paper towel lying nearby, and her crucifix, though the chain was missing.

Then on Sunday they had shipped the body down to Houston, and the medical examiner there, Dr Jachimczyk, had done an autopsy. They were still waiting for the report, but the medical examiner had given him some more stuff – grit and dust from her body, and the pair of white socks which was all she was wearing when she was found. On Monday they had been out to the school again and they found the rest of the dead girl's clothes in a rubbish bag in one of the big dumpsters behind the main building. Everything they had found was on its way up to the Department of Public Safety in Austin, so the laboratory there could have a look at it all.

Although he tried to be upbeat about it, Koerner could not conceal the fact that his investigation was moving slowly, not least because he had allowed his men to take the day off on Sunday, so the trail had been left to go cold from Saturday afternoon right through to Monday morning. By the time his men went back to the high school, the cleaning women had already been round the place with their mops and swept up anything that might have been useful to them.

His men could not even be sure how the dead girl's clothes came to be in the dumpster: they might have been put there by the murderer on the day of the crime or they might have been thrown out by the cleaners who had collected up rubbish bags from all over the school on Monday morning.

His best suspect had been the black janitor. He had had a knife on him, too. But he had passed the lie test. And he had also found the body. The killer had gone to a whole lot of trouble to get that girl's body up into the props loft and hide it behind the wooden screen. Like he wanted to get well away and out of town before anything was discovered. It wouldn't make too much sense to go straight back up there the first chance he got and find it again.

Jim Keeshan listened carefully to Captain Koerner's briefing, told him to get things moving and let him go back to work. He would give Koerner a little longer to get a break in the case, but he was toying with an idea of how he might get things moving himself.

It was Tuesday that Brandley first sensed it, the way you sense a storm coming, from the way the ground darkens without even needing to look up at the sky. Something strange was happening at the school.

It was the way people looked at him and then looked away when he caught their eye. People were acting strangely towards him. Students who usually smiled and said Hi pretended they had not seen him. Teachers who usually talked had nothing to say. He saw strange cops walking round the school, looking at him as if they knew him, as if they were saying 'Oh, yeah, that's the black janitor we all heard about'.

It got worse. It got to the point where he felt he was being watched. And he knew he was not crazy. They couldn't think it was him, they must know he had nothing to do with it. They wouldn't be watching him about that. It must be something else. Unless he was imagining it: but he knew he wasn't. By Wednesday it was really starting to get to him. And it was not just the funny looks. As far as he could tell, the police were paying extra attention to him.

The three white janitors had not had to go to the hospital and give samples from their bodies. They had not had to go down to Houston for a lie test. He found out that he was the only one who had had to give his fingerprints. So what was it all about?

Then he heard on his little black radio the captain of detectives, Monty Koerner, talking about how they were definitely hoping to catch the killer before school started next week.

Brandley was not saying he was frightened. Damn it, he didn't see why he should be. He had hardly ever been in trouble. And he had told them the truth and helped them every way he could. But Minnie Ola kept nagging him, telling him to stay away from the school, going on about Conroe and the way they did things. Finally, he gave in and he agreed with her that they had better do something about it. There wasn't much they could do, except go see an attorney. So on Thursday evening, after work, they went down to Houston to see an attorney there called Ray Reeves, who had helped one of his brothers in the past. Reeves only spent a couple of minutes with them. He said so far as he could see they had nothing to worry about and, anyway, there was nothing much he could do to help them unless Brandley was arrested. If he was arrested, Reeves said, he should be sure to call him.

Cheryl Bradford had been worrying all week. She only knew the dead girl to say hullo to, but she had seen her there at Conroe High School that Saturday. She played volleyball for her school, Waller High, and she was sure she had seen Cheryl Fergeson in the hallway, maybe even walking down towards the restrooms by Sesame Street. But that was not what was worrying her.

The strange thing that stuck in her mind was the two men. They were both white and both young, perhaps in their early 20s. One had shaggy dark hair and the other had sandy hair. She had only noticed them because they had been in the gym and they obviously did not belong there. They had not seemed to have anything to do with the school at all. They had come into the gym from the hallway, from somewhere near the auditorium, and walked across the room and out the other side towards Route 105.

At the time, she had not thought much about it. But later, at home, Cheryl Bradford wondered about the two white men and what they were doing there and where they were coming from. Could they have been coming from the auditorium – where the body was found?

It started to worry her so much that she told her volleyball coach, who seemed to think it was important. So they called the Conroe Police Department to tell them what they knew.

John Wesley Styles was a Texas Ranger. On the Thursday after the murder, he was on holiday at his ageing parents' home in Baylor County near Witchita Falls in north Texas, when the call came through from Ranger headquarters in Houston. He was to go down to Conroe and report to District Attorney Jim Keeshan and try to help him get a break in the rape and murder of a white schoolgirl there.

To Wes Styles, it was just another job. Styles had been a lawman all his life. He had been sheriff in Baylor County, near the Oklahoma border, for 18 years before he decided to join the Rangers. That was in 1969 and he had never regretted it.

He had signed up with Company A, whose job it was to range across east Texas helping local sheriffs and police chiefs with their work, and it was his particular duty to concentrate on three counties – Trinity, Walker, and Montgomery. He had become a familiar sight in many a courtroom with his big, heavy body and baggy green eyes and his paunch sagging over the top of his trousers. He had been in and out of every kind of crime – rape, robbery, murder, including the big siege at Huntsville Gaol in 1974 when four men had died. There were those who said he cut corners and put the fear of God into his witnesses to get them to say what he wanted to hear, and that he was too rough and tough and 'a solid gold sunnuvabitch.' That didn't worry him. He got results and, to a Texas Ranger, that was what mattered.

On Friday morning, wearing his tall leather boots and his white stetson hat, Ranger Styles reported for work in Conroe.

On Friday afternoon in the high school at about four o'clock, an announcement came over the public address system calling Clarence Brandley to the principal's office.

Brandley stopped what he was doing and walked down the long hallway towards the main lobby and the tiger in the glass case. He knocked gently on the door of the principal's office and walked in, and saw a big man with tall leather boots and a white stetson, another guy with a neat suit and sharp blue eyes, a pot-bellied cop who he knew was the captain of detectives, and a whole bunch of other cops, and they all just looked at him with angry faces. Then the big guy with the stetson stepped forward, and in a deep voice said, 'I have a warrant for your arrest on a charge of capital murder', and then the cops took his arms and cuffed his hands behind his back and marched him out of the door.

2

There were several good reasons why Ray Reeves wasted no time when he heard that Clarence Brandley had been arrested, though not all of them were obvious.

The truth about Ray Reeves was that a lot of people did not have a very high opinion of him. That included Ray Reeves. It gave him no pleasure, but he admitted that he was not the greatest attorney in the world and that he had never been considered sharp or worth a damn, and that he had probably pulled more dumb stunts than any other damned lawyer in the whole state of Texas. He admitted it.

He did not even look like an attorney, more like a European peasant, with his stubby fat body and ruddy round face. His language was just as coarse, even foul. He always looked as if he had just walked in from a high wind. God never intended Ray Reeves to sit in the Supreme Court.

Something else he admitted was that he was a racist – not the kind of racist who would do anything very much about it. He was not about to join the Ku-Klux-Klan or pick a fight with black people who wanted to move into his street. But the way he saw it, he was bound to be a racist. Back in the little town where he was born in Gray County up in the Texas panhandle, they would not even let a black person stay overnight. If blacks broke down in a car, they would push the car down the road to the next town. That was the way it was and always had been, especially since there had been a big murder there when a white family had been killed and chopped up and hidden down crevices in the earth, and everyone said it was blacks who'd done that. He had simply never felt sympathy for black people like everyone else, and he had never socialized with them, or wanted to, and he admitted he just considered niggers to be on a different basis from regular people.

Still, despite all that, there were several good reasons why Ray Reeves hurried up I-45 from Houston to Conroe as soon as he could that Saturday morning to see if he could help Clarence Brandley.

One reason was that Ray Reeves did not cheat his clients. He figured he was never going to get rich out of being an attorney, and he was never going to win any prizes, so he might as well try and help a few people. There was always this feeling in the back of his mind that he owed it.

As a young man during the war, he had been shot out of the sky over France on a bombing mission in a B24. Everyone else in the plane had been killed and for a while he had thought he was dead too. He knew he would never have survived on the ground if a family of poor peasants had not taken him in and hidden him and healed him and then passed him on to the French underground, who took advantage of his coarse features to disguise him as a farm worker and smuggle him into Spain. That was probably what had made him feel so restless when he got back to Texas after the war and started working as a sheriff's deputy. He just felt it was chicken-shit work with chicken-shit people and he owed it to someone, if only to a poor French family in a village whose name he could not pronounce, to get out and help people. So he became a defence attorney and, whatever his limitations, he made up his mind never to cheat the people he worked for.

But there was a second reason which kept pricking his imagination as he headed north from his home in Houston. He knew the kind of town that Conroe was.

He drove fast up Interstate 45.

It was a Saturday morning, the road was clear, and it was less than an hour before Reeves swung his car off the freeway, up Frazier Street and into the courthouse square. The sun was warm and the streets were quiet. Reeves had no fancy strategy worked out. He knew next to nothing of what was happening here. Anyway, that was not his style. He just wanted to tell Brandley that he was going to do what he could for him and that, in the meantime, Brandley should keep his mouth shut. He had been in custody for less than a day so they should not have done too much harm. Not yet.

Reeves crossed the courthouse square to the old city jail. But when he asked to see Brandley, the officer on the front desk shook his head and sent him over to the county jail which occupied the top two floors of the courthouse.

Reeves paced back across the square and made his way up to the county jail where he found a deputy sheriff. He explained who he was and that he needed to see his client. The deputy shrugged and turned his mouth down.

'We don't got him here,' he said.

'What you mean? Y'all arrested him, didn't you? Y'all got him in custody, don't you? And I need to see him. I'm his damned attorney.'

'Well, we don't got him here.'

It was happening again. Conroe: Reeves never had liked the place. He might be a racist and a whole lot of other things, but this town was too much. Once these people got it into their heads that someone was guilty, they did not give a damn, especially with a nigger. Reeves looked at the deputy. 'Where's that Keeshan?' The deputy pointed at the floor – downstairs in the DA's offices.

'Is that where I'm going to find my client?'

'Ah reckon,' said the deputy.

That meant one thing, and one thing only: they had already started questioning Brandley. Reeves shook his head and made for the stairs. Keeshan certainly hadn't taken the nigger down there to make him comfortable. Never mind his civil rights; never mind that he was supposed to have his attorney with him. Keeshan was a slick operator, Reeves knew that. He'd always said that Keeshan could crawl bare-assed through a barrel of thistles and never get a scratch. And he was as smart as a whip.

The last time Reeves had been in Conroe, he had defended a man on a murder charge, and Keeshan had thrown so much evidence at him that Reeves didn't even try to beat the charge, but just did his best with the jury to get his man a life sentence instead of the death penalty. Now Keeshan was going to try and do the same thing, try and tie up Brandley with a confession before he had had a chance to talk to his attorney.

By the time he got down to the District Attorney's offices, Reeves was ready with a lungful of law for James Keeshan, but Keeshan was nowhere to be seen. Reeves had to make do with one of the DA's assistants, and when the assistant claimed that they didn't have Brandley with them either, it was a lungful of righteous anger that came out: '. . . Sunnuvabitch Keeshan . . . My damned client . . . God-damned civil rights . . . God-damned, sunnuvabitch town . . . Sunnuvabitch Keeshan . . .'

The assistant said he would see what he could do.

Clarence Brandley felt as if he had been pitched into a circus ring. He had never heard of anybody being arrested this way before. The cops had led him out of the school and driven him down to the courthouse square and, instead of taking him round to the back of the old city jail as they were supposed to do, they had walked him right across the street into the front of the courthouse, and there were people everywhere and reporters and photographers. They must have told the press to be there. It was as if they were putting him on a stage and showing him off, with his hands cuffed behind his back.

Inside, they had made him take off his clothes and had gone all over his body looking for scratches. They had shot pictures of him from every angle and then taken his belt away. Then they had stuck him in some little room and started asking him questions about the dead girl. The big Texas Ranger with the stetson had tried it first, and Brandley had just told him he had nothing to say and he wanted to call an attorney. Then one of the young cops had come in and tried it, and he had told him the same thing. So then they had sent in a black cop, as if that was going to change anything. He knew the way their minds worked.

Finally, they had let him call Ray Reeves, who had told him to stay calm and say nothing. Reeves had told him he would be up there first thing in the morning and he would talk to the cops and make sure they didn't try and question him any more before then.

Brandley had spent his first night in jail, haunted by half-remembered stories from his childhood. Greg Steele had died here, in this building, and at the hands of these white men. Brandley had known him and played basketball with him. But Greg was not the only one. There had been others in the past. Brandley had never met them, but he knew the stories. There was one story in particular that the old people told – about a man called Joe Winters.

He had lived in Dugan years ago, in the 1920s, and worked out at one of the mills near Leonidas on Route 105. He was married to a woman named Anna, but all the same he was going with a white girl. A lot of black people knew they were seeing each other but no white people did, until one day, one Friday afternoon, when they were in the woods together close by the river and a white man saw Joe Winters with his white girl. When she returned home, they asked the girl: 'What you doing in the woods with a nigger?' And in her fear, she said the black man had forced himself on her.

All the old people in Dugan knew what happened next. They still recalled the day when, as children, they had seen the white men with guns and sticks coming down through the streets and into their homes. 'They came to get him. There was white men searching in all the houses. It went on all night . . . Sheriff Hicks came through our house. My mamma was crying. Everybody was crying. I didn't know why. But I started crying, too . . . They had dogs, bloodhounds, searching everywhere. There was white men on horses in the streets. Everybody just stayed inside, hoped there wouldn't be no trouble . . . Just before they came the first time, I saw him walk by my house. Joe Winters. He didn't know he was in trouble. He just walked by and they never saw him . . . They were coming through all the doors, saying they were looking for the man who raped the white girl. There was a lot of men looking for him, white men with torches . . . Everybody was frightened.'

The search through Dugan was only part of the man-hunt, which soon became such a big affair that it made the front page of the newspapers. Within hours of the first report on that Friday afternoon, 19 May 1922, news and rumours were sweeping Montgomery County that a black man had raped a white woman – a girl of only 14 years, according to some. Sheriff Hicks called in the bloodhounds from Huntsville Gaol and by nightfall several hundred men were helping to comb Conroe and the surrounding fields and woods.

At first, the woman did not tell them the name of the man they were hunting, and during that Friday evening the hunters caught a black man named Rudolph Manning, believing he was guilty of the crime. Some deputies took him down to Houston to keep him safe, but Sheriff Hicks went after him and brought him back at three o'clock in the morning and showed him to his supposed victim, who said he was the wrong man.

The hunt went on all night. By Saturday morning, white men had poured into Conroe from all over Montgomery County. Several thousands of them were now hunting the black rapist and, for the first time, they knew the name of the man they were chasing. They went to Joe Winters' house on Avenue J. There were rumours he was hiding underneath it, but he was not there.

They took his clothes to give the scent to the bloodhounds, which chased a trail more than a mile out to the west of Conroe but then they lost it. There was a rumour that the fugitive had taken a mule from a black boy out there. The dogs had given up when word came from Waukegan on the other side of town that Joe Winters had been seen there.

White men converged on Waukegan in trucks, on horses, with their dogs and their guns. Soon the woods were alive with the sound of the hunt, the dogs yelping, the men shouting, all crashing through the undergrowth. This time they were on the right track and early on Saturday afternoon, 20 May 1922, word came through to Conroe that they had caught Joe Winters in the woods two miles from Waukegan, and they were bringing him back.

Just before four o'clock in the afternoon, they dragged Joe Winters into the courthouse square. The whole place was boiling with people, all the men who had come to join the hunt, their wives, children too, hundreds of white faces filling the square and the surrounding streets. Out on the city limits, the sheriff's men blocked the roads and turned away black people.

Joe Winters was in chains when they hauled him through the crowd which jostled and shoved to get a look, to jeer and shout 'Nigger,' and kick him and spit. First they tried to fix him in front of Wahrenberger's store, but Mr Wahrenberger wouldn't let them in case his place got damaged, so they chained him to an iron post at the end of the fence which ran round the old courthouse.

Most of the crowd watched and waited while a few of the men organized everything, fetching old boxes from Wahrenberger's store and piling them up round the black man till they reached up over his head. They they fetched oil and kerosene and splashed it all over all the boxes till they were completely soaked, and one of them struck a match, and all the white men, women and children stood and watched as Joe Winters was burned alive.

In Dugan, the old people still recalled how they heard about the end of the hunt in broken scraps of rumour: '. . . I was only a kid, maybe five or six, and I was riding on a wagon with my mother, coming to Conroe from about nine miles out. When we got to the edge of town, a deputy turned us back. He told my mamma: "You can't come through. They gonna burn a nigger." . . . I remember a man came down our street and he said they had burned him and he said they were trying to burn the heart, which you can't do . . . I heard they tried to take pictures of him, but he wouldn't straighten up . . . There was one man who rode up to him on his horse and hit him so hard he fell out of his stirrup . . . He was trying to make them kill him before they burned him. He was hoping they would shoot him. But they didn't want to do that . . . You could smell it all around. Smell the kerosene and the meat. Burning meat . . . he didn't die straight away, not till the flames went down his throat.'

Later, the fire had died down and, with it, the crowd. Families went home to eat and sleep. The *Courier* reported: 'Joe Winters Burned Here. Negro Pays Penalty for Assault Upon 14-year-old Girl.' The *Courier* described the man-hunt and its conclusion and said: 'Winters was regarded by both white and Negro population as a bad character. He is said to have had three women, one at Waukegan, one at Conroe and one at Leonidas, and his favourite occupation was smoking a cigar as he loafed the streets and refused hard work when offered him.'

Then Conroe got on with its life and all that was left of Joe Winters was memories. In his cell above the courthouse square, Clarence Brandley lay alone with his fear.

On Saturday morning the questioning started again. Brandley protested that they had told Ray Reeves they would stop but it made no difference. By this time Brandley was feeling pretty weak. He had hardly slept and he had not eaten a thing since they took him in. He was hungry, but he was not going to eat anything they gave him. He had heard some of the things that had been going on behind these bars. Earlier that year, in January, some prisoners had tried to pick a lock and the jailer had caught them and taken a dozen prisoners into the freezing night air, made them strip and then hosed them with icy cold water and left them there to freeze for the night. The way Brandley saw it, if they were mean and crazy enough to arrest him for something they must know he hadn't done, then it would be no surprise if they tried to finish him off with something in the food. He would wait till his family brought him a meal.

The Texas Ranger kept asking him a lot of questions. Brandley kept refusing to answer. He had given up thinking he was going to do himself any good by helping these guys. And beneath his fear and weakness he was mad with them, not so mad that he dared to argue with them, but mad enough to stare back, dull and sullen, and be sure he would not play their game. Anyway, he had no idea who had killed that girl. He knew it wasn't him and he guessed it wasn't any of the white janitors. They had all been working. They hadn't had time to do a thing like that. He guessed the girl must have wandered outside, or a vagrant or someone must have got into the auditorium through one of those open doors. The truth was that he did not know.

Finally, word came through that Ray Reeves was kicking up a fuss outside, and the Ranger got up and stood over Brandley and told him: 'If I had my way, I'd take you out now and blow your Goddam brains out.'

By the time Reeves was allowed to see Brandley, the attorney was cursing and swearing about Keeshan and the Ranger. Reeves told Brandley he knew both of them from this other case he had worked on in Conroe where, he said, there had been witnesses who had had the shit beaten out of them and all kinds of other crap. So his advice was to say nothing and keep his head down. Brandley needed more than that. When was he going to get out of here? What did these guys have on him? How could they do this? They talked about trying to raise some money to pay for the defence and Reeves said he would visit Brandley's family and talk to them about it. They discussed bail, though Reeves could not see how he was going to have much luck on a charge as bad as this. Brandley was getting angry. He kept telling Reeves that he had done everything the police had asked him. He had even taken a lie test and passed it. So why had they gone ahead and arrested him?

Reeves had a pretty shrewd idea about why Brandley had caught their eye, but he kept that to himself. Reeves tried to get him to tell him what happened on the day of the crime, but Brandley could hardly remember. It had just been another day. He couldn't even remember what time it was when he turned up at school. All he knew was that he and Icky had found the body and that was the first time in his life he had ever seen this girl.

Reeves leaned forward and looked straight into Brandley's face. 'Clarence, it don't make a whole lot of difference to me whether you done this thing or not. I need to defend you. You gotta tell me the truth, see? Now, did you have a damned thing to do with this?'

Brandley looked straight back and said: 'No, Mr Reeves. I did not.'

Reeves could not exactly explain why, but for some reason he believed him.

It had been a long time since they built a new scaffold in Conroe. In the old days, the city council had often met and set aside $22.50 to pay the carpenter to go to work in the courthouse square. There was one time, back in 1905, when they paid the money and the scaffold was built and the prisoner, who was from Dugan, cheated them by hanging himself in his cell the night before he was due to die. But there had been no public hangings since 1924, when the state ordered that executions should be carried out by the Texas Department of Corrections in Huntsville.

Now Brandley sat alone in his cell and watched the town get ready to stage an execution. The foundation of the scaffold was already being laid.

The Conroe *Courier* carried Brandley's picture on its front page as he was led in handcuffs into the courthouse, his face morose

45

and dull and black. People who did not even know him discussed his guilt in the paper. Everyone in Conroe – everyone who might eventually have to sit on his jury – could read all about this monster called Brandley. A Conroe detective said they had 'an air-tight case' against Brandley. The District Attorney said Brandley would not be entitled to be released on bail. The captain of detectives said he was reluctant to have anybody like Brandley loose in society. The school superintendent said he was so relieved that Brandley had been caught, as now they could start school. The father of the dead girl said he was proud the police had caught their man so quickly and he hoped Brandley would be convicted. Some reporter wrote that 'Conroe can sleep safe at night once again.'

But there was something worse than that – something that had started off so simply, the way bad things often do. It must have been a couple of years back that his mother, Minnie Ola, had been out walking behind the shack on Avenue E, where Brandley had been born and where she still lived. Out along the railway track behind the shack she had spied something in the weeds and, out of curiosity, had taken a closer look. It had turned out to be an old shotgun, riddled with rust and useless, but she decided to take it home and clean it up, in case it came in useful one day for shooting a jack-rabbit or scaring off a prowler.

As it turned out she never had cleaned it up, and it had just lain under the big bed in the front bedroom of the shack – the same bed where he had been born – gathering dust and making a home for a bunch of spiders. He had still been living in Houston at that time driving a Metrobus, and he hadn't known a thing about it.

One weekend, in the spring of 1979, he had come up to stay in the shack on Avenue E. Minnie Ola had gone to Houston to see her doctor, so he was alone up there. This had been at a time when he was still living in the fast lane, drinking in the juke joints and spending all his money on a good time, and he had gone out that night to a place in Dugan called The Doll House.

He had been sitting in The Doll House drinking with some people when a guy had come in and started shouting at a white girl called Mary Zavaba and tried to drag her out by the hair. Brandley and some of the others had got up and helped the girl and told the guy to get lost. After that, he and another guy had started drinking with Mary and a friend of hers, a black girl called Jo Ellen Parrish. One thing had led to another and, many hours and many drinks later, Brandley had ended up taking Jo Ellen back to the shack on Avenue E. Not that he was going to pay for her: it was just a friendly thing. She had been worried because she had some boyfriend – Brandley guessed he was her pimp – and he was going to go crazy if he found out she was with him. In the end, all that had happened was that they had cooked themselves a meal in the shack and Brandley had been so drunk that he had just passed out on the bed. He had woken up in the morning and found that Jo Ellen had vanished and taken his long coat with her. He had thought nothing about it; he had been too hung over to be interested. But the next thing he had known, some cop was outside saying Jo Ellen was accusing him of raping her.

It had turned out that Jo Ellen had found him asleep and then got all worked up about what her boyfriend was going to say. So she had gone off and told her boyfriend that Brandley had made her go back to his place and had raped her or tried to rape her or some such thing. The boyfriend had believed the story and made her go to the police.

The cop had had no search warrant but he had proceeded to search the shack all the same and there, under the bed in the front room, covered in rust and dust, he found Minnie Ola's old shotgun. Brandley had ended up being charged with some kind of sexual assault on Jo Ellen and with unlawful possession of a shotgun. Jo Ellen had soon backed off and withdrawn her story, and the cops had quickly dropped all the talk about the rape, but he had been left with the shotgun. Brandley had wanted to plead not guilty: that gun had been nothing to do with him. But if he said that, the cops were only going to come round and accuse Minnie Ola of unlawful possession. So he had talked to an attorney and been advised to make a deal. He had ended up pleading guilty and getting three years on probation. That had been more than a year back, in the spring of 1979.

The attorney had said it was nothing to worry about. He was not likely to get arrested for anything else so the probation would never mean anything. Just two weeks ago the attorney had filed papers with the courthouse to have the probation discharged. That was the rule: if you did more than one-third of the time without trouble, then you could get the whole thing lifted. All it had needed was for the judge to stamp a piece of paper and it would have been out of the way. But now he still had it hanging over him.

Still, so far as he was concerned, he had never been in trouble before. Well, nothing bad. But that was not the way it looked in the paper. All across the top of the front page of the *Courier*, in big letters, it talked about Brandley being on probation for a felony offence. That damned piece of old rust. They made it sound like he was an armed killer. 'Brandley was serving a three-year probated sentence for possession of a prohibited weapon – a sawed-off shot gun'. All across the front page. It was like he could see this whole town building the scaffold.

Only a few blocks away from the city gaol where Brandley sat watching his fate unfold, a group of men and women were gathered in the office of a Conroe taxi company called City Cab. Like almost everyone else in Conroe, they were talking about the black janitor who had been arrested for the high school murder.

There was the dispatcher sitting behind her desk taking calls and scribbling notes, a couple of drivers sitting around waiting for work, a teenage boy who had stopped in to wait for his grandmother and Connie Millar, a large white woman with light brown hair, who had until recently been the manager there. She had just stopped by to see her old colleagues. It had only been a few weeks since she had left but already there were new faces, like the lean, scruffy young man who had just walked in.

Connie Millar did not like the look of him. Everything about him looked dirty. He seemed drunk or stoned and it looked to her as though he had wet the front of his trousers. She watched in distaste as he walked over to the other drivers and told them he had been signed on as a new part-time driver.

'Name's Gary,' she heard him say, 'Gary Acreman.'

He went in to the back room while they continued to discuss the murder and to agree that they could hardly believe that such a thing had happened in their high school. Connie was just telling

48

the others her theory, that she did not necessarily believe they had arrested the right man.

'Anybody could have come in off the street and done it,' she was saying. 'It would be easy to get in to that school. If you were going to watch the volleyball. Or if you just wandered in.'

That was when Acreman first spoke up, when he came back and settled down on the couch and rested his cup of coffee on an empty chair and told them that he worked up there as a janitor himself and he knew this Clarence Brandley who had been arrested.

'Well,' said Connie. 'My honest opinion is that I feel with school fixing to start that they had to find someone. They had to pin it on someone real quick to clear it up before they started school to, like, calm the community down.'

Connie looked across at Acreman on the couch next to her. 'I mean, I honestly don't think that Clarence Brandley did it.'

Suddenly Acreman was out of the couch. And he was shouting at her: 'Clarence did not kill that girl. I know who did. Clarence didn't do it. But I will never tell.'

She would never forget his eyes like a cat's, and his yellow teeth and foul breath. He was shouting right in her face. She would never forget it.

Then just as suddenly he was back on the couch again, lying with his eyes shut and a dim smile on his face, and the wet patch on the front of his trousers. Connie felt shocked and shaken and the others went quiet. Then they changed the subject.

A few minutes later, Connie Millar got up and left the office of City Cab and drove home. The dispatcher took some more calls. The drivers went to work, and the teenage boy went home with his grandmother. Nobody walked a few blocks across town to tell the black man in the prison cell that somebody out there knew something, that somebody out there said he was innocent.

The Revd John Daviss watched and worried. For 40 years now, Daviss had lived in Conroe and ministered at the First Missionary Baptist Church in Dugan and he had come to know the town well. With his greying hair and his moon-round face, he had a calm, owlish air about him, and on both sides of the railway tracks he had built a reputation as a solid, wise old black man. He had become an unofficial spokesman for the people of Dugan. Revd Daviss knew Clarence Brandley and his family and he wanted to help, but it was hard to know how he could. When he was just a boy, his grandfather had often told him that no matter what you do, there will always be white folks who hate negroes.

It went back to the days of slavery, which were not so long ago. In those days, Montgomery County had been one of the largest slave-holding counties in the state of Texas. They had shipped boat-loads of slaves up the Trinity River to a town called Cincinnati which had since been wiped out by yellow fever, and they had sold them in markets all across the county. The last witnesses of the old days had died in the 1960s: Phillis Bates, who remembered her father being whipped at the post for drinking and trying to run away from his master; the last of the Easley family who had belonged to a rich farmer called Raleigh Rogers, until he gave them all away as a wedding gift to his daughter, Mrs Pleasant Yell.

Conroe had not even existed until the 1880s – 20 years after the slaves were freed – when a Union Army captain from New Jersey named Isaac Conroe set up a sawmill in the Big Thicket from which the new town grew. But John Daviss had come to believe that the old hatreds and inequalities of the county's slave days had become part of Conroe's way of life. Daviss came to Conroe during the oil boom when there was terrible racism, and no black people gained any benefit from the oil. In 1980 he still saw a town that was built to keep blacks on one side of the tracks in shanties and whites up on the hill in big houses. He knew how the Conroe sheriff's deputies used to harass black people who travelled through the town. It seemed to have improved for a while, but now with this killing at the school it was as bad as ever.

Revd Daviss had always tried to hold a hand out to white people. He did not believe in hate. In the 1960s he had worked on the human relations committee that was set up by black community leaders trying to get black people into jobs that were denied them. He persuaded the most liberal of the Conroe bank presidents to hire a black man. He kept working at it, trying to persuade young black people who graduated from Conroe College not to leave town but to stay and build the black community. He visited the more liberal white churches and persuaded them to let him preach to their congregations. He met with the police to work together to keep the young blacks out of trouble. But, in truth, he could not say that he had been able to change very much. The country seemed to have drifted back to what it had once left behind.

Sometimes he had to wonder whether his grandfather wasn't right after all. Only the other Sunday he had been to the Episcopal Church to preach to a white congregation, and afterwards a white man had walked up to him and shook him by the hand and said how much he had enjoyed the sermon. But all the time they were talking the white man's wife stood there, and she didn't shake his hand. She crossed her arms over her chest and scowled at the ground and then, nodding at her husband, she said to Revd John Daviss: 'He may want to shake your hand, but that don't mean I gotta.'

Ray Reeves knew he was in trouble. The town was awash with rumours – that Brandley had raped a whole lot of other women, that he had raped one of his own sisters or maybe his mother, and that there was no doubt that the nigger had killed the girl at the school because they had taken swabs from her vagina and it was nigger semen. Reeves was afraid that the prejudice was becoming overwhelming and had tried to do something about it. A Houston television station had wanted to interview Brandley, but when Reeves had tried to set it up, Keeshan blocked it and they wouldn't let the television people into the jail.

That was only the beginning of his trouble. He had no money. He had a client who had no idea what had hit him; he had no clue about who really killed the girl. He had no witnesses, no scientific evidence. And he could not get one word of sense out of the damned District Attorney who would not even hand over a copy of the statement Brandley had given them on the day of the crime, so he had no way of knowing why they had arrested Brandley or how in hell they hoped to convict him.

The nearest thing he had to a lead was some crazy psychic who called him up and insisted they had got the wrong man – the real killer was a white man with black hair. Reeves had nowhere to go and no way of getting there. Then Jim Keeshan offered him a hand.

Reeves knew he could not trust Keeshan. He told Brandley, he told Brandley's family and he told his wife at home that Keeshan would trick you and twist you, that he was so damned charming but he would cheat you as soon as look at you; and, no matter how much of a gentleman he might make himself out to be, Keeshan never could be trusted. But when Keeshan offered him a hand, Reeves took it.

Keeshan's offer was a simple one: if Brandley would agree to testify to the Grand Jury, Keeshan would not press for a high bail bond. That way, said Keeshan, Brandley would get a chance to put his side of the story to the Grand Jury and he would also be released from jail to help prepare his defence, so it was all fair play.

Reeves could see the danger: the greenest law student, wet behind the ears, could tell you that you should never feed your client to the Grand Jury. Reeves had said it often enough himself: 'The Grand Jury are just a tool for the DA. The Grand Jury will do any damn thing that the DA tells them to do. If they don't, everyone calls them a runaway Grand Jury and they get criticized in the press and looked upon as freaks. The DA just has to come in and say "We can make a case against this ole boy" and so they do. It's a farce.'

There were not even regular rules of evidence at a Grand Jury hearing. Keeshan would be able to throw any kind of rumour and speculation at Brandley, and he would be on his own. Even if Reeves was in the room with him, he would have no right to make objections. Keeshan could slice him up and feed him to the wild hogs. At the end of it all, Brandley would have just about no chance of blocking Keeshan from getting an indictment from the Grand Jury and he would have given the other side a preview of his evidence. Yet Reeves was tempted. He went to see Brandley and explained the deal that Keeshan was offering.

'I tell you, Clarence, I don't know what that sunnuvabitch is up to and I can see where this is a dangerous move. It's extremely dangerous. It could finish up being a foolish move, not wise at all.'

But Reeves explained that he was tempted because, so long as Clarence was in jail, the defence were tethered. He wanted Brandley out so that he could talk to him whenever he needed to, take him up the school and get him to remember every minute of the day of the crime, let him loose in Conroe and see if he could find someone who knew something to help him. More than that, Reeves wanted to buy some time. He had never experienced such a concerted effort to convict a man. It was all moving too fast.

'My God, Clarence. I don't know what to advise you. I can't advise you not to, because I can see where it could possibly help you. But if you're vulnerable, don't go, because that sunnuvabitch Keeshan will get you. You know, he's a pretty sharp ole boy.'

'Mr Reeves, I didn't do it.'

Reeves had that feeling again.

'Clarence, if you really had nothing to do with it, and there's really no shit he can throw at you, then I can't see how it can hurt you too much to go before the Grand Jury. Maybe they'll ask some questions that will shed some light on the sunnuvabitch who did this. And we'll get you out of here on bail.'

Reeves went back to Keeshan and sealed the deal. For what it was worth, he gave Keeshan his personal opinion that he was trying to indict an innocent man here. Keeshan said that was a big, broad statement to make, and for the first time he showed him one of his cards: Keeshan told him that he had a witness who would say Brandley was missing for 45 minutes around the time the girl was killed.

Reeves did not think that sounded like the most powerful evidence he had ever come across, but he could see where it might help a circumstantial case. Keeshan started prodding him, saying that if Brandley was really innocent, he should surely come and tell that to the Grand Jury. Reeves agreed and, in exchange, Keeshan agreed that Reeves could have a transcript of the hearing, that he could sit next to Brandley to advise him – though not to intervene – and, most important, that the DA's office would not try to fix a high bond for his release from gaol.

Reeves told himself it was what Clarence wanted and it would be OK, because, after all, Clarence was an intelligent guy and it would give them a chance to find out what evidence Keeshan was sitting on; but he still could not help feeling that there was something wrong, that somehow Keeshan was making a fool of him.

On Wednesday 3 September, only five days after his arrest and 11 days after the death of Cheryl Fergeson, Clarence Brandley was led into the Grand Jury room on the second floor of Montgomery County courthouse. The room was stark and bare, filled by a long wooden table at which Brandley took his seat.

In front of him sat the 12 jurors. Brandley lifted his eyes and flicked them across their faces. All white. He looked back at the table. Ray Reeves sat on one side of him with a note pad. On the other was the DA Jim Keeshan and his assistant, Jerry Winfree. Both white.

Keeshan spoke. 'Brandley, I'd like you to stand and raise your right hand, please.'

Brandley stood up and swore that he would keep the proceedings secret. Now Ray Reeves spoke. Pointing to Brandley, he apologized to the jurors: 'Sometimes he's a little – you know – a little bit difficult to understand.'

Brandley knew what he meant. He talked the way he had been brought up to talk. These white folk would just have to understand him. He was going to tell the simple truth. Reeves had told him that was all he had to do, and that was all he was going to do.

In gaol he had been feeling angry, feeling the injustice of it all. Some cop in there had been riding him, telling him that if he ever got out of jail on bond, he'd be out to get him and he'd never be seen again. Now he felt a little nervous. He had never done this kind of thing before.

Keeshan started off slowly, explaining that the Grand Jury would decide whether he should be indicted and tried for murdering Cheryl Fergeson, and that he had the right to remain silent; then he asked him some simple questions about his childhood and his work record. Brandley kept saying 'Yessir' and 'Nosir'. Keeshan asked him if he had a criminal record.

'No, sir.'

'Have you ever been arrested for rape before?'

'No, sir,' said Brandley. The end of the answer. Then he thought
for a moment and decided to tell the Grand Jury that Jo Ellen
Parrish had once accused him of raping her but that there was
nothing in it.

Ray Reeves winced. It was all very well being honest but the
odds were already stacked against them without Brandley volun-
teering evidence against himself. He glanced across at Keeshan
who looked like he could hardly believe his luck. Then Keeshan
slashed at Brandley.

'What about a woman by the name of Smith that accused you
of rape one time?'

'No, sir.'

'Do you know a woman by the name of Pokey that grew up
here in Conroe?'

'I know Pokey.'

Reeves did not know who the hell Pokey was. What was Keeshan driving at?

'Is it true that about eight or nine months ago down in Dugan,
you raped her?'

'No, sir.'

If they had been in court, Reeves could have killed this. It was
a rumour without any evidence. Brandley obviously did not know
what Keeshan was talking about. It was pure prejudice. But Keeshan was up and running and dragging Brandley through the dirt.

'Did she report you to the police?'

'No, sir.'

'You don't think she reported you to the police?'

'No, sir.'

Keeshan paused. Reeves knew that the DA had scored his point.
Without producing this Pokey Smith or any other evidence, Keeshan had planted the idea that Brandley had a history of rape, that
he was some kind of bad nigger. Brandley had even helped him
to do it. And all the time, Keeshan was so charming and persuasive
with the jurors. Reeves had to hand it to him.

Now, for the first time, Keeshan started to ask questions about
events at the high school. Brandley told him all about his job at
the school and how his girlfriend, Beverley, had driven him up
there that Saturday morning, about how he had been going about

doing his work and opening all the doors for the volleyball tournament, and all about rubbish bins and toilet rolls. He remembered how Gary Acreman had told him there was a girl in one of the restrooms and how he had said he did not want to go in there, how he had sent the other janitors across to the vocational building while he had a smoke in his office, and finally how he and Icky Peace had joined the search for the missing girl and found her body in the little props loft over the stage.

That was when Keeshan started slashing at him again.

'You had never been up there before?'

'No, sir.'

'Then I take it you had never had any reason to be up there with a girl before?'

'No, sir.'

'And you had never had any reason to be up there by yourself before?'

'No, sir.'

'Never had any reason to masturbate up there or to have sex with anybody up there before?'

'No, sir.'

'Is that right?'

It was the same trick: Keeshan had planted the idea. Reeves had known it all along: the Grand Jury was just a tool for the DA. Keeshan could tell them any damned thing he wanted, and Reeves just had to sit there and let him do it. His only hope was that Keeshan would start throwing some real evidence at Brandley. That was when they might learn something about what the state was really up to.

Keeshan started asking if Brandley had been wearing a belt on the day of the crime. Or carrying a towel. Brandley said sure, he had been wearing a brown belt, and the police had taken it when he was arrested, but he never had a towel. Reeves guessed this had something to do with the state's case but he was damned if he could see what it was. Then Keeshan started slashing again.

'When you worked for Oscar Johnson, did you ever go into the preparation room where the bodies are?'

'Yes, sir.'

'What do you do in there?'

'I mostly assist.'

'What about when you're there at night by yourself, do you have access to the preparation room?'

If this was in court, Reeves would have hit the sunnuvabitch with so many objections he'd think he'd died and gone to hell. What was this? It had nothing to do with Cheryl Fergeson. The sunnuvabitch was just trying to insinuate some idea about Brandley getting off on dead bodies. That damned Keeshan.

'When you stay there at night by yourself, do you have a key?'

'I never stay there at night by myself.'

'Not even when they're having a wake and you're just sitting there waiting for it to be over?'

'No, sir.'

'You've never been there by yourself?'

'No, sir.'

'Why did you go into that kind of work? You had a job at the high school. Why did you go to work around dead bodies?'

The point was made. Keeshan was on a roll. 'You're divorced? . . . Isn't it true that you're fairly rough on women? . . . Have you ever grabbed a woman by the throat and told her to have intercourse with you? . . . Have you ever hit a woman in the head with a gun? . . . How many women have you been having intercourse with in the past two months? . . .'

Reeves could not see how any of this was relevant, or even true. Keeshan was not pretending it was true. It was nothing but prejudice, but he could see that all of it was encircling Brandley tighter and tighter. Then Keeshan moved in and choked him.

'Do you feel sorry for this little white girl that was strangled and raped like that?'

'I feel sorry for anything like that that happens.'

'Are you going to tell the Grand Jury that you didn't molest that little white girl?'

'Yes, sir.'

That was a cheap shot. That was what had worried Reeves from the moment he heard Brandley had been arrested. Okay, the girl may have been white, but waving that around in front of a Conroe jury like that was as good as booking Brandley his own private suite on Death Row. Now, Keeshan was snapping at Brandley's heels like a dog chasing a rabbit.

'Isn't it true that you grabbed the little girl by the throat and took her in through the stage door?'

'No, I didn't.'

'Didn't you have a strap or something and didn't you put it around her neck?'

'No, sir.'

'You didn't? The poor little girl is dead and you had nothing to do with it?'

'I'm telling you, yes, I had nothing to do with it.'

'The poor little girl was a 16-year-old virgin and wasn't ready for anything like that, was she?'

'I don't know. I didn't know or have anything to do with it.'

'You didn't have anything to do with it?'

'No, sir.'

'You swear to God, of course, and all that sort of thing?'

'Yes.'

'You believe in God?'

'I sure do.'

Finally, Reeves could see it. There was no evidence here: no eyewitness; no scientific breakthrough; no confession. They did not even know whether the murder weapon was a towel or a belt or a strap or some other damned thing, never mind whether Brandley had ever been in possession of it, whatever it was. There was only prejudice.

Keeshan had needed Brandley to come and sit in front of the Grand Jury so that he could throw all this trash at him. And if he threw enough, some of it would stick. In Conroe, most of it would stick. Because Clarence Brandley was not the same as everyone else in that jury room and just in case anyone had missed that fundamental point, Keeshan came right back to it.

'You ever had intercourse with a white woman before?'

'No, sir.'

'Have you ever dated a white woman?'

'No, sir.'

'Did you see any other Negro male that day inside the building?'

'No, sir.'

It did not matter how many times Brandley said his Yessir and his Nosir. Reeves could see that all Keeshan needed was for that black man to sit there and talk in his black voice and show his black face at the table. That was all. There was no stopping Keeshan now. And Brandley was still sitting there telling him the truth.

'Do you think any of the custodians beside yourself might have been able to do this thing?'

'No, sir.'

'You don't believe any of the other custodians did it?'

'Not after the experience I've had working around them. They don't seem to be the type of person that would do it.'

Reeves could see that can't-believe-my-luck look on Keeshan's face again as Brandley swept suspicion away from the best alternative suspects. Brandley added that he was not sure about Gary Acreman, because he made sly remarks and he guessed he might tell lies about him. Keeshan kept slashing.

He asked Brandley about his time in Korea with the army. Had he ever killed anyone in Korea? Had he had intercourse with any young Korean girls? Brandley said he had never killed anyone but he had slept with some Korean women. Pause. What about the Monday after Cheryl Fergeson's death? Hadn't Brandley taken some bags of rubbish out to the dumpster, the same dumpster where the dead girl's clothes were later found? Brandley said, Yes, he had taken out some rubbish. What about him and Icky Peace looking for the missing girl? Why had he done that? Was that part of his job? What about Jo Ellen Parrish? Had he raped her? What about Pokey Smith?

'You raped anyone else?'

'I never raped anybody.'

'You haven't raped anybody?'

'No, sir.'

'Isn't it true that you have some kind of psychiatric problem, that you have some problem about sex and meeting girls?'

'No.'

'You don't have any kind of problem like that?'

'No, sir.'

'You don't need any psychiatric help?'

'No, sir.'

'You don't have any mental problems at all?'

'No, sir.'

'You don't want a psychiatrist to look at you?'

'No, sir.'

'You don't want to know what's wrong with you?'

'There's nothing wrong.'

'You haven't got anything wrong with you?'

'No, sir.'

'Have you ever been told you had any mental problems?'

'No, sir.'

'Did your mother ever try to get you to go to a psychiatrist?'

'No, sir.'

'Not one time? Never even suggested it?'

'No, sir.'

'Never?'

'No, sir.'

'What about the time you tied up your sister and beat her, why did you do that?'

'I never tied up my sister and beat her.'

'You never did that?'

'No, sir.'

'I believe that's all. Thank you for testifying.'

Two feelings that had been wrestling their way through Ray Reeves's mind for the last four days had now become certainties. First, Brandley was innocent and there was no damned evidence to show anything different than that. Second, Brandley was going to be indicted and very likely convicted and sentenced to death.

Ray Reeves was still in Conroe that afternoon when he heard that the Grand Jury had decided to indict Brandley and send him for trial. He was not surprised, not after the way that Keeshan had treated Brandley. But he felt bad. He had fallen straight into Keeshan's trap. He had known all along that he should never have fed Brandley to the Grand Jury. He knew the state would always cheat if it got the chance. That was any DA's rule – cheat the opposition. So he had been a dumb sunnuvabitch and let them do it. He had only been trying to help. He guessed he had messed up again.

The one thing he still had to play for was that he could get Brandley out on bail with a bond that was low enough for the Brandley family to afford. Keeshan had promised him that. All Reeves needed was for the District Attorney to play fair.

Back in his cell, Brandley was visited by Minnie Ola. He could see she was trying to be brave, but she could not hide the way she felt. It was like she was carrying a physical weight. Her old head sagged, her shoulders sloped, her arms were limp as string.

He told her not to cry because he hadn't done nothing, but she cried all the same because she felt it inside her. Just like she had felt it inside her before that he should never go back to that school, now she knew in her soul that they were going to try and kill him.

His brother O.T., who was a Baptist minister, came to see him. Brandley told him about Jo Ellen, about how it had been reported in the papers that he had a shotgun, and then how the DA had tried to tell the Grand Jury he had raped Jo Ellen. He told O.T. about Pokey Smith. They all knew Pokey. He used to play in the dirt with her when she was a kid. She was just a dumb little woman from Dugan who spent a lot of time hanging around in the juke joints. He told O.T. he had once had a fight with her when he was drunk, and he had slapped her and she had called the police. He had paid $50 on the spot and that had been the end of it. He was not proud of it. It was the kind of thing that had made him get out of the fast life and try and settle down. But now, this DA was trying to make out he had raped her, too. It seemed like he had raped a whole lot of people, if the DA was to be believed.

O.T. had bad news. O.T. knew a girl whose uncle was a cop, a black cop, and he had told her to tell O.T. that they were going around looking for dirt on Clarence. So far as O.T. could make out, they had gone through their records looking for anything they could get on him and they must have found out about that business of Jo Ellen making out he had raped her, and he guessed they had found something about him slapping Pokey that time. But that was not all.

According to what O.T. had heard, the person who was digging up the dirt on Clarence, who had most likely been round to see Jo Ellen and Pokey, was Ted Morgan.

Ted Morgan was a legend in the Montgomery County sheriff's department. For them, he was the deputy for Dugan Nigger Town – the one man who knew every black face in every black juke joint, who knew all about how blacks lie and cheat because he was black himself. Old Sheriff Gene Reaves used to get on his radio and sing out: 'Where's ma nigger? Where's ma nigger?' And all the other deputies would wait till they heard the gravelly voice come back: 'Ah'm here, boss.' Then they'd laugh at that.

Ted Morgan had iron grey hair cropped close to his scalp and dull, blank eyes like a dead fish. He was a tough old man. They all knew the stories about how he used to get his confessions, how he used to drive the nigger suspects out into the Big Thicket. Then he'd lead them into the trees, hand them a shovel and tell them to start digging a grave so he could kill them and bury them. Most of them never even started digging, just started talking. The white deputies laughed at the stories, especially when Ted Morgan told them himself. He told them how he had once caught some nigger boy who'd been stealing appliances from empty new houses and how he had taken him into the Big Thicket down on the low land by the river, tied his arms round a tree trunk, stripped the shirt off his back and left him there for the mosquitoes to eat him while he went and sat in his patrol car. It wasn't five minutes, he said, before that damned ol' nigger boy started yelling and hollering and begging to confess – and he'd never laid a hand on him.

It was always a big deal when Ted Morgan brought in a suspect. He would lead him up to the desk and wouldn't fill in any forms or register any charge. He'd just croon in that low, black voice of his: 'The nigger done it. Here's the nigger. The nigger done it.' Then they'd all laugh at that, because they knew the reason he never filled in any forms was because he could not read nor write.

If Ted Morgan was down in Dugan trying to dig some dirt, Brandley knew that meant trouble. There was no telling what Jo Ellen and Pokey would come out with.

Ray Reeves visited him, too, full of anger at Keeshan for the trash he had been throwing around at the Grand Jury.

Brandley had a confession to make. He had fouled up on a question: he hoped it was not going to be important. But he had told Keeshan that he had been wearing his brown belt on the day of the crime. Well, that was not right. He had been wearing it with his white trousers when he was arrested. But on the day of the crime, he had been wearing his old blue jeans which had a built-in belt round the top. They didn't need a leather belt. He hoped it was not going to be important.

Reeves told him there was no damned way of knowing if it was going to be important because the damned DA himself couldn't make up his mind what the murder weapon was supposed to have been.

Reeves asked Brandley about the 45 minutes when he was supposed to have been missing while the girl was raped and killed. It took Brandley a moment to realize that they were talking about the one time during that day when he had managed to get a moment to himself, when he had sat in his office and smoked his cigarette and listened to the radio. Was he supposed to have had the girl in there with him? This was crazy. But how could he prove it? He had been alone. He had no alibi. If he was going to rape and kill a white girl, he would surely have planned something better than this. They could not be serious. And what about the lie test? Didn't that prove it? He had passed that damned lie test and that cop had told him he had nothing to worry about.

Ray Reeves told him straight: 'They changed their minds, Clarence. They're saying you failed the lie test.'

Brandley felt the sweat prickle his face.

Ray Reeves was not sure, but as far as he could make out it was the Texas Ranger, Wes Styles, who had done it. On Friday morning, a few hours before they had come to arrest him, Styles had called up Houston Police Department and persuaded a supervisor there to go take another look at the polygraph test. The supervisor had looked at the graph and decided there was one answer where there could have been a deception. It was not the big question – whether he raped and killed Cheryl Fergeson. Not even the supervisor said that he had failed that. It was one of the general questions about whether he had ever had sex with anyone against their will. The supervisor was saying that his answer there might have been a deception and he was saying the man who ran the test might have been a little inexperienced. As far as Ray Reeves could see, that didn't matter a damn to this inquiry.

'It's just like a shrink in a divorce case,' he said. 'You pay him and he'll say whatever you want him to. They gave you that test and you passed the sunnuvabitch. So they got another expert to say you failed it. It's so absurd.'

But it seemed it was good enough for the Texas Ranger, Wes Styles. Now everybody in the DA's office and the Conroe Police Department was going round saying that Brandley had failed the polygraph test.

Ray Reeves still had no money with which to fight this case. He had talked to the Brandleys and, so far as he could tell, he could have taken the whole bunch of them, turned them upside down and shaken them till their eyeballs rattled and he wouldn't have got more than $400 out of the lot of them. He told them: 'From a business point of view, I'm sucking hind tit here.'

But Brandley had put in his savings – the money he had been putting aside for Clarence jr. – and some of his aunts and uncles had put in the bit of cash they had. It was not enough to fight a big case like this, not much more than $500, but it was enough to do one thing that Reeves badly needed.

The day of the Grand Jury hearing, Ray Reeves hired himself a private investigator.

Lorna Hubbell was not exactly Ray Reeves's idea of a private investigator.

She must have been six foot tall and no more than 25 years old. She had lots of bouncy blonde hair and a wide-eyed chatterbox kind of way about her. She was not an ex-cop, like most private investigators, and she had never taken any of the courses that they usually had. Instead, she had a degree in behavioural science. She was not even a Texan. She came from California, somewhere near Los Angeles, and she said things like 'Houston is what happens when architecture catches venereal disease.'

But Lorna Hubbell came highly recommended. She was working for a Houston agency, Burkett and Burkett, which was run
by a husband and wife team – both of them ex-cops. They swore
by her. She had plenty of guts, she could talk her way out of a
tornado, she didn't mind what she did and she would work from
can to can't without stopping to draw a breath.

The day after the Grand Jury hearing, Thursday 4 September,
Lorna Hubbell drove up from Houston to see Clarence Brandley.
She was rather disappointed. She thought this was a big, hot case.
It had been in the papers in Houston and on television just because
it was such a horrible crime. And here she was interviewing the
man in the midst of it all. But he didn't seem to know the first
thing about it. And he was shy with her. Or something. Maybe
he just wasn't used to white women. But he just said 'No, mam'
and 'Yes, mam' in a soft voice.

He tried to explain to her what he had done on the day of the
crime and how he had found all these doors open before they
discovered the body. He seemed credible, but he seemed to have
no idea of time throughout the whole day of the crime. He ended
up giving her the names of the four white janitors and of anyone
else he could think of who worked up at the school.

She went to see Ray Reeves, who told her he knew no more
than Brandley because the DA would not tell him anything, and
they agreed that they were going to have to investigate this whole
crime themselves. They had to clear Brandley but, before they
could do that, they had to try and find out who had really committed this crime and – just as important – what evidence that District
Attorney was working on that made him think he could hang this
black janitor.

The next day, Lorna Hubbell went to Conroe High School in
search of witnesses. They were not pleased to see her.

She spoke to the assistant principal, a tall thin man with glasses,
who told her he was not allowed to discuss the case. She spoke
to Brandley's boss, Mallie Davis, but he said he was not allowed
to discuss the case. He said Brandley was a good and trustworthy
worker, but he refused to put that on paper or say it before a
jury. The volleyball coach told her she remembered Brandley
wandering around the gyms that day and asking her if there was

enough toilet paper in one of the girls' restrooms. She said Brandley must be guilty and that he was the only person who could
have committed the crime because he was the only one who had
keys to the auditorium where the girl's body was found.

Finally she found one friendly face, a woman named Marsha
Porter, who ran all the sports classes for girls in the school. She
showed Lorna round the school, and they tried to retrace the
black janitor's steps down the long hallway with the cafeteria on
the left and the auditorium on the right and the restrooms on the
landing just past the auditorium, where the Sesame Street characters were. They knew from the newspaper reports that the girl
had last been seen looking for a restroom, but they had no idea
which one. She might have gone into the dressing-room by the
gyms and used the restroom there, in which case she must have
been abducted and taken outside the building and into the auditorium. Or she might have walked down to Sesame Street and met
her attacker there, and been dragged off that landing and into the
auditorium. For all her friendliness, Marsha Porter did not disguise
her feeling that Brandley might be guilty. She thought it must be
a janitor who had done it: he would have to have the keys to the
auditorium, he would need to know that the props loft was up
there, and he would need to be inconspicuous. An outsider, she
thought, would surely have been noticed by someone.

Lorna Hubbell left the school feeling almost completely in the
dark. Brandley's keys were obviously going to be used against
him, so they would have to try and prove that these auditorium
doors could have been opened by someone else. Beyond that, all
she had discovered was that someone seemed to have talked to
these people at the school and told them not to talk to the defence,
that someone seemed to want to keep Clarence Brandley in the
dark.

As Lorna Hubbell toured the school, Brandley was making his
first court appearance. He had been taken from his cell and had
walked a gauntlet of whispers to get to court. Ray Reeves had
driven up from Houston, huffing and puffing that Keeshan had
better keep his end of the damned deal. Minnie Ola Brandley had
put on her church clothes and set out across the tracks from

Dugan. Half her family seemed to be crowding round her as she limped up the hard, white steps and through the heavy double doors into Montgomery County courthouse.

The second-floor courtroom was clean and white with a bright blue carpet. At one end, seated on a raised dais, was the judge, Lee Alworth, a small white man in a black gown whose hair was being eaten up by his forehead on both sides of his scalp. He had a tense, impatient air about him and a way of clenching his teeth so that his jaw muscles bulged in his cheeks. Brandley knew his face. This was the same judge who had given him three years' probation for that rusty shotgun.

The hearing was short. Ray Reeves asked the judge to set bail. Minnie Ola's brother, Frank, had come up from Houston to try and help. He went into the witness box and answered some questions. He said the family had talked about raising some money for a bail bond. 'We talked it over. But it's pretty scarce. We couldn't come up with too much. Some of 'em is working and some of 'em is not and I am on disability. I imagine we could come up with ten or twenty thousand dollars for a bond.'

Reeves asked if that would be in cash.

'Cash? Well, that would be about a couple of thousand.'

Could they really not raise any more than that?

'Well, I don't know. Money is pretty scarce the way we are living.'

Judge Alworth said he would set bail at $30,000 and called for the next case.

To Minnie Ola Brandley and her family, the judge might as well have asked for the Empire State Building. They did not have it. But Ray Reeves tried to persuade himself that he was happy with it. He knew Keeshan could have pushed the judge for a much higher bond and he reckoned the Brandleys would find the money if they put their minds to it, although it might take them a couple of weeks. It looked as if Keeshan was delivering his end of the deal. It was just that it seemed a little too easy, and he kept asking himself if there was not something he had missed.

Reeves did not have to wait long for the answer. That same day, the office of the District Attorney filed its first motion in the case of Clarence Brandley.

It was a motion to revoke Brandley's probation. Reeves had never claimed to be a legal scholar, but he knew what that meant. Brandley could not get bail. Not at any price. Not at $30,000. Not at $30 million. No bail. The whole deal with Keeshan was out of the window. The motion said that Brandley had breached the terms of his probation by raping and murdering Cheryl Ferge- son and so he had to serve his three-year sentence. That motion had to go before the court to be ruled on but, in the meantime, the law said that the defendant automatically lost his right to bail.

Reeves was so angry he ran out of curses. It was not just the sheer two-faced deceit of it. What really made him sick was when he examined the papers and found that they had been drafted three days earlier – on Tuesday – before Brandley had been to the Grand Jury. Christ Almighty, that was the same day that Keeshan had made the deal with him.

Nobody in the Brandley family had ever expected an easy life. They had lived in this same shack on Avenue E ever since Minnie Ola had married Buck Brandley back in 1931, when she was only 16. Minnie Ola was not from Conroe originally. She was born 40 miles north, in Huntsville, with seven brothers and sisters who had had a tough time after their mother died when Minnie Ola was little. When she was 13 years old, her father had sent her to live in Conroe, to help his brother Frank whose wife was sick. Uncle Frank worked all night in the sawmill and Minnie Ola looked after his wife and kids for him. Then she had met Buck Brandley and, before she knew it, she was married and having children of her own.

Buck Brandley was born in Montgomery town and raised in Conroe. Most of his life, he repaired track for the Santa Fe railway, like his father, Putt, before him. He and Minnie Ola often had to move to follow the work, even when they had all 11 of their children – six boys and five girls – with them. Silsbee, Somerville, Brenham, Clay, Navasota: they had lived all down the line, but they always came back to Conroe, to the shack on Avenue E.

It was a pretty good place, they always said. Apart from the little kitchen and bathroom at the back, it had two bedrooms and a little dining-room and a front room, too. They usually slept side-by-side, three or four to a room. At the back there was a little land, maybe as much as five acres, and Buck had worked hard on that land. He had a mule to plough it with, and a man called Mr Prince – whom they always called the agriculture man – came from the Government to teach him how to get the most out of it, how to rotate his crops. Buck planted everything on that land: peas, sweet potatoes, corn, Irish potatoes, squash, beets, cucumber, tomatoes, water melon. Even a bit of cotton. He kept some cows and chickens too. They used to work on the land every evening, Buck with the mule and plough, the children pulling up the weeds, putting in the seed and the fertilizer by hand. They sold a lot of what they grew but there was always food. Plenty of biscuits. Chicken. If they had a chicken to eat, they would eat all of it, the feet, the neck, even the gizzard, and keep the best parts for special days and not throw anything away.

Buck was always trying to earn some extra cash on the side. He used to sell peanuts. Everybody in Conroe knew Buck Brandley with his two-foot metal tray full of nuts. He more or less had the peanut franchise for the town. He used to buy a 100–pound sack and then the children would cook them and put them into ten-cent bags and he would sell them at baseball games or at the schools. Some of the schools would not let him through the gate, so he sold them on the pavement outside instead. Buck used to get barrels and sell them to politicians for them to give lemonade to the crowd at their meetings. He would sell the calves that his cows produced. If a mule or a horse died, he used to take it down the street to Miss Griffith's house and she would make soap out of the corpse. Clarence and his brothers and sisters had often wondered how she did that, but they never were allowed to see.

Buck was always working. He might have been a rich man if he had been white. As it was, they scraped along. Minnie Ola used sackcloth to make dresses for the girls. Neighbours gave them hand-me-downs. They never had a car, though they had once had a pick-up truck. They never owned a radio. Once, after Buck had been selling peanuts, he said he had some money and they could buy a television, but Clarence's eldest sister, Ola May, started fussing because she was courting and she wanted to get something fancy to show her boyfriend, so they got a dining-room table instead. Years later, they did buy a second-hand television set for $15 and all the children were happy.

Sunday always used to be the biggest day. They had their Sunday clothes and shoes. During the week, they might look pretty rough, but not on Sunday. They would all go off together to the Church of God in Christ in the white wooden shack a block away on Avenue F and sit there from nine-o'clock until eleven. The children were supposed to pay attention all that time – no talking, no reading, no gum – but they used to let the small ones go to sleep on the bench if they got tired.

Elder Duncan was the preacher then and everybody had a lot of respect for him, a lot of reverence. If people were sick, he would come and put oil on them. What he said really mattered. Each family in the congregation used to take it in turns to give him Sunday lunch. When he came to the Brandley house, all the children were very excited and they all felt blessed and let him have the best piece of chicken.

Clarence had still been young when Buck and Minnie Ola broke up. There had been trouble between them for a long time. Some drinking. Some fighting. Some bad fighting. It got so bad that Buck moved out, around 1962 when Clarence was 11 years old, and eventually they got a divorce. Most of the children had been grown-up by then. But Clarence and his twin sister, Florence, were the youngest and they were left in the shack with Minnie Ola and the two other youngest boys, Tim and Ozell, who was always known as O.T.

Buck gave Minnie Ola $80 a month but she couldn't manage on that, not with four children and bills to pay. She went to Mrs Etheridge who she'd worked for part-time for 35 years, cooking and ironing and minding her children, and she asked for a raise; but Mrs Etheridge turned her down. So she had to go on welfare.

Clarence went to Booker T Washington School, the black school in Dugan, where he was an average student. He played a lot of basketball and once broke his leg playing football. Then while he was in the ninth grade, Minnie Ola had become very ill. She had some mental trouble and couldn't even remember what day of the week it was. It turned out she had a blood clot on the brain. They said it was the size of a golf ball and could have been something to do with one of her old fights with Buck. She was in a bad way. She could not even make it to O.T.'s graduation day. They operated on her but she could not work any more the way she used to, so she moved to Houston with Clarence and Florence and Tim to stay with her sister in the fifth Ward.

For a long time, Houston seemed like home to Brandley. He finished high school, had a baby daughter with a girl and then got drafted to go to Vietnam. At the last moment, they switched him to Korea and he spent 17 months in uniform, mostly in communications. When it was over he returned to Houston, married, had two more kids including Clarence jr., separated and had two further children with another woman. Finally he had got sick of it all and headed back up to Conroe, where Minnie Ola was back living on Avenue E. All he had been looking for was a steady job and a steady life.

The night after Keeshan had broken his deal about Brandley's bail, Ray Reeves and Lorna Hubbell drove round to Avenue E to see Minnie Ola Brandley. Some of her other children were there, and so was Brandley's girlfriend Beverley. They were very bitter. They all agreed that Clarence was being railroaded. And they all agreed why: the police had to arrest someone to stop the panic before school started, and Clarence had been the nearest black man on the scene.

Tim Brandley said he had spoken to a white policeman about it who had said: 'How come they're still holding your brother? Don't you know they found a white man's hair on the girl's body?'

They had all seen a story in the Conroe *Courier* about a 15-year-old schoolgirl in Cleveland, 30 miles away, who had been abducted, raped and strangled and left for dead, though she had survived. Wasn't that where that weird janitor lived? Icky Peace? How come they didn't arrest him? And why was the captain of detectives telling the paper, 'Nothing is going to make me change my mind'?

And how could they take away Clarence's bail like that? And how could they just magically turn that lie test around? And what was all this about Jo Ellen and Pokey? In Dugan, there was talk that they had somehow been persuaded to say bad things about Clarence. Both women had told Ted Morgan that Clarence had raped them. Pokey was supposed to have said he raped her four times. What was it all about?

Ray Reeves said he was doing his best to get on top of the case, but it wasn't easy with a sunnuvabitch like Keeshan. So far as he could tell, Keeshan was working on a circumstantial case. He was going to say Brandley had been missing for 45 minutes, that during that time he had come across the girl in one of the restrooms or somewhere, that he had taken his belt or a towel to strangle her, and then that he had used his keys to get into the auditorium and hide the body there. Keeshan was going to have to say that Brandley changed his mind about hiding her and decided to take Icky Peace and find her again. Reeves did not know. It did not make much sense to him. He couldn't help fearing that Keeshan was hiding some stick of dynamite – a fingerprint or something – that was going to blow them clean out of the water.

But at that moment, it looked to him like a straightforward circumstantial case. And a damned flimsy one at that. He told the Brandleys to stay cool, raise money and hope there was justice in this town.

3

The people of Dugan could offer Clarence Brandley little more than their sympathy. That was the way it had always been, though the Reverend Jerry P. Jones found it hard to believe.

Revd Jones had just moved to Dugan from his birthplace in Birmingham, Alabama, to minister at the Pilgrim Rest Baptist Church on Third Street. He was a commanding sight in his new pulpit, young and tall and strong, with a voice that boomed all the way to the back of the church. He was shocked by Conroe, which looked to him as if it had been completely forgotten by the civil rights movement. It seemed to him that the law might have changed, but the town hadn't.

He looked at the houses in Dugan that were nothing but shinny shacks and said, 'You don't see shinny shacks any more in Birmingham, Alabama because we tore them down and what we didn't tear down, we burned down.' He saw the big, brick-built churches on the white side of town, and it stirred a deep rage in him when white ministers called him up to give him the names of black people who had turned up in a white church, so that he could contact them and steer them back to one of the little wooden churches in Dugan. He saw people in Dugan who were submissive, who did not try to fight for their rights, and he protested, 'Anything they put on you, you just accept.' Most of all, he saw black people who had no power, because nothing in the town belonged to them. 'Everything you want – jobs, loans, credit at the store – whatever you want, you have to get from white hands. You don't own any businesses. You don't have any investment in anything. You don't have any decent clubs, no decent community centres, no facilities at all. The only kind of black business you have here is a juke joint, a hole in the wall where you dance and drink some beer and raise hell and curse.'

The more he looked into Conroe, the worse it got. There were no blacks on the school-board and there never had been any. There were none on the county commission which ran Montgomery County and there never had been. The mayor was white. So was the city administrator. So were all the judges, the district attorney, the county attorney, the sheriff, the chief of police, the captain of detectives, the fire chief, the president of the Chamber of Commerce, the county librarian, the four county constables, the tax assessor, the editor of the *Courier* and all the reporters who wrote for the *Courier*. And they always had been. In the whole town, so far as he could tell, there had never been a black doctor or an architect or an accountant or any other middle-class professional who was born and bred in Dugan. No matter what Congress or the Supreme Court or the *New York Times* might say, Revd Jerry P. Jones could see that Conroe was still a white man's town. The only exception was Oscar Johnson jr.

Revd Jones liked Oscar Johnson, and one of the reasons was that Johnson had no illusions about why he had become the first and only black man ever to be elected to public office in the history of Montgomery County. Johnson readily admitted that he had become a city councillor because he presented no threat to the white man's town.

Oscar Johnson grew up in Willis, just north of Conroe, at a time when he was told his place and what he could do, and he did not argue. He never expected anything else. That was how black people were then. When he went to a football game he didn't try and sit in white seats. When he went to a picture show, he went up the top seats because that was where black people were supposed to be. When he moved to Conroe with his father in 1962 and started running the funeral parlour in Dugan, he knew what kind of town this was. His business often took him up to the courthouse. There were different drinking fountains – 'whites only' and 'coloured'; different restrooms; restaurants where blacks couldn't walk through the front door. He never expected anything else.

He worked hard. He read *How to Win Friends and Influence*

People and kept a copy in his office. He soon had a reputation as a moderate man and so, in 1974, after Greg Steele was killed by the police and black people finally started to say they wanted someone from their end of town who could be on the city council, they looked to Oscar Johnson. They knew no black person could be elected without white votes. The council had made sure that Conroe was never split up into voting districts and so the minority of black votes was always swamped by the white majority. Oscar Johnson, they hoped, might be acceptable to the whites. At his second try, in 1976, Johnson's moderate approach won him a seat on the council, but despite his slow, unthreatening politics, he had trouble. White people called him on the phone and made threats. There were rumours that someone had hired the organized crime group, the Texas Syndicate, to kill him. Once, someone came by his house in Dugan and emptied a .22 rifle through his front door. Oscar Johnson knew Conroe was still a racist town. You might not see the signs up any more; it might not be on such a big scale as it once was. But he saw it every day in his work. In the old days of segregation there had been two cemeteries set aside for black people – Rosewood and Golden Gate – and in all the years since segregation ended, Oscar Johnson had still never buried a black body in a white cemetery and, even though his prices were the lowest in town, no white family had ever asked him to bury their dead.

There were times when the Reverend Jerry P. Jones despaired of Conroe. Around the corner from his church he noticed that there was one building amongst the crumbling wooden shacks that was built of brick with a neatly clipped lawn. He soon discovered that this was the home of the man they called the Head Nigger, who owned most of the shinny shacks and who had become rich off the rent he collected from the inhabitants and who now lived in great comfort off the proceeds. It had been no different in the days of slavery. The white masters would let one or two blacks get the upper hand over the rest and pay them to whip the others into line. The Head Nigger was like some kind of Godfather who handed out favours in Dugan. There was nothing Revd Jones could do about it: the man was also a church deacon.

Revd Jones often heard that things had changed in Conroe. It was the steady refrain of white people in the courthouse and on the city council.

There had been a time in Conroe when white people made no attempt to hide their feelings for the people of Dugan. The *Courier* used to run a column called 'A Little Fun – Jokes To Make You Laugh' in which black people were regular stars: the coloured maid who was about to get married and asked her mistress to keep her savings for her because 'ah hates to keep all dat money in de house wid a strange niggah man'; the black 'mammy' who always signed her name with an 'X', then started signing with a 'Y' because 'Ise done got married yistidy an' changed mah name'; the church committee which met to discuss 'de financial en pecuniary affairs ob dis chu'ch' and was told that 'de treasurer done obscunded wid all de money'; the old coloured lady who refused to go on a carousel because she had seen her friend Rastus on it and asked, 'Rastus, yo' spent yo' money but whar yo' bin?'

The Ku-Klux-Klan had met openly in the town. In February 1923, the *Courier* reported on its front page: 'The Conroe Ku-Klux-Klan enjoyed a most bountiful oyster supper at the Klan Hall in the Foster building last Thursday night in which several scores of Klansmen participated in devouring oysters, cakes and coffee, and several hundred valiant oysters lost their lives that the Kluxers might eat and be merry.'

The history of Dugan was full of victims: an unarmed man shot dead by a deputy in July 1932 because 'he put his hands on the front of his shirt and I thought he was going to shoot me'; young Tommie Goffney, who in January 1951 wrote a letter to a white girl asking her for a date and was fined $100 by a Conroe judge who told him he wished the law allowed him to punish him more severely; Dedward Galveston who had his head split open by a white man with a pair of ice tongs outside the Dude Ranch Cafe in July 1951; the unnamed man who was found dead by a roadside in August 1930 with his legs and arms broken and a hole in the back of his head and who was judged to have died accidentally; a black lumber worker who was given a lift by two deputies who then locked him in a cell, fired tear-gas cylinders at him, beat him over the head with a pistol and asked for him to be declared a lunatic; Marshall Waters and Zeke Rollin, who in June 1922 were shot at a road-block by police who heard rumours that black people were getting drunk on whisky and planning an uprising. Even during the Second World War when Montgomery County called on all men and women between the ages of 15 and 101 to register for civilian defence and bitterly attacked Germany and Japan for their record of 'enslaved people and the destruction of human freedom', the council stated clearly that only white citizens should apply.

All through Dugan's history, the victims showed the same willing compliance in their oppression which so frustrated the newly arrived Revd Jones. It was expressed most clearly on a graduation day in the spring of 1923 at Conroe College, the only college to which black students were admitted. The new graduates – the cream of Dugan's rising young generation – were sitting quietly in their best clothes under the eyes of their proud parents. They were listening to the founder of the college, the Revd J. Johnson, then the most respected figure in the black community, as he outlined for them the brave new future for which they had worked and which was now within their grasp. It was a future weighed down by the past. The new graduates were told to find work as domestic servants. 'All sensible Negroes know that the South only knows the Negro as a servant, labourer and menial in the industries of the country, and we must prove ourselves worthy and indispensable in these vocations before we aspire for the higher industrial regions.' There was no question of these bright young black people trying to influence the nation's future. 'I do not wish to make you a power in the political world, but I am working to make you good in character and useful in life,' their mentor told them. 'You young people must be taught to know what duty means and that all service is honourable, and to know that politeness is cultural gentleness and not cowardice.' In their quest to give satisfaction to the white man, the college founder advised them, they could do no better than to model themselves on the obedience of their ancestors who were slaves. 'Their faithfulness to their mistresses and masters during the war between the states won for them the love and confidence of every southerner. Love, virtue, labour and economy will bring to you a greatness which no race can ignore or despise and this is the education my people need.'

Revd Jones was sure that things had changed in Conroe, but he was not so sure it made a difference. White people still ran the town and black people still let them. 'You can cut the rattles off a rattle snake,' he liked to say, 'but you can't stop him biting like a rattler all the same.'

In the old days, Conroe's politicians never lifted a finger to help black people unless it suited them. There was a famous time in 1968, during integration, when the committee on civic affairs suddenly called on the council to clean up Dugan. The committee had visited Dugan and found piles of rubbish alive with maggots, open sewers spilling waste into yards where barefoot black children played, pigs and dogs running wild, and row after row of dilapidated and unhealthy homes. One Conroe official explained that the reason he wanted to clean up Dugan was that the town's schools were now being integrated. 'And I don't like the idea of those kids bringing diseases from their filthy homes to school and exposing our children to them.' The politicians still did nothing for black people unless they had to. Even when federal law compelled them to integrate the schools, they had held a referendum and voted by 2,337 votes to 218 to ban the busing of children between racially segregated areas. Earlier that year, in May 1980, the Justice Department in Washington DC had ordered the school board in Houston to stop discriminating against black schoolchildren, and Conroe's schools superintendent, Chuck York, had stood up and attacked the Justice Department for interfering.

As far as Revd Jones could see, most of the changes seemed to have driven the racism a little way underground but not to have stopped it. White people in Conroe might not print jokes about niggers in the paper any more, but he didn't doubt they told them in private just the same – and what was more, they still liked to believe that black people were just as stupid and dishonest as the niggers in the jokes. Black people in Conroe still became domestic servants and gardeners and store cashiers, even though the white schools pretended to be grooming them for professional careers. They were still victims. There was a white woman on trial right now who had paid someone to kill her daughter because she was going out with a black man. The Klan was still active in Texas. It had little of the political power it once had, but it had been running 'white youth self-defence and survival camps' and it was planning a protest against Vietnamese immigrants which its Grand Dragon, Louis Beam, described in the papers as 'an old time political rally with a fish fry, flag-waving, some speechmaking, maybe some apple pie and a cross-lighting.'

There were very few people in Dugan who would even think of fighting. Charles Henry might have fought if he had believed anyone would join him. He had been at school with Brandley and, unlike many of his classmates, he had not only left Conroe but travelled around the world a bit, particularly in the Middle East where he worked as an oil hand, so he had learned that life did not have to be the way it was in Conroe. Charles Henry had tried to get Dugan moving by launching the Montgomery County Black Awareness Committee. People said they supported it, but joining was another matter. So far as Henry could see, people were too frightened of trouble. As long as they had bread on the table, they said 'What the heck'. Charles Henry and his wife held an annual Black History week where they elected a black beauty queen. That was a victory of a sort, to give black women pride in themselves; but it was a defeat, too, to admit that they had no chance of winning in the rest of Conroe. Henry had no doubt that Conroe was still essentially the same in 1980 as it had been when he was a child in the 1950s and used to go down to the river and lie quietly in the bushes to watch the white men burn their crosses there. Things had changed enough that his white boss felt OK about inviting him to his wedding recently. But they had not changed too much: as soon as he sat down in the church, some white man came up and started asking who he was and what he was doing there. To his mind, they might not call him nigger to his face any more, but white folk still didn't think his children were good enough to marry their children and, so long as white men ran this town, he guessed they never would.

He and Revd Jerry Jones were isolated. Revd Jones liked to think he was not just a preacher but a fighter too. There was no point in being afraid. 'If you don't have something worthy dying

for,' he used to say, 'you don't have anything worth living for.'
It made him want to cry that a black man could still be railroaded
in this day and age just because he was black. It reminded him of
the Crucifixion, when the crowd freed Barabas and called out for
Jesus to be killed. It was as if Conroe was calling out 'Give us the
nigger. That will satisfy our thirst.' Yet there seemed to be no one
in Dugan who would stand up and fight for Clarence Brandley.

The young minister could only stand in his pulpit and warn
them in his big booming voice: 'They talk about justice being
blindfolded. That's the biggest lie. That woman can see. She knows
the colour of your skin.'

If Clarence Brandley didn't kill that girl, then who did? So far as
Ray Reeves could see, it had to be either one of the white janitors
or an outsider of some kind – someone who had got into the
school that morning and tried to assault her, or someone who
knew her and maybe even met her there by arrangement, perhaps
a boyfriend who wanted to have sex with her when she didn't. It
could have been anyone.

To narrow down the suspects, Reeves needed to know about
the scene of the crime. Had the attacker left anything there? Any
item of clothing? Something that might have fallen out of his
pocket? A footprint? Were there blood stains or signs of a struggle
to show whether she had been raped there, or raped in some other
place and then dragged up to the loft when she was dead? But the
District Attorney would not let him look at the photographs the
police had taken of the scene.

He needed to know about the dead girl's body. Had she
scratched her attacker and got his skin or blood under her nails?
Did she have semen on her body or in her vagina? Were there
bite marks on her? Or even fingerprints, which could sometimes
be lifted from a corpse? Were there bruises round her wrists to
suggest that she had been tied or handcuffed? Were there cuts or
scuff marks on her legs to show whether she had been dragged or
carried? What was this mark round her neck like? Had she definitely been strangled and, if so, with what? But the District
Attorney would not let him look at the autopsy report.

He needed to know the results of scientific tests. If semen or blood had been found, then what blood group was it? If there were fingerprints, to whom did they belong? Was it true that there was a white man's hair on the body? What other hairs or types of hair were there? But the District Attorney would not let him look at any of the scientific reports.

He needed to get hold of the dead girl's clothes, samples of her hair and of any other little clues that had been found in the school that day, so that he could send them off to be tested by his own scientists. But the District Attorney would not release the girl's clothes or anything else that had been found.

Most important, Reeves needed to get blood and hair samples from the white janitors and from Frank, the dead girl's boyfriend, as well as from anyone else who might have been near her. But the District Attorney would not give him anything and, even worse, he did not seem to be interested in getting them for himself.

That was what really bothered Ray Reeves. Clarence Brandley did not kill that girl. Someone else did. But the District Attorney and the Texas Ranger did not seem to want to find out. It was as if they were so focused on the black man that they were blind to everything else.

Lorna Hubbell was still looking for clues, but she felt that someone had been there before her and swept them all away. People were so clammed up, they would not even tell her why they were clammed up; the other janitors, high school students, teachers, Brandley's bosses, they were all the same. Someone had always been there before her and silenced these people.

As the weeks passed, she began to feel more strongly that Brandley was innocent. It was not just that his story was credible. It was this sensation she felt of working against a whole town which was determined to see this man convicted, even if it meant sweeping away the truth. She could taste the prejudice.

She began to develop her own theory about the crime. She could see why people believed the murderer must be one of the janitors. They were in the building, they were inconspicuous, they would know about the props loft, and they could easily have got hold of keys. But, in her mind, Brandley was probably the least suspect of any of the janitors. It was not as if he had ever had a problem with women, and she had met Beverley and seen how crazy she was about him.

Lorna Hubbell's suspicion turned to Icky Peace. Brandley had told her that Peace was always complaining that women did not like him and that he had tried to get the other janitors to find a woman for him. So Peace had the simplest possible motive for trying to rape someone. Brandley also said the little janitor had been on his own in the teachers' lounge for more than an hour that morning, so he had had the opportunity.

But he was so small. How could he have abducted a healthy teenage girl and forced himself upon her? That was what most excited Lorna Hubbell's suspicion. If Brandley was telling the truth, Peace was carrying a small armoury in his car that day and had previously brought his hand-gun into the school. If Peace had had his gun with him it would have been simple for him to confront the girl, take her at gunpoint up into the props loft, tie her up, rape her and then strangle her. The big problem with her theory was that Brandley rejected it. He liked Icky Peace and he would not believe that he was capable of committing such a terrible crime. Lorna Hubbell wanted to see for herself.

Within days of the murder, Peace had been transferred away from Conroe High School and word at the school was that he had been moved to stop him talking. Lorna Hubbell traced him to a junior high school in the town, drove there before he was due to start work, spotted him waddling away from his old green Chevrolet and bounced up to him like a long-lost friend. Peace said he would be happy to talk. 'I got nothing to hide,' he piped, peering up at the girl, who was a full twelve inches taller than him. But before she could start asking him any questions, he said something that sounded like an echo from every interview she had ever started on this case.

'I can't say anything,' he said. 'I better call my attorney.'

Lorna Hubbell watched him, fascinated. He was like a little child playing at being a grown-up. He strode purposefully into one of the school offices, pulled out an address book, and, frowning with concentration, dialled the number of his attorney. As soon as the attorney came on the line, Peace passed the phone to Lorna. The attorney said he had spoken to Jim Keeshan about the case and he did not want Icky Peace to talk. 'He's a little slow, you know.'

Lorna was not so sure. Peace was watching her the way a dog watches a bird. He was not missing a thing. And he was beginning to look nervous, moving in a jerky kind of way, even trembling a little, she thought. She said goodbye to the attorney and started gently chatting with Icky. She did not want to push him about the crime. She let him talk instead about the police and how they had treated him. For the first time, she began to understand why people were refusing to speak to her.

'They treated me real bad,' he said, his eyes staring up at her through his spectacles. They had called him names. They had mistreated him. He had been scared. They had made him sign a statement and he never even knew what was in it. He did not know how to read: he had just had to sign it. Then there was the Texas Ranger. He had come by a week after the murder and scared him out of his wits. Peace fingered a silver chain round his neck. It had a tag on the end which said he was diabetic. He said the Ranger had threatened him and grabbed this chain and tried to choke him with it. Now he couldn't sleep, and he had nightmares about what had happened. It had all gone blank in his mind. He could not remember what had happened, except when he tried to sleep, and then he could see the girl lying there.

'She was pretty,' he confided. 'Very pretty.'

Lorna Hubbell watched him talk. She could not see why Brandley was so sure he was innocent. If she had been a cop, she would have been much more interested in this little guy than in the black man. And that was another thing: if Peace was carrying all those clubs and guns around in his car, why hadn't the police charged him with unlawful possession of weapons? If Peace had that hanging over him, he would surely do anything these cops told him to. They could bust him and get him fired in hours if they wanted to.

She started to press him on the crime and was shocked to find that he did not share Brandley's feelings of friendship. Instead, the little janitor was damning. He was sure Clarence had done it. Clarence had a problem with women, he said, and he worked in a mortuary at weekends, which was mighty strange. Clarence must have done it, because he had kept sending him up into that props loft and getting mad with him until he found the girl's body. He must have known it was there.

That was news to Lorna Hubbell, and bad news, too. If that was what Peace was telling the police, that would look very damaging to a jury.

Peace said he had to get on with his work. Lorna Hubbell let him go and drove off to look for more clues. She could not quite make up her mind about him. He was obviously going to be a hostile witness. Maybe that was because he was guilty himself and he wanted to cover it up. Maybe he was just too scared of the cops and the Texas Ranger to dare to quarrel with their version of events. She could not be sure.

It was the same way with these stories that the District Attorney was spreading around, that Brandley had a history of raping women in Dugan. She had been trying to find Jo Ellen Parrish, the black prostitute. The defence needed to know whether Brandley really had taken her out of The Doll House and raped her in his mother's shack, or whether she had just said that to keep her boyfriend quiet. Lorna Hubbell suspected she was lying: if the rape had really happened and she had had the strength to get through the difficult part of reporting it and getting the police to believe her, she would surely not have dropped the complaint without explanation a few days later. It sounded like she had made up the story for her boyfriend and never meant it to reach the police.

Now she drove across town to find an elderly black lady named Rosie Holmes. She was Jo Ellen's grandmother, and somebody had called Ray Reeves' office to say that she knew the truth about Jo Ellen's rape story. Lorna Hubbell stopped outside a small, wood-framed house on the edge of Conroe. After a lot of knocking, a round old black lady with grey hair and a cotton housecoat opened the door. She stood back in the shadows of the house, talking through the screen door and saying she was not feeling well because she was just out of hospital where she had been for ten days. Lorna Hubbell explained why she had come.

'Oh, yeah!' said the old lady. 'Now my granddaughter said all that stuff about being raped and all, and she told me that she never was raped, that there was never time for him to rape her.'

Lorna pressed her for more details. The old lady did not have many. All she knew was that Jo Ellen had told her that this man had cooked her some food because she was hungry and that nothing had happened. That was all she knew. Except that she was sure Jo Ellen had just said the other day that she had lied to the cops about it. But she didn't know why and she didn't know whether Jo Ellen would speak to Lorna about it.

It took several more days, but Lorna Hubbell finally found Jo Ellen and got her talking. She was sitting in a broken-down old red and white Cadillac outside a shack in Dugan. Someone was working on the engine, jerking the throttle cable and making it roar. The car radio was playing loud music and there was a baby crying on Jo Ellen's lap. Jo Ellen talked through the waves of noise.

She had told lies to the police. She admitted that straight away. She agreed now to tell the truth. She told her story. Then she changed it. Then she wanted to change it again. It was as if, every time a different song came blasting out of the car radio, a different version of the facts came out of her mouth. The one thing she was always sure of was that Clarence Brandley had never raped her. Sometimes she said Ted Morgan, the old black deputy, had made her say that. Sometimes she said that Ted Morgan had taken her up to the courthouse and it was Jim Keeshan who had threatened to drag her name through the dirt if she did not co-operate. Sometimes she said she never had told anyone that Clarence had raped her.

Lorna Hubbell took her statement denying that she had been raped. It was reassuring to know that Brandley had not raped her, but she could see that, if Jo Ellen ever got anywhere near a witness-box, there was no telling what she would say, and if it was the police who put her there it was not going to do Clarence Brandley any good.

There was still Pokey Smith to worry about. The Brandleys had heard that Ted Morgan had got hold of Pokey and that instead of complaining that Clarence had slapped her, she was now saying that he had hauled her off and raped her four times in one night.

Again, in Lorna Hubbell's eyes, the story made no sense. If she had really been raped four times, she would surely have mentioned it to the police at the time and they would not have just fined Brandley $50 for slapping her.

She found Pokey in the Holiday Inn, south of Conroe on I–45, where she worked as a maid. Pokey was short and skinny with small eyes and a dull look to her. Her hair was tied up in little cornrows and she was chain-smoking. She did not want to talk. After some prompting she started to say that it was true that Clarence Brandley had raped her. Lorna Hubbell did not believe her. Her guess was that she was scared of Ted Morgan, and if she had just sworn a statement saying that Brandley had raped her four times, she was not going to risk a load of trouble from Ted Morgan by going back on it the first time anyone asked her about it.

A few days later, one of Brandley's sisters contacted Lorna Hubbell to say she had spoken to Pokey, and Pokey was now willing to tell the truth. Lorna Hubbell went back to Conroe and met her once more. This time she was ready to talk and even signed a statement. Pokey said she had never been raped by Clarence Brandley. What had happened, she said, was that she had been in a bar in Dugan with a bunch of people and she had gone to the restroom and when she had come back she had found $20 missing from her purse. She had been very upset and blamed Clarence, because he had been sitting next to her where he could easily have got inside her purse and taken the money. So she had gone to the police and told them he had raped her. She was sorry now and she did not think he had taken her money at all.

Her story made almost no sense. If she had told the police at the time that Brandley had raped her, why had they let Brandley off with a $50 fine? Pokey said that maybe she had not told them he raped her, just that he kind of assaulted her. But why hadn't she told them that he had stolen her money, if that was what she thought?

The truth, it seemed, was that Brandley had slapped her and she had told that to the police at the time, so they had fined him $50. Simple as that. But now both sides wanted to tell lies about it. Ted Morgan or someone had persuaded her to produce a grand story about rape so that Conroe could have its bad nigger. And Brandley's family or friends had got her to tell this tale about stolen money because it explained why she had gone to the police but it made Clarence out to be completely innocent. The simple truth – one slap in the face – was too dangerous for him in this climate of prejudice. It was a story born of fear and bred by years of life in Dugan.

Lorna Hubbell took Pokey's statement. It said: 'Ted Morgan came to my house and asked me to come downtown and state that Clarence Brandley had raped me. I guess he wanted me to lie. I don't think that Clarence messes with white women. I have never seen him force himself on a woman. I do not believe that Clarence is guilty of murder. I do not believe he is a rapist.'

Lorna Hubbell drove away to report her findings to the attorneys. The bottom line was that Brandley had not raped Pokey any more than he had raped Jo Ellen. But this whole crossfire of lies only served to remind her that the people in the courthouse badly wanted to put that black man on Death Row, and they were not too worried as to how they went about it.

In gaol, Brandley felt as if he had become a bystander at his own lynching. It was all happening so slowly. He was trapped – physically trapped by bricks and mortar and iron bars, and beyond that he was trapped by this whole tangle of prejudice. Nothing anyone did seemed to make any difference. It was as if they had built this scaffold for him and they had bound him so tight and now they were dropping the noose around his neck, getting ready to squeeze the breath out of his body.

The other day Ray Reeves had come in to see him and said that Minnie Ola had found an alibi for him. She was saying she remembered that Clarence had come home on the day of the crime at around ten in the morning. She remembered the time because the postman had just been by. Clarence had been driving an orange pick-up truck, she was sure of it. She had checked with one of her daughters who had been there, and she agreed. Clarence had been at home on Avenue E when the girl was killed.

Clarence shook his head. 'I'm sorry, Mr Reeves. She's just trying to help. But it ain't true.'

Reeves had thought as much. In a way he was relieved. An alibi would have been good for the defence. But if he had heard Brandley try to pick up a phoney alibi like that he would have been worried. But Brandley was not so happy. He needed some help – not phoney alibis, but real help. And he needed it fast. He was beginning to think Ray Reeves was not up to fighting this town.

On 25 September, Ray Reeves went back to court.

The dumpy attorney had given up trying to persuade Keeshan to play fair in this case, so he had gone off to see the District Clerk, a lady by the name of Peggy Stevens whom he found very charming. She smoked long thin cigarettes in a holder and carried her spectacles on a dainty gold chain around her neck, and her fingernails were beautifully painted the same red as strawberries. He had filed two heavyweight legal motions with her. One said that District Attorney Jim Keeshan should stop interfering with witnesses and allow them to talk to the defence. Keeshan was guilty of 'unethical and unprofessional conduct', he complained. The second motion listed 18 different types of evidence that he said the District Attorney had to hand over if Clarence Brandley was going to have a fair trial.

Peggy Stevens had filed the motions with the court and now Reeves was back in the courtroom, trying to persuade Judge Lee Alworth to order the District Attorney to comply with these motions. The judge did not seem to be very interested. Ray Reeves began to wonder whether this judge had been fed some of the stories about Brandley raping half the women in Dugan. He stood up and tried to explain to the judge that all the witnesses whom they had approached were scared to talk, and that it was his belief that the District Attorney was the cause of the problem. Keeshan stood up and said this was all untrue.

Ray Reeves put Lorna Hubbell in the witness-box and asked her to tell the judge what had been happening. She started to explain, but Judge Alworth cut across her and stopped Reeves's questions.

'There is no evidence that the state has interfered,' he said. His voice seemed testy and impatient. It was up to the witnesses to decide whom they spoke to. The court was not going to help.

Reeves switched to his second motion and pleaded to be given access to the 18 different types of evidence he had asked for. Judge Alworth looked at the list and declared that the wording was too broad and that Reeves was asking the DA to do his work for him. Finally, he agreed to let the defence have a handful of items. Reeves was not impressed. They were to be allowed a transcript of Brandley's evidence to the Grand Jury. Since Keeshan had already promised him that as part of his deal to encourage Brandley to appear before the Grand Jury, Reeves saw that as no gain at all. They were to be given a copy of the statement which Brandley had made on the day of the crime – but they could have no access to anything that had been said by anyone else. So they were not only unable to speak to these witnesses, they were also unable to read what they had already said. The judge gave Reeves two things which he needed badly – access to the dead girl's clothes and some of the photographs of the scene of the crime. That, at least, gave him something to start work on.

But there was still a lot missing. The judge had refused to give them a copy of the autopsy report. Reeves had never come across such a ruling in any case he had ever worked on. So far as he knew, it was just plain illegal. Nor would the judge give them the photographs of the dead girl's body, from which they might have been able to glean some clues; nor any photographs of the rest of the school on the day of the crime; nor anything on the criminal records of any of the witnesses in the case – like the white janitors, for example.

And Reeves still had none of the scientific evidence. No blood or hair or semen swabs: none of the contents of the rape kit – the physical evidence which was routinely collected from the body of a rape victim. Jim Keeshan had pre-empted the judge by announcing in open court that he would give the defence all the scientific evidence that he had. But Reeves had yet to see anything, and time was moving on. Pretty soon now they were going to start talking about fixing a trial date.

In the county jail that day, Brandley marked his birthday. He was 29.

It was Brandley's oldest brother, Lawrence, who first worried out loud that Ray Reeves might not be doing the best possible job here and who said that perhaps they needed a Conroe attorney who knew the town and its ways of working. Lawrence Brandley knew nothing about attorneys himself, so he went to a well-respected white man, Mr Gentry, who ran a menswear store on the courthouse square.

Mr Gentry suggested that the Brandleys take their case to a couple of attorneys who worked upstairs from him. They were called Morris and Brown.

George Morris and Don Brown belonged together like a horse and carriage. They would sit up in their dark, cramped little offices over Mr Gentry's store in an old building just across the street from the courthouse. In their waiting room, the same brown carpet that covered the floor also climbed up the wall; the radio played country music; the ashtrays overflowed with old cigarette ends and the words under the painting of a cowboy at a watering-hole read: 'Surely the Lord is in this place. Genesis 28:16.' There, they would prepare for battle.

Then they would emerge – two silver-haired men with bundles of legal papers under their arms, Morris well over six feet tall and stately as a Dickensian schoolmaster; Brown a well-rounded, shambling figure, like a bear in a brown suit. In court they were a natural double act. Morris liked to play to the gallery. He would tease a friendly witness, slash a hostile one to ribbons and try to play with a jury's affections. Brown was more of a scholar who could pick apart the fine print of a scientific report and who knew the Texas code of criminal practice in such intimate detail that people used to say he must be sleeping with it. Both of them habitually fought to the last drop of sweat.

Unlike many law partners, they were friends. They spent evenings drinking and smoking together in the Iron Horse on the courthouse square, swapping gossip about the courthouse, chewing over their cases, wheezing into their cigarettes and occasionally stunning the room into silence with the volume of Don Brown's low, dark, rumbling voice. But there was something deeper that held them together, a lesson they had both learned years earlier when growing up in small-town Texas.

Morris learned it through his father, an old-fashioned family doctor with a battered bag and a never-ending list of patients in the old sawmill town of Magnolia, 15 miles south-west of Conroe. As a child, Morris used to go out with his father on house visits and help him deliver babies. He got so good at it that, by the time he was a teenager, he would go out on his own to see women through their labour.

Some doctors picked their patients carefully, staying in the nice part of town, on the right side of the tracks. But George Morris followed his father through white ranches, black shacks, clean-as-a-whistle town houses and isolated backwood trailers, and in all of them he saw life with the special intimacy that is granted to doctors. So he learned at first hand about the facts of life in Texas, about the rich and the poor and the black and the white, and when he went back to the comfort of life on his side of the tracks and he heard people talk in their ignorance, he learned in particular – and in a profound and passionate way – to loathe and despise those of his neighbours who were racists.

Don Brown arrived at the same point by a different route. He grew up picking cotton with his nine brothers and sisters on a small farm his parents owned in a tiny community called Cotton Gin, about 150 miles north of Conroe. He started his education in a one-room schoolhouse where most of the other children were his cousins and nephews. From the age of 13 he worked in the oil fields, earning money to stay at school. He was always set apart from the others: first he was just the brightest kid in the class, then he was the one who was going to go all the way to college and become a chemist and, finally, by the time he had got his chemistry degree, he was the owner of an intellect like a bulldozer with emotions to match.

Brown would take an issue and simply tear it apart to get at the truth; then doggedly defend his position against all comers. He was that way with his chemistry and with his politics (he fastened on to the liberal wing of the Democratic Party when he was still a child and never let go) and he was that way, too, about racism. It was a political target, a social disease, a moral evil, a human absurdity. No matter how Don Brown looked at racism, his intellect destroyed it.

Morris was the first to bring the fight to Conroe. When he came out of the Navy at the end of the war, he set out on a career whose course was always dictated by his passion for fairness. For a while he worked in Houston with Percy Foreman, then one of the most famous defence attorneys in America, cheating the executioner of hundreds of intended victims, but Morris rapidly moved on to set up his own practice in Conroe in 1952. The little office soon became a garrison in a permanent war with the courthouse across the street. Morris fought not only as an attorney but also as a member of the city council, to which he was elected in the 1970s with a combination of black and white votes.

Don Brown had tried at first to become a professional chemist and worked for Monsanto Chemical. He raised hell when he discovered that the lunch-room was segregated. Then he ran into a storm when he refused to join the staff social club until blacks were allowed to use the sleek white clubhouse instead of the dingy little place which had been set aside for them.

He left to study law and to run for the state legislature in 1962. He was elected from Galveston County and then scandalized the redneck wing of his own party by insisting on hiring a black woman as one of his aides. His party bosses ordered him to sack her and said she would not be paid. There was no black employee in the state capitol of Austin at that time above the rank of janitor. But Brown told them to 'go screw themselves' and led his new aide on to the floor of the house and won his point by sheer dogged defiance.

Then he drafted a bill to repeal every statute in the state of Texas which mentioned race, particularly the one that outlawed marriage between the races. He knew the bill had no chance. Two years later, he narrowly lost his bid for re-election and set out to be an attorney instead.

For more than a decade he worked in La Marque, south of Houston on the road to Galveston. Then in May 1978 he decided to join forces with an attorney whose reputation attracted him, and he moved north and settled into the offices over the menswear store on the courthouse square. So the double act was born.

When Lawrence Brandley first came to see them about his brother,

Morris and Brown were not too sure whether they wanted to get involved. They had too much work already and they could see there was little prospect of the Brandleys ever paying them. They knew too that Jim Keeshan was going to use every trick in his private book to get a conviction, because the case was such a big deal in town. Yet something struck them about it all: it gave them an uneasy feeling. Don Brown had had it ever since he had looked out of his window one afternoon at the end of August and happened to see a bunch of police officers leading the black school janitor into the courthouse with his hands cuffed tight behind his back. It had struck him then that it was all too simple and easy – the white girl killed, the black man arrested. It was all too familiar.

Morris and Brown agreed to help Ray Reeves, just to sit by him and see if they could advise him at all. George Morris went into court on 25 September and watched Reeves get almost nowhere with his two big motions. He and Brown took Reeves across to the Iron Horse and heard all about the dumb deal he had made with Keeshan over the Grand Jury and how Keeshan had given him a royal screwing. Morris and Brown began to wonder how Reeves had got through law school.

When Reeves started talking in his usual way about 'nigger this' and 'nigger that' at the top of his voice in front of the young black kids who worked in the Iron Horse, they wondered how he had ever come to take the case at all. It was not long before they realized that if Clarence Brandley was ever going to have a chance of beating this town, they were going to have to do Ray Reeves's job for him.

Morris and Brown decided to mount an offensive. From their base camp overlooking the courthouse square, they unleashed a volley of writs and motions at the DA's office. They found themselves fighting tooth and nail to obtain what they believed was theirs by right.

They needed the autopsy report on the dead girl. As far as Morris and Brown were concerned, they had an absolute right to it. Don Brown went straight to the paragraph in the code of criminal procedure that declared: 'The detailed findings of an autopsy shall be part of the record and such records shall be public records'. They had never been denied one before, but in this case they could not get it – not from the Justice of the Peace, who was supposed to have a copy, nor from the District Clerk, who was supposed to have one, nor from the District Attorney nor from the judge, not from anyone in the courthouse. So far as they could find out, Jim Keeshan had cornered every copy in Conroe and he would part with none of them.

Don Brown tried to outflank Keeshan by going direct to Dr Jachimczyk, the medical examiner in Houston who had performed the autopsy. Brown knew him slightly from law school. But when Brown contacted him, the doctor claimed that he had performed the autopsy on Cheryl Fergeson not as a public medical examiner but as a private physician hired by Montgomery County and, therefore, that his report was private. Brown became heated. He got nowhere and suspected that Keeshan had got to the doctor before him.

Finally, Morris and Brown compiled a stinging motion in which they accumulated all the facts and all the law and submitted it to Judge Lee Alworth with the threat of an appeal to a higher court.

On 3 October – a full 40 days after the autopsy – the judge finally conceded that Clarence Brandley's attorneys should be allowed to read the report.

It was all they had. Despite Ray Reeves's small victory on 25 September, the District Attorney had still not handed them any of the evidence which he had been ordered to provide: no transcript of Brandley at the Grand Jury; no copy of his statement on the day of the crime; no photographs of the scene of the crime; no clothes from the dead girl; and none of the other scientific evidence which Keeshan had promised to release.

On 10 October, Keeshan finally told Don Brown that he would hand over the clothes and the scientific evidence. On 15 October – 20 days after the court order – the Texas Ranger Wesley Styles collected a plain brown box from the Department of Public Safety's laboratories in Austin and drove it up to Dallas, where a scientist named Irving Stone was prepared to study its contents for the defence.

The box was full of mysteries. For a start, there was no rape kit. It was standard procedure in every county in the state of

Texas that when a woman was raped, the police and the doctors made up a kit of physical evidence – especially any swabs of semen – and kept it for any subsequent trial. The semen was key evidence and it was particularly attractive to any defence attorney because its potential to help was much greater than its potential to harm. If the semen matched the blood group of the defendant, that merely meant he was one of millions of men who might have committed the crime. But if the semen did not match his blood group he was innocent, and the defence was home and dry. But there was no rape kit in the box. No swabs. No semen. And no chance for the defence to be home and dry.

Other things were also missing. There was supposed to be a yellow gym mat on which the girl had been lying in the props loft. Perhaps it would have shown some semen stain. But it was not to be found. And then there was the girl's underwear. It was there, but a small patch in the front which had been stained with semen had been cut out.

It was all very mysterious. Strangest of all was the pubic hair – or rather, the lack of it. When Don Brown was told the contents of the box, he thought it was surprising that the police had not taken samples of Brandley's pubic hair. His sample of head hair was in the box, but no pubic hair. At first, Brown assumed it was just another example of Captain Monty Koerner's sloppy work, until he mentioned it to Clarence Brandley. Brandley vividly remembered the nurse with her tweezers plucking out his head hair and his pubic hair. Brown rummaged around in the case papers and found that Brandley was right. The pubic hair was listed. But it was gone.

It was another mystery. Morris and Brown set out to find an explanation.

Meanwhile, Lorna Hubbell was still looking for clues and sending reports to the attorneys. She was at last beginning to find some that had not been swept away.

She spent a morning speaking to a man named David Harris who had once worked at Conroe High as a janitor, and who was now one of Mallie Davis's assistants, running the janitors for all the schools in Conroe. She found him very impressive. He was a tall, heavily-muscled black man who had fought in Vietnam and who appeared to be highly educated. He played the violin and trumpet and spoke Swahili as well as English, with no trace of a southern accent.

Like everyone else, he had originally refused to talk. He had been frightened of losing his job and had been explicitly ordered by the school superintendent not to talk to anyone. But Brandley's girlfriend, Beverley, had gone to see him and finally he agreed to talk, because he had something to say.

He believed Icky Peace might have killed the girl.

He had a low opinion of most of Brandley's co-workers. He said Acreman was an underminer, always complaining and trying to cause trouble. John Sessum, he reckoned, was certainly a drunk and also a racist. Sam Martinez might be OK, but, in his view, Icky Peace was psychotic and capable of just about anything, rape and murder included.

Harris said he had personally seen Icky Peace showing off a pearl-handled gun in the school. He had also seen Peace brandishing the identity card which was supposed to show that he was working for the police as an undercover narcotics agent. Harris knew it sounded crazy, but he had seen the card and talked to Peace about it, and he believed him. Peace had even offered to recruit him and told him a senior officer would be in touch with him. Peace could easily have used that card to trick the girl into going with him into the auditorium.

Harris also had information about the auditorium. In the first place, he said, it was common for doors to be left open. Some of them were broken and had never shut properly. So it was nonsense to claim that Brandley was the only person who could have got in there to hide the body. But more than that, he knew that Peace had a set of keys to the auditorium. He was not supposed to have them but during the previous summer he had been issued with a set and then failed to return them, claiming he had lost them.

After six weeks on the road, Lorna Hubbell could barely believe her ears. This all slotted together with what she already knew. Peace was now a prime suspect.

Harris also gave her an account of the way the police were treating witnesses. He said he had been visited by the Texas

Ranger, Wesley Styles. 'He has a big stomach, a big head and a narrow mind,' he told her.

And Harris had been in the high school one day about a week after Brandley's arrest when the Ranger had been questioning Icky Peace, walking him up and down the hallway. According to Harris, the Ranger had been coaching Peace, rehearsing his story with him and then recording only the final version.

Finally, Harris believed he was being harassed because he was not co-operating with the police. A cleaning woman at the high school had recently reported that she had been raped in the grounds of the school. She said she had been attacked by a white man, but that had not stopped the police from arresting one Mexican and three black men, including Harris himself. Even now, after spending the morning talking to Lorna Hubbell, he was nervous of being seen with her. If the police heard that he was dealing with white people, there could be trouble. He said he would stay in touch through Beverley. It was safer that way.

Buoyed by her success, Lorna Hubbell made one more attempt to get to the white janitors. She drove out east of Conroe towards Cut and Shoot, and after an hour of tracking up and down and checking post boxes, she found John Sessum in a trailer house. David Harris had told her that according to the records in his office Sessum was 39. But he looked much older. His face was deeply lined and his body bowed. His clothes were dirty. She did not need to be told he was a drunk.

Away from the school, he was willing to talk to her. She needed to know what he had told the police so that she could try and solve one of the biggest mysteries in this whole case – how the police expected to be able to convict Brandley. Sitting hunched up outside his trailer, scratching frequently, Sessum explained that he and Gary Acreman and Sam Martinez had finished laying out the tables and chairs in the school cafeteria and wandered into the hallway to wait for Brandley. They had seen this girl walk up the steps to the restroom on Sesame Street. They had noticed she was blonde and pretty. Then Brandley had come along the hallway with some toilet rolls in his hand and sent them to the vocational building and left them all waiting there for some time before he came across with a key. That was it.

On the face of it, that meant nothing. It all depended on timing. The janitors might have had time to drag the girl into the auditorium and kill her before Brandley got there with his toilet rolls. An outsider – or even Icky Peace – could have caught her coming out of the restroom after Brandley and the other janitors had moved on, and then killed her while Brandley was smoking in his office and the others were in the vocational building. Alternatively, Brandley would have had time to kill her himself if he had waited for the white janitors to leave and then cornered her in the restroom. It was all a matter of timing and nobody she had spoken to seemed to be sure of the timing in this story.

Sessum started to ramble on about his wife who had divorced him and all the fights he had been in and how he must have a thousand different stitches in him. He also refused point-blank to give a statement. Lorna Hubbell left him and went off to find Gary Acreman. Her luck held, and when she cornered him at the high school he agreed to talk.

To begin with, he was fine. He rehearsed the events of that day, just as Sessum had. But when Lorna Hubbell told him that she already spoken to Sessum, his mood changed. His hands started to shake. He could not sit still. He was smoking as if he couldn't breathe without nicotine.

He kept saying: 'What did John say? What did John tell you?'

He, too, refused to give her a statement. Clearly he was hiding something. And he also obviously believed John Sessum was hiding something too. Neither of them was ready to say what it was.

Just like Ray Reeves before them, Morris and Brown had given up hoping that Jim Keeshan was going to play fair.

On 13 November, they went back to court, just as Ray Reeves had, to try and compel the District Attorney to co-operate with them. He had still not given them the rest of the evidence he had been ordered to hand over on 25 September – fifty days earlier. They still had no transcript of Brandley's appearance before the Grand Jury, nor a copy of his statement on the day of the crime, nor any photographs of the scene of the crime.

In court Keeshan was suave and charming. Ignoring the long

delay, he stood up at the beginning of the hearing and asked to speak first. 'May I make a brief representation to the court?' he asked politely. 'Most of these matters are all available and the State is prepared to voluntarily turn them over to the defence attorneys. If they are willing to come down to my office and not take up the court's time, I will be glad to convey all these matters.'

Don Brown rumbled under his breath that Keeshan made it sound as if this was the first time they had asked him for any of this stuff. He asked the judge to order Keeshan to produce the evidence in court now. The judge brushed him aside. Morris and Brown then explained that there was more evidence that they needed. They explained their needs, one by one. One by one, Judge Alworth brushed them aside.

It had become vital for Morris and Brown to sort out their suspicions about the white janitors. Judge Alworth had already refused to order Keeshan to hand over the statements they had made to the police. None of them would give them a statement to the defence and, although they had now started to talk, none of them had done so in any real detail. All claimed that they had been told to keep their mouths shut.

Morris and Brown asked the court to order the white janitors to give a deposition of facts to the defence. They said this was essential if Brandley was to get a fair trial. Keeshan and the judge said no.

Morris and Brown pleaded that, at the very least, the court should order the white janitors to provide samples of their blood, hair and saliva. The attorneys still found it inconceivable that the District Attorney had not done this himself. They now knew from their scientist in Dallas, Dr Irving Stone, that the rumour about a white man's hair being found on the girl's body was true. It was a reddish-brown hair and had been found on the girl's inner thigh. It was a vital clue. Samples from the white janitors were equally vital if they were to be able to make sense of it. Keeshan and the judge said no.

They asked for the notes that the schoolchildren had written for the police about the day of the crime, for a list of witnesses who had spoken to the state about the crime, for a transcript of the whole Grand Jury hearing. Keeshan and the judge said no.

Morris and Brown then closed in on the mystery of the missing rape kit. Keeshan shrugged them off as if he had no idea what they were talking about. 'There is absolutely no other evidence in the nature of semen in my possession or in the Conroe Police Department's possession or in the Department of Public Safety's lab's possession or, to my knowledge, in the pathologist's possession.'

Morris and Brown were dumbfounded. What on earth were these clowns doing? If that was true, then either the State was so dumb that it had failed to gather some of the most vital evidence in the inquiry, or so corrupt that it had deliberately destroyed it in case it helped Clarence Brandley.

Brown tried to find out what had happened to the missing patch from the dead girl's underwear. He was told that it had been used up during tests which had failed to disclose anything conclusive about the semen. Brown turned to the judge and asked him to order that Keeshan produce either the semen or the results of any tests which had been conducted on it. Judge Alworth cut him short. 'I believe the DA has already told you that he has no such sample, Mr Brown. How can I order him to produce that which does not exist?'

That was it. There was no question of this judge ordering an inquiry or castigating the DA or the police.

Brown called Monty Koerner, the captain of detectives, to the witness-box. He shrugged and stammered and said he had no rape kit and he had never asked for one. For Morris and Brown, this was too much like the Keystone Cops, even for Conroe. These cops might be dumb – just the other day two of them had driven into town with their uniforms in tatters because they had tried to capture an escaped lioness without any back-up – but this kind of stupidity bordered on corruption. They refused to believe that there were no semen samples, that there was no scientific evidence which might prove Brandley's innocence. Brown had only one option left.

During the lunch break he called the medical examiner, Dr Jachimczyk. Surely he could help. If the police had really not asked for the swabs, they must still be in his laboratory. But if the police had asked for them and taken them and thrown them away, then the doctor would be able to testify that they were lying. But Jachimczyk did not see it that way.

'Oh, gosh,' he told Brown on the telephone. 'That case was back in August. That's more than 30 days ago. I throw everything away after 30 days.'

Brown's temperature started to rise. 'What? On a rape homicide? You throw everything away? Just throw it away?'

'Well, I don't have the room to keep everything here.'

'But didn't you give it to the police?'

'If they ask me for it, I give it to them.'

'Well, did you give it to them on this occasion?'

'I don't know. I couldn't say. I just identified it as human semen.'

'Yes, but, Doctor Jachimczyk, we're trying to identify which human it belongs to.'

It was no use. Brown found it all hard to believe. Here was a professional medical examiner, highly experienced, indeed one of the most experienced in the country, who threw away the most important medical evidence in a rape homicide when the trial was still pending. Here was an experienced and intelligent District Attorney who claimed not to have noticed that this evidence was missing when all the material was sent to the DPS laboratories a few days after the crime.

Brown did not believe a word of it. He believed Keeshan was a ruthless careerist who was going after a poor black janitor with nothing but circumstantial evidence and he did not want any evidence that could get in his way – not the autopsy report nor the semen samples nor the hairs from the white janitors nor even the statements of witnesses. They were holding a blind focus on Clarence Brandley. He believed this whole prosecution was dedicated to stringing up the nearest available black man and that what was happening in that courthouse was close to a conspiracy. But what could he prove?

And there was one more mystery that he was afraid they might have cleared up – the missing pubic hair. There was still no sign of the original sample which had been taken from Brandley on the day of the crime. Morris and Brown had arranged for Brandley to provide a new sample. But in the meantime, their scientist in

Dallas had reported to them that the reddish-brown white man's hair was not all that had been found on the girl's body. There were also several Negro hairs. They appeared to have been forcibly removed from their owner.

But what could they prove?

Morris and Brown's day in court was not yet over. That afternoon, they returned to Judge Alworth's courtroom to fight for an issue on which they believed they were so completely in the right and Jim Keeshan was so obviously in the wrong that not even Montgomery County courthouse could deny them justice. They wanted Clarence Brandley released on bail.

As soon as Morris and Brown had got a grip on the case, they had fired off a motion demanding a court hearing at which Keeshan would have to prove that Brandley had breached his probation by murdering Cheryl Fergeson. The law said the hearing must take place within 20 days. If Keeshan did not come to court within the 20 days, then Brandley would be entitled to bail again.

Their motion went into the courthouse on 3 October. A few days later, Judge Lee Alworth went elk-hunting in Colorado without setting a date for the hearing. The 20 days passed. Morris and Brown still heard nothing. Brandley was now entitled to be released on his $30,000 bail. But he was not. So on 24 October, Morris and Brown fired off yet another motion, this time a writ of Habeas Corpus, the traditional legal device used by lawyers to prise their clients out of the gaoler's grip. They quoted the law which declared that this writ must be heard 'at the earliest practicable time'. In the courthouse, Judge Lee Alworth, who had by now returned from this hunting trip, agreed to consider the matter on 13 November, nearly three weeks away.

Like many big men, Don Brown maintained an air of gentle courtesy but, under pressure, he was capable of exploding with mighty force. Now, Brown was beginning to get angry. So far as he could see, the State was playing crooked games with them. Keeshan did not want to prove that Brandley had breached his probation by murdering Cheryl Fergeson because he would have to disclose the evidence he had collected. Nor did he want to release Brandley. So he did neither and never mind the law. Brown said they had no right to leave Brandley in jail without a hearing and there was no damned way that 13 November was the earliest practical time they could go to court. He could see Keeshan's game: he was playing for time in an attempt to get Brandley tried for murder before the defence ever had a chance to hold a hearing on his bail.

Brown and Morris reached for the big gun and went to the Court of Criminal Appeals in Austin, the highest criminal court in the State of Texas, and asked them for a writ of Habeas Corpus. By Thursday 13 November, when Judge Alworth was finally due to consider Brandley's freedom, everyone in the courthouse knew that the judges in Austin had heard details of the case. Everyone knew that they were due to make their decision in a few days and everyone understood the message: if Conroe did not put its own house in order, then the judges in Austin would do it for them.

Morris and Brown heard that Judge Alworth was furious with them for trying to cause him embarrassment. They didn't mind about that: the main point was that the courthouse had failed to give Brandley his hearing within 20 days. That meant that they could not revoke his probation. So now, the law said he could be released on the $30,000 bail which had been set on 5 September.

That morning, George Morris and another law partner, Nat Davis, went over to the sheriff's office to tell him that they had raised the $30,000 for Brandley's bail bond, using their own property as collateral, and that they wanted to make sure that there would be no hitch in releasing Brandley once Judge Alworth had finished his hearing. The sheriff, Gene Reaves, did not seem pleased to see them.

'I'm not gonna let him out,' he said. 'I don't care how much bond you post.'

Morris, who knew the sheriff was an old-fashioned East Texas racist, suggested that he would have to obey the court. The sheriff scowled and Morris and Davis went off to court, marvelling at the idea of a sheriff who so openly defied the law.

That afternoon in court, Keeshan fought to keep Brandley behind bars. But Don Brown said the facts and the law were cut and dried: there should have been a hearing on Brandley's probation within 20 days of their request; there had been no such hearing; Brandley had to be released. He told the judge that the court in Austin would be handing down a ruling on the issue within the next week.

In Brown's eyes, Alworth was not as bad as some of the other Conroe judges. Brown knew the judge had a reputation for being bad-tempered and overbearing, but at least he knew the law and was capable of upholding it. Just the other week, he had enraged the rest of the courthouse by throwing out the confession of a man accused of killing a 12-year-old girl after hearing that the interrogators had threatened to feed the man maggots from the dead girl's body. Not every judge in Conroe would have done that.

That was what Brown was counting on – that Alworth knew the law was clear and that there was no point in pretending anything different with the Court of Criminal Appeals in Austin waiting to pounce. Sure enough, a stoney-faced Alworth agreed that Brandley should have his probation back and that if the state tried to revoke it again, he should be allowed out on bail of only $1,000 until a hearing took place. In the meantime, he could be released on bail of $30,000.

Brandley's family wept and cheered with relief. After 11 weeks of doubt and confusion, Clarence would be released that evening. Don Brown felt a bitter relief: Brandley might now have his freedom, but he had been denied it these past 11 weeks by trickery and prejudice. And even now, after the judge's ruling, Brown was not sure. He knew Sheriff Gene Reaves; he could be a mean old boy. It looked as if he had been telegraphing his punch that morning. So before the hearing ended, Brown asked the judge if he would agree to stay in his chambers in the courthouse so that he would be available in case there was any problem with the sheriff. Alworth agreed. Then he gave Brown a withering stare and swept out of court. Morris and Brown might have won, but they had made an enemy out of the judge by threatening him with the court in Austin.

Brown led George Morris and Ray Reeves off to one of the jury rooms, where there was a little coffee bar, to talk tactics. Most of

Brandley's family followed. So there were plenty of witnesses present a few minutes later when Judge Alworth followed them in.

At first the judge said nothing, just poured himself some coffee. Then, with his jaw-muscles bunching in his cheeks, he walked towards the huddle of defence lawyers.

'Don, so that you will know where you and I stand, I want you to know that I ruled the way I did because the law says I have to. But I do not appreciate a lawyer doing what you did.'

His voice was loud. Everyone stopped talking to watch.

The judge was accusing Brown of deliberately asking for a hearing on Brandley's probation just as he was about to start his vacation in Colorado. Brown was starting to explain that it had nothing to do with that, but the judge was already on his way to the door, where he turned.

'And, furthermore, I do not appreciate some of the words you used in the petition that you filed with the Court of Criminal Appeals.'

Brown muttered that that was fine.

The judge jabbed a finger across the room at him. 'You are going to regret those words,' he shouted. 'I guarantee that you will answer for them when this case is over.'

Brown, who had never seen a judge behave this way, looked back at him and said: 'That's all right with me.'

Now the judge was white with anger. 'You are going to eat those words,' he yelled, his voice whipping past the dazed spectators, 'because I am going to stuff them down your damned throat!'

Then he was gone.

'OK,' said Brown.

It was only half an hour later when George Morris headed up to the fourth floor of the courthouse to deliver the $30,000 bond which would secure Brandley's freedom. Outside, Minnie Ola and the family waited. Less than five minutes later, Morris returned without Brandley. The sheriff had kept his promise: he was not interested in the bond. He did not care what the court had ordered;

he did not give a damn what the law said. He was not going to let the nigger go.

Minnie Ola started to weep.

Morris and Brown were outraged and immediately stormed up to Judge Alworth's chambers. Alworth had promised he would stay there to make sure Brandley was released. Brandley was now being held captive illegally. They would just have to ask the judge to intervene directly to force the sheriff to obey the court. But when the two attorneys arrived at the judge's chambers, they found he had abandoned his promise and left for the weekend.

Morris and Brown agreed that promises did not count for much in Montgomery County courthouse and trudged back across the courthouse square to their offices with the useless bond. In all their years of dealing with small-town prejudice, they could not remember a more brazen abuse of power.

Minnie Ola and the family went slowly home across the tracks to Dugan, all downcast.

The black man stayed behind bars.

For four days, the defence camp was paralysed while it waited for Judge Alworth to return from his long weekend and enforce the rule of law in Conroe. Friday, Saturday and Sunday passed, and when the judge finally returned to the courthouse on Monday morning, he announced that he was too busy to consider the matter until the evening. In the meantime, news of the row swept through the town, harming Brandley at every turn.

Keeshan was quoted in the paper as expressing his surprise that the judge had agreed to let Brandley keep his probation, and the sheriff baldly declared that he had personal reasons for defying the court. 'I just don't think a man like the accused should be on the ground,' he told the *Courier*.

Judge Alworth finally agreed to consider the Brandley case in his chambers at 5.15 on Monday evening. It was a tense meeting. Don Brown was there with his other partner, Nat Davis. Keeshan was there with Sheriff Gene Reaves by his side. Judge Alworth opened the meeting by asking the sheriff if the bail bond was sufficient.

'Sure. The bond's sufficient. There's no problem with that.'

'So why don't you let him out?' asked the judge.

The sheriff looked straight back at the judge and said: 'Because that little nigger don't belong on the ground.'

Brown exhaled sharply and resisted an urge to accuse the sheriff there and then of being a racist who was not fit to wear a badge. The judge was still talking. 'But, Sheriff, that is not sufficient reason.'

Now Keeshan intervened. Brown sat in silent horror and heard the DA say: 'I agree with the sheriff. That little nigger doesn't belong on the ground.'

Judge Alworth seemed not to notice their language, but he held his line. Brown guessed he did not want to be threatened again with the judges in Austin. The judge said that if Brandley could put up the $30,000 bond there was no lawful reason to keep him in custody. 'I'm ordering that if that bond is sufficient that the prisoner be released,' he said.

Keeshan was not happy. 'If you're gonna do that, I ask that the amount of the bond be increased.'

'Jim, I can't do that,' said the judge. 'We had a hearing on that and you didn't choose to put on your evidence so that I could find that there was proof evident that he committed this offence. I'd have to conduct another hearing to raise the bond.'

'That is correct,' said Keeshan, his eyes fastened on the judge.

This was too much for Brown. Keeshan had made a deal with Ray Reeves that he would not press for a high bail bond. It was bad enough that he had tried to bypass that deal by revoking Brandley's probation. Now he was going right back and breaking the deal in two, pushing for a higher bond.

'We've had the hearing,' said Brown in his deep bass voice, 'and we have the judge's decision. I suggest we just come up now and get him out.'

It was already 5.30 p.m. Keeshan could not mount a hearing that evening. He lapsed into silence.

The sheriff, too, appeared to be accepting defeat: 'They'll be feeding them now in the jail and trying to get them put away to bed. How about y'all come round in the morning to get him, about nine?'

Brown guessed that the sheriff was trying to save face. He didn't want to cause any more problems .

'OK,' he said.'We'll be there at nine in the morning, tomorrow.'

After all, he thought, what difference could one more night make?

The very next morning, Tuesday 18 November, shortly before nine o'clock, two deputies came to Clarence Brandley in his cell in the county jail on the top floor of the courthouse. They told him his attorneys were standing bail for him.

They let him gather his few possessions from the cell. They marched him along the corridor, took his photograph and his fingerprints, filled in some paperwork and told him to wait for his attorneys. Downstairs in the first-floor lobby of the court-house, Don Brown, George Morris and Nat Davis were standing waiting for the elevator to take them up to the cells when Sheriff Reaves came by. He seemed a lot more relaxed and stopped to chat with them about the weather and one thing and another.

Just then Jim Keeshan's secretary, Kathy, came up with an envelope and handed it to Don Brown. Brown was explaining to the sheriff that they were on their way up to the cells with their $30,000 bail bond to get Brandley released. The sheriff nodded. Brown was starting to open the envelope as the elevator doors slid open to let them in. All three lawyers were in the elevator and the sheriff was just nodding goodbye when Don Brown exploded. 'That son of a bitch!' he shouted.

The envelope contained a motion from Jim Keeshan to raise Brandley's bond from $30,000 to $75,000 – and an order signed by Judge Lee Alworth that morning agreeing to the increase. How the hell could they do that? They hadn't even had a hearing. It was just plain illegal. The sheriff retreated. Brown thrust the papers into George Morris's hands and told Nat Davis what they con-tained. By the time the elevator reached the fourth floor, three very angry men walked out.

Back in his cell, Clarence Brandley was angry too. It seemed they wanted to torment him before they killed him, by dangling his freedom in front of him – just so he knew that no matter how close he got, he could never have it back.

As soon as they had finished telling Brandley the bad news, the attorneys returned to their office to take a step they had resisted but which now seemed inevitable. They would force Judge Lee Alworth off the case by 'recusing' him – filing a formal motion complaining about his behaviour and, if necessary, holding a public hearing to prove that he should be removed.

They had not wanted to do this. No attorney wants to make an enemy out of a judge. But it had gone too far. That morning, Morris and Brown sat down together and drafted a damning indictment of the judge's performance.

They accused him outright of bias and prejudice. They complained that he had refused to let Brandley defend his right to probation within the 20 days allowed by law and that he had refused to hear Brandley's writ of Habeas Corpus in good time. They said he had displayed 'a generally sarcastic and intimidating demeanour' towards them and had shouted abuse at Don Brown. And they raised the issue that had made their blood boil – the sudden raising of Brandley's bail bond to $75,000.

They were outraged that Keeshan and the judge had decided to go behind their backs. There had been no hearing, no chance for Brandley to put his side of the story. They had not even tried to contact them. Raising his bond like this was a breach of Keeshan's deal with Ray Reeves, a violation of Keeshan's code of conduct, a flagrant contradiction of the judge's own ruling that Brandley should be released on a $30,000 bond, and a denial of their agreement the previous evening that Brandley would be released at nine o'clock that morning. It also drove a horse and buggy through Clarence Brandley's civil rights. They were outraged.

Keeshan, it seemed, had just gone to see Alworth as one good old boy to another, trying to find any way they could to keep the nigger in jail. Keeshan had produced a motion that was full of holes: it was not even sworn. Keeshan had even tried to pretend that since the $30,000 bond had been set on 5 September, he had learned of new evidence that Brandley was a threat to public safety – the alleged rape of Pokey Smith. Morris and Brown knew that was dishonest. Not only had Pokey withdrawn her allegation but also, Keeshan had known all about Pokey Smith on 5 September. He had been using her story two days earlier with the Grand Jury.

He was simply pretending that it had come to light more recently in order to give a phoney justification for raising the bail bond. As far as Morris and Brown were concerned, Keeshan was nothing but a snake, and a racist snake at that, and this whole motion was the purest horseshit.

Keeshan had wreaked maximum possible damage with his motion to raise the bond to $75,000. Clipped to the back of it was a copy of Pokey Smith's statement to Ted Morgan. It was a powerful story: Brandley had abducted her at gunpoint, beaten her with a stick and raped her four or five times and he had done the same thing on other occasions to Pokey's sister and to one of his own sisters.

There was no indication that Pokey had now withdrawn her statement and, by filing it publicly with his motion, Keeshan had instantly advertised its contents to the Press, who could be relied upon to reproduce them with yet more prejudice to Brandley.

Morris and Brown poured their feelings into their demand for Judge Alworth's recusal. By midday they had dropped their bombshell on the courthouse. Later that afternoon, Judge Alworth replied with a couple of his own.

First, he voluntarily stepped down from the case. In doing so, he issued a statement in which he rejected the charges laid by Morris and Brown. He had not been denying Brandley a hearing: he had been away elk-hunting and then he had been too busy with other cases. He claimed he was quite entitled to raise Brandley's bail-bond. He agreed that he had made aggressive remarks to Don Brown, but this brought him to his own reason for standing down.

'I have a great dislike for Don Brown,' he said, 'whom I find to be the most completely obnoxious individual it has ever become my displeasure to know and I certainly conveyed that thought to him in my remarks. Unlike Will Rogers, who never met a man he didn't like, I can only say that Will Rogers never met Don Brown.'

Morris and Brown were relieved to see the back of the judge. But even as he left, they admired his clever footwork: by identifying obnoxious Don Brown as his reason for stepping down, he avoided the embarrassment of a recusal hearing without having to admit any of the complaints that were laid against him. But Judge Alworth was still not finished.

Having stepped down, he had to contact the Administrative Judge who covered Montgomery County, Max Rogers, and ask him to appoint a replacement. But Judge Alworth went a little further: he contacted Max Rogers and told him that he himself would find a replacement.

He selected Judge Sam Robertson jr. of Houston.

'The son of a bitch,' said Don Brown when he heard. 'Sam Robertson is the most prosecution-minded judge in the whole area. That Lee Alworth has malice in his heart.'

Jim Keeshan wanted to start the trial. The courthouse set a date. Clarence Brandley would go on trial for his life on Monday 1 December.

After Judge Alworth stepped down from the case on Tuesday 18 November, Morris and Brown had less than two weeks to prepare for trial. They still lacked basic information about the case and their client was still trapped in jail, unable to help them.

The two attorneys went to a bail bondsman who specialized in lending money for defendants who were trying to make bail. Despite the Brandleys' poverty, they succeeded in borrowing $75,000 to make the new, higher bond which Keeshan and Judge Alworth had arranged. They could still get Brandley out of jail before the trial. But before they could do that, they had their first encounter with the new judge.

On Wednesday 26 November, Judge Sam Robertson jr. came to the courthouse in Conroe to hold his first hearing in the case of Clarence Brandley. First, he wanted to discuss three procedural motions, known as Motions In Limine, which Don Brown had filed. They were designed to prevent the State from referring to Brandley's conviction for possessing a sawn-off shotgun, or to Pokey Smith's claim that Brandley had raped her, or to any suggestion such as Keeshan had made in the Grand Jury that Brandley suffered from an obsessive desire to have sex with white women. Brown said any reference to any of these would be highly prejudicial, even if the judge then told the jury to disregard them. 'That would be throwing the skunk in the jury box and taking the skunk

out, but leaving the smell there,' rumbled Brown. Keeshan agreed
not to mention any of them without first consulting the judge.

Then Jim Keeshan filed a new motion – asking to revoke Brandley's probation.

Morris and Brown could hardly believe it. Keeshan must have
heard that they had got their $75,000 bond. This had all been dealt
with. Even Judge Alworth had admitted – with a little pressure
from the court in Austin – that the State had lost its right to
revoke Brandley's probation by failing to hold a hearing within
20 days. And he had also ruled that if the issue ever arose again,
Brandley could be released on $1,000 bail until the DA came to
court and proved that he had breached his probation by murdering
Cheryl Fergeson. But Keeshan was trying it on again.

Morris and Brown fired back their own motion calling on the
judge to stop the District Attorney from harassing Clarence
Brandley with his attempts to revoke his probation.

Brown led the judge through the whole saga, calling himself as
a witness, then Jim Keeshan, then the sheriff Gene Reaves, who
now claimed that he had refused to release Brandley because the
signatures on the bond were rather faint. Brown pleaded with the
judge not to revoke Brandley's probation, not to uphold the
$75,000 bail bond, not to sweep aside their few hard-won legal
gains. His speech was long and detailed and sometimes passionate.
Judge Robertson listened in silence.

First, the judge agreed that Jim Keeshan could file his motion
to revoke Brandley's probation. Thus Brandley had lost his right
to bail again. Then he dismissed the idea that Brandley was entitled
to $1,000 bond while he waited for a hearing on his probation. 'I
am not going to set bond on the basis of what Judge Alworth said
he would do.' So Brandley had lost the escape route which had
been guaranteed him. Then he agreed to uphold the $75,000 bail
bond. That no longer mattered since Brandley could not now have
bail at any price, but it rubbed salt in the attorney's raw wounds.

Brandley hung his head. Brown slammed his files shut and
clenched his fists in anger. This was not even remotely fair: it was
old-fashioned redneck justice.

Hour after hour, George Morris and Don Brown sat in their

smoke-filled cave overlooking the courthouse square, talking to Lorna Hubbell and Ray Reeves and the Brandleys, shuffling the few facts that they had managed to gather, trying somehow to put together a coherent picture of what had happened at the high school that Saturday.

The autopsy report and the scientific evidence from their expert in Dallas had turned out to contain hidden treasure.

There was the mark round the girl's neck, left by whatever she had been strangled with. It was four and a half inches wide, and one and a quarter inches high. It was the last measurement that mattered. Brandley was worried that Keeshan was going to use his mistake at the Grand Jury hearing to make out that he had used his belt to strangle the girl, even though he had not been wearing it on the day of the crime. The autopsy report put an end to that: his belt was one and a half inches high and could not have left such a narrow mark. As confirmation, his belt showed no traces of the dead girl's skin tissue. His work knife, which had been seized by the police, had no fibres from the girl's clothes, even though the killer had cut some of them from her body. And none of the fingerprint testing on the girl's body and clothes revealed any of his prints.

There had been a point, soon after they had first taken the case, when Morris and Brown had not known for sure whether Brandley was innocent. They had asked for all these tests, knowing that if they had found anything it would have been devastating. But they had found nothing. Now they began to feel keenly that their client was innocent. It was not just the striking absence of any evidence to link him to the crime. There were now also clues which clearly pointed away from him.

The most important, they believed, were the numerous hairs on the dead girl which could have nothing to do with Brandley, since they were not negroid. If only Keeshan had allowed them to take hair samples from the other janitors or from anyone else, they might have been able to crack the case. Even so, the white man's hairs must surely raise real doubt about Brandley's guilt. How in God's name could Keeshan explain them away?

But there were also the two negroid hairs. They were giving Morris and Brown a headache. They were more than ready to believe that they had been planted. They had fought this court-house long enough to believe that if the people over there per-suaded themselves that they had got the right man, they would plant evidence and never suffer a moment's bad conscience about it. The trouble was that they could not prove anything, and if they produced such an allegation in court without any proof they would surely alienate the jury – particularly a Conroe jury trying a black man. That could only damage Brandley.

Then there were a number of clues which caused endless specu-lation in the smoke-filled attorneys' office. First there were the girl's finger-nails, which were unbroken and showed no trace of her attacker's skin or blood beneath them. Then there were strange bruises on her upper arms and on her palms at the base of both thumbs; and finally, there was the eerie indentation on her back in the shape of her crucifix.

After much debate, Brown put the clues together and concluded that the girl had been attacked by two men, not one: her hands had not been free to scratch; she had been held down on her back, the crucifix pressing into her skin, with one man raping her while the other crouched behind her head and held her arms back over her head and possibly even kneeled on her palms, bruising her as he trapped her. The clues did not fit the theory of a one-man attack, no matter what colour he was.

Finally, there was the whole cluster of clues round Icky Peace. And this, they concluded, was their strongest single line of defence.

So far as they could see they were facing a case of circumstantial evidence. For weeks they had waited in dread of hearing that Keeshan had produced some devastating new breakthrough. But there was still no sign that he had anything more than circumstance to go on. Keeshan would say that Brandley was alone near the restrooms at the time when the girl disappeared, that he was the only one with the keys to the auditorium, that he knew about the props loft, and that he had been missing for at least half-an-hour. The classic defence against a circumstantial prosecution like that was to produce a reasonable alternative. All the defence had to do was to show that there was another suspect against whom an equally good circumstantial case might be built. They did not have to prove that another suspect had committed the crime, only that an equally strong case could be made against him. If they did that, they had won. That was the law.

And – although they did not believe that Peace had committed the crime – the circumstantial case against him was demonstrably stronger than it was against Brandley. Just like Brandley, Peace had been alone at the time the girl disappeared – supposedly buffing the floor in the teachers' lounge – and he had keys to the auditorium and he knew about the props loft and he had spent more than an hour out of sight of the other janitors. But in addition, he had a strong motive in his problems with women, the right means in his gun and his narcotics card, and furthermore, unlike Brandley, he admitted that he had been having nightmares and anxiety attacks about the crime.

It was frustrating to push a theory which they did not believe. But that was the direct result of the other side's activity. If Captain Koerner had not allowed the high school cleaners to sweep all the clues away after the crime and had not lost or destroyed the semen swabs; if the Texas Ranger had not gone round threatening witnesses; if the District Attorney had not kept a blind focus on the black janitor, it might all have been different. But Morris and Brown had to face the fact that they had only fragments of the truth to work with.

There was one other thing they also had to face. They appeared to have removed a bad judge from the case only to have him replaced with another who was even worse. All Brandley needed in order to become a free man was a fair hearing. Morris and Brown did not believe that Judge Sam Robertson jr. would give them one.

For the second time in only eight days they would have to try and recuse a judge. Chain-smoking over their word processor, they constructed a legal torpedo. Its thrust was straightforward: Judge Robertson had endorsed the sins of his predecessor and was therefore just as biased and prejudiced as he had been.

'Sam Robertson jr. has demonstrated by the foregoing actions that he cannot be fair and impartial to this defendant,' they wrote. 'He has arbitrarily and illegally deprived the defendant of his liberty.'

But unlike his predecessor, Robertson refused to step down. So on 1 December, it was not the trial of Clarence Brandley which opened in Conroe but the recusal hearing of Judge Robertson, staged in front of a regular Conroe judge, Lynn Coker.

Brown rehearsed his argument and the injustice which had been handed out to the black school janitor. He put Judge Robertson in the witness box and challenged him that he could not be a fair and impartial judge. Robertson said he could be.

Brown boomed out his demand for justice for Clarence Brandley. 'We know he has had no due process up until now. Is this man going to have due process for the rest of the time that he is going to be tried for capital murder?'

Judge Lynn Coker listened in silence. Then he agreed to let Judge Robertson stay on the case. The trial could start immediately.

It occurred to Don Brown that times had indeed changed in east Texas. Once, it had been common practice for lynch mobs to collect money to pay the bail-bond of some nigger they wanted to get their hands on, so that they could get him out of the courthouse and put him to death. Now all that had changed, and a black man in trouble was denied his bail and trapped under lock and key. But that was where the real danger was – for now the lynch mob was inside the courthouse.

4

Bill Srack was not a Conroe man. He was born in Oklahoma, and he had grown up in Houston and spent most of his working life there, running around with a clip-board and a hard hat managing construction projects for an oil company. It was only ten years since he had sold his house in Houston and bought a plot of land outside Conroe in one of the new satellite communities, River Plantation, south of Conroe. It was a green, sculpted landscape with a golf-course and the deliberately quaint feeling of an old English village about it. He and his wife had designed their own home and moved in permanently in 1971. They liked it.

Bill Srack had never visited Dugan and never intended to. He was not concerned with civil rights or integration and was happy to vote Republican at elections and mind his own business in the meantime. He had never heard of Clarence Brandley and, though he was dimly aware that there had been a murder at Conroe High, he had not followed the case and had no interest in its rights or wrongs. Until Tuesday, 2 December 1980, when he was called to Montgomery County courthouse for jury duty.

The truth was that he had been called before, two weeks earlier, and he had done something quite out of character: even though he had written it in his calendar and made a mental note of it, he had completely forgotten to go to the courthouse. He was on the other side of Houston that day before he realized his mistake. He had apologized to the courthouse and been called, instead, for the first week in December.

His wife, Lajewel, a religious woman who regularly attended a bible study group in Conroe, said that that was no accident, that was providence; God had wanted Bill on the jury in this murder trial. And when he set off that Tuesday morning to answer his jury summons, Lajewel went to her bible study group and told them, and they agreed that they would all pray for him to be selected for the jury if that was what God wanted, and for him to have wisdom to discern the truth and strength to stand up for it.

For his part, Srack would rather he was not selected. He had already served on four juries in Houston, including two federal cases, and he was beginning to feel that he had done more than his fair share for the community. But there was no stopping it. In the second-floor courtroom, each of the 50 prospective jurors was given a number. He was number two. The first juror was questioned and rejected because he said he had already made up his mind about the defendant's guilt. Srack stood up and said he knew nothing about it but he would do his best to follow the evidence. He was the first juror chosen.

Conroe was still stricken by the schoolgirl's murder.

In the three months since her death, it seemed, there had been one outrage after another in the town. Someone had taken a high-powered rifle and shot up some of the stores near the courthouse, just for the hell of it. Someone else had broken into the church on Hillcrest Drive and stolen all the musical instruments.

In Willis, ten miles north of Conroe, Montgomery County sheriffs had arrested a man for repeatedly sexually abusing a nine-year-old boy. 'There are more reported cases of sexual abuse of children than there have been ever before,' said the arresting officer, Richard Reyna.

A woman was abducted from a convenience store on Route 105 and brutally raped. A schoolgirl in Cleveland was assaulted and strangled and left for dead. A woman in Porter was raped by a man to whom she had given a lift in her car. A female cleaner was attacked and raped in the grounds of Conroe High. A maintenance man had gone missing from Runyon Elementary School and the police said he had been molesting a young girl there. A Conroe minister had been indicted for stealing from two old ladies in his congregation.

The Brandley case was never out of the newspaper. It was on the front page every day for two weeks after the murder. Pictures of Brandley; details of his past; speculation about his guilt. Every time there was another twitch in the case, it was back on the front page. The Montgomery County Rape Coalition were up in arms. They set up a panel of eight expert speakers to advise the county's women on how to protect themselves. They also called for volunteers and trained them to inspire more vigilance. Sgt Berle Johnson, Conroe's Crime Prevention Officer, started running rape prevention workshops to meet the demand. The Conroe YMCA announced free classes in rape prevention, to be held during daylight hours. 'The next rape could be you,' the *Courier* warned its readers.

The town had elected a new sheriff to replace Gene Reaves who was retiring at the end of December after 20 years. The new man, Joe Corley, promised to be tough on criminals, to make this town safe again, and no messing around.

But there was no easy cure for the fear – only the chance of punishing the guilty. With death – ordered by a jury, sanctioned by a judge and welcomed by all.

The stricken town looked to the courthouse.

It was Monday of the next week, 8 December, before Bill Srack was called back to the courthouse. The whole of the previous week had been consumed by arguments about who should sit on the jury. It had been a bad-tempered business. The defence had been trying to ferret out anyone who had already formed an opinion against Brandley. Some jurors admitted they thought he was guilty because they had read it in the paper; one or two even admitted they thought he was guilty because he was black. But Judge Sam Robertson jr. had complained that the defence was taking too long and was playing with the jurors. Morris and Brown felt the Judge was trying to do Jim Keeshan's job for him, making objections to their questions, ruling against them all the time and even interceding to defend jurors who admitted they were prejudiced. Keeshan, for his part, seemed to be determined to stop any black person getting on to the jury. He challenged some of them because they admitted they did not believe in the death penalty. Others he removed with a peremptory challenge which needed no explanation. The judge allowed him to do this and the result was inevitable: a jury of nine men and three women, all of them white.

Now, on a warm, cloudy morning, when all the rest of the world seemed to be in a state of shock about the murder of John Lennon in New York, Bill Srack climbed into his half-ton blue pick-up, drove north a few miles up I-45, swung off on to Frazier Street, parked in the First Baptist Church where he and Lajewel worshipped every Sunday, and walked across the street to the imposing white building that rose like a temple over the square.

Srack was in sombre mood. He knew he was going to be dealing with murder and rape and with a defendant whose life was at stake. It was going to be an important trial. He could not imagine a more serious set of circumstances and he deliberately tried to prepare himself mentally for what lay ahead, clearing his mind and telling himself that all he had to do was to be honest and fair. He believed he could do it. He had a mind like a tram track which went straight to the point without distraction. Sometimes he was a little short on humour but he always thought logically and clearly. He was certainly not about to be swayed by any feelings against Brandley because of his colour. The truth was that he had had his troubles with black people. They were the reason he had uprooted his wife and three children and left Houston. Black families had started moving into their neighbourhood in the south of the city and it seemed to Bill Srack and his family that the area started going downhill fast – more litter in the streets, more crime. He was no racist, but he was happy to live in a white neighbourhood like River Plantation.

Srack found his way to the jury room, where most of the others had already gathered. He did not know them. Some of them introduced themselves.

On the other side of the courtroom, in the office where Judge Lee Alworth usually ran his affairs, the small, bespectacled figure of Judge Sam Robertson jr. was making his final preparations. It was a familiar routine. He had been prosecuting criminal cases for 19 years with the District Attorney in Houston before his appointment as a judge two years earlier, on 1 January 1978. His critics said he had spent too long in the DA's office and was too prosecution-minded. That kind of criticism had never been known to worry Judge Sam Robertson.

On the first floor, Jim Keeshan and his assistant, Jerry Winfree, were checking their paperwork in the District Attorney's office. This was an important case. Conroe did not elect its District Attorneys to allow black rapists to run round murdering young white girls. But it was not going to be easy to put the evidence across. And it was all slightly complicated by the fact that this was really two hearings rolled into one: the jury had to decide beyond reasonable doubt whether Brandley was guilty of capital murder, and the judge had also to decide whether it was more likely than not that Brandley had breached his probation by committing a murder. It meant that even if the jury decided to acquit Brandley, the judge could still make him serve his three years for breach of probation.

In the courtroom above them, spectators already lined the public benches: white men in faded denims and battered baseball caps; a knot of anxious white faces belonging to the dead girl's relatives; a second knot of anxious brown faces belonging to the Brandleys; some black ministers and observers from Houston civil rights groups, drawn to the courthouse by rumours that a black man was being railroaded; everyone gently murmuring their speculation, exchanging their opinions, confirming their foregone conclusions.

On a solitary chair at the front of the court sat Clarence Brandley, wearing his blue Sunday suit. He looked around at the white faces lined up in rows like gravestones: the white jurors, the white District Clerk with her bright red fingernails, the white reporters with their notebooks, the white deputies at the door. All he could do was to hold on to his hope and fight the fear inside him.

At a long wooden table at his side, just in front of the judge's raised dias, sat the defence team – George Morris and Don Brown occasionally leaning into each other to swap whispers; Ray Reeves sitting apart working a pinky finger into his ear. Despite the futility of their struggles since they had come into the case, they were feeling good about their defence, just so long as that judge didn't try and cheat them again.

Now, on the other side of the defence team, at a second long wooden table, Keeshan and Winfree took their seats.

Just before nine o'clock Sam Robertson swept into the room, and the case of the state of Texas versus Clarence Lee Brandley began.

Brandley sat still and silent. People he had never seen before started to act out a strange ritual. Its language was foreign to him; its form was alien. It unfolded around him, yet it seemed to have no role for him. The white people in the jury box solemnly swore that they would a true verdict render according to the law and the evidence submitted to them, so help them God. The white clerk with the long, glossy, strawberry-coloured fingernails stood up and said that the Grand Jury – duly selected, empanelled, sworn, charged and organized – had indicted a defendant. This defendant had, on or about 23 August 1980, intentionally caused the death of Cheryl Fergeson by choking and strangling her by means to the Grand Jury unknown in the course of committing and attempting to commit the offence of aggravated rape of the said Cheryl Fergeson. From time to time people mentioned Clarence Lee Brandley, the name he had grown up with.

Witnesses started to reappear. A tall, grey-haired man with a deeply lined face, the father of the dead girl, was stooped with grief. When he tried to describe how he had last seen his daughter, through his kitchen window as she drove off one Saturday morning with her blonde hair catching his eye, his face crumpled and he had to stop to wipe away his tears. School-teachers told how the girl had disappeared and they had started to worry. Girls who had been playing volleyball remembered searching the school. Policemen talked about calls they had received over their radios and then about the calls they had made to summon the detectives when the dead girl's body was found. From time to time they mentioned Brandley's name.

The white volleyball coach from Conroe High said Brandley had told her to keep everyone away from his end of the building. He didn't remember that. They said he had helped with the search and then taken the police to the body. Nobody said he was guilty of anything, or not so far as he could tell. Then the four white janitors told their stories. They all said pretty much the same as each other. Brandley could not see how any of it meant that he had killed the girl. Not at first.

They described the plain facts about right, all of them getting to the school around 7.30 a.m., Icky going off to buff the floor in the teachers' lounge while Acreman, Sessum and Martinez set out the chairs in the cafeteria; how they all waited around in the hallway till Clarence came along with an armful of toilet rolls. They all agreed that Acreman had said something about a girl being in the restroom and that Brandley had sent them all over to the vocational building, where they had waited for some time before Brandley came over with the key to the door. It was all true enough. Brandley remembered it clearly. It was Gary Acreman who started to worry him.

He slouched in the witness chair with his hair slicked down and his long, thin legs spidering out across the floor, fidgeting all the time and talking in that whining voice with the east Texas twang. Right away he said something that set Brandley thinking. Nothing important: just that he claimed that they were friends. 'Me and Clarence worked together and we got along real good and he had even bought my lunch for me.' Who was he trying to kid? Acreman had never liked him, never liked a black man being over him, and never made any secret of it.

Then he started to say some other things, none of them that big on its own. All of them put together did not really add up to anything. But they were not true, and that worried Brandley. Like when he was talking about how they all waited in the hallway for Brandley to come and give them another job to do. Acreman reckoned that he and the others had started their wait at around 9.15 a.m. and that they had been standing there for a full 15 minutes before they noticed a girl walking towards them down the hallway, go up the little staircase about 50 feet away from where they stood and enter the Sesame Street restroom.

Brandley winced. Why was he saying that the girl went down the hallway at 9.30 when all the teachers and volleyball players had agreed that it was 9.15? Acreman had somehow lost 15 minutes. And another thing: those white janitors had not been 50 feet away from Sesame Street; they had been right there on the staircase. They must have been. Acreman himself said he had been able to read the girl's name on the back of her belt: CHERYL.

Brandley had no time to think about how all this mattered before Acreman said something else that was not quite right. According to him, Brandley was following along right behind the girl, walking just ten feet behind her as she came down the hallway. Brandley knew he had never seen that girl alive, that the first time he laid eyes on her was up in the little props loft when Icky screamed and then he saw her lying there, naked. He had never seen her going down any hallway. Still, it didn't mean much. It surely didn't mean he had killed her.

Acreman carried on talking. 'I told Clarence there was a girl in the restroom and he said he wasn't going to go in there.'

That was true. He had gone down there to put new toilet rolls in the boys' restroom. He never did go in the girls' restrooms. Acreman recalled how Brandley had sent them all over to the vocational building and how they had waited there for some time before Brandley finally came over with a key to open the doors. That was all true, except for one other little thing which he added: 'Clarence had a white towel around his neck which I had never seen him wear before.'

What was he talking about? Brandley couldn't remember any towel, but he did remember how the DA had been on at him about a towel with the Grand Jury, trying to make out that he was carrying one. Acreman was playing some kind of game here. He had always been a sly one, always mouthing off. What was he trying to do? It was as if someone had got to him and told him to nail Brandley to the crime. Acreman hammered once more: 'Clarence seemed to act kind of strange,' he said. 'He seemed to act strange like he wanted us to go, so me and John Sessum went and got my truck and took off.'

Brandley could feel his heart thumping. Acreman was out to get him here. There was no telling why, but Acreman was taking every change he got to point a finger at him. He had always tried to treat Acreman like a human being. Why would he do this to him now?

Still, Brandley couldn't see how anyone could say he had killed the girl. No way.

In the jury box, Bill Srack watched carefully. He did not like the look of Gary Acreman. He was cocky; he was nervous. Srack watched his little eyes twitching around the room, now at the floor, now at the ceiling. Srack was not at all sure that Gary Acreman was an honest witness. It was not just his manner. Sam Martinez had been very tense and John Sessum even worse – so nervous he was almost incoherent. It was something more subtle than that.

Srack pushed the facts a little further down his tram-track mind and finally came to a conclusion: all these white janitors were telling the same story, not just in general shape but in all its essential details and particularly in any detail that tended to make Brandley look bad. They all said the same thing. But real people, honest people, didn't do that. Honest people recalled all kinds of different things and, with the best will in the world, gave different versions of the same events. But these white janitors were all agreeing about who had arrived at what time at the school, all agreeing that Brandley was the only one with keys to any of the doors, all agreeing that Brandley had been walking right behind the girl, all recalling that Gary Acreman warned him that she was in the restroom, all rehearsing the same sequence of events in which they moved away, leaving Brandley alone and unobserved, and which ended with Brandley returning and all of them noticing that he had a towel around his neck and all of them thinking to themselves that he seemed nervous. It was too pat. It was not real.

The more he thought about it, the more convinced Srack became that the white janitors had put their heads together and agreed on a story. But there was something wrong with that, too. In Srack's mind, these white janitors were obviously unintelligent men. Sessum, in particular, looked like a complete derelict. These men were not sharp enough to have put their heads together and agreed a story. They had to have had some help. Somebody had got them all together and helped them to sort out the story.

On the defence bench, Morris and Brown had arrived at the same conclusion. This was the first chance they had had to question these white janitors. They began to see more of how the police and the Texas Ranger had been acting. They discovered that Gary Acreman, John Sessum and Sam Martinez had all made two statements. First, they had been down to Conroe Police Department on the Monday after the crime while Brandley and Peace were in Houston taking lie tests, and put their stories down on paper.

Then, five days later, on the Saturday immediately after Brandley's arrest, they had all been taken back to the high school by the Texas Ranger, Wesley Styles, and walked through the hallway re-enacting the day of the crime. After that, they had made another set of statements. And they had changed their stories. It was their second version of the story, compiled after their walk-through with the Ranger, which contained all the details that were causing the defence trouble.

In their first statement, none of them had suggested that Brandley was the only one with keys to the auditorium, nor that the girl had appeared at 9.30, nor that they had been standing at least 50 feet away from Sesame Street when the girl arrived, nor that Brandley later had a towel around his neck, nor that he was then acting in a nervous fashion. But after their walk-through, all three agreed that all of these details were correct, and even used the same words and phrases to describe them. And it was not just that they were adding damaging details to fill holes in their first version. They were completely contradicting themselves. Both John Sessum and Sam Martinez had said originally that the girl had come down the hallway behind Brandley, but after their walk-through they all agreed that the black janitor had been following the girl. In their original statements, they guessed Brandley had left them waiting outside the vocational building for as little as five minutes. Now, they all agreed he had left them for 45 minutes.

George Morris did his best to put pressure on the white janitors, to point out all these changes and to try and make them admit that they had been coached by the Texas Ranger. At one point, John Sessum started to say he had been scared by the Ranger, but Morris could not break through. It left Morris and Brown with a frightening picture of a town in which the investigation of a crime was stood on its head. First they arrested a man and then they started work. It was only after Brandley had been arrested that the Ranger extracted these damaging details from witnesses, just like it was after the arrest that Ted Morgan was sent down into Dugan to find some dirt to justify what they were doing.

Bill Srack was impressed by only one of the white janitors, Icky Peace, who seemed to have more poise about him than the others despite the fact that he admitted to being illiterate and to having attended a special school for those with learning difficulties.

The little fat janitor with the squeaky voice started his evidence by following the well-trodden path through the day of the crime. Then he came to the point when he and Brandley joined the search for the missing girl, checking the lobby doors and then going into the auditorium where, he said, Brandley had told him to go up and check in the props loft over the stage.

According to Peace, he had taken a quick look and come straight back down. He said Brandley had then sent him back up to look properly. 'I went back up there and started moving stuff around, not looking real good, but I moved a few things around.' He had come down again, he said, without finding anything and the two of them had then gone off around the school, looking in the gyms and out on the football field before coming back to the auditorium where, he said, Brandley had sent him up to the props loft yet another time. 'This time, I did look. I just got disgusted and I just decided I would go ahead and look real good. I started moving boards around and everything and then I picked up this sheet of plywood . . . I saw the girl laying there . . . I screamed and called his name . . . He ran over to where I was at. He just said: "Oh, my God. I'll go get the police and you stay here." '

Srack could see the point plainly enough. The State was trying to suggest that Brandley knew the girl's body was there and wanted it discovered by Peace. He could see some of the other jurors nodding their heads knowingly. But why, Srack wondered, would a killer go to so much trouble to conceal a body and then, one hour later, go to such trouble to uncover it? The truth might just as easily be that it was Peace who had hidden the body and that he was deliberately avoiding uncovering it until Brandley made it impossible for him.

Anyway, Srack wondered how he would have handled someone like Peace himself if he had been in Brandley's shoes, working as a supervisor; if you sent a man to do a job and he failed to do it, you had to send him back and keep sending him back until he did it right. That was what a supervisor was for.

Now Srack watched as the defence tried to make a very different point about Icky Peace. As George Morris questioned him, Peace started to reveal some strange things about himself.

Morris asked him about the police searching his car on the day of the crime. 'Did you have a gun in it?'

'Yes, sir. I just forgot about it being in there. I had just got it fixed.'

'Did they also get a club out of your car?'

'Uh. Yes, sir. It was a souvenir at the school where I used to work at, the kids all made it and gave it to me.'

'Have you ever showed that gun to David Harris?'

'I showed it to him once.'

'Was that in school?'

'No, sir. It was a picture that I showed him.'

'Isn't it a fact that you carried that gun underneath your bill-fold?'

'No, sir.'

'You didn't show David Harris that gun while you were working on the job there at the school?'

'I showed him a picture of it.'

'Do you have a card showing you to be a narcotics agent with the name *Four Seasons* written across it?'

Srack watched Peace's face closely. Peace seemed to be making this up as he went along. Had he been showing off a gun in school or not? What was he doing with a gun and a club? There was something about his story that was just not right. Srack could see that the defence were driving at something. Suddenly, his thoughts were torn away from him. It was the Judge, barking at George Morris.

'Counsel, what does that have to do with this?'

'I think I can connect it up, Your Honour. If it please the court, I would like to be able to show . . .'

But the judge barked again. 'Members of the jury, I'd like you to step back into the jury room.'

Puzzled, Srack allowed himself to be shepherded out of the courtroom with his fellow jurors.

Brandley watched them go. He had not been enjoying Icky's evidence one bit. It was just the same as Acreman – like this business about him repeatedly sending Icky up to the props room. It couldn't be true. The first thing that he and Icky had seen when they left the vocational building to go and lock up the main building was a police car. The cops themselves said they had not got to the school until 11.40. The girl had been found at about 11.50. There was no way they could have straightened out the cafeteria, searched the auditorium and then gone off on Icky's grand tour of the school and then come back and found the body in only ten minutes.

But why was Peace saying it? Maybe he was just scared the police were going to pin the murder on him if he didn't point the finger at someone else. He always had been good at talking himself out of trouble. Brandley knew he was lying about the gun he had been showing off in school. But all these little lies were adding up. And now this judge was acting funny. Every time George Morris opened his mouth, the judge seemed to snap at him.

As the jury disappeared behind a closed door, Morris started to explain that he was trying to demonstrate how someone other than Brandley could have committed the crime: 'We would like to show another reasonable hypothesis as to . . .'

'First let the jury retire,' said the judge in a tone which suggested he was dealing with a disobedient brat, 'and ask him some questions.'

'Oh, I thought you wanted to know the purpose.'

'No, sir. I am not going to permit this. I am not going to permit questions to be asked of this witness that doesn't have anything to do with any matter that is on trial.'

Morris opened his mouth to say that the fact that Icky Peace may have killed the girl was all that mattered. But he thought better of it and started to ask Peace if it was true that he had originally been a suspect.

'Did they tell you that you were a possible . . .'

The judge barked again. 'This is not what the jury retired on.

Ask him the question that you asked him, that I had the jury retired on.'

Morris started again, asking Peace whether he had been in the habit of showing people, including David Harris, an identity card which claimed that he was a narcotics agent with the code name *Four Seasons*.

'I showed the whole crew a bunch of cards.'

'I'm talking about a particular card showing you as a narcotics agent.'

Peace then launched into an explanation involving a toy city which he said he played with at home with his little nephews and nieces. It was a hobby, he said, and to make it more real he had himself made some plastic ID cards complete with his photograph. 'I have a whole bunch of them made up – doctors and lawyers and druggists and FBIs,' he said. 'I'm head of the narcotics division of my play city.'

Had he ever shown his narcotics card to David Harris and asked if he would work undercover for him? Peace said no. Morris moved in for the kill: he was sure that Peace was lying and if he could just draw him out and . . . But the judge barked again.

'All right, now, hurry up. What is the materiality of this?'

Morris sighed and tried to explain. 'I am demonstrating to the jury that this man also could have committed this offence. It would have been very easy for him to induce some little girl, 16 years old, by showing her a narcotics card to get her to go anywhere with him. And I think it is admissible.'

The judge shook his head. 'I am not going to permit this witness to be questioned about this matter in front of the jury. Bring the jury out.'

Morris took a deep breath, shook his head and sat down.

Brandley watched in silence as his best shot was stolen from him.

Bill Srack came back with the rest of the jury and tried to figure out what he had missed. It seemed to be important. But it was clear that they were not going to be told.

The Reverend J. J. Roberson had travelled up to the courthouse from Houston, where he was pastor of the Mount Hebrew

Missionary Baptist Church. He was concerned by the rumours he had heard about a railroading. Now, looking round the court-room, his heart felt heavy. Not that it was any surprise to him: he knew all about Montgomery County. He remembered a particular time, back in 1955, when he was a younger man and had bought himself a brand new Mercury and driven it up through Montgomery County. The police had stopped him in Conroe. He had not committed any crime, so he had asked them: 'Why did you stop me?'

And they had told the young minister to his face: 'Any nigger that comes through Conroe driving a '55 Mercury is gonna get stopped.'

It seemed to him that, 25 years later, the atmosphere was still the same. Every time a black person got up and left the court, one of the white deputies would get up and follow him. Not say anything, just follow him. The deputies were even following black people into the restroom. All around the court, the minister could see the same look on every white face – an angry, hateful look. And he was not just talking about a few redneck spectators. He meant the white people who were running this court. They all had the same look, and that included the judge.

This was a white man's court.

As the trial progressed, Morris and Brown retired as often as possible to the Iron Horse across the street from the courthouse to discuss each day's events. They agreed that they were happy enough with the way the trial had started, but they were worried about the judge.

'Anyone would think he was working for the prosecution,' grumbled Brown. 'He's not even waiting for Keeshan to make objections. He's just coming out and doing the DA's job for him.'

Ray Reeves had started keeping a note of every time the judge did the District Attorney's job for him. The writing on his notepad was getting bigger and bigger as his anger at the judge's behaviour got the better of him.

The crucial test would come when the defence tried to put their own witnesses on the stand to outline their theory about Peace, and Morris and Brown had both seen something that worried them greatly: Keeshan slipping into the judge's office on his own.

It would be totally improper for the judge to start discussing the case with one side while the other was excluded. But after both of them had seen Keeshan disappearing into the judge's room and closing the door behind him, Morris and Brown had complained and asked if they could join in these meetings. The judge had told them that the meetings were nothing to do with the case. Keeshan was just in there talking about other things, never even mentioning the trial.

'Bullshit,' said Brown.

'Damn right,' said Morris.

For three days, Bill Srack listened to Jim Keeshan as he paraded his witnesses. Some of it was worrying; some of it seemed to him to be irrelevant; some of it was plain embarrassing. Like the evidence of Mr E. H. Hoffmeister, a fingerprint specialist from the Department of Public Safety in Austin. Mr Hoffmeister had no fingerprint evidence of any significance to offer the court, but he had a sorry story to tell. He said, for example, that he had not been able to take any prints from a wad of paper which had been screwed up and possibly used to gag Cheryl Fergeson because the police had failed to pass it on to him. He added that he might have been able to take prints from the girl's body if the police had given him access to it soon enough after her death, but the police had failed to do that. He had, however, found one fingerprint on the rubbish bag in which the dead girl's clothes had been found – that of a detective who had not bothered to wear gloves while he handled the evidence.

Srack found even less comfort in the evidence of the short, hefty Captain of Detectives, Monty Koerner. Koerner proudly told the court that he had been a law enforcement officer for 15 years and Captain of Detectives for Conroe Police Department for nine of them. He explained how he had set about tackling the crime. On the day of the murder, he had ordered one of his sergeants, 'Woody' Allen, to take photographs of the scene of the crime and of the people who were there.

'What about those photographs?' he was asked. 'What happened to them?'

'The – Sgt Allen had the uh – wrong setting on the camera. And the film did not come out.'

On the defence table, the attorneys grimaced.

Had they tried to develop the photographs? Not exactly, said the captain. They had taken them to Fox Photo. The defence attorneys laughed out loud. Fox Photo? Not the FBI in Houston or the DPS laboratory in Austin or even the Montgomery County Sheriff's Department? Conroe's Captain of Detectives had allowed his scene-of-the-crime photos in the biggest rape homicide in the history of the whole town to be taken down to North Hills shopping mall and chucked into the Fox Photo deposit, where little kids took their happy snaps of family pets to be developed? That was so, said the captain.

The defence attorneys shook their heads in wonder.

The captain was asked about the autopsy on the dead girl. Yes, he had been there. Yes, he had been investigating rapes for some ten years now. Yes, he knew what a rape kit was. And yes, he knew that swabs of semen collected from a rape victim could reveal the blood type of the rapist. But no, he had not collected the swabs and washings which contained the semen collected from this girl's body. He had thought that someone else was going to do it.

Srack sighed.

Srack found little to reassure him in the testimony of Dr Joseph Jachimczyk MD, JD, Forensic Pathologist, Attorney at Law, Chief Medical Examiner for Harris County, and medical examiner upon request and upon payment of the appropriate fee for Montgomery County. Srack listened respectfully to the portly medical examiner with the owlish face as he outlined his findings. Cheryl Fergeson had died of asphyxia due to ligature strangulation and she had been the victim of a sexual attack. His belief was that it would have taken at least 30 seconds for her to lose consciousness and at least three minutes to die.

The doctor disclosed that the girl's bladder was completely empty and said that this was striking since a bladder would fill with urine at the rate of two millilitres a minute. The District

Attorney said this proved that she had been attacked as soon as she had tried to leave the restroom – timing which tended to point to Brandley as the attacker. The defence suggested that if Brandley had attacked her as she left the restroom, then in the three minutes it had taken her to die her bladder would have accumulated six millilitres of urine, so Keeshan must be wrong. It seemed to Srack to be more likely that the girl's bladder had emptied after she was dead when her muscles relaxed, and that its emptiness told him nothing at all about when she had died. He was surprised that the doctor had not suggested it himself.

The doctor also said that the girl's hymen had still been intact, even though the presence of semen showed she had been raped. Srack assumed that meant her attacker had simply failed to penetrate her, but the doctor had a more disturbing theory. It suggested to him that the girl had been killed and then raped when she was already dead, and that her hymen had been so relaxed in death that it had not broken. Some of Srack's fellow jurors stared at Brandley with deep revulsion.

Srack was not impressed, but his respect for the doctor's evidence began to crumble completely as he was led through the sensitive question of the missing swabs. At first, the doctor declared confidently that he had passed the swabs to Captain Koerner during the autopsy. Then he backtracked and said it was possible that he had not. Then he said he would have given the captain anything he asked for. He could not be sure.

The point was rubbed in by Sally Williams of the Forensic Science Institute in Dallas who specialized in analysing body fluids for the police. Don Brown asked her if it was unusual to have no vaginal swabs from a rape victim.

'It's not only unusual,' she said. 'That's the whole purpose of doing the examination.'

Srack despaired. There was no way of knowing whether this was cock-up or conspiracy. It was certainly no way to run a murder inquiry.

Brandley did not know what to believe. All this mattered. The lost fingerprints might have identified the guilty man. The photographs they had messed up could have shown that he was not carrying a towel around his neck and that he was not wearing a belt – or carrying anything else that they might try and say he had used to kill this girl. The swabs were even more important: they could have blown the lid off the whole case. It seemed like more than just bad luck that they had all been lost. Lost and gone forever. And there was more bad luck with the judge.

Before Captain Koerner retreated from the witness chair, George Morris tried to get him to admit that there were some similarities between the rape of Cheryl Fergeson and another rape in the town – a rape in which a man who had no connection with Clarence Brandley had been identified as the rapist. Could there not be a link? Was this not a reasonable hypothesis to put to the jury? But the judge sent the jury out of the room. Then he listened to the evidence and announced: 'There will be no reference to this in front of the jury.'

Srack was still waiting for the state to land its big punch. So far, it seemed to him, they had been swinging hard but never making contact. Even supposing the other janitors were all honest, which he doubted, all their evidence meant was that Brandley could conceivably be guilty and that he had had the time to commit the offence. But that did not seem to him to be anywhere close to proving beyond reasonable doubt that Brandley had really done this thing. What other evidence was there? Icky Peace said Brandley had kept sending him up to the props loft. Maybe, maybe not. So what? It still did not prove a thing. They were trying to say that Brandley had been the only one with a key to the auditorium, but Srack had worked in places like this where keys were given out and soon got left with all kinds of people who shouldn't have had them and in this school, so far as he could see, they hadn't changed the keys since Methuselah. Anyone could have got into the auditorium. The fact was that there was not enough circumstantial evidence to pinpoint Brandley, and so far there had been nothing – no fingerprints, no photos, no swabs – which linked him with this crime.

Morris and Brown launched into the scientific evidence, trying to alert the jury to the clues they had found in the autopsy report and to their expert's work. Keeshan fought back.

The jury were told that the line across the girl's neck was too narrow to have been made by Brandley's belt. The defence attorneys sat, mute in disbelief and admiration, as the District Attorney took Brandley's leather belt in both hands, stretched it with all his strength and suggested that if it was pulled with maximum force, its width would be reduced by the tension so that it might, after all, fit the line on the girl's neck.

The jury were told that scientists for both sides had studied Brandley's belt and his knife and all the girl's clothes and found nothing – no fibre, no skin tissue, no fingerprint – that could conceivably link Brandley with the murder. It was only then that the defence finally understood the importance of the towel which the white janitors now all remembered seeing round the black man's shoulders. Of course, he had used it to wipe away all this missing evidence.

Then they came to the hairs.

Keeshan called his expert, Tony Arnold, who worked at the DPS laboratory in Austin, and the defence called Dr Irving Stone, their expert from the Forensic Science Institute in Dallas. They had examined 13 different hairs or fragments of hair which had been found on the dead girl's body or clothes. Both men agreed that you could never be too sure about hairs: you could sometimes say that a hair came from a black or a white person, but you could never show a definite link between one particular hair and one particular individual.

Two of the hairs, they thought, could have come from the dead girl. They had compared the remaining 11 hairs to the samples which they had been given from Clarence Brandley and Icky Peace. Eight of the hairs had no resemblance to the samples from either man.

The defence quietly cursed Keeshan for his blind focus on Brandley. Why had he refused to test anyone else's hair? Still, those eight hairs should be powerful evidence for the jury, they thought. They were eight clues to the real culprit.

The court pored over the origins of the remaining three hairs. Two of the three hairs had been rescued from the girl's inner thigh by the detective who had stashed them in his cigarette pack. One was black and the other was reddish.

The black hair, according to Keeshan's expert, could have been one of Brandley's pubic hairs. However, the defence expert said it was not a pubic hair at all, never mind being one of Brandley's. Morris and Brown had no idea what it was – whether it had been taken from Brandley and planted, or whether it belonged to one of the black volleyball players or even the dead girl's boyfriend, who was a black-haired Hispanic. But the confusion between the experts gave them plenty of room to dismiss the hair as real evidence.

The red hair from the girl's thigh, according to Keeshan's expert, could have been one of Icky Peace's pubic hairs. Morris and Brown were delighted to hear that, but their own expert disagreed. He thought it was a pubic hair, but he believed it probably belonged to someone other than Icky Peace. He could not say who. For Morris and Brown, this red pubic hair was a powerful reason to find Clarence Brandley not guilty. There were also two other hairs on the girl's thigh which could not be linked to any known suspect. But the District Attorney had an answer. He suggested that while the dead girl had picked up the black hair in the course of being raped by Clarence Brandley, she must have picked up the other three from a toilet seat. Morris and Brown thought this was a desperate argument, since it meant the girl must have been lying across the toilet on her abdomen.

The final hair had been found in one of the dead girl's socks. Keeshan's expert said it probably came from a black person and had some similarities to Brandley's. The defence expert said that he could see no difference at all between this hair and Brandley's, but before anyone in court had a chance to think that he might be offering a conclusive clue, he explained that all that he meant was that 'there are a number of people in the population from whom this hair could have come and it's not just one person.'

Did that mean, asked Don Brown, that he was merely putting Brandley into a segment of the general population who could have committed this crime?

'No sir,' replied the expert with searing precision. 'It just puts him in a segment of the population that could have gotten the hair on that sock.'

The Reverend C. Anderson Davis had also travelled up from Houston to witness the trial of the black janitor. He worked for the Baptist Ministers' Association and he wanted to observe the quality of justice in this courthouse. He was not impressed. It was not just the judge with his hostile attitude and his way of talking down to black people who dared to make a sound in court, nor the atmosphere in the room. What most disturbed the elderly minister were his conversations with a Montgomery County deputy. The deputy never went into any detail and, if he had not been such a reliable source, the minister would have paid it no attention at all, but the one thing that this deputy kept coming back to was that this trial was rigged.

Late on Wednesday afternoon, after three days of evidence, Jim Keeshan declared that he had completed the State's case. For a moment, Morris and Brown were confused. They had never quite shrugged off the fear that Keeshan had some secret weapon to throw at them. The fear had dogged them ever since they had taken the case. But now Keeshan was sitting down. That was it: there was no secret weapon.

George Morris immediately hauled himself to his feet and invited the judge to instruct the jury to find Brandley not guilty.

With the jury dispatched to their room, George Morris put the argument. 'I'd like to state to this court that there is a difference between possibility and probability, and that even though it might be possible for this defendant to have committed this crime, it's also possible that other people might have committed this crime. The probability is great that other people could have committed this crime.'

Morris tried to make the judge focus on the law covering cases of circumstantial evidence and, in particular, on the need for the State to exclude all other reasonable hypotheses, leaving the guilt of the defendant as the only reasonable explanation for the crime. He pointed in particular to the hairs which had been found on the dead girl and for which no owners could be found.

'It gives rise to the proposition that somebody other than this defendant could have committed this crime,' said Morris. 'Your Honour, since the court knows the law on circumstantial evidence,

we feel that there is another hypothesis, there is another theory –
that somebody other than the defendant could have committed
this crime. We feel that because the state has failed to exclude
every other reasonable hypothesis that this defendant is entitled
to that law – and that law should be an instructed verdict.'

Morris believed he was right. And yet it was no surprise when
the judge, without pausing to hear any further discussion, said:
'All right, sir, your motion will be denied. Mr Morris, it is a fact
issue to the jury.'

Morris and Brown were not too worried. Brown, in particular,
had gone backwards and forwards over all the evidence.

'No reasonable jury could possibly convict anyone on this evidence,' he kept saying. 'The state has not made its case. It's as
simple as that.'

When the defence opened on Thursday morning, Morris and
Brown had a simple strategy. All they wanted to do was to show
that someone else could have raped and killed Cheryl Fergeson.
Their best suspect was Icky Peace. Their best theory was that he
had used his ID card to pretend to be a narcotics officer; he had
stopped the girl and told her he wanted to question her in the
auditorium, where he had used his gun or his club to subdue her
before raping and strangling her. They did not know whether it
was true, but they knew it was at least as reasonable as the State's
case and it was enough to cut Brandley free of the flimsy web of
circumstantial evidence which Keeshan had tried to throw around
him.

Their first major witness was David Harris, the black Vietnam
veteran who helped to supervise all the janitors in Conroe's 19
schools. He had become a key figure for the defence. For a start,
he could tell the jury how he had personally seen the Texas
Ranger, Wes Styles, coaching Icky Peace in his evidence at the
high school. But as soon as Don Brown asked Harris to describe
what had happened, Jim Keeshan leapt to his feet.

'I would object to hearsay, Your Honour.'

'Sustained,' said the judge.

Brown was open-mouthed. 'You Honour, we are asking . . .'

'I have ruled, counsel. I'll hear you in the absence of the jury on what your contention is, but I have ruled on it.'

George Morris tried to help. 'I don't believe this would be hearsay. Mr Peace is already . . .'

'I have ruled, counsel, I have ruled. I have told you I would hear it in the absence of the jury if you want to argue the point. Now, move along.'

Brown struggled on, trying to explain that they wanted to warn the jury that Peace might be lying. 'Your Honour, we're not offering this to the proof of any facts. We're offering it for the purpose of impeachment.'

The judge glared at him. 'Counsel, do you understand me when I say I have ruled?'

Eventually, the judge sent the jury out of the room, listened to Don Brown, who was barely suppressing his desire to bellow like a bull, and told him he could not put this evidence before the jury.

But that was not the end of David Harris. He could also testify that Icky Peace had carried a gun in school and had posed as a narcotics officer and he could vouch from his own experience that Peace made a convincing job of it. This, too, would show that Icky Peace had not necessarily been telling the truth when he was in court earlier in the week.

The jurors were back in their seats. Don Brown had settled Harris into his evidence and was just bringing him round to the big questions when – without any hint of an objection from Jim Keeshan – the judge intervened and sent the jury out of the room again.

Brown tried to persuade the judge to allow the evidence. With the jury out of the way, he asked Harris to tell his story. Harris was clear that Icky Peace had shown him a pistol in the school, not a picture of a pistol. He recalled, too, how Peace had shown him his narcotics ID card with the code name *Four Seasons*.

'Did he say anything about this was part of his play city or play world?'

'No, sir.'

'Did he inquire of you as to whether or not you wanted to participate in narcotics work?'

'Yes, sir.'

'What if anything did you tell him when he inquired of you if you wanted to participate?'

'I told him to let me think about it.'

Brown was pleased. This was a direct contradiction of what Peace had told the jury. If he could just show the jury that Peace was a liar, they might not only discount anything bad he had to say about Brandley but they might also see that perhaps he had some reason for lying, including the possibility that he was trying to cover up his own guilt. Brown started to draw out more detail from his witness, but the judge intervened.

'Is there any other evidence other than just this? All this doesn't have anything to do with any matter here before me.'

Jim Keeshan stood up and asked if he could put some questions to the witness.

'You can ask him a couple, but as far as I'm concerned, I've heard all I need to hear. If you want to, I'll let you ask him.'

'I won't ask him, Your Honour,' said Keeshan.

With that, the judge dismissed the witness. 'I'm not going to permit this in front of the jury.'

Brown tried to plead with him, saying he was offering the evidence to show that Icky Peace may have lied to the jury.

'Your offer is refused,' barked the judge.

The defence had lost their first big witness.

Brown and Morris were not beaten yet. They had other witnesses. They called Officer Wayne Kremenak, one of the detectives who had searched Icky Peace's car on the day of the crime. The gun and the club were not all he had found.

But the judge said that this was not for the jury. So once again, Don Brown found himself questioning his witness in the absence of the jury in an attempt to persuade the judge to allow the evidence into the case. Brown went straight to the point.

'Did you recover any pictures from his car of nude women?'

'No, sir.'

Brown straightened up his considerable bulk and looked the officer straight in the eye. 'You don't recall recovering any pictures of nude women from his car?'

'No, sir, I don't.'

Brown was not going to let him go. 'Are you saying you didn't recover any pictures of nude women or you don't remember whether you did or not?'

'I don't believe I recovered any pictures of nude women.'

Brown was still not persuaded. 'Did you recover any pictures of nude people of any kind?'

'There were some on the dash of the car.'

At last.

'These were nude pictures of people?'

'Yes, sir.'

'And they were women?'

'Women I believe.'

'Then you do remember there being some nude pictures in his car.'

'Yes, sir.'

The detective went on to recall that there were two pictures of naked women pasted to the front of the dashboard of Icky Peace's car. He believed they were drawings cut out of a magazine.

The judge made no move to reprimand the officer for trying to mislead the court. Brown let it go. All he wanted to do was to get this in front of the jury, so that they would see that although this strange little man might seem like a child, he had some advanced adult obsessions.

But the judge said: 'There will be no mention of this to the jury.'

Then he warned the attorneys to behave themselves and told Brown to call his next witness.

Morris and Brown were beginning to worry.

As Bill Srack shuttled backwards and forwards to the jury room with his fellow jurors, a troubling idea began to form in his mind. After serving on four other juries, he believed he knew a little bit about how judges should behave. He understood, too, that there was some evidence which a jury could not hear – things that were prejudicial or inadmissible for some technical reason, but this judge seemed to be blocking the defence for the wrong kind of reason. It appeared to Srack that the judge was being unfair, as if he was on the side of the prosecution. He did not even seem to be hiding it; it was as if he was deliberately trying to show the jury that he believed that Brandley was guilty. His whole demeanour was hostile to the defence, as well as his rulings. That troubled Bill Srack.

He had been around courts long enough to see what was happening and not be swayed by a judge doing something like that, but he was not so sure about some of the other jurors. They might just decide that if the judge thought Brandley was guilty, then it would be all right for them to think so too.

Clarence Brandley was determined not to lose hope, but he was finding it hard.

Each morning, two white deputies came to his cell and led him out in chains. Before they got to the courtroom they would pull out their keys and release the locks because the jury were not supposed to see that he was a prisoner. It made no difference to Brandley. OK, so he could move his hands around. He was just as trapped, all the same.

He watched the judge and the way his face seemed to go as red as a brick any time Morris or Brown dared to stand up to him, and he watched the people in the courtroom on the public benches and he saw the way they stiffened and shifted away any time a black person came and sat down next to them. Black people were treated like intruders in this courthouse. It was as if black people only came to court as criminals.

Each day, before the hearing began, Brandley's family and friends would stand in a circle in the hallway outside the courtroom and join hands and pray for justice in America. Brandley found it hard to pray or to hope. Today, especially. Today, he had to get into that witness stand and give evidence in that courtroom. He had to stay cool.

George Morris had told him that he was going to ask just a few simple questions to start with and then leave it to the prosecution to make the running.

Brandley sat with his hands folded in his lap, trying to concentrate on Morris and ignore the unyielding stares that surrounded him. Nothing at school or in his work had ever prepared him for this. It was as if he was talking to save his life.

Morris led him through his life history for a few minutes. Then he asked him: 'Clarence, do you believe in God?'

'Yes, sir.'

'Clarence, did your mother raise you . . .'

Keeshan was on his feet objecting. He never explained why. The judge sustained the objection. Brandley thought that was no surprise.

'Clarence,' persisted Morris. 'Do you know right from wrong?'

'Yes, sir.'

'Clarence, I ask you: did you commit this murder rape that you have been charged with?'

'No, sir. I did not.'

George Morris sat down. Brandley saw Keeshan's assistant, Jerry Winfree, rise to cross-examine him. Winfree was a short man with a barrel chest and an untidy moustache. Brandley hardly knew him, and yet here he was, dissecting the tiny details of a day in his life, a day he could barely remember. For Chrisesake he had been half asleep all day. He never knew people were going to want to know every move he made. If he had known he would have written it down.

Winfree started asking him about the white lady, the Conroe volleyball coach, and how he was supposed to have told her to keep everyone away from his end of the school. As if he was already planning to murder someone up there. He knew that was what they were trying to say. But he had never said any such thing. Why would he? Anyway, no white lady teacher was going to take orders from some no-account black janitor. So he told Winfree it had never happened.

Then Winfree started on at him about where he had been while the white janitors were waiting outside the vocational building.

Brandley told him: 'I sat down and smoked a cigarette and listened to the radio.'

Winfree paused for a scornful moment. 'How long did you smoke the cigarettes there in the office?'

Brandley could not remember. He had had no watch. He had not been interested. 'I would say . . . I couldn't say how long. I couldn't give you no time, how long it took me. I stayed in the office maybe 15 to 20 minutes.'

'How many cigarettes did you smoke?'

'I smoked one.'

'What made you decide to get up and go on over to the vocational building?'

'I decided it was time to go on over because the main reason I didn't proceed right on over – I wasn't in no big hurry. We had to try to make at least half a day.'

'You wanted those janitors to just kill some time in front of that vocational building then?'

'That was normal.'

Brandley could see Winfree did not believe him. But what did some attorney from the DA's office know about a janitor's life? What did this jury know about it?

Winfree started pressing him on his movements and the timing of his movements. Brandley felt his memory collapsing. He could not even remember what the other witnesses had all been saying, let alone what had really happened.

He said he had gone down the hallway and seen the white janitors standing by Sesame Street soon after ten past eight – at least an hour earlier than anyone else's timing. He said he had started searching for the girl at ten o'clock and not found her until noon.

Winfree gave him that scornful look again. 'So you are now testifying that from ten until twelve – for two hours – you and Icky looked solid for the girl?'

Brandley shook his head, lost between anger and helplessness. 'I am not saying we didn't look for no two hours. I'm saying that if that was the time, then undoubtedly I am mistaken with my times.'

Winfree got him to describe exactly what he and Peace had done during their search for the girl, and then dug at the same sore point. 'So it took two hours for you to do this – what you have just described?'

'No, sir,' said Brandley, his frustration building. 'It didn't take no two hours.'

Winfree dragged him backwards and forwards across the events of that morning, tearing him to shreds with his times.

Bill Srack was beginning to despair of ever hearing anything persuasive in this trial. The prosecution case had been a shambles. Now the defence was being ruled out of court by the judge, and their one star witness, Clarence Brandley, seemed to him to have nothing helpful to say in his own defence. It was all very well Brandley saying he was innocent. Anyone who was accused of capital murder would say that but, so far as Srack was concerned, he had said nothing to clear his name.

Morris and Brown were also unhappy with Brandley's performance as a witness. He had rambled on too much and got all his timings in a mess. They knew he was nervous: he was charged with a capital murder. But he seemed dishonest. He looked like the bad nigger that the jury were expecting him to be. And it had done him no good to challenge the white volleyball coach about whether he had told her to keep everyone away from his end of the building. It would have been fine to admit that he had said it to her. But he did not remember saying it, so he said what he believed was true. The trouble was that this jury was not going to believe a black janitor over a white teacher. Not in Conroe.

They had to press on with their chosen strategy, to somehow get that jury to understand that the circumstantial evidence was just as strong against Icky Peace as it was against Brandley. They had one last witness who could bring the point home – the private investigator, Lorna Hubbell.

But the judge did not like it. Once again, Don Brown found himself pleading: Icky Peace had told Lorna Hubbell a number of things that he had then denied to the jury. The jury needed to know that Peace might be lying to them. And some of the things he had said to Lorna Hubbell suggested he had something to hide. The judge agreed that he could once again rehearse his witness's evidence in front of him in the absence of a jury. Brown rapidly took the investigator through her recollection of the day in September when she caught Icky Peace on his way to work and persuaded him to talk a little about the case. She said Peace had told her that the Texas Ranger had choked him with his necklace, that he had nightmares since the murder, that he had trouble talking about the case and that Conroe police had wanted to hypnotize him because he was blocking out the truth in his mind. Brown told the judge that these were all things which Peace had denied in his evidence. Jim Keeshan objected that there was no proper basis upon which to introduce this evidence.

The judge said: 'I sustain the objection and I will not permit her to testify before the jury.'

Their strategy had just lost its final witness.

By 2.40 p.m. on Thursday, just half a day after they had started to present the case, the defence team had finished. With their three key witnesses ruled out of court they had nothing left to offer.

Don Brown was in a volcanic mood, barely able to contain an explosion of rage at the judge. Brandley was despondent. George Morris was talking about how bad all this would look if it ever got to the Court of Criminal Appeals in Austin. But this trial was not over and the one thing that they clung to was that, so far as they could see, Jim Keeshan had failed to touch their client.

With the jury locked away in their room once more, George Morris tried again to persuade the judge to order a verdict of not guilty. He rehearsed the same argument and got the same response.

Judge Sam Robertson said: 'Your motion is overruled.'

That Thursday afternoon, Bill Srack was thoughtful as he drove the blue pick-up truck back to River Plantation. They had now heard all the evidence. Tomorrow, they had only to listen to the attorneys delivering their final speeches before beginning their deliberation. In his mind, he took each of his fellow jurors one by one and considered how he thought they would vote.

Some of them were easy.

There was one particular group, three men and a woman, none of them very old, who had eaten together at the midday break and who seemed to wear the same kind of rough denim clothes and spent a lot of time laughing at the same stupid things. They were a certain type which he knew well and he did not like to use the word, but if someone had put the word to him, he would have had to agree that they were rednecks. He was pretty sure he knew how the four of them would vote. In their eyes, this black school janitor was a guilty man.

But he fancied the other jurors might see things his way. He really could not say whether Brandley was guilty or innocent. He did not know. It seemed to him that the whole inquiry had been badly mishandled, and if they had got the right man they had certainly failed to prove it beyond reasonable doubt. And that was his job – to look for reasonable doubt. It was nothing to do with personal feelings, only logic. That was what he was good at. He could not possibly vote to convict Brandley on this evidence and so it was his duty to vote not guilty, and he reckoned that that was how most of the other jurors would see it.

Shortly before 8.30 the following morning, Friday 12 December, Bill Srack returned to the courthouse. For the next three hours, the attorneys heaved and pulled at the jury's sympathy in their final speeches.

The defence assailed the police inquiry. 'This was a Keystone cop investigation,' said Don Brown. 'Why were no semen traces preserved? Why were no fingerprints lifted from the body?'

'Clarence Brandley deserved that evidence,' boomed Brown.

And what about these janitors and their story? George Morris argued with all his force that they must have been coached by the Texas Ranger, Wes Styles. There could be no other explanation for the way their statements changed after their walk-through at the school.

What about all these unidentified hairs on the body? Who did they belong to? Not Brandley. All the experts agreed on that. They belonged to the rapist, to the girl's killer, who had not been caught. Maybe it was Icky Peace. Maybe it was someone else they had never heard of. The evidence did not tell them who it was, but it certainly did not tell them that the killer was Clarence Brandley. They had to vote not guilty.

By the time that Jerry Winfree and Morris and Brown had spoken, Bill Srack was confirmed in his view that not only should he vote not guilty, but that at least seven of his fellow jurors would agree with him. Then Keeshan spoke.

Vividly, he described his version of the crime: the black janitor ordering everyone to stay away from his end of the building; the innocent girl looking for a restroom; the black janitor pointing her down the hallway where he could get her on her own and then follow her; the black janitor sending the other janitors out of the building and then unlocking the auditorium door and waiting outside the restroom with his belt until the unsuspecting girl emerged; then throttling her and dragging her into the darkness of the auditorium, and killing her and raping her and hiding her naked body while he disposed of her clothes, cleaned up with a towel, then calmly going back to his work. Clarence Brandley was the only man with keys, a man who knew his way around the building, a man who was absent unobserved when the girl went missing, a man who owned a belt, a man who would naturally use rubbish bags to dispose of the dead girl's clothes. Keeshan's passion was rising.

'Doesn't this bear the tracks of a janitor?' he cried. 'If you listen to the defence, this could have been the Murder of the Rue Morgue or the Phantom of the Opera. I think if you really use your imagination, you could imagine some ape swinging in through the window to do this.' Keeshan paused and then struck. 'But this is a janitor! And we know which one, don't we?' Keeshan appealed to their emotions. 'This is a crime against all of us,' he shouted. Brandley, he said, was bestial and monstrous. There could be only one verdict – guilty.

As Keeshan sat down, Srack thought he saw tears in his blue eyes. It had been quite a performance. Nothing in it had changed Srack's opinion about how he should vote, but he wondered about some of the others.

Finally, at 11.40 a.m., Bill Srack and his 11 fellow jurors were sent to their room to reach a verdict. Just as he expected, the group of three men and a woman settled down together up one end of the table, and one of the men, a loud young man named Joe, began rubbing his hands and grinning. 'Let's get that old judge in here,' he said, 'and get us some cards and some beer and have us a good time.'

Srack looked at him sternly and told him the judge would have nothing to do with them until they had finished their deliberations.

By now, they were all seated round the table. Srack had found a chair in the middle of one side. To his left was an intelligent-looking man, a teacher, whom Srack had marked down in his mind as a definite ally. To the teacher's left sat the three men and the woman, still snickering about Joe's call for beer, then the two other women on the jury and the rest of the men ranged round the table to Srack's right, ending with a nervous man with whom Srack had exchanged a few remarks during the case. Srack knew from these conversations that this man wanted to vote not guilty.

They had to choose a foreman. Someone asked if anyone had ever served on a jury before. Srack confessed that he had and added that he had been a foreman twice and did not want to do it again. He turned to the teacher on his left.

'Why don't you be foreman?' he asked. 'I'll sit right here next to you and advise you if I can and we'll see if we can't get through this.'

The teacher agreed and Srack suggested that they should hold a secret ballot to test opinion. Each juror took a piece of paper, marked it, folded it and passed it round to the teacher, who counted them out into three piles. Four had voted guilty – Srack guessed he knew who they were – but only two had voted not guilty. Srack reckoned that must be the nervous man on his right and himself. The other six said they were undecided. It was not far from what he had imagined.

He suggested that they go round the table giving each person a chance to explain their vote. The teacher gestured to his left, inviting Joe and his friends to speak first. Srack instantly regretted it. All three men spoke bluntly and forcefully in favour of finding Brandley guilty. They all pointed to the other janitors as good witnesses – good enough for them – and they agreed that Brandley had no explanation for where he was when the girl went missing. He was guilty, they had no doubt. The three men had set the tone. Anyone who wanted to say Brandley was innocent was now going to be coming uphill against the mood of the room.

To his surprise, the rough-looking woman who had hung around with three men said she was undecided. The rest of the jurors started echoing her, mumbling their indecision, until it came to the turn of the nervous man on Srack's right.

'What about you, sir?' asked the teacher.

'I think he's guilty,' came the answer.

Srack was dumbfounded. This man had told him he thought Brandley was innocent. Srack was sure he had just voted not guilty in the secret ballot. He just did not dare to say so.

If only they had gone the other way round the table. Then he would have spoken first and explained how they had to vote not guilty. Then the nervous juror might have spoken up for himself and the mood would have been quite different. It was Srack's turn to speak now.

'I am voting not guilty,' he said in a firm voice. The room was still. 'And I want to tell you right now that I will not change this vote. I want you to understand that it doesn't matter what happens in this jury room, because I believe this is right and I must not change my mind.'

There was silence all round the table. Then the teacher on Srack's left spoke.

'I am voting guilty,' he said.

Srack hung his head. He had pushed the wrong man for foreman and let the whole mood go wrong. Now he was isolated, the sole vote for not guilty against five who wanted to convict and six who were undecided.

But now they were all talking, some in pairs, some to the room in general. Someone was rifling through the stack of evidence, pulling out pictures of the dead girl. Someone was saying they were not sure and someone else was saying they had to be sure. 'Just look at these pictures . . . You heard them janitors . . . Poor little dead girl . . . negroid hair . . . Look at these pictures.'

Only ten minutes later – and only 20 minutes since they had come into the room – the teacher suggested that they should take another vote. A show of hands, he said. Who wanted to vote not guilty? Srack alone raised his arm in silence. And who wanted to vote guilty? A ripple spread around the table: all of them had raised their hands.

Srack thought of Lajewel at home, and the bible story group and the prayers, and he remembered his oath to find a true verdict according to the evidence. And so he tried to explain about the janitors, and the story that was just too pat; and how it made no difference anyway because even if they were telling the truth, it didn't prove Brandley was guilty. It just proved he could have been guilty.

They all kept interrupting him. Voices were getting louder. The heat was rising. Srack talked on. About evidence that had been lost and evidence that had been bungled. About hairs that did not prove a thing, except that Clarence Brandley was one of several million people who might have left a hair on the dead girl's sock. And still their voices got louder, shouting sometimes, swearing sometimes. 'Can't you see? . . . It's so damned obvious he done it . . . What's wrong with you for Chrisesake?'

And he talked on. About reasonable doubt and circumstantial evidence and about a man's life being at stake here. They shouted, especially the three men at the end of the table; they shouted and slumped back in their chairs and slapped the table in their anger. 'Dammit, who do you think done it? . . . All them janitors agree . . . You only thinking about Brandley. What about that poor little girl?'

Then he heard them. Not shouting. Just leaning back and muttering at each other: 'Nigger lover. He's nothin' but a nigger lover. Peterhead. What kind of peterhead is he? He's a nigger lover.'

Srack fell silent, a deep despair sinking over him.

The teacher spoke up, suggesting that they write a note to the Judge to explain that, since noon, 11 of them had been agreed on a guilty verdict but that one juror was holding out and would not change his mind. Maybe the judge would declare them a hung jury. But the note came back from the judge's office. 'Continue deliberating,' he had written.

Now everybody was angry. How long were they going to be stuck in here? A woman said she wanted to do her Christmas shopping. A man said he had left his dog locked in the house and he was worried about it. Someone else had a Christmas party to go to.

Srack said: 'Listen. You all can't be worried about parties and dogs. Our commitment is here. There's a man here in life and death circumstances. I'm not going to change my mind just to get out of here.'

The shouting started again. 'What are you? Some kind of professional juror? . . . Brandley done it. He's guilty . . . How long

we got to stay in here? . . . What about that poor little girl? . . .
Change your damned vote and get us out of here . . . Nigger
lover . . . Nothin' but a nigger lover.'

Srack gave up talking. He was never going to persuade these
people. He did not even believe Brandley was innocent himself.
He just did not think he had the right to convict a man on such
weak evidence. And that was the beginning and the end of it: it
was a matter of plain and simple logic. His duty was to vote not
guilty and no amount of name-calling was going to change his
mind.

The jurors stopped while the teacher wrote the judge another
note. The same reply came back.

Outside, in the courtroom, the defence attorneys were on the edge
of a precipice. The tension had been getting steadily worse since
the jury retired.

First, Jerry Winfree complained that he had been threatened by
a member of the Brandley family. It turned out that Brandley's
brother, Tim, who considered the whole prosecution was dishonest and twisted, had seen Winfree in the corridor and told
him: 'You need more churching.'

Since Winfree liked to think of himself as a Christian – defence
attorneys used to say he belonged to 'the radical Shi'ite wing of
the Protestant Church' – he had taken offence and complained to
the judge. Morris and Brown had little sympathy for him. In their
eyes he was the kind of white bible-thumper who thought all
black men were naturally criminal.

Then Judge Robertson had done his bit. He had called the
attorneys for both sides into the chambers and told them that, as
far as he was concerned, it did not matter what the jury decided.
He had made up his mind that Clarence Brandley had breached
the terms of his probation by murdering Cheryl Fergeson. The
jury had to come to a decision 'beyond reasonable doubt', but all
the judge had to do to take away Brandley's probation was to
find it was 'more likely than not' that he had killed the girl. Even
if the jury decided that he was not guilty, Brandley was going to
have to serve his three-year sentence for possession of a shotgun.

Morris and Brown were hardly surprised. They had been telling each other all through the trial that the judge was on the side of the opposition. So now he was admitting it. Still, it rankled.

In the corridor outside the court, Don Brown broke the news to Minnie Ola Brandley and her family. Brown started to fume about the judge and his rulings. The judge was not even obeying the law, he said.

'But if it ain't the law, why's he doing it?' asked Minnie Ola.

'Because,' said Brown, his voice quaking in anger, 'the Judge is a mean and spiteful person.'

Brown carried on talking and then went back into the court. He never saw the reporter from the *Houston Post* lurking nearby and noting down his every word for the next day's paper.

Amidst all the tension, the defence heard that the jury had sent out notes. They saw Jim Keeshan going into the judge's chambers but they were not allowed in themselves. Ray Reeves cursed loudly that they had no damned right to be discussing notes from the jury without defence counsel being present – especially if what they had heard was true, that the jury was split eleven to one. If that was one juror voting for the defence, they wanted a chance to call off the deliberation before he got so bullied or exhausted that he changed his vote. But Jim Keeshan only smiled and said they were not discussing the case at all.

Across the road in the Iron Horse, the betting was all one way among the reporters gathered there. If it was split eleven to one, it must be in favour of not guilty. Just for once, they reckoned, Jim Keeshan had missed his mark. The truth was he hadn't put on much of a case. Poor old Keeshan. The reporters started drafting stories about the acquittal of Clarence Brandley.

It was late afternoon now. Srack got up from the table in the jury room and went and sat by himself in the little coffee-room off to one side. Behind him, he could hear them talking, complaining about being stuck in there, muttering about him, using that same word.

After a while, Srack went back in and told the teacher that nothing had changed and that since he did not imagine the other 11 were about to change their minds, they should draft a third note, making it as plain and simple as possible. Srack helped him write it. 'Judge, one person on this jury has stated in his mind there was no evidence to suggest the defendant is guilty beyond a reasonable doubt. He will not change his position regardless of our deliberations.' The reply came back the same.

Finally, at 10.30 p.m., after nearly 11 hours in their room, the jurors were told that they could leave – but not to go home. They were to be sequestered for the night, taken off to the Holiday Inn just south of Conroe, sealed off from contact with outsiders and then returned to their room the next day to continue their deliberations. The other jurors were angry.

By the time they got to the Holiday Inn in their court bus, the others jurors had begun to unwind. Joe and his friends were talking about beer again, though nobody was talking to Srack.

The court ushers shepherded them out of the hotel to the Feed Store restaurant – 'Chicken Fried Steak a Speciality'. There, they helped themselves to steak and french fries and ice-cream and plenty to drink and all sat down together and jabbered and talked, all that is, except Bill Srack who could not bring himself to try and cross the great gulf that had opened between himself and these 11 other people.

He took a baked potato and shuffled off to the other side of the restaurant, where he sat in solitude and longed for another day.

Judge Sam Robertson jr. had no reason to be happy. In the *Houston Post*, one of the defence attorneys was calling him 'mean and spiteful' and, in the case of the state of Texas versus Clarence Lee Brandley, the jury had run into the sands.

On Saturday morning, the judge received a fourth note from the jury, pleading to be released. Finally, he agreed that there was no alternative: this lone juror was not going to change his mind and this trial had failed to come to a verdict.

In the jury room, it had been a desultory morning. They had been locked in there since 7.50 a.m. No one was even pretending to be discussing the case. No one was even angry any more. Srack had kept a discreet distance, sitting in the little coffee-room, looking out of the window and waiting for this to be over. The others had sat round their table, talking about one thing and another, often not talking at all.

Occasionally, someone – usually the teacher – would try and get them back to the case. But it was never too long before someone – usually one of the three men at the end of the table – said this was a waste of time because they had been through this before and that sunnuvabitch in there was never going to agree to anything.

Midway through this idle morning, one of the male jurors entered the little coffee-room and pulled a chair up next to Srack. For a moment he said nothing, just stroked his forehead with one hand. Then in a quiet voice, which shook a little, he said: 'I'm thinking I might change my vote, I might vote not guilty.'

Srack looked into his face and saw tears in his eyes.

'Don't do that,' he said. 'It won't make no difference. They're never going to change their minds. It's OK for me. I work down in Houston, but you got to go back into this town and earn a living. If word gets round that you held out on this jury, you'll be finished. So don't do that.'

The juror shook his head and sighed and shuffled back to the jury room.

And that was the truth, thought Srack. A few of these jurors might be nothing more than rednecks and might have that redneck way of thinking about a man like Brandley. But that wasn't the whole story about this jury.

These were small-town people, decent enough folk who did not want to be racists or rednecks, who only wanted to get on with their lives without trouble, and they had to go back and live in this small-town community and tell their decent ordinary neighbours how they voted. How could they go back there and tell them they let this black man go free among them all again? Who was ever going to forgive them if they did that? If they let this horrible crime go unpunished?

It was not the same for him. He was not a Conroe man. If he was really part of this small town, maybe he would feel the same way. But he was not. So he could understand why they must just want to look away. He could even forgive them for it. In a way they were only bystanders. But he did not have to join them.

Finally, around eleven o'clock, the defence attorneys were told that the jury were being brought back so that the judge could declare a mistrial. It was a victory of sorts but it was not what they had wanted.

When they learned that eleven jurors had been voting guilty they felt the hollowness of it all. Don Brown, in particular, felt frustrated that the jury had been even tempted to convict on this evidence. Yet it was better than defeat.

Judge Robertson swept into court, eyed the jury, fired a few questions at the foreman to confirm that they were completely deadlocked, and discharged them.

Then without pausing, he turned to Clarence Brandley. 'Stand up, Mr Brandley. I find you have violated the terms of your probation by committing the offence of capital murder on 23 August 1980. Your probation is hereby revoked. Do you have anything to say why sentencing should not be pronounced against you?'

Brandley looked towards his attorneys. The three of them were shaking their heads and muttering 'sunnuvabitch' to each other. That judge had let Clarence Brandley stay an innocent man for approximately ten seconds. Don Brown looked towards Brandley and lifted his eyebrows in a gesture of helplessness. 'A mean and spiteful person,' he thought.

Once again, Brandley had the feeling he was watching some strange ritual which was only remotely connected with him. He looked back at the judge. 'No, your Honour,' he said.

The judge was saying something. 'You having nothing said for thereof, it's the order of this court that you, Clarence Lee Brandley, who's been convicted of the offence of possession of a short-barrel firearm and whose punishment has been assessed to be confined to the Texas Department of Corrections for a period of three years, you are to be delivered by the Sheriff of Montgomery County, Texas to the Director of the Texas Department of Corrections who will confine you in the Texas Department of Corrections for not less than two years nor more than three years in accordance with the laws governing the operation of the Texas Department of Corrections and you're now remanded to obey the direction of this sentence.'

Brandley guessed that he was being gaoled.

Don Brown stumbled to his feet again and asked for bail while they lodged an appeal and waited for a retrial of the murder charge.

The judge eyed Clarence again. 'Believing that you are likely to commit another offence while you are on bond, if you were allowed one pending appeal – hereby denied.'

Then, in case anyone had missed the point he was trying to make, he added: 'I am entering the following order denying bail pending retrial of the capital murder case, in that I find proof is evident in that a dispassionate jury would not only find you guilty of murder but would assess his punishment at death.'

He paused. Don Brown had never heard a more brazen declaration of prejudice.

'The court is adjourned.'

The judge brought his gavel down once, hard, with a noise like a trap door dropping.

Srack was dazed. He barely understood what the judge had said. The judge's verbal dart about what a dispassionate jury would have done had flown over his head. All he wanted to do was to get home and see Lajewel and talk to civilized people.

He walked from the jury box and started pushing his way through the milling crowd outside the court. As he left, he heard one of the redneck men being interviewed by reporters.

'I think I can pretty well sum things up,' he crowed. 'There has been an injustice done.'

Obediently, the reporters wrote it down. 'Who was it who held out?' they asked. 'Which juror?'

'There he goes,' Srack heard a voice reply. 'There's the little sunnuvabitch.'

The stricken town took the news badly.

At the high school, they said they did not care what the jury had said, they did not want that black janitor back. Brandley would never be hired for any job where he would be anywhere near their schoolchildren, they said. 'We would go to court to keep from rehiring him if possible.'

The *Courier* printed every word.

The jurors tried to explain that they had done their best. The evidence of the other janitors was most incriminating, they said.

All of Conroe read about it in the newspapers.

Jim Keeshan tried to reassure the town: he would bring this man to trial again. He would do more work, find more clues. He had some ideas he was working on.

5

Justice was not a total stranger to the Montgomery County court-house. Morris and Brown recognized that the judges and prosecutors who had worked there over the years did not think of themselves as being racist or corrupt. For the most part they took a real pride in their profession and, day by day, they were happy to administer justice with the appearance of reason and fairness. But under pressure – particularly from their voters – many of those who had been proud to uphold the law would glibly brush it aside. In those moments it was like watching a spoiled child who cannot bear to lose a game, who suddenly complains that all the rules are unfair and that he is the winner, no matter what anyone else says and, just like an angry child, the courthouse would then defend itself with such open-hearted dishonesty that those who watched could only shake their heads and wonder.

The history of the courthouse was riddled with allegations of bribes, vote-buying, ballot-stealing, illegal campaign contributions and political favouritism. Most of the allegations were never resolved. There was a notorious incident in the 1920s when Conroe's richest citizens complained bitterly about the new, higher taxes they were being asked to pay, only to find themselves saved when all the papers detailing their dues simply vanished from the courthouse. Officials explained that they had been blown away by a gust of wind which had left behind only the papers of less wealthy townspeople.

As Morris and Brown prepared to return to the courthouse to save Clarence Brandley's life, they could not help but be worried. This struggle was becoming an eerie repeat of a notorious case in Conroe's past when pressure on the courthouse to nail a bad nigger had seen the law torn up and thrown away. It concerned

160

another black man who, years earlier in the summer of 1941, found himself sitting alone in the same courthouse in the middle of Conroe while angry white people debated his fate. His name was Bob White and he, too, was accused of assaulting a white woman. There were those in Conroe who remembered his fate which was recorded in all its bloody detail in bundles of official papers, and now they worried about seeing a repeat.

Bob White's family lived and worked in the cotton fields near Livingston, 50 miles north-east of Conroe. The land which they worked belonged to a wealthy white man named Dude Cochran who lived with his wife, Ruby, and their two boys in a big house across the fields from their shacks. Bob White's life began to unravel one hot and humid night in August 1937.

Dude Cochran was away in Houston. Ruby was in bed upstairs in the big house while the boys, Joe and Laddie, slept out on the porch where the sticky air was just a little cooler. Ruby had been asleep for an hour or so when she was suddenly snapped awake. She lay still as death. She could have sworn she heard something. Something quite close. She slid her hand up on to the bedside table and slipped her fingers round the pistol lying there.

'Joe, is that you?' she said and the words were hardly out of her mouth when she was fighting for her life, the hard, heavy weight of some foul-smelling man on top of her, grabbing her hands, knocking the pistol to the floor, swearing 'God damn you, God damn you' in her face, and then slicing her fingers with his blade and telling her he'd cut her throat if she didn't stop struggling. She was afraid to fight, afraid that if he killed her, he might go down and kill her boys too. So she threatened him with something that should have put fear in his heart.

'Don't you know what them Cochrans will do to you?' she said, but the gruff voice told her he didn't give a God damn what they did to him.

Later, after the intruder had finished with her and slipped back into the night, Ruby Cochran staggered to her nearest white neighbour to raise the alarm. They called her brother-in-law, Ernest, and the sheriff, and, when they arrived, she sobbed out her story to them. Who was it, they asked, who had done this thing to her? She did not know; all she could tell them for sure it was a nigger.

By the time day broke the next morning, a terrible turbulence had swept across the cotton fields. White families heard of the outrage and cursed the nigger who had done this thing; black families felt a cloud of anxiety sweep over their homes. At the big house, Sheriff Roscoe Holliday had found some bare footprints running away down the dirt road and put a bucket over them to preserve them. He called in the bloodhounds from Huntsville jail, and their yelping and howling blew across the plantation like an ill wind. There was a fingerprint man scattering white powder over the scene. There were the Texas Rangers, big white men with leather boots and pearl-handled pistols at their hips, striding round the house and looking out across the cotton fields at the black men.

At the heart of the storm were Dude Cochran and his two brothers, Ernest and Carey, three angry men who knew one thing – the nigger who did this was going to pay. They set out in their cars to round up as many blacks as they could find in the shacks and fields, and within a couple of hours they had 16 of them herded into the yard at Ernest Cochran's house. The law might have said the three Cochran brothers had no right nor authority to arrest 16 black men without a warrant, but no one raised a word against them.

Bob White had left his girlfriend in Houston a few weeks earlier to come up and pick cotton and to stay with his mother, Martha, in her shinny shack a couple of miles down the dirt road from where Dude and Ruby Cochran lived. He knew the Cochrans. He had lived on their land for most of his 27 years.

Bob White was in the fields picking cotton at about nine o'clock that morning when Ernest Cochran drove up alongside the sagging wire fence and told him to climb on the car's fender and come with him; so he did as he was told and rode back to Ernest Cochran's house, to the yard full of black men.

Bob White's family heard no more than rumours for the rest of that week. All the men had been taken to the county jail in Livingston. The Texas Rangers were questioning them. There were stories – fearful things that people said were going on in the jail house – but no one really knew. It was nine days before the news came through: Ruby Cochran had listened to the voices of all the men in the county jail and she had picked out Bob White, and now he had confessed; he was guilty and he was going to be tried and put to death just as soon as it could be done.

The trial was a sensational event when it opened before Judge W. B. Browder in Livingston a few weeks later. The courtroom was crowded. The three Cochran men were there, stern and subdued. White friends came from all over the county to see justice done and to stare at the black animal who sat alone in chains at the front of the court. It took less than two days for the business to be done and for the Livingston jury of 12 white men to declare that Bob White was guilty and should be sentenced to death.

The county was ready for him to be hanged as soon as possible, but Bob White's attorney, J. P. Rogers, who came from Houston, lodged an appeal. Rogers said that the trial had been unfair from start to finish because of the prejudice in the courtroom; he said the trial should never have been held in Livingston, where feelings against the black man were running so high. A deep fury spilled over white families in the town when, seven months later, on 16 April 1938, the Texas Court of Criminal Appeals in Austin overturned the verdict and ordered a new trial in a different venue. J. P. Rogers went back to court in Livingston and Judge Browder agreed to move the case, and so Bob White was sent to face his accusers a second time, in Conroe.

There, on 2 August 1938, a special persecutor, 'Zimmie' Foreman, hired by Dude Cochran, paraded his witnesses again. There was Sol Bergman, the town doctor who had examined the hysterical victim. 'The sperm was plenty active,' he said. 'I could tell that it was from some male person.' He said he had not kept any sample of it.

There was Sheriff Roscoe Holliday who assured the court that Bob White had made his confession freely and without duress. 'The nigger was never mistreated in any way,' he said.

There were the Cochran brothers grimly recalling the events of that night, and Ruby Cochran tearfully describing her ordeal.

Then the defence mounted its case and soon ran into trouble: many of their black witnesses refused to testify, or claimed they could remember nothing; J. P. Rogers asked them in open court if he had not seen them being spoken to in the hallway by Texas Rangers, but the witnesses said they did not remember that.

Finally, Bob White took the stand and told his story. On the first day, after Ernest Cochran had rounded him up, he was taken to Livingston jail and there, he said, sometime after nightfall, some Rangers came and led him from his cell and put him in their vehicle and drove him up into the woods somewhere and handcuffed him to a tree with his face against the bark; and then they whipped his back with something that he thought was a rubber hose, something that gouged deep stripes in his flesh. They whipped him until his shirt was torn into shreds by the blows, he said, so that when they finally took him back to the jail house, the sheriff's son had had to give him one of his own shirts to cover him.

Bob White said the Rangers had done the same thing for the next three or four nights: once they made him drop his pants before they tied him to the tree and whipped him; each time they beat him they told him that sooner or later he was going to confess, and before they dumped him back in his cell they always told him not to tell anyone about what they were doing to him. Then, around midnight on the eighth day, the sheriff drove him all alone down to the jail house in Beaumont. The Rangers who had been beating him were there, with the special prosecutor, Zimmie Foreman, and a man who was then the county attorney, Ernest Coker.

All night long, Bob White said, they kept him there crying on the floor, and every so often the Rangers gave him a kicking and, at the end of it, Ernest Coker had typed out a complete confession. Bob White said he didn't really know what was in it. He could not read nor write. He did not even know whether he had made a cross on it for a signature. He said he didn't know what was happening, although he was sure he had never had an attorney there and no one had told him anything about having any rights. He lifted his shirt to show the court his scars.

Ernest Coker attended the trial in Conroe and said he had seen no sign of injury on Bob White. He said he had certainly told Bob White his rights and he was sure that every word in the confession had come freely and voluntarily from the Negro's own mouth, and all he had done was to type it out 'exactly as he related it to me'. Bob White said there were words in that confession he had never heard of and that it was just plain wrong. Even the size of his shoes that was mentioned in there was wrong. Zimmie Foreman took the stand himself and swore that 'nobody did any-thing to him except treat him just as nice as they could'.

Then J. P. Rogers ordered the Rangers and other law officers to stand up at the back of the court, and Bob White pointed to two of the Rangers, named Williamson and Davenport, and to a Polk County deputy called Coleman Weeks. They were the ones who had beaten him in the woods, he said.

The sheriff said it was all lies. No one had taken the nigger out of his jail. Ranger Davenport said he didn't think it had happened, but it was hard to say. Then Ranger Williamson came to the stand and admitted they had taken him out so many times that he had lost count, but it had nothing to do with whipping him.

'We took him out of jail to talk to him,' he said. 'The jail was crowded. There was lots of them in there and we took them out where we would be by ourselves, to talk to him.' Coleman Weeks agreed with that.

But Zimmie Foreman was not tolerating any of this. When J. P. Rogers asked Bob White if he had recently been injured and Bob White replied 'Yessir', Zimmie Foreman jumped to his feet and said it was prejudicial, so Judge Browder agreed to strike it from the record. When Bob White was first asked to identify the men who whipped him, Zimmie Foreman interrupted. 'It could have been John D. Rockerfeller,' he joked. When he made his final speech, Zimmie Foreman looked straight at the jury and told them that Bob White's attorneys didn't care what had happened to Mrs Cochran. 'As far as they are concerned, their innocent Negro should be turned loose,' he said.

After three days of evidence, the Conroe jury of 12 white men declared that Bob White was guilty and sentenced him to death again.

J. P. Rogers launched a volley of appeals. He said Bob White was the victim of race discrimination, and that black people had been excluded from the Grand Jury and from both trial juries that had dealt with the case. 'It has been, was and still is the custom in Montgomery County, Texas to use white men exclusively for jurors to serve in any and all cases,' he said in his legal submission. The DA and his officials in Conroe said it was just chance that all the jurors had been white. The judge said that anyway it was too late in the proceedings to be raising such issues.

Rogers said the confession was involuntary because Bob White had been repeatedly chained to a tree and beaten before giving it and because it had been taken by Zimmie Foreman and Ernest Coker – 'both men who were highly prejudiced against the defendant and seeking his conviction'. The judge in Conroe said they had been into all this at the trial. Rogers went to the Court of Criminal Appeals in Austin, but in March 1939 they turned him down and said there was no evidence of race discrimination and no reason to be disturbed by the court's use of Bob White's confession. So Rogers went all the way to Washington DC, to the Supreme Court of the United States.

On 25 March 1940, the Supreme Court reached out to save Bob White. After reviewing all the details of Bob White's eight days in jail and of his confession to Zimmie Foreman and Ernest Coker, the court concluded: 'Due process of law, preserved for all by our Constitution, commands that no such practice as that disclosed by this record shall send any accused to his death'.

The Supreme Court ordered a new trial. Back in Livingston, the Cochrans were furious. Dude Cochran paid out of his own pocket to send Zimmie Foreman and the Montgomery County DA, W. C. 'Cleo' McClain, up to Washington to demand a rehearing, but the Supreme Court stood by its decision. In Conroe, Bob White prepared to face his third trial.

The Conroe courtroom was packed with spectators as the notorious case began again on 11 June 1941 with the exhausting process of selecting a jury. Bob White sat in chains at the front of the court with his attorneys. Behind him on the public benches sat the three Cochran brothers side by side. All morning, the attorneys questioned jurymen, and by 12.20 p.m. they had exhausted their supply and had chosen only nine jurors. The court bailiff was just leading the last chosen juror out of the room; the attorneys were just stretching their legs at the front of the court; Judge Browder was shuffling his papers and chewing his wad of tobacco; Bob White was slumped silently in his chair as usual, when Dude Cochran rose quietly to his feet and started to walk forwards.

No one even noticed the stoney-faced white farmer as he pressed through the little wooden gate in front of the public benches and stepped up to the defence table, up behind Bob White, up behind his black head and still no one noticed as he drew a .38 calibre pistol from his pocket and shot Bob White dead. The bullet crashed into Bob White's brain from just behind his right ear. He slumped over sideways, spilling blood on the courtroom floor and he was dead before his body fell out of the chair.

'Don't you know what them Cochrans will do to you?'

For a moment, the courtroom was frozen with fear and shock. Then Dude Cochran handed over his pistol to Zimmie Foreman and stood still and cold while spectators surged forward from the benches, leaning over the railing to slap him on the back, reaching out to shake his hand, calling out their congratulations. Black spectators who had been sitting at the back of the courtroom vanished quickly. Sheriff Grover Mostyn came running to the court and took Dude Cochran into custody. Outside there was jubilation. 'General satisfaction over the killing of Bob White was apparent in the business district of Conroe which is practically all within one block of the courthouse,' the *Courier* recorded.

The jubilation was renewed a few hours later when the white farmer was released from custody on a nominal bond of $500.

A week later, Dude Cochran was back in the Conroe courthouse, but this time he was the defendant, charged with the murder of Bob White. The trial took less than two hours. Montgomery County DA, W.C. 'Cleo' McClain, led the prosecution by taking the unusual step of urging the jury to find the defendant not guilty. McClain told them that he fully understood Dude Cochran's actions. 'It is unfortunate that Mr Cochran was forced to do that which was done,' he told them. 'It was his wish that the law handle the matter. In my opinion the guilty party got justice, but it was unfortunate that it had to be at Mr Cochran's hands.'

The District Attorney, aided by Zimmie Foreman, read the jury a history of the case which included the full text of Bob White's confession and omitted any reference to Bob White's account of the beatings he had received. McClain took the jury of 12 white men to the heart of the matter: 'The time has not come in this state when any man, black or white, can assault a white woman and go free by reason of legal technicalities.'

The District Attorney left no doubt as to the course of action he was recommending to the jury: 'If I were going into that jury room, I wouldn't hesitate, I wouldn't stand back a minute in writing a verdict of not guilty. When you have done that, I say justice will have been done in this case. I ask you to return a verdict finding Mr Cochran not guilty.'

Dude Cochran's attorneys thanked the District Attorney for his kind remarks and the jury retired. It took them less than a minute to make up their minds, and they returned to declare Dude Cochran innocent. The *Houston Post* reported the next day: 'The jury's report set off an impromptu celebration in the crowded courtroom, filled largely with friends and neighbours of the Cochran family. Applause had begun when District Attorney McClain finished his argument. Cochran, a slight sun-browned man wearing a tan business suit and high-heeled cowboy boots, was unable to leave the courtroom for nearly 15 minutes after his acquittal. Spectators formed in lines to pass behind the rail and shake hands with him, some still cheering and whistling.'

The rejoicing spilled out into the street, and Dude Cochran emerged into the courthouse square to be greeted as a hero. Bob White's body was taken to a funeral home, where it lay unclaimed by his fearful family.

It was Christmas in Conroe. In the drug-store on the courthouse square, they stuck sprigs of plastic holly in the window and played Christmas carols on the hi-fi system. On the outskirts of town there were Santas in the shopping malls and business was brisk. Clarence Brandley sat in his cell in the county jail. It would be more than a month before they put him on trial again, he had been told, and now that he had finally lost his probation there was no chance of joining his family for Christmas.

In the office over the menswear shop, Morris and Brown talked tactics and returned always to the same point. It did not matter how good their evidence was, or how weak the prosecution was, or how hard they tried to overcome the bias of the jury, they were never going to get a fair shot in this trial while Judge Sam Robertson jr. was presiding. Robertson had to go.

Even in the quiet days since the trial, he had been giving them a hard time. Morris and Brown had noticed a technical foul-up that had been made in the rush to revoke Brandley's probation at the end of the trial. Keeshan had failed to prove that the Clarence Lee Brandley in the courtroom was the same Clarence Lee Brandley who had been given a probated sentence for possessing a prohibited weapon. It was only a technical point, but Morris and Brown had filed an appeal on it. And they felt the appeals court might run with it.

But then Keeshan had realized his mistake and had gone to the judge to ask if he could have a new hearing so that he could straighten out the record. Morris and Brown said that was not allowed, because the state had rested its case and sentence had been passed and they had already filed their appeal. But Judge Robertson had let him do it.

Then at the hearing, George Morris had complained bitterly that the State could not go re-opening its case and presenting new evidence after sentence had been passed. It was just not proper. And the judge had said the strangest thing: 'I doubt seriously, legally, that I have the authority to permit them to re-open, but law is never made unless there is a ruling made contrary to some-one, and I will permit them to put the evidence on.'

So, without even pretending that he had the law on his side, Judge Robertson had given Keeshan his way, and the technical point of their appeal had been destroyed.

At the same hearing, Robertson had also announced that he would be presiding over the retrial and ordered that it should begin on 19 January. Don Brown said he was more damned sure than ever that Robertson had to go. And he had noticed something that might just help.

By sheer good luck – possibly the first piece of good luck Brown could think of in this case – the state of Texas, in its wisdom, had decided that on 1 January 1981, it would overhaul certain administrative rules affecting the running of its courts – including the right to recuse judges. Brown studied the new rules and found that they made it easier to move a prejudiced judge off a case. Last time Robertson had beaten them off, but now he might not find it so simple. Brown cornered Morris in his office looking over the courthouse square. 'George,' he said. 'Let's take another shot at recusing Robertson.'

'Don, I don't mind if we do.'

As Christmas Day approached, Morris and Brown began to wonder whether their luck might not be changing permanently. Their relationship with Ray Reeves had broken down completely. They had told him what they thought of him and he had given them several paragraphs of technicolour abuse in reply. Then Morris and Brown had gone to the Brandley family and told them that they would agree to handle the retrial if they were paid a fee and, if it was all the same to them, that they did not intend to share any fee with Ray Reeves. The family agreed, and Ray Reeves was out of the case. Then, as if that were not enough of a Christmas bonus, Sheriff Gene Reaves retired. The *Courier* ran a glowing profile of his 20 years of service. They quoted his view that: 'Some times you kind of think the laws were written for the criminal.' They put his picture on the front page. 'Into the sunset,' the caption said. But goodbye was good riddance as far as Morris and Brown were concerned. But there was still a little more good luck in the wind.

In Christmas week, Morris and Brown held their annual Christmas party. They draped decorations all around their offices, stacked plenty of drink up on the tables, called a temporary truce with everyone in the courthouse and invited all the judges and attorneys and court reporters, and even Jim Keeshan, to come on over.

The party was swinging. Everybody was having a good time, drinking and yelling and smoking too much. Morris and Brown found themselves jammed into a corner with a group of lawyers including John Martin, one of Morris's closest friends, a handsome, clean-cut defence attorney who had just been elected to become a district judge in Conroe. Morris and Brown had worked for John Martin's election. They liked the man and, simply out of friendship, they had wanted him to do well. But they could also see that it would do them no harm to have a friend on the bench in the courthouse. They had put money into his campaign, distributed leaflets, advised him, got sunburn standing outside polling stations, and babysat him through election night to day-break, when the last box of votes had come in and given him the most narrow of victories.

Now, amidst all the backslapping of the Christmas party, John Martin quietened the conversation for a moment and told the group of lawyers in the corner that he had heard an interesting rumour: Sam Robertson might not hear the retrial of the Brandley case. And what was more, said Martin, he had heard that he himself would be in line to get the case. He turned to Morris and Brown.

'I know y'all got a screwing from Robertson. I want y'all to know that if I'm assigned to hear the case, you will receive a fair trial.'

Morris and Brown beamed through the smoke and chorused almost as one: 'John, that's all we ever wanted.'

As soon as the new rules came into effect on 1 January, Morris and Brown polished up their motion to recuse Judge Robertson. They read it over and liked it. The charge of bias and prejudice ran through the motion like the chorus of a Christmas carol. Before the trial, they complained, Judge Robertson had upheld the illegal $75,000 bail-bond and overturned the court's promise that Brandley should be released on $1,000 bail if the state ever repeated its attempt to revoke his probation. Judge Robertson had interfered in the selection of jurors, tried to do the DA's job for him, and then done the same all through the trial, making the DA's objections for him, and capped that by refusing to let the defence put on any of its evidence about Icky Peace. The judge had held private meetings with the DA, refused to let the defence take part, concealed the contents of the jury's notes from the defence and then, when the trial was over, he had allowed the DA to re-open the case to put on new evidence. 'He has a personal bias or prejudice against the defendant in this proceeding,' they concluded. It was strong stuff. They liked it.

Their only problem was that they would have to file the motion at the courthouse where some Conroe judge would wind up ruling on it – just like last time when Judge Lynn Coker had stopped them recusing Robertson before the trial. They mulled it over and decided it was only fair to let Robertson himself decide what to do. That way, they might just be able to persuade him to go gracefully.

On the first Monday of the new year, 5 January, Morris and Brown went into their office, took a phone each and dialled Sam Robertson in Houston.

'We want to know what your intention is about trying the case again,' said Morris.

'Well, I've told you I intend to try that case.'

Then they told him about the new rules of recusal which made it easier for them to get to him, and about their motion, they read him some of the strongest passages, and then they asked him whether he thought they should file their motion.

'I told you I intend to try that case,' said the judge.

'Well, that's just fine,' said Morris. 'We'll go ahead and file this motion.'

It looked as though he was going to fight them again.

Two days later, Don Brown was reading his newspaper.

'Goddam,' he said out loud. 'The sunnuvabitch stood down.'

Judge Sam Robertson had announced that he had too many trials competing for his attention and had decided that he would not be able to try the Brandley case.

The next day, it was announced that the newly elected Judge John Martin would take over.

The ritual began again.

Brandley sat in the same blue suit, his hands clasped in his lap, and looked round the courtroom. The faces danced before his eyes: the jurors, the attorneys, the clerk with the strawberry-coloured fingernails, the jailhouse deputies, the judge, all moving together through the same routine. Some of the faces were different this time, but still they were all the same colour.

He had been sitting there already for ten days. While the rest of the world had been watching the new President, Ronald Reagan, being inaugurated in Washington DC, he had been staring at the bright white walls and listening to the fans slapping the air overhead.

After ten days, there was still not one word of evidence. The attorneys had been scrapping all that time, mostly about who was going to sit on the jury. Brandley could not see how it made that much difference. This time around, there had been four black people called for jury service and they had sat in court while the jury was selected, but all four of them had been rejected for one reason or another at the request of the District Attorney.

Now finally, on Thursday morning, 29 January, they were going to start hearing some evidence. Spectators had crowded on to the benches, mostly white faces, the curious and the concerned. Some of the men stared at him while they chewed their gum. Brandley was glad to see some friendly faces down there, not just his family but people from Houston who had come to show their faith in him. Right in the front row, there were two black men bravely displaying badges that announced their support for the National Association for the Advancement of Colored People.

He was glad, too, that they had got rid of that last judge. He had been even worse than the first one. Now his attorneys had told him for sure that this new Judge Martin was going to be OK. They knew him. They said he would give them a fair shot which was all that they needed. That was what the attorneys said. Then Brandley heard the judge speak up: he ordered the two black men to remove their badges for the National Association for the Advancement of Colored People and banned anyone from wearing any more badges at any time during this trial.

Brandley guessed he must have had some good reason for doing that.

Morris and Brown, hunched over a table full of trial papers, were feeling confident. They had a reasonable looking jury and they had managed to get rid of some jurors who admitted to racism and prejudice, though they had had to fight for every inch of ground, and they had lost all the blacks along the way. And there was John Martin, their friend, whose election they had fought for, sitting up there on the bench. They had high hopes that he would give them a fair shot, although the truth was that he had already done some rather worrying things. In some of the pre-trial hearings he had been short with them, and had ruled against them when he did not need to. Morris and Brown had told themselves that he was just trying to prove that he was not in their pocket, that he was independent. That was fine.

Then, during one of the pre-trial hearings in chambers, he had gone a little further. Don Brown had been arguing some legal point, bulldozing away at Jim Keeshan, and the new judge had suddenly snapped at him in the meanest of voices. 'Brown, shut your damned mouth so Jim Keeshan can talk.'

Brown had been so shocked that he had walked straight out of the room. It was bad enough to hear any judge address an attorney like that, but worse when the judge was supposed to be a friend. Outside, Brown had recovered himself and gone back in and continued the hearing. Then, when it was over and they had lost the argument, he had turned to George Morris as they left the room and asked him: 'What kind of monster have we created?'

They just hoped that he would remember his decency and all the times that he had been screwed by Keeshan when he was a defence attorney.

Keeshan sat calmly across the other side of the court from Morris and Brown, dapper as ever in his sharp suit, chuckling with Jerry Winfree and waiting to call his first witness. The defence attorneys knew he had been working hard since the first trial and probably had a few surprises of his own planned in order to win himself a famous victory and salvage his reputation.

The evidence began. To Brandley, it was like sitting on a train watching familiar scenes flash past the window. Questions. Evidence. Cross-questions. Objections. More evidence. More questions. The volleyball coaches. The shy young schoolgirls. The times that they did things. The things that they saw. The day of the crime. The day his life got lost. By the evening, Brandley had had enough. He was almost happy to see his cell again. The next day, Friday, was a rest day. Brandley stayed in his cell. The attorneys took it easy and worked on their papers.

On Saturday, the phone rang in George Morris's home. Morris heard the creaking east Texas cadence of a man who said he was John Payne from Houston and he wanted to talk to him about this here Brandley case. He wanted to tell him something about his family and about his brother, Ed.

Morris waited for him to get to the point. This Ed lived out in Grangerland, ten miles south-east of Conroe, and he had a daughter. She was called Cynthia, though she was known as Cindy, and she lived right next to old Ed in a trailer with her husband. Cindy's husband was a young feller named Gary Acreman.

Morris started to listen. John Payne explained that he and his wife Mary had been talking to Ed about this here Brandley case and about Ed's son-in-law, Gary Acreman. And Ed had told them something. According to Ed Payne, Gary Acreman had come home on the day of the crime, very nervous and pacing up and down, saying that a girl had been killed up at the high school.

Morris was now rivetted. This was not the story they had been told in court. According to that, Acreman had left school without knowing that a girl was even missing, let alone that she had been killed. He had told the police that the first he knew of the killing was when he read about it in the newspaper the next day. How could Acreman have known about it on Saturday? John Payne had some of the answer.

According to Ed, Acreman had been really worried because he knew where the dead girl's clothes were. He had told Ed that they were in a dumpster behind the school. Ed had not known what to make of that, but when it came out a few days later that the police had just found the girl's clothes right where Gary said they were, Ed got really worried too.

Morris, hardly daring to breathe, nudged John Payne on into the rest of his story. The way his brother Ed had told it, Gary had wanted to go back to the school that Saturday afternoon to find the clothes. He never exactly said why he wanted to do that and he never said how he knew those clothes were in the dumpster. But Ed could think of only two explanations: either his son-in-law had seen the killer dumping the clothes and he was wanting to cover for him, or he was the killer himself. Whatever it was, Ed Payne was frightened.

Morris saw that this was dynamite. If it were true, it would turn the whole case around. If Acreman really knew the truth about this killing and he was covering it up, that was dynamite. Morris took some more details from John Payne, arranged to stay in touch, thanked him and called Don Brown. The two of them spent the rest of the evening talking like kids at Christmas. They could not believe what they had got here. Goddam, if they could just get this into court. They had to get this Ed Payne, get an affidavit out of him, get him to come to court and say all this to the jury. Goddam, it was dynamite. But how would they get to Payne? He seemed to be living more or less on top of Gary Acreman, whose trailer was in his yard. If they went up there, there was no way of knowing whether Acreman would be around or not. If Acreman saw them or if he saw his father-in-law talking to them, that would be an end of it. Acreman would shut the old boy up; he might even kill him. They needed to talk to John Payne again, but it was late now. Morris and Brown arranged to meet the next morning, Sunday, in their office.

There they called John Payne, who got his wife Mary on the extension and they talked it all through again. The story was still the same. The way the Paynes saw it, Ed was crying out for help. He had a bad conscience about sitting on the story and he wanted something to be done. It was just a question of getting to him without alerting Acreman. Morris and Brown thanked them and talked together some more. Finally, they hatched a plan. They would send someone else up to Ed Payne's place as an intermediary, someone they could trust who would not be known to Acreman and who would do this confidentially. They picked Charlie Hayden.

Hayden had just been elected to the office of county constable, responsible for civil cases involving Montgomery County, gathering the evidence, serving the papers and so on. Hayden was only a young man, but Morris had known him for some time, and he liked him and believed he had a good relationship with him. So Morris called him up and asked if they could come over to his office to talk to him about something urgent. Half an hour later, the three men sat down together, Charlie Hayden behind his big brown desk, Morris and Brown on the edge of their chairs in front of him.

This was urgent, they said, and it was confidential. This was such dynamite, they said, that if word of it got out there was no telling what would happen. Did he understand that everything that was being said here had to be absolutely confidential? Charlie Hayden said he understood.

George Morris told him their story and explained their difficulty, and asked if he would help them by going up to Ed Payne's house and bringing the man back down to the office here so that they could all interview him together. Hayden said he understood what they were saying, but it worried him that perhaps he was being asked to conceal evidence from the proper authorities. Morris reassured him. Once they had interviewed Ed Payne, he would no longer be bound by confidence.

'All we're asking is that we get a chance to get this old boy's story first. Then you're free to disclose this to the District Attorney. No question. This is all completely legal. But you know what Jim Keeshan's like. If he gets first shot at him he won't talk. We have to get his story down before Keeshan gets to him.'

They chewed it over a little more and came to an agreement: Hayden would visit Ed Payne; Morris and Brown would stay by the phone in their office; as soon as he had got Payne's co-operation, Hayden would call Morris and Brown and they would all meet in his office for the interview. In the meantime, all of them would hold this in the utmost confidence.

'I got one other thing to do,' said Hayden. 'Y'all wait by your phone. I should be talking to you about noon.'

'We'll be there,' said Morris.

Don Brown was smoking far more than he ought to have been. Morris was as bad. It was the excitement. They sat in their office overlooking the courthouse square, talking about the case and swapping cigarettes and trying to get on with some work. Every so often they checked their watches.

Noon came and went. It was one o'clock and then it was coming up to two, and still there was no call. But Hayden had said he had something else to do first. They called his office and were told Mr Hayden was out, interviewing a witness. They smoked some more, called his office some more and then the afternoon was getting old and the light outside was dimming, and they began to wonder what was happening out there. How could it take

Charlie Hayden this long just to drive out to Grangerland? They called Hayden's home. No answer. They called his office. No damned answer there either. It was dark now. They began to feel truly anxious. Could Hayden have screwed them? Goddam, what was going on?

It was well into the evening and Morris and Brown were knotted with worry before George Morris finally got Hayden on the phone at his home.

'Where have you been? What the hell's going on?'

'The man is not going to co-operate with you.'

Pause.

'What do you mean? Why isn't he going to co-operate? What the hell happened?'

'All I can tell y'all is that he is not going to co-operate.'

'Did you talk to him?'

'All I can tell y'all is that he . . .'

'What he tell you? Why didn't you call us?'

Hayden would only tell them that Ed Payne was not going to co-operate.

A total blank. It had all gone wrong. They could only guess at what had happened, but somewhere out there they had been screwed. And what had they lost? Maybe more than just the chance to get some justice into that courtroom. Maybe they had just lost the chance to catch the bastard who killed that poor girl.

Soon afterwards, the two attorneys stumbled off into the darkness, split up and went home to worry alone. All they could do now was to subpoena Ed Payne, just like any other witness. But as soon as they filed the papers for the subpoena on Monday morning, everyone in the courthouse, including Jim Keeshan, would know what they were doing. And they would be subpoenaing a witness with no idea what he was going to say.

Janet Dial was new to the courthouse. She had only taken this job out of friendship for John Martin. He had handled her divorce when he was an attorney, and she had liked him. She had liked his politics, too. He seemed to be the perfect liberal defence attorney and, to someone like her, who lived and breathed Democratic politics and feminism, John Martin had seemed a really good guy. So when he became a judge and asked her to come and be his secretary and kind of advise him on politics, too, she jumped at the chance. She thought it would be so interesting to be inside the courthouse, where all the political power in this county was concentrated.

It was not working out quite the way she had expected. Now that he was a judge, John Martin seemed different. He was so concerned about acting as a judge should. He kept calling her into his office in the morning, asking here whether his robe looked alright. And he was not the great liberal any more. He was getting to be unapproachable, and they had a bad argument because he started to assume that Janet was going to run round fetching coffee for him. An old defence attorney she knew said that Martin was getting too close to the District Attorney.

She was new to the courthouse, so she was not sure how things were supposed to be, but it seemed to her that John Martin had been caught up by the whole atmosphere of this place – and of the Brandley trial.

Janet Dial thought they were all supposed to be impartial, but the truth was that it felt like they were working on some kind of project to convict Clarence Brandley. She had asked one of the court clerks if she really thought Brandley was guilty, and it was as if she had said something really scandalous. It was all anyone talked about in the courthouse – the Brandley case and how they were doing. That meant how the prosecution was doing. No one was interested in the defence. If you were going to work in the courthouse, you had to believe that Brandley was guilty.

The atmosphere was so powerful – and John Martin seemed to have been taken over by it. The way it had changed him reminded Janet Dial of one of those religious cults which preys on vulnerable people.

On monday morning, the trial continued. Sam Martinez served up the now familiar story. It seemed so harmless the way he told it – how Brandley had come down the hallway right behind that girl, how he had disappeared for 45 minutes, how he had been in a hurry to send them all home. It seemed harmless, but it was lethal. Brandley watched Martinez and wondered what could be in his mind. Martinez would not return his gaze.

George Morris tried hard to make him admit that the Texas Ranger had been coaching him in his evidence, but Martinez shrugged him off. Morris did dig one point out of him when he described how they had got bored waiting outside the vocational building for Clarence. Martinez said he and Acreman had gone off to the gas station on Route 105 to buy some cigarettes. Martinez had bought himself a cold drink. Then a few minutes later, back outside the vocational building, Acreman had gone off alone into the main building. Acreman said he was going to get himself a cold drink from a machine in the teachers' lounge. But Morris wanted to know why, if Acreman was really looking for a drink, he had not bought one two minutes earlier in the gas station when Martinez had. Martinez did not know. Morris left the little cloud of doubt hanging over Acreman's name.

Doubt was all that Morris and Brown had where Gary Acreman was concerned. Could he be the killer? Or was it just that he knew who the killer was? Or was it all baloney? All day, sitting in court, they were rubbing their chins and chewing their thumbs, wrestling with the problem of how to salvage Ed Payne's story. First thing that morning, they had filed subpoenas to call Ed Payne and his daughter Cindy as witnesses. But they could not just call them to stand and tell them to recite what Gary had told them. For one thing, they had no idea what they would say: they might stand up there and say, 'Gary always said the nigger done it' and then the defence would be screwed.

More than that, the law just plain did not allow a witness to come out of the blue and start repeating hearsay like that. They would have to go through a legal manoeuvre: they had to wait for Gary Acreman to give evidence first and ask him if it was true that he had come home on the day of the crime and said all these things. If he said yes, then they were home and dry and Jim Keeshan was wrecked on the rocks.

But if Acreman denied saying all these things, then the law would allow them to call his father-in-law, Ed Payne, and his wife, Cindy, to impeach him, to show that he had been lying. But that was very risky because, thanks to the efforts of Charlie

Hayden, they still did not know what Ed or Cindy might say. And Morris and Brown knew that if they raised all this with Gary Acreman in front of the jury and then failed to follow it through, or, even worse, called witnesses who agreed with Acreman, Jim Keeshan would wipe the floor with them and Acreman would come out looking like an honest man while the defence looked like no-good rumour-rakers. It was a tough one.

It came down to a race with time: Morris and Brown had to talk to old Ed and Cindy and find out what they were going to say before Gary Acreman gave his evidence. If Ed and Cindy were prepared to help, they could throw it all at Acreman in the witness-box. If not, it was all lost. It looked like they had most of the rest of the day to play with: there were two policemen waiting to give evidence before Acreman was due and some legal argument, too.

Don Brown posted look-outs on the courthouse steps to watch for Ed Payne to show up in answer to the subpoena. By the midday break there was still no sign. And Jim Keeshan was starting to do something that hooked Morris and Brown right out of their nervous distraction.

Judge Martin had sent the jury out of the room. Keeshan had called Icky Peace to the stand and in his mild-mannered and charming way had started to ask him a string of questions which rapidly brought Don Brown to boiling-point.

'During your testimony in the last trial, outside the presence of the jury, Mr Morris got to ask you some questions about a pistol. As I remember, you had a .25 automatic pistol in your car on 23 August. Is that true?'

'Yes, sir,' piped the familiar childlike voice.

'And as I remember, Mr Morris asked some questions as to whether you had a pistol in your pocket on a previous occasion at the school.'

'Yes, sir.'

'Remember that?'

'Yes, sir.'

'Do you remember that you told Mr Morris that you showed Harris a picture of a pistol?'

'Yes, sir.'

'OK. Is it true that you sent your sister to tell me that that testimony was not true?'

'Yes, sir.'

Brown shook his head in despair. 'Jesus . . .'

'OK. And did you send your sister to tell me that before I found out or anybody found out that that testimony was not true?'

'Yes, sir. I told her to come tell you.'

'OK. Did you later have an occasion to explain to me that you did have a pistol in your pocket on a prior occasion, some weeks or months earlier at the school?'

'Yes, sir.'

'And did you explain to me that you had showed such a pistol to Harris?'

'Yes, sir.'

At last, thought Brown. At last they had got to a tiny piece of the truth. Except that it was too damned late for the first trial, when it could have helped Clarence Brandley. And except that Jim Keeshan was still getting it wrong. This evidence had not been outside the presence of the jury. Peace had told the jury on oath that it was only a picture of a pistol which he showed to David Harris. The evidence that was held back from the jury was David Harris's story, where he said Peace was lying and that it had been a real gun. Judge Robertson had refused to let the jury hear that. Now it was too damned late. The battles at the last trial were already lost. Still, there was something else that was troubling Don Brown, something that might be worth a battle right here and now. He rose to his feet and started putting questions to Peace.

'Mr Peace, I believe Mr Keeshan asked you if you sent your sister to tell Mr Keeshan that you had told a lie about having a pistol at the high school earlier. Is that right?'

'Yes, sir.'

'When did you send your sister to tell him? Was it during the trial or do you not remember?'

Brown could see Keeshan stiffen behind his table.

'I don't really remember that.'

'Did you, at the time that you said you showed Harris only a picture of the pistol, did you think that was the truth?'

'No, sir.'

'You knew you were lying about showing Harris that pistol then, on the other occasion?'

'Yes, sir.'

'Well, did you go right home and tell your sister that "I lied on the witness-stand today"?'

'I went home and told her that I did something I shouldn't have done.'

Brown could smell blood here. If this dumb little sunnuvabitch had told Keeshan the truth while the first trial was still going on, and if Keeshan had deliberately suppressed the information, it would be the most improper abuse of his position. It would be disbarment time for James Keeshan. It had nothing to do with this present trial, but Brown pressed on.

'Did you send your sister then to tell Mr Keeshan?'

'I told her to tell him what it was I said.'

Keeshan sat motionless. Peace's eyes were swivelling nervously round the court as he tried to work out what was happening here.

'Do you know if that was during the trial?'

'No, sir. I think it was after I went home. I don't really remember.'

'It was after you went home, after you testified the first time?'

'I believe it was.'

'That day? Do you know if your sister went that day and told Mr Keeshan?'

'I don't know when she told him. But I had told her that day.'

Keeshan had had enough. 'Judge, I kind of resent this crap,' he said, his mild manner and charm dissolving. 'I'm here offering this man's testimony. I asked him to straighten up his testimony. The trial ended in a hung jury and it appears to me that he's trying to show misconduct . . .'

Brown held his hands up in a gesture of innocence. 'No, no, no,' he cooed. 'We've got an appeal on a revocation of probation growing out of the same facts, and I just sort of wondered.'

John Martin intervened from the bench. 'Well, let's just confine ourselves to the purposes of this trial today, and this witness.'

'Fine,' said Brown. 'Nothing further.'

He could still smell blood.

Keeshan continued to question Peace, outlining his story about the gun and the club and the narcotics badge and the smutty dashboard pictures, trying to persuade Judge Martin that it was not the kind of stuff that should be put before a jury.

Meanwhile, Brown had received a message that Cindy Acreman was in the building. But she was not the important one. So far as they knew she had not heard Gary talking about all these things on the day of the killing. She just might be able to confirm some of the circumstances.

Brown started chewing his thumb again, wondering where the hell Ed Payne was and whether he would get to court before Gary Acreman was called and what Jim Keeshan was going to do about the subpoenas, when Keeshan suddenly stopped asking Icky Peace about life in his toy city, turned to Jerry Winfree at his side and casually asked him an innocent question.

'Say, Jerry, what do you think about changing the order of our witnesses a little bit and having Acreman testify now? And then the two policeman?'

They could come back to this argument about Icky Peace later in the day, he said, after the jury had gone home. His only concern, he said softly, was the convenience of the jury.

'I hate to have the jury waiting so long,' he explained.

The judge said that would be fine by him. Keeshan said it kind of messed up the order of his witnesses. 'What do you think, Jerry?'

'That's fine with me.'

Morris and Brown felt their hearts sink. Now they only had a couple of hours to play with. Keeshan was right up to speed. He knew what was going on all right. There was not much they could do now, just try and keep Cindy Acreman out of the State's clutches and hope that Ed Payne showed up before Acreman finished on the witness-stand.

Brown rose and explained that they had subpoenaed Cynthia Acreman, and they wanted her brought in and sworn as a witness and ordered not to speak to anyone about her evidence. Before the Judge could reply, Jerry Winfree spoke up.

'You've also subpoenaed another member of the Acreman family.'

'Right,' said Brown, 'but he's not here yet.'

Right up to speed.

That Monday afternoon was as tense a time as Morris and Brown could ever remember spending in court. Acreman took the stand and told his story. But all the time, they were checking their watches and drumming their fingers and waiting for some word that Ed Payne had answered his subpoena.

Finally, it came: Payne was in the hallway outside.

Keeshan was still taking Acreman through his evidence. There was still time. If they could just check out what Payne was going to say they could confront Acreman and, if he denied it all, they could bring in Ed Payne and knock him sideways – and then Clarence Brandley would be as good as free.

Brown gathered up all his papers and scuttled out of court, leaving Morris to watch Acreman's evidence. He spotted Ed Payne as soon as he got out of the door. He was a strange-looking character, a skinny, scrawny little guy – he looked like a plucked chicken – with grey hair and a heavy pair of dark-framed spectacles straddling his nose and something very badly wrong with one of his legs. It appeared that the whole foot was missing from the ankle down. He was hobbling on a wooden stick.

Brown walked up to him with his biggest grin.

'You Ed Payne? Hi, I'm Don Brown. I'm the one that sub-poenaed you. We're really sorry to trouble you like this.'

Brown shook him by the hand and steered him gently towards a conference room, conscious all the while of the eyes of Conroe policemen boring into them as they passed. All Brown hoped was that this guy was going to come up to scratch.

His hope was soon dead.

As soon as Brown started putting his questions, he hit a wall. Ed Payne shrugged his skinny shoulders and turned down his mouth. No, he didn't know what Brown was talking about. He didn't remember any conversation with Gary. He had never heard anything about any clothes in any dumpster. Brown tried to move up a gear.

'We've talked to your brother John. And to Mary. Now, they say you told them all this.'

'Well, they're lying.'

'Now, Mr Payne, why would your brother lie like that? He told us he wasn't even interested in this trial till you started telling him about all this.'

'I never told him nothing.'

'Well, why would he say that?'

Payne said he was having a dispute with his brother John about some property. This must be some kind of way of getting at him and his family. Brown tried a different line.

'Mr Payne. You know there's a man's life at stake here. Clarence Brandley is being tried for capital murder. And I don't believe he's guilty of that crime. There's a man may be executed for something he did not do.'

'Well, I don't know nothing about it.'

Brown did not believe him. He tried some bluff.

'My Payne, you know we're going to have to call you on to that witness stand and put you on your oath. And we can call John and Mary, too, to tell about this. All I want is the truth. But if you get on to that stand and perjure yourself, you're in serious trouble, Mr Payne.'

But Payne would not budge. After 20 minutes Brown gave up, told Payne that if he changed his mind they would like to hear from him, and bade him farewell.

Back in court, Acreman was still being questioned by Jim Keeshan. Brown leaned into Morris's shoulder and whispered: 'Don't ask Acreman the questions. Payne's going to deny the whole thing. We got to approach this some other way.' Morris nodded.

Brown could not remember feeling so frustrated. They had lost the lead. They had been beaten. God alone knew how it had happened, but someone out there had screwed them. Brown tried to calm his rumbling fury.

Now George Morris was cross-examining Acreman, trying to chip away at him, pressuring him to admit that he and the other white janitors had been coached in their story. Brown could see he was doing a good job, but Acreman was standing up to him. It was pretty much over. Then Keeshan got up and asked a few final questions. The District Attorney made to sit down and then he stopped and lobbed one final query to the witness-stand.

'Do you know whether or not your wife and your father-in-law have been subpoenaed by the defence lawyers to be here today?'

'I know they've been subpoenaed,' said Acreman. 'I don't know by who.'

Brown clenched his fists very tight and glared down at the table. That was a piece of dirty, rotten bad faith. Keeshan must have heard from his people outside that Brown had talked to Payne and got nowhere. So now he was trying to tip off the jury, trying to push the defence into calling Ed Payne and Cindy so that their private problem would become public.

When the hearing ended for the day, Morris and Brown went straight to their office and got on the phone to John Payne and told him what had happened. John Payne told them that his brother had lied to Brown. There was no property dispute between them, he said. He did not know why, but his brother had lied.

Morris and Brown went back to the courthouse and found Jim Keeshan. Brown was seething. 'Do you know what this scumbag Acreman's father-in-law has been telling members of his family? Do you?'

Keeshan calmly asked him to explain. Morris and Brown rehashed their story.

'Do you know about this? Have y'all talked to Ed Payne about this?'

Keeshan smiled. 'I have had it drawn to my attention that Payne may say something about his son-in-law.'

'OK,' said Brown. 'Will you instruct Wes Styles or one of your investigators to go out and interrogate this man?'

Keeshan smiled and shook his head. 'I feel comfortable with the case as it is,' he said. 'If Brandley's acquitted, I'll follow it up.'

'If he's acquitted?' Brown burst out. 'If he's acquitted?'

Brown wanted to ask how Brandley was ever going to be acquitted if people suppressed the truth, and he wanted to ask whether Jim Keeshan had ever read the code of conduct which said his job was not to convict but to see that justice was done, and he wanted to pick him up and shake him. But there was no point. Keeshan had won. They were dead in the water.

The Revd John Daviss was taking a personal interest in the trial of Clarence Brandley. Nothing had happened since the day of Brandley's arrest to erase his anxiety that this case had released the worst instincts of Conroe's people, the kind of instincts which he hoped had been laid to rest long ago.

Sitting in court from day to day, Revd Daviss could not make out this Judge Martin. He had started out all right. Then one day, early in the trial, Revd Daviss had been sitting in court when they called a recess and most people had left the room. He had just been gathering his thoughts and getting ready to go when he had seen a whole crowd of people coming through the court and heading for the judge's office. These had been powerful people. Revd Daviss had recognized members of the school board among them and maybe one of the other courthouse judges. They had all trooped into the judge's office and shut the door.

Revd Daviss never did find out what happened in that office, but it seemed to him that the Judge had never been the same again. When he came back into court he looked as if he had been scolded, and he started coming down hard on Brandley's attorneys. Revd Daviss did not mention it to anyone. He assumed everyone must know.

Brandley watched the frantic efforts of his attorneys to get to the truth. But he didn't know the truth himself and never had. He didn't know whether Gary Acreman knew about the clothes being in the dumpster or not. He didn't know how Acreman could have known. Acreman surely wasn't a killer. He didn't know why anyone would want to stop all that coming out in court. Maybe the killer had got to Acreman's father-in-law. He didn't know. The only truth was that he had never killed a white girl. That was just about all he knew.

Morris and Brown told him that even without Ed Payne, it would all be OK. They still had their strategy and they still had John Martin on the bench. But privately, Morris and Brown were beginning to admit that their old friend John Martin was slipping away from them. They guessed he was just trying to please this town – perhaps he thought he could walk through the next election if he could send this bad nigger to Death Row. It was like he had some kind of private deal with Keeshan where the two of them were working together. They had become a well-oiled machine. Morris and Brown had been fighting tooth and nail for the right to tell the jury everything they knew about Icky Peace. They had won a small victory: they could tell the jury about his narcotics card and about how he had tried to recruit David Harris as an agent. But on everything else, Judge Martin was walking in the footsteps of Judge Sam Robertson.

They could mention the gun and the club that Peace had been carrying in his car, but they could not show them to the jury so that they could see just how threatening they were. Nor were they allowed to talk about the smutty pictures Peace carried around on the dashboard of his car. Nor could they tell them about Peace's set of handcuffs – ideal for restraining the girl. Somehow the police had failed to mention the cuffs in the first trial, but now Morris and Brown had found out that Peace had been carrying them, too. Judge Martin said they could not tell the jury about those either.

While they were struggling to introduce their evidence, Keeshan seemed to be able to pull any stunt he wanted. He wanted to call one of the school officials, a Mr Collier, to relate a conversation he had had with Peace on the day of the crime. In this conversation, it appeared that Peace had described how Brandley had made him search the props loft three times. Keeshan said it was powerful confirmation of Peace's story. Morris and Brown said it was obviously hearsay and could not be admitted. But the judge said Keeshan could have his way. They had objected to some of the pictures of the dead girl, some of which seemed to Morris and Brown to be so obscene and offensive in their violation of the girl's privacy that they were likely to stir up prejudice in the jury. They had asked for them to be held back from the jury since they added nothing except offence. But the judge had let Keeshan put them in.

It was galling. Keeshan was getting so cocky that he was starting to wink and grin at them every time he won another ruling from the judge.

Janet Dial found she got bored with her work and, as often as she could, she would leave Judge Martin's office on the ground floor of the courthouse, go up to the first floor and slip into the big trial. She was sitting at the back of the courtroom one day during the first week of the trial. John Martin was up on his dais. The attorneys were all bunched round him, arguing about something. She was watching Brandley, trying to figure out what was going on behind his face. Then she heard a strange noise coming from somewhere just in front of her, a sort of muttering. Only it was more like chanting.

She shifted in her seat and saw that the sound was coming from a woman sitting two rows in front of her, an elderly white woman, statuesque, wearing an old mink that was just on the edge of being shabby and a nice hat and some fancy jewellery. The woman was sitting stiff-backed and chanting in a strident whisper.

It was only a whisper but it was loud enough now for Janet to make out the words. At first she could not believe it. Then she looked across the aisle at Brandley's mother to see if she could hear it. There was no doubt what the white woman was saying: 'Kill the nigger. Kill the nigger. Kill the nigger. Kill the nigger.'

Captain Monty Koerner was on the stand. George Morris was cross-examining him. Morris was in powerful form. He had no respect for Koerner, and as a city councillor he had tried to get him fired for incompetence. Now he was hitting him from all sides.

At the climax of his attack, Morris started challenging Koerner to justify his decision to arrest Clarence Brandley on the Friday after the murder. He made Koerner list all the evidence which he did not have on that day. The Ranger's walk-through at the school with the white janitors had not yet taken place. There had been no clues from vaginal swabs, no fingerprints, no report yet on the foreign hairs found on the dead girl's thigh.

Morris looked at him in mocking disbelief. 'You went ahead and filed a complaint against the defendant charging him with capital murder?'

Koerner said that he had.

Morris pursued him. What about the knives that belonged to

Brandley and Peace? Had he received any scientific reports on them by that day? No, Koerner admitted, he had not. Morris had now got Koerner right where he wanted him. He opened up a new line of attack.

'Were you making daily reports to the administration of the Conroe Independent School District?'

'No, sir. Not every day.'

'Not every day. But how often were you making any reports?'

'Officer Williams was coming by and would ask us – he's the chief of their security – would ask how the case was proceeding, but there was no reports made to the school board.'

'School was fixing to start the next Monday, wasn't it?'

'Yes, sir.'

'Did anybody put pressure on you to get somebody in jail, because school was fixing to start?'

'No, sir. I had no political pressure.'

Morris paused to let that sink in, to give the jury a chance to wonder about that. Then he moved in and finished him off.

'Did you have any more evidence on Friday, when the complaint was filed against this defendant, than you had had on Monday?'

Koerner shifted in his seat and asked him to repeat the question.

'Did you have any more knowledge about this crime on Friday, when you filed a complaint against this defendant, than you had the preceding Monday?'

'No, sir.'

'I pass the witness,' said Morris and sat down, victorious. He had taken Monty Koerner right to the heart of this case – to the blind focus on the only black man near the scene of the crime, who had been arrested before they started gathering evidence to fit round him like a noose.

Jerry Winfree stood up and was attempting to rescue the captain of detectives.

'Now listen to the question carefully,' he was saying, 'and answer yes or no. As of Friday August 29 1980, other than the facts that you had learned of this case at that time about what happened at the high school, did you have knowledge of a previous history of this defendant that might have a bearing upon what happened . . .'

Morris could not believe it. Don Brown was already on his feet, objecting. Dammit, Keeshan had agreed not to go into any of that crap about Jo Ellen and Pokey. They had a Motion in Limine all about it. It had nothing to do with the facts of this case, and anyway, both women had retracted their allegations.

Judge Martin immediately told the jury to disregard the question. But the skunk was in the jury box. The attorneys huddled around Judge Martin's desk, whispering their protests and jabbing their fingers. Judge Martin sent out the jury and let the battle begin.

Keeshan spelled it out. 'By Friday, they had learned that he had kidnapped and attempted to rape another woman in connection with the possession of a sawed-off shotgun, for which he was earlier convicted. So they had that information as well.'

Morris protested that the girls had admitted they were lying and that he had their statements to prove it. Keeshan said it was all George Morris's fault: he had opened the door for this by questioning Captain Koerner's motive for arresting Brandley.

Clarence Brandley sat and watched the attorneys snarling and snapping over his life like coyotes fighting over a kill. The judge was trying to calm them down. He was agreeing that George Morris had been criticising the captain.

'Counsel had completely emasculated the witness,' said the judge.

'True,' said Jerry Winfree.

'He had the cords to the testicle running all the way to his counsel table,' continued the judge.

'Are we off the record now, Your Honour?' It was Mary, the court reporter, worrying over her notes.

Don Brown told her to keep writing and turned back in time to hear Keeshan claiming that he was worried that George Morris had made such a bad mistake in cross-examining the captain that Brandley might be able to win an appeal by claiming that he had ineffective counsel.

Brown felt his internal volcano beginning to bubble over and launched into an emphatic appeal to the judge.

'You're hurting my ears,' whined Keeshan.

'Well, I don't care,' said Brown.

On and on they wrangled, Keeshan saying he had to be able to show that Koerner was justified in arresting Brandley because he had found out about his history as a rapist; Morris saying the information was untrue, irrelevant and inadmissible.

Finally, Judge Martin ruled in favour of Keeshan: he could ask the question again and get Monty Koerner's answer, but he could not go on from there to explain exactly what Brandley's previous record was. Morris said the damage was done and this would only make it worse and he filed a motion for a mistrial. But his old friend, John Martin, whose election to the bench he had fought for, turned him down.

One day, during a short recess, George Morris wandered over to Keeshan's table and smiled at him broadly.

'Well, Jim, I knew you'd do it, but how did you do it so quickly?'

'Do what, George?'

'Get John Martin in your pocket.'

Keeshan smiled back, his blue eyes twinkling.

As Keeshan unfolded his case, he started slotting in fresh evidence. He called new witnesses from the school to testify that the auditorium would have been locked on the day of the crime. The killer must have had a key. He stressed that the two negroid hairs on the girl's body were unlike any of the others: they had been forcibly removed, as if in a struggle. Morris and Brown swept the idea aside, saying you could forcibly remove a hair with ordinary combing or just by running your hand through your hair. Brandley wanted to stand up and shout that a nurse's tweezers would do just as well, but the attorneys did not wish to fight a battle about planting hairs unless they could win it. Keeshan called a drama teacher and made much of the fact that one of her students had tied a towel round a pulley rope up near the props loft over the stage, and that the towel was no longer there. The implication was clear that this must have been the towel which the janitors said they had seen around Brandley's neck. Morris and Brown were not worried. It was just another circumstantial hint. No proof that a reasonable jury could be moved by.

Then Keeshan pitched his screw ball, a black teenager named Danny Taylor, who had spent a few days the previous summer working at the high school as a janitor alongside Clarence Brandley. According to Danny Taylor, they had been standing in the hallway one day, just outside the teachers' lounge, when a group of schoolgirls had walked by, and Brandley had said: 'If I got one of them alone, ain't no tellin' what I might do.'

Morris and Brown were horrified. This could do terrible damage to Brandley. Surely John Martin would stop it. They even had a Motion in Limine from Judge Robertson which blocked Keeshan from suggesting that Brandley had any kind of special sexual interest in white women. But Keeshan said he wanted the judge to remove that block. He seemed very confident. Judge Martin sent the jury away and listened to arguments. Morris and Brown pleaded that the evidence was not true and that even if it had been true, it would be nothing more than locker-room talk and it would mean nothing, and it would tell them nothing about what was going on in Brandley's mind on the day of the crime and it would be the purest prejudice. But the judge agreed that Keeshan could have his way.

Don Brown was furious that after all of the times they had been blocked from getting Icky Peace's background into the trial, Keeshan was going to be allowed to put this kind of stuff in front of the jury.

'The evidence is irrelevant,' he boomed. 'It's immaterial to this case and can serve only to prejudice and inflame the jury against the defendant . . .'

'And unconstitutional . . .' interjected Morris.

'And it is mere speculation as to his intent,' added Brown.

But what really worried them was a much deeper point, one that had nothing to do with legal technicalities.

It was the myth that mattered – the myth that black men slavered after white women and longed for any opportunity to sexually abuse them, the myth that black men not only spent every waking hour lusting after white men's women but that they were endowed with special sexual prowess beyond anything that a white man could offer. It was this myth which moved every white man who ever laid hands on a nigger and accused him of raping a white woman, or attempting to rape a white woman, or even just watching a white woman. It was the myth that moved lynch mobs. And the myth could move this jury, this all-white Conroe jury, just the same way. It was the most potent poison.

Calmly, Jim Keeshan explained that this was evidence from which an inference could properly be drawn by the jury and that it showed that Brandley was looking for an opportunity to get one of these girls on her own. Equally calmly, Judge Martin repeated that Keeshan could have his way.

While the jury were being brought back into court and Danny Taylor was led back to the stand, Don Brown went into a huddle with Clarence, trying to find out who this boy was and what this was all about. Taylor started his evidence. George Morris kept rising to his feet to repeat his objections so that at least the jury would know how outrageous he believed this was. The judge kept overruling him. Finally, Taylor uttered the words that Keeshan was waiting for.

'Brandley said if he got one of them alone, ain't no tellin' what he might do.'

All along the jury box, all along the public benches, hostile eyes glared at the black man.

George Morris tried to salvage what he could, taking Taylor back through his story and then, without warning or change of pace, asking: 'Now, when did you pull a knife on your supervisor?'

Now Jerry Winfree was bouncing up and objecting. There was a brief squabble. George Morris explained that Danny Taylor had attacked the then supervisor, David Harris, at the school with a butcher's knife, that Brandley had tried to stop him and that Taylor had been sacked because of the incident. To Morris's relief the judge agreed that they could tell this to the jury, since it raised the possibility that Taylor was inventing his story to take revenge on Brandley.

Morris put his questions, but Danny Taylor argued with him. He said David Harris had attacked him by slapping him and that, anyway, Brandley had never intervened. The attack on Taylor was weak. It was certainly not strong enough to lift the mythical cloak that had now been so deliberately draped around Clarence Brandley's shoulders.

Janet Dial did not pretend to know about courthouse procedure. She was new. But she had always thought that the judge and the District Attorney were supposed to be separate from each other. The longer she spent in the courthouse, the more she began to feel that things were not quite right.

She could see how charming Jim Keeshan was. Most of the time she thought he was probably the most charming person she had ever met. Other times she worried about him, and he struck her as a textbook case of someone who had been emotionally damaged somewhere along the line and had come out with this charming mask to hide behind. She could see how he was charming John Martin. It seemed somehow that Keeshan was not just being friendly for friendship's sake. Sitting there in the trial each day, she could see that the judge was ruling more and more for Keeshan and against the defence.

She remembered the judge's odd behaviour with the internal phone book which listed the extensions numbers for everyone in the courthouse. When she had first started work at the beginning of January, Martin had taken the book and put plus signs by the people who were alright to talk to, and minus signs by those who were enemies. Then, a little while later, he had come back and changed the minus sign opposite Keeshan's name to a plus.

But what most worried her – what seemed not to be the right procedure at all – was the way that almost every morning, before the Brandley trial started, Keeshan would come by Judge Martin's office, go in and shut the door. The defence attorneys never did that. She guessed the defence attorneys did not even know these meetings were happening. To her, it just did not seem right.

Most evenings, Morris or Brown visited Brandley in his cell after the hearing to talk about the day's events and to plan their strategy for the following day. Brandley kept on at them about the photographs which the police had taken at the high school on the day of the crime. He was sure they had taken photographs of him standing around while they started their investigation, and he was just as sure that those photographs would show that he had not been wearing a belt that day.

'They saying they lost all them pictures,' he told them. 'I don't believe it. They just won't give them 'cause they'll show I'm telling the truth. I had no damned belt.'

When the police photographer, Sgt Woody Allen, came to the stand, George Morris took him once more through his failed attempts to photograph the scene of the crime. The sergeant repeated his evidence from the first trial – that he had taken two rolls of film that day, one colour and one black-and-white, and that only a few of the colour shots had come out.

Then he disclosed that it was only the colour film which he had taken to Fox Photo in the shopping mall – the Fox Crime Lab as Morris and Brown now called it. He had given the other roll to Officer Wayne Kremenak to develop. And, for all he knew, Kremenak still had the black-and-white negatives. Keeshan immediately volunteered that if George Harris was really so interested in these photographs, he could arrange for Officer Kremenak to dig out the negatives.

That night, Brandley was on the edge of being happy. He asked Don Brown: 'Do you think they know what we're after, why we want them so bad?'

Brown chuckled. 'Damn right they do. They're no fools.'

On the next day of the trial, Keeshan called Officer Kremenak to the stand. The detective described how, obeying Jim Keeshan's instructions, he had dug out his old negatives and taken them to the DA's office, where Ranger Styles had taken a look at them and agreed that they might be able to develop the pictures after all. It was not until George Morris cross-examined the officer that he admitted that he was not talking about the black-and-white film at all – only about the colour film which the Fox Crime Lab had returned to him.

The black-and-white film, he confessed, had disappeared. He could not explain it. It had been in the file along with the colour one, he was sure about that. Both rolls of film had been in there. Right next to each other. But now there was only one.

The black-and-white film was lost and gone forever. He just could not explain it.

Don Brown could explain it all right. That evening in Brandley's cell, he exploded. 'I told you those scumbags knew what we were after. They've destroyed that goddam film. Clarence, these people are too damned determined to get your ass.'

A few days later, Jim Keeshan triumphantly presented a pile of glossy colour photographs of the high school on the day of the crime. Using the most advanced technology, he smiled, they had succeeded in developing these pictures. A couple of them showed Brandley on the day of the crime. None of them showed his waist.

Keeshan called the Texas Ranger, Wes Styles. Styles sat stiff and proud in his uniform and described how he had worked for more than 500 hours on the case. Morris and Brown could see it was good theatre. The Ranger appeared to know what he was doing: a special breed of man. George Morris tried to score a point off him by asking why, in all his 500 hours of investigation, he had never seen fit to take any samples of blood, hair or saliva from Gary Acreman, John Sessum or Sam Martinez to see whether they compared with anything found on the dead girl.

The Ranger answered in a firm voice. 'I did not because they hadn't been in contact with her. That's the reason.'

Morris sighed. He was back in the heart of this case again, back with the blind focus and the grabbing of the nearest black man. How could this big-bellied old Ranger possibly know that these white janitors had not been in contact with the girl? Why had they picked on Brandley to give his samples? Even when they found that there were all those hairs on that girl which could not conceivably have come from Brandley, why did they stick with Brandley? But Morris had got into trouble before by pursuing that line, so he had to let it go.

Besides, something else had surfaced. As soon as Styles started giving evidence, Morris and Brown were entitled to see the offence report which he had written for Jim Keeshan. It made interesting reading.

For example, there was a tape-recording which he had faithfully transcribed in his report, of a conversation between the Ranger and Icky Peace soon after the Ranger had joined the inquiry. The little janitor chattered on about how Gary Acreman had come across to the vocational building on the day of the crime and told them all that Brandley was fooling around with a girl in the main building and that there were girl's clothes scattered around.

Morris and Brown had no idea what it meant nor why the prosecution had never mentioned this apparently important clue. And it was clearly a dangerous statement to start putting in front of this jury. But Peace had never said it in his evidence, nor had Acreman. Morris and Brown wanted the jury to know that these witnesses were not telling the whole story. But Judge Martin said no.

'Ranger Styles's investigative report and any investigation that he conducted regarding any interview with Icky Peace, is not signed, has not been read by Icky Peace, is not a statement.'

Morris and Brown thought it was uncanny how every time the defence needed a break from this judge, he came up with some kind of procedural objection. He and the District Attorney might as well have been partners. Morris and Brown watched glumly as Keeshan started to pull the kind of tricks that attorneys normally only dream of.

At one point, a Conroe High School teacher was talking about keys to the school auditorium. Keeshan smiled politely at her and said: 'I believe the evidence will show that Clarence Brandley had a set of keys to the auditorium for about a month before 23 August.'

The teacher nodded and Keeshan continued in the same gentle tone. 'Did you, before that time, did you ever have anybody raped and murdered in the Conroe High School auditorium?'

Morris and Brown went off together like both barrels of a shotgun: 'Objection – irrelevant – immaterial – prejudicial – slurry.'

'OK,' said Judge Martin. 'Sustained.'

Keeshan smiled and said he had no further questions.

The manoeuvre that most deflated Morris and Brown came right at the end of the State's case. They had been waiting for John Sessum to come to the stand. The other three white janitors had already testified. But Sessum was the one that Morris and Brown wanted. They felt that Morris had come close to cracking him when he cross-examined him in the first trial and they hoped that if they could start to pull his story apart now, they might get a glimpse of the truth that was being concealed.

All through the state's case they waited for him. With all the legal argument and some extra witnesses that Keeshan called, the state took eight working days to present its evidence. But there was still no sign of Sessum. Then, finally, on Tuesday 10 February, Keeshan rose and turned to the court bailiff.

'Would you bring John Sessum in?'

Morris and Brown sat up and watched. This was not the way that Keeshan usually called a witness. Sessum shuffled into court, chewing his lip and looking unsteadily from one face to another. He looked as though he was seasick. Keeshan gestured him towards the front of the court. He was all courtesy.

'Mr Sessum, would you stop and stand right there, please? May it please the court, this is Mr John Sessum. We would tender him, at this time, to the defence counsel, and, at this time, State rests, Your Honour.'

It was brilliant. Morris and Brown had to admit that it was brilliant. By offering Sessum as a defence witness, Keeshan was destroying their ability to cross-examine him. If Sessum was their witness, the rules said that they could not attack him. They would just have to let him tell the same story as the other janitors to get the truth out of him. And by offering Sessum to them in public, Keeshan was scoring a point with the jury who would think that the defence had something to hide if they failed to call him. It was brilliant.

While Sessum was sworn in as a witness, Morris and Brown tried to gather their thoughts. Morris stumbled to his feet and asked if they could have copies of Sessum's two statements to the police. At this point, Keeshan performed his next manoeuvre. Since Sessum was now a defence witness, they were not entitled to any statements he had made to the prosecution. 'They know this is improper,' he scolded.

Morris tried to fight back. He told the judge that it was the defence that had arranged for those statement to be put into evidence at the first trial. That made them defence exhibits, so they must be entitled to them. Jerry Winfree bobbed up and said that the state had only loaned them to the defence and had never given them away. Don Brown was bubbling over again.

'That case was a mistrial. The revocation of probation has been appealed and those statements – defence exhibits – should be kept by the clerk with all exhibits and they have no right to take our exhibits out of our appeal on revocation.'

Judge Martin snapped back: 'This court is not concerned with revocation or the prior trial. The witness sits up here. If you want him, fine. If you don't, just dismiss him.'

George Morris asked: 'Is it the ruling of the court that we will not be given the two statements of Mr Sessum, any of the statements?'

'Not prior to his testimony,' said the judge.

Morris shook his head. 'Your Honour, Mr Sessum is not now and never was our witness. We will pass him back.'

'All right,' said the judge.

'No questions,' said Keeshan.

'Mr Sessum,' said the judge, 'you may step down.'

Beaten again.

Morris and Brown did their best to fight back. It was extraordinary to see, but after four days of the State's case in the first trial, and after eight more days of the State's case here in the second trial, after the 500 hours' work by the Texas Ranger and after all the efforts of the Conroe Police Department, there was still not one witness, nor one piece of scientific evidence, nor one hard clue of any kind, to link their client to the crime. It ought to have been easy to fight this case. All they had to do to knock the state over was to run the case against Icky Peace. They could not see how the circumstantial evidence against Brandley could stand up against it. But it was not that easy. This was not a regular fight. This was Conroe.

Morris and Brown started calling their witnesses, chipping away at the role of Icky Peace, using David Harris to confirm that the little janitor had carried his gun in school and had shown off his narcotics card and even tried to recruit Harris as his agent. Over Jim Keeshan's objections, Harris added that the card which Peace had now produced in court was not the one which he had shown off in school. That one had been bigger and Peace had told him soon after the murder in the high school that he had torn it up.

They called a drama student who said he was the one who had tied a towel round a pulley rope up near the props loft. But he said it was not a white school towel like the one the other janitors claimed Brandley had round his neck. It was a little hand towel that he had taken from a motel where they once stayed on a school trip.

Morris and Brown called a string of witnesses to challenge Keeshan's claim that Brandley must be the murderer because he was the only one present who had a key to get into the auditorium that day. There was talk of damaged doors and doors routinely left open and doors whose keys were borrowed and never returned.

David Harris spoke of the set of keys that had been loaned out to Icky Peace and never seen again. George Morris urged him to tell more. Harris said Peace had evidently given the missing keys to a man called Clarence Robinson, a white man who had briefly worked as supervisor to the janitors at Conroe High before Brandley was promoted. Over Keeshan's objection that this was heresay, Morris probed a little further.

'Do you know of your own personal knowledge whether or not Clarence Robinson turned in a set of keys that Henry Peace said that he returned to him?'

'He did not.'

'You know of your own personal knowledge that Clarence Robinson did not turn in the keys that Peace said he gave Clarence Robinson?'

'That is correct.'

Morris left it at that. The keys were clearly missing – either this Robinson had them or, as Morris hoped the jury would conclude, Peace had never passed them on and still had them in his possession.

After little more than a day, the defence had made their points. The one thing they had not done was to call Clarence Brandley to the stand.

They had discussed it endlessly. They had talked to other attorneys who had watched Brandley's evidence at the first trial, and they said that he came across badly and that he had damaged his case by contradicting white witnesses. Brandley insisted that he had only been telling the truth but, in Conroe, that could be dangerous. Morris and Brown decided it was better to let the facts that they had already produced speak for themselves and not to antagonize this all-white jury with the image of a black man calling white people liars.

They believed they had done enough, and they received an unexpected bonus from one of Jim Keeshan's scientific witnesses, a serologist named Pat Lux, who had examined the dead girl's clothes and the various stains on them.

Brown had been trying to find out about a bloodstain on the dead girl's shirt. It was potentially important evidence. If it was not Type O, then it was not Clarence Brandley's blood. The serologist, however, said that she had not tested the stain so she did not know what type it was.

Brown became irritated and challenged her failure to do the test.

'But these items were all packaged together in one package,' complained the serologist. 'It's hard to say if that bloodstain came from those socks that were packaged in there . . .'

Brown leaped on her words. 'Well, now, wait a minute now. I didn't know you found any blood on the socks. I don't believe you testified about that.'

'No, sir. I didn't testify to any of that.'

Hardly daring to hope, Brown pushed forward. 'Was there blood on the socks?'

'Yes, sir.'

'And did you do any testing on the blood on the socks?'

'Yes, sir.'

'And what did you find?'

'I found blood group A.'

Brown could hardly believe his luck. That was not Clarence Brandley's blood. So whose was it? In Brown's mind, there was no doubt: it came from the same person who owned all these mysterious hairs that had been found. Not Brandley. Someone else – the murderer.

There was, however, one problem. The dead girl had Type A

blood. Yet there was no evidence that she had been knifed or that her nose had bled. She had certainly not got up that morning and put on a bloodstained shirt and socks. The blood had been spilled during the attack, and it must be from the attacker. The girl could easily have struggled and given him a bloody nose.

Jim Keeshan fought back. The girl's vagina had been slightly torn, he said. The attacker might have used her shirt, or her sock, to wipe himself, transferring her Type A blood onto the clothes. Don Brown found it hard to imagine the attacker doing that to the girl's sock while it was still on her foot – which was where the police had found it. But Keeshan had an answer for that, too. He pointed to a scuff mark on the girl's right shin and suggested that that was the source of the blood on the sock. It was pure speculation, but Morris and Brown feared that, weak as it was, in this courtroom it might suit the jury to accept it.

Late on Thursday morning, 12 February, the defence rested their case.

The court took a brief recess, but before they could move on, George Morris sent a shiver of speculation across the court by announcing that the defence wanted to reopen its case. They had a new witness. It was a dramatic moment, but the tension soon faded.

The last-minute witness was a white air-conditioning engineer called Joe McFarland who had been following the case and who had contacted Morris and Brown during the recess to tell them that he had often worked at the school and had found the doors to the auditorium unlocked almost all the time.

Jim Keeshan struck him with the speed of a snake. Had he been there on the day of the crime? No. The day before? No. Had he been drinking before he gave evidence? Wasn't it true that he had been sacked by the school? And why had he come forward at the last minute like this? McFarland finally snapped. 'The reason I came forward with this information was that I think you're railroading somebody. Everybody had access to the keys to that door.'

Morris and Brown knew that McFarland meant well, but he came across like an obnoxious pipsqueak and Keeshan had just

needled him into destroying his own credibility. He sounded like
he was crusading for Brandley.

The defence rested again. It was getting late. Judge Martin sent
the jury home and told them to come back the next day, on Friday
13 February, when they would listen to final speeches and then
retire to reach their verdict.

Clarence Brandley was ready to be free again. He looked across
the room at the jury. He looked at them a thousand times. He
had always believed that most people weren't all bad; they were
just people. Sure, they were white people, but there was no reason
why they should want to blame him for this crime. It was not
like a judge or a district attorney who wanted to be powerful and
wanted to use him. There was no way they were going to accept
this evidence, no way they were going to find him guilty. That
night, Brandley went back to his cell in the county jail and prayed
– really prayed – that tomorrow morning that jury was going to
set him free again.

At 8.30 on Friday morning, the attorneys began their speeches,
following the tracks of the first trial. Jerry Winfree spent 45
minutes summarizing the evidence from prosecution witnesses.
Don Brown rehearsed the scientific evidence, returning again and
again to the mysterious hairs that had been found on the dead girl
and that had never been traced to anyone, let alone to Clarence
Brandley. George Morris attacked the police inquiry, which he
said should be written up in a book called *How Not To Investigate
A Case*. 'They fumbled the evidence. They used poor judgement.
And they ignored very important facts . . . You can't expect the
police and the Texas Ranger to find a needle in a haystack. But
you can expect them to find the haystack.' Morris went back to
the autopsy report and raised the theory that two people must
have been involved in the attack on the girl. He returned to the
unidentified hairs. He argued that the killer had not wanted the
body found. He moved Icky Peace to the centre of the stage. And
he pleaded: 'I want you to ask yourselves: "Where is the proof?
Where is the proof?" '

Then it was Keeshan's turn. He moved into a discussion of the

evidence which held no surprises for Morris and Brown, until he
started to remind the jury that Brandley had worked part-time in
a funeral home. 'Dr Jachimczyk told you from the medical evidence that it appeared that this girl had been molested after she
was dead or unconscious. We know also that the person who
committed this offence had to have stayed with the body . . .'

Morris was on his feet. 'Your Honour, we are going to object
to this. This is inflammatory . . .'

'Overruled,' said the judge. And Keeshan continued.

'We know that whoever did this was not repelled by a dead
body. Somebody stayed there and took the clothing off that body.
Somebody had intercourse with that body, apparently after she
was unconscious or dead. It is not just everybody who is going
to be involved in that kind of offence. This man was not repelled
by the fact that she was deceased.'

Don Brown made a mental note that if this jury ever convicted
Clarence Brandley, they would go straight to the appeal court and
complain about this kind of dirty prejudice.

Keeshan went on – sketching out his chain of circumstances –
the path of the janitor, the keys, the negroid hair, the opportunity,
the ability, the motive. Then, pacing up and down in front of the
jury box, he moved away from his evidence and started to appeal
to something else. He talked about the dead girl, her hopes and
fears, her innocence and the mark of the crucifix stamped into her
flesh. 'Cheryl was part of all of us,' he cried. He talked about
Conroe, a community for families, a community that needed to
send out a message, a message that this kind of crime would not
be tolerated. A hung jury was no good, he warned. That would
not relieve the dead girl's family or help the town.

'It would be a disservice to your community to go back there
and decide: "We just can't agree". I'm going to ask you to help
make your community safe and a good place to live. A place
where you want your children and grandchildren to grow up,
where people can go to a school function without fear that some
monstrous person is going to commit an offence like this. And
when you reach a proper verdict in this case, when you go back
to find this defendant guilty according to the evidence, and you
get to go home tonight, I'd like to have you hug your children or

whoever you love and tell them you've done something for them today.'

Keeshan sat down. The jury had a choice. They could listen to George Morris asking for proof, or they could heal their town.

Just after two o'clock, for the first time in his new career as a judge, John Martin sent away a jury to reach a verdict in a capital murder case. Before they went, he reminded them that this was a case of circumstantial evidence and he read them the required rule of law.

'It is not sufficient that the circumstances coincide with, account for, and therefore render probable the guilt of the defendant; they must exclude to a moral certainty every other reasonable hypotheses except that of the defendant's guilt.'

To a moral certainty.

Just over an hour later, the jury came back and said that they had found the black janitor guilty of capital murder.

Clarence Brandley watched the woman with the brightly coloured fingernails come in to court to read the verdict. Peggy Stevens. He knew she should not even have been there. She was the District Clerk, not the Clerk of the Court. But she came in and took the verdict from the foreman of the jury and held it in her elegant hands and read out 'Guilty' loud and clear. And then she clapped her hands together and smiled.

Brandley saw that smile. It was like pure joy on her face.

And the judge was doing the same. Smiling.

Why had they done this to him? He was no murderer. But now he felt like he could be. He could reach out and grab them and just murder them. Look at them: all around the court they were smiling.

At the prosecution table, Jim Keeshan sorted out his papers. He had one last courtroom manoeuvre to perform – to persuade this jury to order that Clarence Brandley be put to death for this crime.

The jurors were taken away for the night and sequestered, like their predecessors, in the Holiday Inn. On Saturday morning they returned to the courthouse, where Clarence Brandley's fate now hung on the answers to two questions. Had he killed this girl deliberately? And was there a risk that he might commit more violent acts? If the jury believed the answer to either question was no, he would be sentenced to a lifetime in jail. If the jury believed that the answer to both question should be yes, then he would be sentenced to death. The District Attorney stood up and set about persuading the jury to say yes twice.

First, he called the old sheriff Gene Reaves out of his retirement and asked him what kind of reputation this Clarence Lee Brandley had in the community. 'It's bad,' came the reply. That was all.

George Morris got up and went straight for the sheriff's jugular. Wasn't this hearsay that he was reporting? Wasn't hearsay most unreliable? Hadn't he himself been the victim of hearsay? Hadn't he been the victim of hearsay in an election campaign when people said he had been stealing gasoline from the county? Keeshan was jumping up and down objecting, but Morris pressed on.

'You can't really believe everything you hear, can you?'

'No, you sure can't,' muttered the sheriff with a face like flint.

Then Jo Ellen Parrish came back, like a bad spirit. Coaxed along by Jim Keeshan, she said she was a 19-year-old girl with a husband and a baby son and that one night in March 1979, she had been walking past her friend Mary Zavaba's car when she saw that Mary was being choked by a man she now knew to be Clarence Brandley. She had made him stop. Then she had gone with Mary to a drinking club called The Doll House, but Clarence Brandley had followed them there with a sawn-off shotgun pushed down the back of his trousers and he had abducted her and made her wait behind The Doll House until everyone had left. Then he had taken her to his house and made her strip to her underwear and tried to have sex with her. Her husband had knocked on the door but he had choked her to stop her crying out. Then he had cooked her a meal and got into bed and she had run out of the house wearing her underwear and Clarence's coat, and hidden at her friend Lillian's house until the morning. Then she had gone to her husband and told him what had happened and he made her contact the police.

Brandley had heard that Jo Ellen was telling some story about him, but he never realized it was as crazy as this. At least now he understood why she had run out on him that night. If her boy-friend really had come round knocking on the door while he had been asleep, it was no surprise that she had panicked. She must have waited for her boyfriend to go and then worked out this story to cover herself.

Don Brown set out to demolish her story. Jo Ellen soon admit-ted that she was not married at all. She denied being a prostitute, but said she was not sure about Mary Zavaba, even though she was supposed to be her best friend. Brown suggested to her that she and Mary had met Brandley and his friend and that she had invented the story of abduction to hide her infidelity from her boyfriend. She denied it and then spoiled her denial by admitting that Mary's boyfriend, Ralph, had come looking for Mary that night and had dragged her out of The Doll House by her hair at gunpoint. She admitted, too, that Brandley had not been choking her when her boyfriend came knocking on the door of the house looking for her, and she could not explain why she did not scream for help. Nor could she explain why she had not run away while he was cooking her a meal.

Don Brown showed the jury the rusty old shotgun and hoped that they shared his view that it could not have fitted down the back of anybody's trousers without splitting them in two.

Finally, Brown asked Jim Keeshan to produce Jo Ellen's two statements – the one she had made immediately after this incident in March 1979 and the one she had made 18 months later, after Brandley's arrest for murder, when Ted Morgan had taken her to the courthouse. He wanted to show how she had embellished this story in the meantime. Keeshan sent someone out to look for the statements. The court waited. Keeshan then reported that they could not find them. He could not explain it, he said. He was sorry. They were gone. Lost and gone forever. Brown was hardly surprised.

He was not surprised either that at the last moment Keeshan changed his mind and decided not to call Pokey Smith to tell her story of Brandley's violent assault and multiple rape. Jo Ellen Parrish had fared badly under cross-examination. Pokey Smith was likely to collapse completely and spoil the show. Anyway, in this atmosphere, Keeshan did not need any more evidence.

The court broke for lunch. Judge Martin called all the attorneys into his office, and there, Morris and Brown witnessed a rare sight. They saw Jim Keeshan drop his guard.

It started with the judge reporting that a toy pistol had been found in the courthouse. 'We have reached a point in the trial where it might pay all of us to be extremely careful and cautious,' he said. Everyone agreed and then, perhaps buoyed by his success in the trial, Jim Keeshan launched into a speech in which he complained that some of the spectators had been unruly, giggling and talking during the evidence, and that some black woman had sat on a white woman's hand. He suggested that police officers should be seated along the front of the public benches 'looking directly down the throats of that audience.'

While he was explaining this, he said something that finally confirmed what Morris and Brown had always suspected. It was only a little thing, almost in parenthesis as he talked, but to them it said everything. 'I haven't made any announcements to the white people out there,' he said, 'and I know y'all haven't felt obligated to make an announcement to all the black people.'

That was all. Jim Keeshan – the white people's District Attorney. He was not going to talk to any black people in court. They were nothing to do with him. They might technically be members of the community he served, but he would speak only to the white people, because they were his people. He had simply taken that for granted in talking to them. As he had done throughout this trial.

Morris and Brown said nothing. It had already occurred to them that if Clarence Brandley had been acquitted, there were people in this town who would be willing to take revenge on two nigger-loving attorneys. They all agreed that they should take proper security precautions and they returned to court to finish the day's business.

The two defence attorneys had reached a point where they had just about lost all confidence in justice in this courtroom. Now they had to argue to save Brandley's life, but with this judge and this jury, it seemed to them that there was no rational argument that had a chance of succeeding. If rational argument were succeeding, Brandley would never have been convicted. And perhaps that was the angle to work on – the possibility that some of these jurors knew they had returned an irrational verdict, that maybe some of them had a lingering doubt.

Don Brown decided that instead of making the usual attempt to present mitigating evidence and challenge the other side, he would simply appeal to that lingering doubt.

As Brown began his speech, his depression showed through his threadbare attempt to respect the court. Breathing sarcasm, he said: 'I will just say that I know that you have heard Clarence Lee Brandley's terrible record this morning, what a terrible person he is. And I'm not going to dignify the evidence they put on this morning by arguing about it. We have argued until we are blue in the face about the evidence in the first phase of the trial with obviously little success. Perhaps Mr Morris and I just failed.

'I would like to say this: that each of you took an oath on your God that you would a true verdict render in this case, and I am telling you now that under the oath you took in this case, if you believe from the evidence that you have heard beyond a reasonable doubt and to a moral certainty that there is no reasonable possibility that someone else could have committed this crime, you should assess the death penalty . . .'

Keeshan was interrupting. 'Your Honour. Your Honour.'

Brown waded on. '. . . and you know the other alternative if your conscience bothers you at all because of your verdict. Thank you.'

Keeshan was still talking. 'Your Honour, may it please the court, ladies and gentlemen of the jury, it is not considered professional to attack the verdict of the jury or quarrel with the verdict . . .'

Don Brown could not believe it. Was there nothing they could do in this case without Keeshan trying to trip them up? He rose to his feet and insisted he had not been attacking the verdict at all.

'Okay,' said Judge Martin. 'Over . . . Let's proceed.'

For a moment, Brown hesitated. Had the judge overruled him? He appeared to have done, but he had swallowed the word. Brown let it pass. He had had enough. Keeshan continued his plea for the death penalty. He commended the ladies and gentlemen of the jury for their verdict. He said Brandley had had his chance to be rehabilitated when he was given probation in 1979. Don Brown objected that this was not an issue. The judge overruled him. Keeshan reminded the jurors of the photographs of the dead girl. 'The look of stark terror on her face. It's fair for you to think about the feelings of the father who lost his baby daughter and it's fair for you to think about how you would feel if you lost your children.'

Morris and Brown did not think that that was at all fair. And for once, Brown's objection was sustained. Brown then complained that it was not enough just to sustain his objection when these inflammatory remarks had already been made to the jury. The judge overruled him. Keeshan had finished. The jury retired.

Three quarters of an hour later they were back. Just as Jim Keeshan had asked, they said yes to both questions.

Clarence Lee Brandley must die.

Brandley felt nothing. He was numb. Physically numb, all over his body. He thought nothing. But a strange thing happened in his head. He saw his life. Just like drowning people do. Real pictures. Nothing he would ever remember. But it was his whole life: the life he once had.

Reporters crowded round his family. His brother, O.T., told them: 'I think the state knows who did it and has known it all along. They just wanted somebody caught for it and it's easier to prosecute a black man.'

His mother cried quietly on somebody's shoulder.

Then white policeman came and led Clarence Brandley from the court, and he was lost, one black face in a blizzard of white faces, lost like one simple fact in this blizzard of lies – he had not done this thing.

Don Brown felt sick to his heart. He had never thought this could happen. Sure, he had seen people who appeared to be innocent being convicted by juries. But never in a case like this – where a man's life was at stake. He had never thought it could happen in a death penalty case. And on such weak evidence! He had never thought that jurors could be so indifferent to the oath which they had sworn, to find guilt beyond reasonable doubt. But this was not really about jurors. This was about Conroe.

This was about corruption and dirty tricks and about ruthless men who would twist the truth and bend the rules to get their way. This was about politics and power, and about ambitious people who would happily sacrifice one innocent man's life in their pursuit of success. This was about a town where black people had always been victims, the town that killed Bob White in this very courthouse.

Sure, times had changed. Not so long ago, a bunch of white men would have done their manly duty and dragged Clarence Brandley out of his wooden shack and hanged him from the nearest tree while the rest of the town turned its back. But not any more. Now they had to use the courthouse and the law instead of the stout tree and the rope. But the end result was just the same. One dead nigger boy. One big white lie.

Part Two
Heroes of Faith

Faith is the substance of things hoped for, the evidence of things not seen.

Hebrews 11 (i)

6

High up on a hill, 40 miles north of Conroe, in the town of Huntsville where Sam Houston is buried, there is a building which looks like a shadow in the sky, a giant stockade with a soaring 25-foot redbrick wall topped with razor wire. Guards ride shotgun at every corner. This is the headquarters of the Texas Department of Corrections, the biggest jailhouse in East Texas. It is also the home of the Walls Unit, a bright bleached-white room with no windows, where doctors strap men to stretchers, plug catheters into their arms, run a solution of sodium thiopental pavulon and potassium chloride into their veins, and wait for their hearts to stop beating.

One sunny day early in the spring of 1981, a patrol car from Montgomery County Sheriff's Department sped northward out of Conroe along Interstate 45 and brought Clarence Brandley to Huntsville.

For Brandley, this was the scariest moment so far. He had no idea what to expect. He had never had to deal with anything like this. He had never even been in jail before all this started. And here he was, on his way to Death Row.

The sheriff's car sped through Huntsville, past the building in the middle of town where the killing is done and out into the desert of empty grass and swamps, to the Ellis Unit, where condemned men are kept until their date to die comes round. A few dead trees rise out of the bayous, their branches bearded with Spanish moss. The sheriff's car prowled through the high redbrick gateway and up the long tarmac driveway. To one side, there was a work party, almost like a chain gang: about a dozen black men, dressed in white from neck to ankle, standing in a line, all holding hoes and hacking the ground in unison, sending little clouds of dust up round their ankles. Beside them, white men sat on horse-back, resting easy in the saddle, cradling rifles in their laps, chewing slowly on unlit cigars, their eyes masked by the reflecting shades of their sunglasses. Further up the driveway, over to the left, Brandley saw a firing range.

Then he saw the unit: the high wire fence, the second fence inside that – just as high – the towers at each corner with the shadows of the sentries and their guns, the long, low redbrick building with the bars, bars on every window he could see, painted blue.

They took him inside. They stripped him, cut off his hair, sprayed him with powder, put him in regulation all-white clothes from neck to ankle and gave him a new identity. He was number 680 on Death Row.

The trial was over.

The *Courier* reported: 'The guilty verdict ended the Halloween-ish atmosphere lying heavily upon the community for the past five months. In less time than it takes to mow the lawn, Brandley was found guilty of one of the most heinous crimes in Montgomery County history.'

Yet it was not over.

In River Plantation, a little way south of town, in an elegant ranch-style bungalow on a quiet road with the look of an old English village, the phone was ringing. Nowadays it was always ringing. Bill Srack answered it yet again.

Yet again he heard the angry silence, and then the sound of breathing before he hung up. It had started that Saturday night only a few hours after he had got home from court, desperate for peace. The reporters had followed him from the courthouse. He had sent them away, but that had not stopped them from announcing on the radio and television and in the newspapers in Conroe and in Houston, that the dissident juror who had refused to convict the black janitor was William A. Srack. So the phone had started ringing that Saturday night.

By Sunday, it was ringing so often that he had to take it off the hook. Then he would try and put it back on again and it would start ringing again almost immediately. Day after day it was the same, even now after a second jury had convicted the man. Mostly there was just the silence, but sometimes someone spoke. Like that very first call on Saturday evening.

Srack had answered the phone, all unsuspecting, and a man's voice had said: 'I'm calling you from Houston.'

It seemed a strange introduction. Srack waited. Then his heart sank as the man's bitter voice went on. 'You're a nigger-lover. You turned that nigger loose. You're a nigger-lover.'

Srack had started debating with him. 'You don't really know what all happened,' he said. 'I did what I thought was right.'

But the man from Houston was not interested. He used those words on him again and hung up. If they spoke, it was always those words. Sometimes it would be a man, sometimes a woman who said it. But mostly it was just the angry silence.

Bill Srack was struck by the sheer frequency of the calls. He could leave the phone off the hook for as long as he liked, but as soon as he put it back on it would ring again. Within seconds. It made him wonder whether there was some kind of electronic gadget you could rig up which would automatically keep dialling someone's number, or whether there really could be that many people out there who hated him that much for what he had done.

He called Jim Keeshan and told him about it. Keeshan said it was outside his jurisdiction, but he would see what he could do. Soon afterwards, the sheriff started sending patrol cars to drive past the house and occasionally knock on the door to make sure he was safe. Then an officer came down from Conroe Police Department.

He wanted to make a report. Srack told him that the phone rang every few seconds, though it was off the hook at that moment, and told him that it must be some kind of electronic gadget.

'You got any witnesses?' asked the officer.

Srack pointed to his neighbour who happened to be visiting, and she agreed that she had seen it happen.

'Well, we need two witnesses,' said the officer.

Srack asked him: 'Could you be a witness yourself?'

The officer agreed. Srack walked over to the phone and replaced the receiver in its cradle. He had just turned to walk back to his chair when it rang. The officer picked it up and listened. The line was silent.

The officer started yelling into the receiver. 'Now, listen here, you no-account son of a bitch, you got no damned business carryin' on like this. You hear me?'

Then a woman's voice answered. 'We gonna get you, nigger-lover.'

That was no gadget. Srack felt almost awed at the idea that there were real people out there who would devote so much time and energy to persecuting him. The officer hung up and said he would contact the phone company to see what they could find out.

Weeks later, he came back and said they had traced the calls and spoken to the people involved. But no one was going to be charged with anything and Srack would have to get a court order if he wanted to find out who they were. Anyway, the calls would stop now, the officer said. But they didn't. They just became a little less frequent as the months went by.

The case of Clarence Brandley was not over for George Morris or Don Brown. They wanted to get their client a new trial and so, pushing aside all their doubt and despair about Conroe and its courthouse, they set out once more to appeal to the selfsame courthouse for justice.

They produced a motion. It ran to 11 closely-typed pages and it spelled out 28 different reasons why Clarence Brandley should have a new trial. Their most important point was that there had never been enough evidence to justify a conviction and that the state had failed to exclude other reasonable explanations for the girl's death.

They exhumed the defeats of the last six months: the samples of blood and hair that were never taken from the white janitors; the depositions that were never ordered from them; the secret tape of Ranger Styles and Icky Peace; Brandley and dead bodies; Icky Peace and guns and clubs; Jo Ellen Parrish and her mysterious missing statements; the flare-up over whether Don Brown attacked the jury's verdict; Keeshan inviting the jurors to put themselves in the shoes of the dead girl's family; the jurors who had never been selected; the objections that had never been sustained; the questions that had never been asked. They added it all up and concluded that Jim Keeshan was guilty of a catalogue of misconduct, that he had repeatedly withheld evidence and deliberately misled the jury in order to harm Clarence Brandley. And they castigated Judge Martin and his predecessors for helping Keeshan along.

On 23 February, only nine days after the end of the trial, Morris and Brown filed their 28 different arguments with the court. The next day, they took it back and added two more – recalling the furious row over Brandley's bail – and filed it again on 13 March. Six days later, they were in court – the same court with the same bright blue carpet and the four gilt fans stirring the air overhead. And there was Judge John Martin on his dais and there at their side was Jim Keeshan, clean and smart and unfailingly polite as ever.

Morris and Brown had subpoenaed ten witnesses to give evidence about their 30 different arguments. Keeshan immediately attacked them. He wanted to quash all the subpoenas and send the witnesses home, but Judge Martin would not let him. Morris and Brown wondered if their old friend might be ready to fight free of the courthouse.

They called their first witness, Oscar Johnson. They wanted him to explain that Clarence Brandley had never had anything to do with dead bodies in his part-time work at Johnson's funeral home, and that Jim Keeshan had known that and had been misleading the jury when he suggested that Brandley's work there meant he had some kind of special indifference to corpses. Keeshan went on the attack again, insisting that Johnson should not give evidence, and that Morris and Brown had no business trying to bring in new evidence after the trial was finished. After a long debate, Judge Martin overruled Keeshan, and Morris and Brown began to feel that there might be justice in Conroe after all. Oscar Johnson said his piece.

Morris and Brown then tried to call Ranger Styles. They explained that they wanted him to talk about his secret tape-recording of Icky Peace and the fact that Keeshan had known all about the tape and about how it could help Clarence Brandley, and how Keeshan had been guilty of misconduct by failing to pass it to the defence. Keeshan attacked again. They should have brought all this up at the trial, he said. It was too late now. Don Brown said they had tried to bring it up at the trial, but this same Judge Martin had refused to let them use the tape as evidence and had refused to let them recall Icky Peace to question him about it. This was their first chance to bring it up. Judge Martin paused and then agreed with Keeshan. Ranger Styles could not give evidence.

Morris and Brown tried to call Icky Peace to talk about the things he had said to Ranger Styles in the secret tape. Keeshan said Peace should not be allowed to give evidence, and Judge Martin agreed again. Morris and Brown tried to call Gary Acreman to talk about how he had never had to give samples of his blood or hair. Keeshan said Acreman should not be allowed to give evidence, and Judge Martin agreed again.

Morris and Brown watched helpless as one witness after another was sent away without testifying. Keeshan kept objecting and Judge Martin kept agreeing. Seventeen times in a row, Keeshan objected to the defence strategy and 17 times Judge Martin agreed with him. Finally, Morris and Brown tried to call Keeshan himself to give evidence. Keeshan objected strenuously and said he should have to testify on only one issue – his attempt to find Jo Ellen Parrish's statements in which she claimed that Brandley abducted her with his old shotgun and tried to rape her. Judge Martin agreed.

Keeshan then told the court that he and his staff had searched diligently for the woman's statements but had found nothing except a few notes of his own. The defence – still hoping to prove that Jo Ellen had embellished her story at the prosecution's request – asked to see them. Keeshan claimed the defence had no right to see them, and Judge Martin agreed. Keeshan concluded that Jo Ellen Parrish had never made any statement. Then Brown landed a blow. He reminded Keeshan that at the end of the first trial, after the jury had failed to come to a verdict, Judge Sam Robertson had revoked Brandley's probation and refused him bail, and later written an order in which the judge explained that one of his reasons for doing this was that: 'The defendant is presently on probation for possession of a short-barrelled firearm, during which offence a female named Jo Ellen Parrish was allegedly raped.'

But Jo Ellen Parrish had not given this evidence until the second trial, five weeks later. So Brown wanted to know how Judge Robertson could possibly have known about it – unless Jo Ellen Parrish had made a statement about it all which had been given to the judge.

Keeshan started talking fast. He was not sure. Perhaps he had mentioned it to the judge on the telephone when he first took the case. Perhaps the judge had somehow learned the woman's name himself. Or perhaps not: he believed the judge must have asked Jerry Winfree for the name. Or perhaps the judge had just seen the name on the witness list for the trial?

Pressing his advantage, Brown asked for Judge Robertson's order to be put into the record of this hearing. Keeshan objected that it should not be, and Judge Martin agreed. Brown said he would call Sam Robertson to ask him in person how he had learned about Jo Ellen Parrish and her alleged rape. Keeshan objected that Judge Robertson should not be allowed to give evidence. The judge said he would recess for a while to think about it, and then he came back and agreed with Jim Keeshan. Judge Robertson would not be called.

Morris and Brown said they had run out of witnesses. Between them, the District Attorney and the judge had dismantled their entire case. All they now asked for was a few days to prepare briefs outlining their points of law. Keeshan objected and said the court should rule now, and Judge Martin agreed. Keeshan then argued that there was no reason to hold a new trial. And Judge Martin said he agreed.

Finally, Keeshan asked him to pronounce the formal sentence of death on Clarence Brandley. Judge Martin agreed and told Clarence Brandley he would be kept in the Texas Department of Corrections until the Court of Criminal Appeals in Austin had heard his appeal, after which a date could be set for his death.

Morris and Brown went back to their offices to lick their wounds. Brandley was taken northward back to Huntsville.

The Brandley case was not over for *Houston City Magazine*.

That spring, the magazine ran a story, which spanned two issues and became a landmark in the case. For the first time, someone outside the defence camp with no axe to grind suggested plainly and publicly that Clarence Brandley was being railroaded. And the magazine had new evidence to support the claim. The story succeeded for the first time in peeling a layer off the secrecy which concealed the police and the Texas Ranger and Jim Keeshan as they worked to convict Clarence Brandley. It was Icky Peace who showed the way.

Peace talked to *Houston City Magazine* a few months after the trial. Away from the courthouse and the limelight, the little janitor relaxed and told for the first time how a police officer had turned to Clarence Brandley and told him that, since he was a nigger, he was elected to hang for this crime. He went on to say that he had told Jim Keeshan all about this, but the District Attorney had not seemed pleased. Peace recalled: 'They started shutting doors and everything else and said: "Don't you dare open your mouth about that. It would help get Clarence off because it would prove you were both threatened. How would you feel having a murderer out roaming the streets?" '

Peace then confessed that he had lied under oath at Brandley's trial: he had been asked if he had been threatened and he had denied it. He said it had got worse. Jim Keeshan had later warned him that if he ever told anyone about any of this, he would be prosecuted for perjury and could get two to ten years in jail. At the second trial, he had been asked if he knew that he could be jailed for two to ten years for perjury, and he had lied and said that was news to him.

The magazine recorded the denials of the District Attorney and the Conroe police. But to Clarence Brandley and his family, and to George Morris and Don Brown, it seemed like confirmation of what they had always believed: the people in the courthouse had been playing dirty behind the scenes.

They had to fight on, somehow uncover a new witness, retrieve a hidden clue and throw everything into an appeal to the court in Austin. This was not over yet.

The machine stalled. Brandley sat in jail, waiting for his attorneys to put an appeal together. His attorneys sat in their offices, waiting for the courthouse to produce the official record of his case. The courthouse produced nothing.

Every week or so, Don Brown would track down the court reporter whose job it was to type up a transcript of Brandley's trial and put all the evidence together for the official record. Brown liked the court reporter, a cool, elegant – in fact, beautiful – woman named Mary Johnson who had been hired by Judge Martin. Her hair was so blonde it was white and she wore it in a tight bun, drawn back from her handsome face. She was well into middle-age, but every man in the courthouse seemed to be in love with her. Brown and Morris sometimes drank with her over at the Iron Horse. Every time Brown asked her how she was getting on with the Brandley record, Mary Johnson told him that she was working on it. She apologized: it was such a long trial. Brown said he understood. It was not unusual in a big case like this.

Every month or so, Don Brown would track down the District Clerk, Peggy Stevens, in the courthouse and explain that they were still waiting for the record and he would file a motion asking for an extra 60 days to prepare their appeal. The District Clerk was not warm and friendly like Mary Johnson.

Peggy Stevens was always immaculately dressed and perfectly poised and entirely polite. She was as sweet as saccharin, and just as genuine. She had worked in the courthouse for more than 20 years, ever since she left college, and she looked upon the people who ran it as her family. Jim Keeshan was her favourite boy. Anyone who criticized the courthouse was picking a fight with Peggy Stevens.

Courteously, Peggy Stevens would pass the motion to Judge Martin, who would grant the defence their extra 60 days.

Brandley sat in jail. He wondered how his children were, one hundred miles away in Houston. He missed almost everybody. But he did his best to keep his cool as the months rolled by. August came. He had spent one whole year behind bars. September came. It was his 30th birthday – his second birthday in jail. Maybe he would be free by the time the next one came around. Maybe not. Maybe he would die here. His life had stalled.

Brandley's family were becoming desperate with impatience.

They had been trying to raise more money to cover the cost of this appeal. It was going to be at least $25,000. Where were they going to find that kind of money? They scraped out their savings. Tim had sued his old employers because they sacked him for whistling at some girls, and he gave his $10,000 settlement to the defence fund. They put the message out far and wide through the black churches and community groups: an innocent black man is being railroaded. They asked for help and they began to get it. Money started to trickle through, from Conroe and from Houston, even from as far away as Dallas. People heard their preachers talk about this Brandley case and they reached into their pockets to send a dollar for a good cause. But where was the appeal? What were Morris and Brown doing up there?

It began to seem to the family that they were not doing enough. Some of them began to say they should never have lost this case in the first place and they should never have let that jury sentence Clarence to death like that. Some of them began to say they needed new attorneys for the appeal.

By the time November came, the family decided to try something new. They had gathered together the $25,000 they needed, but instead of taking it into the courthouse square for Morris and Brown, they headed southward down I-45 to Houston, to the office of the most famous defence attorney in Texas, Percy Foreman.

In November 1981, Foreman was past his prime. Now aged 79, his big, broad frame was just beginning to sag with age, his hair was white, his face was like tree-bark, but he was still a powerful figure, still able to pummel and pound a witness into submission, still joyfully chopping down district attorneys and liberating his clients, still churning out orders from behind his king-sized desk where all the legal papers and the uncashed cheques almost buried the sign which warned his visitors 'Don't Fuck With The Wizard'.

The Brandleys wanted the wizard. Like anyone else who had ever read a newspaper in the state of Texas, they knew his reputation. He was fearless and completely contemptuous of all forms of authority – particularly district attorneys. He pulled tricks and staged stunts that had never been written up in any law book. He got into fights. He was rude and he was a bully, even to his clients.

He would often refuse point-blank to take a case. But he was a winner. He won cases where other attorneys begged for a plea-bargain. He had robbed the executioner of so many victims that he had lost count – at least 1,500 of them. If he took a case, he would fight until he won it. The Brandleys wanted a winner.

The first Morris and Brown knew of the family's decision was a week later, on 3 December, when Peggy Stevens passed them a formal notice which she had received from Percy Foreman's firm, announcing that they were now representing Clarence Brandley.

The two attorneys felt as though they had been slapped in the face. When they found out that the Brandleys had paid their fee to Foreman, they felt as though they had also had their wallet taken. But it was not just a matter of pride, or even money. This case was now really important to them. It had become a symbol of everything that they had been fighting against all these years. Small towns and mean people. White people and black victims. If ever they had wondered, they had stopped doubting long ago that Brandley was innocent. He was the ultimate victim. They believed they could prove it and, if they kept fighting, they could win a great victory. If they were not going to be paid, that was bad news, but they still wanted to fight.

George Morris called Percy Foreman. He knew him from years back when he was fresh out of law school and had gone to work for him briefly in Houston. Foreman was instantly embarrassed, and angry at the Brandleys who had not told him that other attorneys were still working on the case. He told Morris that they must all work on the case together. They would sort out the fee as they went along. So a new team was born.

In January, the stalling finally stopped. And instantly, Don Brown knew that something was wrong.

It was 21 January when he got the formal letter, headed 'State of Texas vs Clarence Lee Brandley', from Peggy Stevens. 'This is to advise you that the record is complete in the above styled and numbered case. You now have fifteen days in which to file any objection to said record.'

Brown managed to get Brandley sent down from Huntsville to help him check the record. It was a big job making sure that everything was accurate. If there was a mistake, it could cause them trouble later at the appeal. And it was not just the transcript of the last trial, which Mary Johnson had finally finished and which ran to more than 2,000 pages. There were xeroxes and descriptions of all the exhibits: the precious few witness statements the defence had managed to obtain; the photographs they had finally salvaged; the 13 hairs and all the expert reports on them; the autopsy report; the dead girl's clothes with their spots of blood; Icky Peace's little armoury and his narcotics card. They were all registered and copied into the official record, while the originals were stored safely in the courthouse. They all had to be checked within 15 days. That was when Brown, with his bulldozer mind, first became suspicious.

Each day he would go over to the courthouse, take the elevator up to the fourth floor and sit quietly with Brandley in his cell while they both read through all the papers. Odd things soon caught his eye. Some of these witness statements, for example, had been put into evidence during the first trial when there was a different court reporter there who always marked her exhibits with little stickers – blue ones for the defence and yellow ones for the state. Brown knew them well. But these xeroxes did not show the stickers. Then there was something wrong with some of the exhibit numbers: the xerox of the exhibit in the record would have one number, but when it was referred to in the trial transcript it would have another. That made no sense. They were all numbered during the trial. How could the numbers have changed so that they no longer matched? There was something else, too. There were two exhibits which had not been copied into the record at all. The xerox of Icky Peace's narcotics card, for example, was nowhere to be seen.

Brown went off to see Peggy Stevens. He told her there was something wrong with the record. 'It's like it wasn't made up from the originals or something,' he said. 'There's something wrong.'

Peggy Stevens shrugged and smiled at Brown. 'I'm sure I don't know what could have happened,' she told him.

'Well, I want the originals.'

The District Clerk smiled sweetly again. 'They are up in the exhibits room, Don. I'll see what I can do for you.'

'All right, then. I'll come by and have a look this afternoon.'

'Sure, Don. I'll be sure and get them for you.'

Brown had the feeling he was on to something, but he was damned if he knew what it was.

That afternoon, Brown returned to Peggy Stevens' office. The District Clerk showed him a box of papers, but as soon as he looked at them he could tell they were not right.

'These are the same as the copies we've got already,' he grumbled. 'They got no stickers, Peggy.'

'Well, I don't understand that, Don.'

Brown shook his head. He was beginning to simmer. He was not sure he understood either, but he had an idea of someone who might. 'I got to go see Keeshan about something in a minute. I'm gonna find out what he knows about this.'

Brown strode off to pick up some papers and then found his way to the District Attorney's office, pondering the mystery, scenting trouble. But he got no joy at the DA's office, just Keeshan's secretary, Kathy Olson, telling him that Jim was not there at the moment and she really couldn't say when he was going to be available. She was real sorry.

Brown's temperature was now well past boiling-point. As politely as he could, he told Kathy Olson that he knew damn well that they were up to something and he was going to get to the bottom of it. Then he shambled off, cursing Keeshan under his breath.

Don Brown's difficulties were soon the joke of the month all over the courthouse. Everyone was talking about how he had stood in Peggy Stevens' office, raving and raging at her, and then how he went and stood outside Jim Keeshan's office, raving and raging at Kathy Olson. In the DA's office they loved it. Poor old Don, they said. Best joke in a long time.

The truth was that not everyone enjoyed the joke.

People in the courthouse knew things, things they had heard in the offices, or had read in private papers. They let them go by. They heard stories about Jim Keeshan and the Brandley case and they put them out of their minds. They knew all about the project to convict him, but it was not exactly their business. But the truth was that not all of them enjoyed it. Some of them were beginning to feel bad about it. Some of them were feeling it was maybe time to stop being innocent bystanders.

It was only a couple of days after Don Brown's run-in with Peggy Stevens. He and Brandley were still poring over the record of the case, trying to list all the mistakes and missing exhibits. They had less than a week before their work had to be complete. Brown was now convinced that there was something seriously wrong, and that Peggy Stevens was deliberately covering up, but he was still trying to find out just what it was. Brown was also trying to earn a living, and every so often he would have to leave Brandley to go down to the courts to represent other clients. It was on one such visit that Frank Robin took him aside.

Robin was new to the courthouse. He was a sharp young attorney, only in his late 20s, tall and dark with a clean-cut Superman kind of look about him. He had just been hired out of private practice as an assistant to Jim Keeshan. Brown had dealt with him on a couple of cases and found him personable enough. Now Robin took him into his office and closed the door. He was nervous.

'Look, Don. I'm going to tell you something. But you must hold it in confidence. I'll get fired if this gets out. You understand?'

Brown said he understood.

'I got to tell you this thing.' He paused again and then plunged: 'You see, the evidence in the Brandley trial has gone.'

Brown looked at him. 'Gone?'

'It's gone. Almost all of the original exhibits, so far as I know. I thought you ought to know.'

'Well, I've been trying to figure it out. What in the hell happened?'

Now Robin told his story. Mary Johnson had been working on the trial transcript and she had not got round to making xeroxes of all the exhibits for the record, when the whole lot had just disappeared from her office. He did not know how it had happened, whether it was accidental or deliberate, but he knew it was a big secret. This had happened several weeks back, around the second week in January, and ever since then they had been trying to cover it up. They had agreed that the defence would not be told. Judge Martin was in on it. So were Keeshan and Peggy Stevens. Jim Keeshan and his secretary had been making copies of everything that they had in their files and then trying to reconstruct anything that was missing. They had been desperate to throw the defence off the scent. Keeshan had been saying privately that he was going to blame some janitor who worked in the courthouse for throwing everything away. Keeshan had even been out to the rubbish dump with Judge Martin and Mary Johnson to dig around in an effort to find the exhibits, though there was no telling if they had just been going through the motions.

Brown laughed for a moment. He had seen them. He remembered looking out of his window several weeks ago and seeing the three of them going off somewhere in the middle of the afternoon. He had wondered about it at the time. Now, he could just imagine Keeshan and Martin in their sleek suits, and Mary with her $200 shoes, all poking around on some fly-blown rubbish dump in the freezing cold. Still, this was serious. The more he thought about it, the more serious it got.

He thanked Frank Robin and promised he would keep his confidence, and then padded quietly back across the courthouse square to his office to think. There were several angles to this.

First, there was the deceit by the other side. The District Attorney, who was supposed to have a code of conduct, had been conspiring with the District Clerk, who was supposed to be an impartial public official, and with the judge, who was supposed to be independent of all sides, to cover up the destruction of this evidence. Brown found it hard to believe that this cosy little club had only just been formed. All through the trial and then during the hearing to win a new trial, Morris and Brown had felt that they were somehow the victims of a conspiracy. Now, for the first time, he could prove that the bastards had been working together. Improperly. Unjustly.

Brown could see that they were trying to stall him so that his 15 days for filing objections to the record would be over before he could find out the truth. He remembered Peggy Stevens, about ten days after the destruction of the exhibits, primly informing him that 'the record is now complete in the above styled and numbered case'. That was a lie. And then smiling sweetly and saying 'Yes, Don, of course, Don', and promising to get him the originals when she already knew they were gone. Then leaving him standing helplessly outside Keeshan's office.

But this was not the first time in the history of Texas that exhibits had been lost. There was an established procedure for both sides to come to court and reconstruct the record. But in the established procedure, the courthouse was not supposed to cover up the loss. Why had they done that? Brown could only begin to guess, but it smelled of foul play.

First, the semen swabs from the dead girl. Then Brandley's pubic hair. Then the photographs from the day of the crime. Then Jo Ellen Parrish's statements. Now, everything else. All lost and gone forever. How were they ever going to impress the Court of Criminal Appeals with Icky Peace's narcotics card if they could not show it to them so that they could see how realistic it was? Or his gun, or his club? Icky Peace could now start pretending they were just toys from his imaginary city.

The photographs were gone too. There was one particular picture of the dead girl which Brown thought was vital. It had been taken in the morgue, and it showed some sort of reddish-brown stain on her backside. That stain had not been there in the earlier pictures taken in the props loft. Brown saw this as evidence that she had emptied her bladder after she was dead, on the way to the morgue, staining herself with her blood in the process. That knocked a big hole in the timing of Jim Keeshan's version of events, since it suggested that she had been killed before she went to the restroom, before anyone claimed that Clarence Brandley arrived on the scene. Now the evidence was gone.

Then there were the hairs. Perhaps they would ultimately prove to be the most important evidence of all – the best clues to the real culprit. Now they were lost and gone.

How many coincidences does it take to make a conspiracy?

Brown went to see George Morris. Then he talked to Percy Foreman's office in Houston. They had to do something about this. The real irony was that, whatever they decided to do, they had to go back through the same courthouse to do it.

They moved cautiously. They could not confront the

courthouse with their knowledge without running the risk of exposing Frank Robin as their source. Besides, it would be interesting to watch Keeshan and his friends trying to keep up their charade without realizing that the audience had seen through them.

They scheduled a hearing for 5 February, just inside their 15-day limit and filed a straightforward motion, in which they listed all the discrepancies which Brown and Brandley had noticed in the record, and innocently asked for the originals to be brought to court. At the hearing, they listened politely to the other side's poker-faced explanation that it might take them a while to prepare for such a hearing. They agreed to wait a week. All that the defence asked was that Brandley should be allowed to stay in gaol in Conroe in order to help them to continue to review the record. Judge Martin immediately ordered that Brandley be returned to Huntsville that day.

A week later, Judge Martin agreed to give the State a little more time to prepare themselves before having to produce the original exhibits in court.

The defence watched them play. Don Brown was still wrestling with the tactical problem of how to confront the courthouse without exposing Frank Robin. He could not tell how many people knew about this and whether Robin could be identified as the source if he went public with what he knew. He was slumped in his office late one afternoon, trying to clear a patch through the problem, when his phone rang, and he heard a familiar voice.

'It's Jan.'

Jan? It was Janet Dial, Judge Martin's old secretary. Brown had not heard from her for months. She had left the courthouse a few months after the Brandley trial had ended, disenchanted with the atmosphere she had found there.

Janet Dial was not the sort of person who wasted time making her point. 'Don,' she said. 'Mary Johnson just called me from the courthouse. She's scared to call you direct but there's some things you ought to know. It's about the Brandley case.'

Brown had not confronted Mary Johnson about the flaws in the trial record she had produced. Now he suggested that he and George Morris should meet the two women.

'I don't know if Mary will do it,' came the reply. 'I tell you,

Don, she's frightened of those people in the courthouse. But I've told her that you have to know what's happening. I'll try and get her to come, but we can't meet in town. Someone might see us.'

Brown started to take notes as Janet Dial directed him to some God-forsaken spot out by Lake Conroe. They were to meet there at seven that evening.

'You won't tell anyone, will you, Don?'

'Don't worry. Y'all be there and we'll meet you. We won't say a word to anyone.'

That courthouse was fraying at the edges. Brown hurried through to Morris's office to tell him the news.

It was the kind of night when trees come down on power lines and anyone with any sense stays at home. George Morris pointed his old Plymouth Sedan up Interstate 45 and peered through the windscreen wipers at the lights ahead. He had given up smoking, but that did not stop him coughing. Brown lit up another Malibu in the passenger seat in what he hoped was a discreet fashion.

They had spent the last hour trying to anticipate what it was that Janet and Mary could want with them, whether it could be the missing exhibits or something else. This was obviously no social engagement. They just had to wait and see. Twenty minutes out of Conroe, Morris swung off the freeway and headed west down an old farm road that cut a narrow path through the pitch black shadows of the pine-trees. The wind was thrashing the rain against the windscreen. There were no more lights now. Ten minutes down the farm road, Lake Conroe opened up like a black hole on their right-hand side. Then Morris saw what he was looking for: a rectangular patch of asphalt leading down to a jetty at the water's edge. On a spring day it was a peaceful little cove for a quiet picnic, a good place to launch a pleasure-boat. On a night like this it was plain scarey.

As soon as he turned off the road, his headlights caught the outline of a black Chevrolet, sitting still and dark at the edge of the asphalt. Morris stopped and switched off his lights. For Chrisesake, thought Brown, what were they doing here? Two men of advancing years playing around like Burt Reynolds. Supposing it was a set up?

Clutching their jackets to the front of their chests, the two attorneys ducked out of the car, butted their way through the splintering rain and heaved themselves into the back seat of the waiting Chevrolet. The two women had been trying to smoke themselves out of a nervous breakdown. Brown lit up again and Morris coughed quietly.

Mary spoke first. She was plainly frightened – of losing her job or her court reporter's licence or of getting into trouble with the courthouse. 'You can use what I'm going to tell you,' she said. 'Just don't use my name.' Morris and Brown agreed that they would not use her name unless there was no alternative. Then Mary poured out the whole story of the missing exhibits. She had to tell them because there was a cover-up in the courthouse. The exhibits had all been in a box in her office while she had been working on the record, and she had come in one Monday morning – she thought it was 11 January – and they had vanished. She just could not believe it. She was so worried. Then there had been this cover-up.

Morris and Brown, still anxious to protect Frank Robin, pretended that this was the first they had heard of any missing exhibits and encouraged her to tell more.

As soon as she had found they were missing, Mary said, she had gone to Judge Martin and told him. He had told Keeshan and Peggy Stevens. She had assumed they would try and sort it out with the defence, but instead the judge had ordered her to keep it quiet, and on no account to say anything that could leak to the defence attorneys because they would just make a big deal about it.

'Damn right we would have,' said Brown.

According to Mary, Keeshan and the judge had tried to fix it so that the defence would never find out what had happened. They had all agreed together that Peggy Stevens would keep fobbing them off, so that they would have time to fake everything they needed to make it look like they still had the originals. And that day when Don had been left standing outside Keeshan's office, he didn't know the half of it, she said. The truth was that as soon as Don had told Peggy Stevens that he intended to raise the matter with the District Attorney, Peggy had called the DA

and the judge to warn them. That was why he had been left
standing outside – because Keeshan had heeded the warning and
sent his secretary out to fob him off. Peggy Stevens had been
laughing about it.

Don Brown shook his head in disgust. It was hard to believe
that there was a man's life at stake in the middle of all this. These
people just did not give a damn about that black man.

Mary said that Keeshan had worked out a story to explain
everything if they got caught. He was going to say that one of
the janitors in the courthouse had thrown the exhibits away by
mistake. It was nonsense, she said. The janitors never went into
her office. They were under permanent instructions not to go in
there. She did her own cleaning. And even if for some reason they
had gone in there, they could not possibly have mistaken the
exhibits box for rubbish: Peace's gun and the knives were clearly
visible.

But there was someone else who did have keys to her office:
Jim Keeshan. Mary described how her secretary had been working
late one evening when suddenly someone turned a key in the lock
and opened the door. It was Jim Keeshan with his investigator,
Charlie Ray. They had been surprised to see the secretary there,
and had said something about wanting to make a diagram of the
office and that they would come back another time. Mary was
not saying Keeshan had taken the exhibits. She really did not
know. She was just saying she never believed a word of this story
about janitors.

In the back seat, Brown's mind was whirring, trying to figure
this out. If it was no accident by the janitors, it had to be either
the State or the real murderer. The murderer could never have got
into Mary's office without breaking the door, so it had to be the
state. They must be worried about losing the appeal and figured
it would be better to tell the town that they could not stage a
retrial than to go to trial and lose.

Now Janet had something to say. She explained that she had
been very worried all the time she had worked for Judge Martin
and she had felt there was such prejudice against Brandley in the
courthouse.

Then she told them the secret that had been worrying its way through her memory for months now – how Jim Keeshan and Judge John Martin had been holding secret meetings all through the Brandley trial. She knew these were no social get-togethers, because sometimes they were still talking as they came out and she had heard them discussing the Brandley case.

Mary Johnson cut in. She, too, knew about the meetings. 'They were kind of rehearsing things,' she said. 'Rehearsing rulings and objections, you know, so that they could get things their way in court.'

Morris and Brown swore gently through the smoke. All these years they had worked with the law, believing in what they were doing, believing in the system, believing that even a black man in a white town could get something like justice if they worked hard enough at it. Now this. This was even worse than the missing exhibits. It struck right at the heart of the justice that was supposed to reign in that courthouse. If the judge and the prosecution were colluding, then the whole trial was a charade, just a fancy ritual with a foregone conclusion, and this whole system they believed in wasn't worth a handful of dust. Yet it was no surprise. So many times in that trial, they had fought and lost and failed to see the reason why.

'Those scumbags,' said Brown. 'I knew it. I just knew it.'

The secrecy that had surrounded the investigation of the Brandley case now had a fair-sized hole in it. Looking through it, Morris and Brown were torn between disbelief and anger.

The four talked a little longer in the back of the smoke-filled Chevrolet and then parted through the storm.

Now they could go on the attack. Morris and Brown spoke to Percy Foreman's office, and on 16 February they fired a new motion into the courthouse in which they said explicitly that 'the defence has reason to believe that the original exhibits are missing' and insisted that all the available exhibits should be produced in court. Judge Martin finally agreed that this should happen on 5 March. The defence prepared for a show-down.

Before the hearing, however, Frank Robin surfaced again. Once more he took Don Brown into his office, recited his prayer for confidentiality and then told Brown he had discovered that the

District Attorney had deliberately suppressed information which he should have passed on to the defence during the Brandley trial. According to Robin, the DA had received a call from a woman who said she believed Icky Peace might have killed the girl at the high school. Her reason was simple and personal: Peace had once lived with her family and, when she was 18 years old, he had tried to sexually assault her. Keeshan's investigator, Charlie Ray, had taken a statement from the woman and then they had buried it. Robin showed Brown a copy of the statement but insisted that he could not keep it.

Brown was no longer surprised by what he heard. There was no telling whether the story was true. This woman could be telling a pack of lies, but any District Attorney in the country knew that that kind of information should have been shared with the defence, particularly when they were trying to show that Icky Peace was a reasonable alternative suspect. But what could he do with it now? The trial was gone. He could not even put it into the appeal since new facts had to be entered within 30 days of the end of the trial, and that time had long passed. They could only store it away and try to find a use for it later. Brown thanked Robin and pledged to cover his footsteps.

Next it was Judge Lynn Coker's turn to break cover. Morris and Brown had never distrusted Judge Coker the way they had most of the judges in the courthouse. He was always affable and he meant well. His problem, they had always found, was that he did not have the heart to stand up to the courthouse. He was the judge who had allowed Sam Robertson to keep his grip on the Brandley case when Morris and Brown had first tried to recuse him.

He came from a family of East Texas attorneys. His father, Ernest, had a fearsome reputation. As a county attorney in the 1930s, he took the controversial confession from Bob White which was later rejected by the Supreme Court in Washington. As a judge, Ernest Coker later presided over the trial of the police officer who was cleared of murdering Greg Steele. His reputation for toughness and harsh dealings had not prevented Don Brown from recusing him back in 1978. Shortly after that the old man had stepped down, and his mild-mannered son Lynn had been put up to replace him. Lynn Coker had probably never in his life stood up to his father and he would not now stand up for anything if it was going to cause trouble. Almost shyly, he approached Morris and Brown in the courthouse and called them into his office.

'Has anybody told you that the Brandley evidence is missing?'

Don Brown wondered just how many more informants they were going to develop in this courthouse.

'No one has told us officially,' he said. 'But we've heard scuttle-butt around the halls. We know that Peggy Stevens won't produce the exhibits.'

'Well, it's no longer rumour,' whispered the judge. 'I have it from an unimpeachable source.'

'Well, thank you, Judge.'

'What I can't understand,' Judge Coker confided, warming to his theme, 'is how they could carry on like this without telling the defence attorneys. It just boggles the imagination.'

'It boggles ours too,' said Brown.

'Anyway, I can't tell you any more,' said the judge, who was already scurrying away. 'I can't tell you anything officially. You understand.'

Early in the morning of Friday 5 March 1982, a jailer led Clarence Brandley out of his cell. He had been in the cell for a year. It was nine feet long and three feet wide. The front was made of bars so that he could always be seen by a passing guard. It contained his bed, his Bible and his library book. Brandley had been learning to live on Death Row. He found he had to fight a little. There were officers there who liked to give him a hard time, put him on discipline charges when he had done nothing; that kind of thing. But he could handle it, mostly by keeping his head down and minding his own business. The real big fight was inside himself.

He felt so bitter and so angry, but he knew he could not let himself feel that way. It would just destroy him, eat through him like acid. So he tried to get a grip on himself. He stopped smoking. His brothers thought that was strange – to quit cigarettes right when he needed them. He made himself fast for one day each week. So he felt clean and he felt like he was making a decision about himself. Everything in here was taken away from you, not just freedom, but self-respect. Every little thing in your life was decided for you: what to watch on television, when to eat, what to eat, what to wear. But when he fasted, he got a grip.

He taught himself to meditate. He would get up early, not when they decided – but when he decided: about 4.30 every morning. And he would read his Bible and sit, calm and quiet with his eyes shut, and just be easy, try and drain all that bitterness away.

Right now, he couldn't say that he was winning the fight. But he was trying.

Morris and Brown spent the morning in their office making final preparations for the big show-down. If they played it right at the afternoon's hearing they just might be able to find out who had taken those exhibits, and that might just take them to the heart of the conspiracy in the courthouse. The phone rang. Brown answered.

'It's Jan.'

Morris watched as Brown's face hardened and his intake of smoke increased dramatically. He stopped work and waited. Brown finally hung up the phone and banged his fist down hard on his desk. It seemed that Mary Johnson had just been talking to Janet again. Mary was terribly upset. She had sat in on a meeting the previous evening between Jim Keeshan and Judge Martin. It had been a late meeting, after everyone else had gone home, in Keeshan's private office. The subject of the meeting had been today's hearing. Mary said she had watched the District Attorney and the judge plotting together to fix the hearing so that the defence would not be able to call any witnesses or uncover any evidence about what had happened to the exhibits.

Right in front of Mary, the DA and the judge had agreed that as soon as the hearing started, the DA would offer to save time by giving evidence in person about his investigation into the disappearance. The judge would agree and Keeshan would then explain that, after a diligent investigation, he had concluded that unnamed janitors had accidentally thrown the exhibits away. He would go on to say that there was no evidence of criminal intent, and therefore no janitor would be put on trial for anything. Then, when the defence tried to call their own witnesses, Keeshan would object that he had already given all the facts and that the witnesses should not be called, and Judge Martin would agree. So the defence attempt to get to the truth would end.

George Morris was deeply offended. 'It's like a banana republic. Except that you probably couldn't get away with that kind of thing in a banana republic.'

There was little time to act. The two attorneys quickly agreed that, for the third time in the case of the State of Texas vs. Clarence Brandley, the judge had stepped so far out of line that he would have to be removed by recusal. In haste, they drafted a motion to remove John Martin from the case. This too was quickly achieved, since they now had the format for a recusal permanently filed in their computer.

They had no time to revive the long history of their unhappiness with the judge during the trial and the subsequent effort to win a new trial. Nor did they touch on the secret meetings which, Janet Dial had now told them, had been taking place since the judge first took on the case. They simply accused their former friend John Martin of meeting secretly with the District Attorney to rig that afternoon's hearing and of plotting for nearly two months to conceal the disappearance of the exhibits – 'the clear intent of such conspiracy being to illegally deprive the defendant of an effective appeal.'

Just before 1.30 p.m., the two silver-haired attorneys crossed the street to the courthouse where they found Brandley waiting in the courtroom, and told him what was happening. Brandley smiled quietly and shook his head – how could he not be bitter when people treated him like this?

As the clock in John Martin's court moved round to 1.30 p.m., Morris and Brown felt a terrible weight settle over them. John Martin, once their friend, had sunk so low. The man they had once had such faith in had succumbed to all the rottenness in the courthouse and all the lowest and nastiest demands of this community. He had put Clarence Brandley's life in jeopardy. George Morris felt particularly bad. He was the one who was going to have to stand up and confront Martin. They had decided they would do it in private, in chambers. It seemed to have helped with Sam Robertson that they had given him the chance to go gracefully without public exposure, and it might make it a little easier on them too. It was 1.40 p.m. when the judge finally walked into court.

Morris immediately rose to his feet and asked to go into chambers. The judge agreed, the press and the few spectators trooped out and Morris rose again. Brandley stared unblinking at the judge in his robe as Morris explained that they understood about the missing exhibits and the various steps that had been taken. He paused, and his voice broke a little as he stumbled on.

'We also understand, judge, that we are not going to be able to put on any witnesses here this afternoon in regard to our motion; that it is all going to be conducted by the District Attorney where he is going to take the witness-stand and testify to his investigation and so forth.'

Brandley could see the fear creeping over Martin's face. He watched this man who had sat in judgement over him fumble for his pack of cigarettes, his fingers trembling.

Morris trudged on. 'We would like to ask the court, so that we can keep out any publicity or anything like that, for you to voluntarily recuse yourself from hearing this matter.' Morris paused. 'If you don't, then we have a motion in our file right now to recuse you from any further hearings.'

He had done it. Judge Martin was speechless, but Keeshan was quickly on his feet. To the astonishment of Morris and Brown, he started confirming their story. Yes, he said, he had been planning to save time by taking the witness-stand himself and he had asked the judge to let him do that. 'But as far as you not having the opportunity to put on witnesses, I am sure that was not my intention.'

Morris and Brown had learned not to underestimate Keeshan. He was quick. He could see that Morris and Brown were not just guessing here, that they had got some kind of informant, so he was not going to tangle himself up in denials. But he was still fighting, trying to limit the damage.

He had been conducting a criminal investigation, he said. He had no need to go telling the defence about such a thing. And Judge Martin should certainly not recuse himself. He knew more about the case than anyone. Morris and Brown started hammering away at the judge, Brown quoting chapter and verse from the canons of judicial conduct.

The judge finally managed to speak and admitted he was not sure of the correct procedure. Brandley was still gazing at the judge in silent contempt, watching now as he reached for a second cigarette. Suddenly, the judge seemed to feel the condemned man's eyes on his face, and he glanced up and instantly dropped the pack of cigarettes, like an admission of guilt.

The attorneys wrangled on. Finally the judge decided that he needed time to think. 'I might decide over the weekend to recuse myself. I don't know. At this time, I am just going to recess the case.'

They agreed to meet again in a week, by which time the judge would have decided whether to step down or face a formal recusal hearing in public. Judge Martin walked briskly out of the room.

By the end of the week, the Brandley case had its fourth judge – affable, ineffectual Lynn Coker. John Martin had never come back to the defence to tell them that he had decided to step down. Morris and Brown heard about his decision in the corridors of the courthouse and then read about it in the *Courier*, where the Judge claimed that he was leaving the case because he had 'personal knowledge of some missing exhibits'. Morris and Brown could not remember a case which had generated such bitterness. It was rare enough to recuse any judge, but to recuse three in one case in only 18 months was unique in their experience.

It was by no means certain that it was worth it. One after another, judges seemed to succumb to the oppressive influence of the courthouse and to the town's demands for the black man's life. Lee Alworth had become enmeshed in Jim Keeshan's plot to deny the defence evidence in the case and to cheat Brandley of his bail. Sam Robertson had plunged into the same tangle and then more or less joined the prosecution during Brandley's first trial. Now John Martin had been exposed for making secret deals with the DA.

One after another, they went the same way. As far as Morris and Brown were concerned, the judges were no different from any of the other good old boys who ran this town. The truth was that if they wanted to be re-elected every four years, judges could not afford to be any different. Morris and Brown held out little hope that things would change with Lynn Coker, the courthouse's cowardly lion.

On Friday 12 March 1982, Lynn Coker sat for the first time in the Brandley case to consider the vexed question of the missing exhibits. He opened the hearing by announcing that some janitors had apparently and inadvertently thrown away the box containing the exhibits and they had now been bulldozed into the ground at Montgomery County Sanitary Land Fill. With the help of Peggy Stevens, Judge Coker started listing the 166 exhibits which were lost and the 143 other exhibits which were not.

Don Brown was on his own in court. George Morris was ill. Now was the time to fight, now that finally, after two months, they had been told officially about the loss of the exhibits. Don Brown rose and said it was not good enough for the judge to announce a version of events like this. How could anyone be certain that this version was correct? They needed a public hearing with witnesses and evidence to try to establish the truth. Jim Keeshan objected that there was no need for any such hearing, at which point Judge Coker made his first ruling.

'That's what I think,' he said. 'I see no reason to have any type of evidentiary hearing in connection with how the exhibits became lost. The fact is they are no longer present in the courthouse.'

Keeshan claimed that it was the state that had suffered from the disappearance because they had to bear the burden of reconstructing the record. He took a swipe at the defence by suggesting that he could not have told them of the disappearance, since he was conducting a criminal inquiry and they were among his suspects. Brown insisted that they had a legal right to make a record of how they were lost, and that some of the missing originals were vital to their appeal.

'We have nothing on the record that is competent evidence to show that the exhibits were even lost,' he said.

'Well,' said Judge Coker, 'I'm competent and I say they're gone.'

'I still object to that because it is hearsay.'

'OK,' said the judge. 'You're overruled.'

Once again, the truth was being buried. And surely, thought Brown, this District Attorney would not be so keen to bury it if he honestly believed that the truth could hurt the defence. No, if Keeshan was not involved in the disappearance of the exhibits, then at the least he knew something about it which he was frightened of. But Judge Coker was not interested.

The two sides then embarked on a detailed negotiation in which they agreed to correct the errors in the record which had been made by Jim Keeshan and his friends in their hurried efforts to cover up the disappearance of the originals. But there was nothing they could do about the dead girl's bloodstained clothes, or Icky Peace's narcotics card or his weapons, or the photographs, or the vital hairs that had been left on Cheryl Fergeson's body. They were all lost forever – and with them, perhaps, the chance of proving Brandley's innocence.

It was during that April of 1982 that George Morris learned that he had cancer of the lung. By the summer he knew he was dying. Don Brown found it hard to imagine working in Conroe without him. It would never be the same. Brown's only hope was that Morris would survive for long enough to see them somehow break through on the Brandley case. Now that they had finally got the official record, they could file an appeal. And it would be a strong one. They could describe the flimsy, insufficient evidence, package up all the bias and all the prejudice and present it to the Court of Criminal Appeals in Austin.

The court in Austin was not always reliable. Its nine judges were elected by the public and had in the past been guilty of allowing their politics to interfere with their judgements. There was obviously a risk they might think that a ruling in favour of Clarence Brandley would alienate some of their white voters. But this appeal would be strong enough, Brown believed, to cut through any political undergrowth.

The trouble was that Brown was finding it almost impossible to put the appeal together. Foreman's office was so busy in Houston that they could not work on it. Morris could not help. Brown himself was still working unpaid and was trying to run other cases through the courthouse to earn a living. Then in July, his 18-year-old son, Bo, was almost killed in a car crash. That threw Brown off the tracks for a while. He had brought up Bo and his daughter, Celia, alone. Their mother had died when they were children and now he took time off to heal his son, whose head, neck and back had been badly crushed.

Finally, in the autumn, Brown decided that Brandley was never going to get an appeal unless he took it on his shoulders alone. He stopped all other work and buried himself in his office. After several weeks of solid study, he emerged with 75 pages of pure aggression. Here was the whole horrible saga – the factual details, the legal arguments, the relevant cases, and the inescapable conclusion that an innocent man had been wrongly convicted and sentenced to death.

He filed it with the Court of Criminal Appeals.

Several months later, the court replied. Appeal briefs could be no longer than 50 pages, they said. Brown would have to cut back his argument.

This made Don Brown angry. He knew all about the 50-page rule. He had been told that all he had to do was to file a motion asking to go over 50 pages and, in an important case like this, it would be all right. He had done that and the judges in their wisdom had decided that their bureaucratic rule was more important than the truth about an innocent man on Death Row. Brown was not about to give up. He took his 75-page brief to his secretary.

'Can we print this a little bit smaller and reduce the margins and kind of run it right down to the bottom of each page?'

The secretary said that was no problem. A few days later, the brief had been magically reduced to only 47 pages without losing a word. Brown then added a few extra points to take up his full 50 pages and sent a copy off to Percy Foreman for his approval.

In January 1983, a full two years after the trial, the appeal was finally lodged in Austin, where the judges accepted it without comment. Morris, though terribly weakened, saw it on its way.

Two months later Jim Keeshan filed his brief, and the court in Austin rolled slowly into action. They announced that they wanted both sides in the case to travel to Austin to argue their points.

By this time, Percy Foreman had passed the Brandley case to his young partner, Mike De Geurin. Foreman and De Geurin were one of the oddest couples ever to grace a courtroom. Foreman was as tough as a tree, a big-boned, bare-fisted, heavy-handed prize-fighter of an attorney. Mike De Geurin was a clear 12 inches shorter, as gentle as a child, with his face almost permanently creased by his impish grin. He was everybody's favourite guy. De Geurin was a boyish, blond version of Peter Falk playing Columbo – the same air of harmless innocence and twinkling charm, the same rather deferential stoop and then the same sudden outbreaks of high-speed insight and lethal intelligence. District Attorneys had learned to fear his charm, just as they had learned to respect his old partner's aggression. Foreman loved him like a son.

Don Brown and Mike De Geurin agreed that they would go to Austin together to share the arguments. Austin was familiar ground to both men, but particularly to De Geurin, who had worked there as a clerk when he first left law school. Some of the judges there remembered him, if only because he had once ruined their ceremonial exit from the court at the end of a case by secretly locking the door through which they paraded, with the result that all nine judges stood up together, wheeled to the left, headed for the door and then piled into each other, creating a human concertina at the back of the court.

Before they left for Austin, Brown and De Geurin reviewed thousands of pages of transcribed hearings, checked witness statements and scientific reports, talked to Brandley in Huntsville and finally felt that they were ready for anything that the court could throw at them. They hardly dared to admit it, but they could not see how they could lose. Even without the missing exhibits, no serious court could ignore this wealth of argument.

The hearing started badly. The judges announced that each side could have only 20 minutes to state their case. Brown and De Geurin took ten minutes each and did their best. Jim Keeshan was there to reply. Despite the restriction on their time, they felt they had done well. De Geurin had never seen a circumstantial case that was so weak, and he doubted if the court had either.

Now they waited.

Brandley waited on Death Row – a place which had now become more scary than ever. For years, no one had been executed in Texas. The US Supreme Court had closed the door at the end of Death Row and made the executioner redundant. But on 7 December 1982, as Brandley waited for his appeal to be filed, the courts had opened the door again, and a young black man named Charlie Brooks had been led through it, to the big building in the middle of Huntsville, to the stretcher in the brightly lit room and the doctors with their catheters. Brandley would never forget that day.

Charlie Brooks had been on his wing, three cells down, and during recreation periods Brandley had got to know him. He had told him all about how he was being railroaded. On the day that Charlie Brooks was taken away, they had let him come down the wing and shake hands with people through the bars at the front of the cells. He had stopped outside Brandley's cell and said goodbye and shaken hands. Then as they led him off he had turned and said: 'You hang in there, man.'

As if there was some consolation for him in thinking that Brandley, at least, might one day be free again.

Everything changed on Death Row once Charlie Brooks had gone. Until then, everyone there had always believed that the death penalty was finished and that their sentences would all be overturned and commuted to life in jail. Then when Charlie Brooks went, and they started the killing again, nobody was safe any more. Nobody knew who was going to be next. Nobody knew what to expect.

Brandley tried to stop worrying about it, while he waited.

Don Brown waited, too. It was a miserable time.

Frank Robin, his old contact in the District Attorney's office, succumbed to disaster. Robin had left Conroe in July 1982 and gone to work for the US Attorney's office in Houston. There, he had been accused of soliciting a $200,000 bribe from drug dealers he was investigating. The Justice Department had been scandalized by the case and the US Attorney General in Washington DC had played tapes of Robin allegedly extracting money from the criminals to President Reagan to stress the need for a war on drugs. Now, in the summer of 1983, Robin was jailed for ten years. Brown wanted to believe it was all a mistake.

Then there was his son, Bo. By the spring of 1983, he had been climbing back to health and he no longer wore the halo brace around his head. Brown started to hope he would recover completely. Then in June, the boy was involved in another car crash, and this time it killed him.

Brown was still reeling from the blow when, two months later, George Morris finally succumbed to his cancer.

Now, Brown waited alone for the court in Austin.

A year rolled by. It was 1984. Still there was no word from Austin. The sticky summer heat enveloped Conroe. Clarence Brandley was just approaching the end of his fourth year in gaol when a group of people he had never heard of, and who had never heard of him, dealt him a bruising blow.

The US Supreme Court in Washington DC, hearing a completely unrelated case, decided that if a man had a hung jury and was then convicted in a second trial, it was only the most recent trial which should be considered in his appeal. Previously, the courts had always said that both trials should be considered: if the man's first trial ought really to have ended in his acquittal, then it was unfair to expose him to a second trial. Now the Supreme Court had changed the rule.

By doing so, they had wiped from the record the whole history of Clarence Brandley's first trial and the behaviour of Judge Sam Robertson, and they had kicked one of the legs out from under Don Brown's appeal.

Brown cursed their luck and cursed the long delay.

It was around this time that he found himself out on Route 105 in a roadside diner. He was just stopping for a glass of iced tea when he saw a bunch of Montgomery County deputies sitting at a table, talking and laughing. He went over to say Hi and they showed him what it was they were laughing about – faded photographs of a black man being burned at the stake outside the

courthouse in Conroe. Brown glanced at them just long enough
to see the boxes and the flames and the white people watching.
Then he left and cursed Conroe too.

Still the judges in Austin had more important things to do than
to consider whether Clarence Brandley was innocent. It was the
spring of 1985. Just outside Conroe, a black student who was
hitch-hiking on I-45 was abducted by four men, who bound
him, beat him and then covered him with tar and feathers before
abandoning him in a field. In May, four and a half years after his
conviction, two years since his appeal was filed, the judges finally
published their ruling. It was a disaster.

The judges in Austin tore the defence apart point by point and
emphatically confirmed Brandley's conviction. At every turn, they
supported Judge Martin and Jim Keeshan.

The judges not only satisfied themselves that there was plenty
of evidence to show Brandley's guilt, but added that there was no
evidence to even suggest that anyone else had committed the
offence. They approved the use of Danny Taylor's claim that
Brandley had lusted after a group of schoolgirls. They were content that Monty Koerner had been asked about Brandley's previous record. They were happy with the restrictions on evidence
about Icky Peace's armoury and about his taped conversation with
Ranger Styles.

At one point, they considered the moment when Jim Keeshan
had accused Don Brown of attacking the jury's verdict by appeal-
ing to any lingering doubts they might have. Brown had objected.
The judge had started to overrule his objection but had swallowed
his words. According to the transcript, Judge Martin had said:
'Okay. Over . . . Let's proceed.'

The Court of Criminal Appeals decided that this meant that
Judge Martin had not really overruled Don Brown's objection
and, therefore, that he had nothing to complain about.

The nearest they came to conceding anything to the defence
was over Jim Keeshan's suggestion to the jury that they should
put themselves into the shoes of the dead girl's family. That had
been an error, the judges conceded. But it had been a harmless
one, they added, and needed no action on their part.

The defence immediately asked for a re-hearing of their appeal. The court refused. It was over.

Don Brown and Mike De Geurin could only guess at the reasons for their failure. Maybe it was electoral politics and those judges were plain scared of taking on their white voters. Maybe it was judicial politics and they preferred not to join such heated criticism of the Montgomery County courthouse. Maybe the missing exhibits had harmed the defence. They could only guess. All they knew was that they had been beaten and that Clarence Brandley's life was now in real danger.

The despair in the defence camp was matched by the excitement in the courthouse. The mood there was sparkling. Not only had they won the Brandley case, but Jim Keeshan had been rewarded for his years of service as District Attorney by being promoted to a judgeship in a new court which was being created in Conroe.

Before being sworn in by Judge Lee Alworth, Keeshan was praised to the skies in the courthouse, where his supporters boasted that he had won 99 of the 100 jury trials he had fought. Keeshan accepted his new power with modesty. 'I intend to be the best kind of judge as I know how,' he told the *Courier*.

Judge Keeshan's first job was to swear in his successor as District Attorney. The man chosen was Peter Speers III, a lanky, fresh-faced young attorney from Pennsylvania who had settled in Conroe, where he had been working as Keeshan's assistant for three years. Speers had little of Keeshan's sharpness or experience, but it was a popular appointment in the courthouse: what Peter Speers lacked in charisma, he made up for in loyalty. He was brother-in-law to Judge Alworth. Peter Speers was reliable.

The excitement did not stop there. Now that the court in Austin had thrown out Brandley's appeal, there was only one more move to make to put the black janitor out of their lives.

On 22 November 1985, Clarence Lee Brandley was led through the corridors of Montgomery County courthouse. He was surrounded by armed men. His wrists were handcuffed and locked to a chain which ran around his waist. He was steered through a set of double doors and into a chair.

The room was full of people. Some of them he recognized:

Mike De Geurin; Peter Speers, the new DA; that Peggy Stevens woman with her strawberry-coloured fingernails. Keeshan was there, too, making small talk with his friends. Back on the public benches, Brandley could just make out his mother. She was hunched into a ball, crying into her fists. Brown arms held her tight. Now the judge came in. Brandley knew him, too. It was John Martin.

It only took a minute. The words just trickled past him and left no trace. Except for the date. 16 January. Less than two months. The words said that on 16 January he had to go through the door and be strapped to the stretcher like Charlie Brooks so they could finish him off. Brandley tried to show nothing on his face. He did not want to look sad in case his mother saw him.

The judge was trying to make a big deal about how he was not going to have him put to death before Christmas. As if he were doing him some big favour by killing him three weeks later. Brandley looked straight into the judge's eye. He did not want to yield to these people. He kept his grip.

As they led him back through the corridors with the chains and the armed men, his mother rose from her bench and her eyes rested on the shape of James Keeshan, and her voice soared over the courtroom like a hovering hawk: 'I'm gonna pray for you,' she sang, like a slow chant: 'I'm gonna pray for you, Mr Keeshan. How can you kill Clarence for something he didn't do? I'm gonna pray for you.'

Keeshan dropped his head and hurried from the room.

Mike De Geurin watched him go. So they had an execution date. He had hoped and believed it would never come to this. It was a sickening moment. And there was something wrong with the way it had finally happened. What was John Martin doing setting the date of execution? He had been forced to step down from this case more than three years ago. This case was no longer any of his business.

De Geurin guessed he could have stopped him doing it, but he let him go ahead. It might give them some handle to grab hold of, to get the execution stalled if all else failed. All the same, it seemed wrong.

In the beginning, only a few people in the courthouse knew the truth.

Mary Johnson, the elegant court reporter, knew. She had been sitting next to Judge Martin when the District Clerk, Peggy Stevens, had come up, as excited as a schoolgirl at her first dance, and talked to Judge Martin about it. Some of the people who worked in the District Clerk's office knew. They had been there when Peggy Stevens had come in and started boasting about it.

Soon, the truth was being whispered all over the courthouse. Judge Martin had got back on the Brandley case because Peggy Stevens had asked him. She had no business doing that, but that was how things were in the courthouse. She had a special reason. It was the date. That was what she wanted. 16 January: because 16 January was her birthday. She wanted the black man to die on her birthday. As a gift, so they could all celebrate. She had asked the judge to fix it for her. And the judge had agreed.

7

Mike De Geurin was at home in Houston. It was a Sunday evening and in amongst the children's toys and the television, he was shuffling through his paperwork trying to get ready for the Brandley hearing in Conroe the next day.

He was just finishing off when the phone rang. It was W. B. Etheridge, a veteran attorney from Conroe who had worked on the courthouse square all his life. He had been born in Conroe and his father had been editor of the *Courier*. Etheridge had a reputation as a decent man, and he had followed the Brandley case, not just because the whole courthouse was still talking about it but also because he knew the Brandley family. Minnie Ola had worked for his mother and had more or less raised him. When Clarence had got into trouble over the rusty shotgun back in 1979, Etheridge's firm had represented him and settled the plea-bargain.

He told De Geurin he had read that there was a hearing coming up on the Brandley case. 'I just wondered if Peter Speers ever told you about Brenda Medina.'

'Brenda who?'

'Brenda Medina,' said Etheridge. 'She's a client of mine.'

'I never heard of her.'

'Well, she came to me a while back and told me that her husband had confessed to killing that girl up at the high school, right back when it happened, he confessed. So I took her over to Peter Speers's office so she could tell him.'

De Geurin's mind was spinning trying to get a grip on this.

'You telling me that this woman says the murderer confessed to her?'

'That's right. She says her husband confessed it.'

'And she has told this to Peter Speers?'

'I took her over there. That was several weeks ago now. They interviewed her. Speers didn't tell you?'

'The son of a bitch never said a word.'

'Well, I was afraid of that,' said Etheridge. 'So I thought I'd give you a call.'

'And I'm very grateful to you. I can't think of any better way to wind up a weekend than to get news like this.'

De Geurin paused a moment and then asked the big question. 'So, who is her husband?'

'He's called Robinson. James Dexter Robinson. He used to work at the school.'

De Geurin loved his work. People used to say he won cases because he put his heart out on the counsel's table and let the jury feel the way he felt. It was not a matter of tactics. There were some times when he just got caught up in the emotion of it all. That Monday morning was one of those times.

He left home early to drive to Conroe, with W. B. Etheridge's words playing in his mind and a tight knot of excitement sitting in his stomach.

Ever since Judge Martin had set a date for Clarence Brandley's death the defence camp had been fighting for time, using the ancient legal device of applying for a writ of Habeas Corpus to force the court to justify Brandley's incarceration. They had started raising any issue that had not been destroyed by the court in Austin.

De Geurin had brought in reinforcements. He had been working on his own with Percy Foreman, who was now too old to make court appearances and could do little more than lie on the couch in his office, barking orders and playing the wizard. De Geurin had told Foreman they had to get help and Foreman, irascible as ever, had said that was fine by him so long as De Geurin did not mind paying for the help out of his own wages. De Geurin had agreed and hired Paul Nugent.

Nugent was an odd addition to the odd couple. Foreman and De Geurin, for all their differences, were both full-time Texans, as happy on horseback out on their ranches or telling tall tales in a bar in the boonies as they were raising hell and bending rules in a courtroom. But Paul Nugent grew up in New Jersey and went to law school in Boston, on the other side of the universe, and he looked, sounded and even thought, uncannily like Bobby Kennedy.

Still, De Geurin liked him the very first time they met, down in Galveston in the federal court where Nugent was working as clerk to one of the judges. That job said a lot. A bright, well-groomed, well-spoken young lawyer like Nugent with a good degree could have walked into one of those $300-a-minute law firms in Manhattan and sat there with his meter running, earning a fortune working for some big corporation. But he had avoided that and deliberately looked for work out on the edge, where the money might not be so good but the cases would mean something. The fact that he had landed a federal judge as his first employer suggested he knew his law. And he laughed at De Geurin's stories.

The first day Paul Nugent walked into his new office, half-way up a skyscraper in downtown Houston, he shook hands with the wizard, hailed Mike De Geurin, and was pointed at the Brandley 'file', which consisted of a dozen big cardboard boxes, stuffed with thousands of pages of legal papers. Nugent devoured it all. He had no affection for the death penalty. At college, he had taken up public speaking so that he could attack capital punishment. It was that experience which had persuaded him to become an attorney.

Within weeks of the date being set for Brandley's death, De Geurin, Nugent and Don Brown had put together enough arguments to apply for their writ of Habeas Corpus. Their strongest pitch had been one of the little nuggets of information passed to Don Brown by Frank Robin – that the DA had suppressed evidence of Icky Peace having once attempted to assault an 18-year-old girl. They said that this suppression had denied Brandley due process. They had added three more issues: the photographs which had been lost by the Conroe police and which might have proved that Brandley was not wearing a belt on the day of the crime; a juror from the second trial who, they had discovered, had been discussing the case with friends while the trial was still going on; and the deliberate rejection of any juror who opposed capital punishment, a policy which, they said, inevitably produced a 'conviction prone' jury.

Peter Speers had fought them, but on 6 January, just ten days before Brandley was due to die, the defence had succeeded in winning a stay of execution. Now six months later, on 17 June 1986, they were preparing to stage a hearing on the four issues they had raised in their Habeas Corpus writ.

Until now, De Geurin had not had much to fight with; but now, as he drove through the outskirts of Conroe, with the knot of excitement still tightening his stomach, he was looking forward to the next round.

He parked on the courthouse square, which was already warming up for another day at melting point, and hurried over to Don Brown's office with his battered briefcase full of papers. He passed old Mr Gentry's menswear shop on the ground floor, now abandoned and empty, and the blown-up black-and-white photograph of a smiling George Morris which Don Brown had fixed at the top of the stairs, as if Morris was still watching over his old work.

De Geurin had already discovered that Brown's brain was like a gigantic filing cabinet. He not only had an entire library of Texas criminal justice tucked away in there, but also the whole history of the case of Clarence Brandley, stretching back over nearly six years now, all dated and catalogued and ready to be retrieved. De Geurin told him all about Brenda Medina and James Dexter Robinson.

'Robinson?' asked Brown. 'There was a Robinson came up in evidence.'

De Geurin could almost hear Brown's brain clicking and whirring. Then he retrieved what he wanted: towards the end of the second trial, Brandley's old supervisor, David Harris, had talked about a set of keys that had gone missing. They had belonged to Icky Peace, but Peace had given them to a white man who had briefly worked at the school with the janitors. That white man's name was Robinson.

'The son of a bitch,' said Brown. 'But he wasn't James Dexter. He was Clarence – Clarence Robinson. But they've got to be connected.'

The hearing was due to start in the courthouse. The question

was how to use this new information. There was no point in
throwing it straight into court without following it up. They
needed to find this Brenda Medina, and check out everything they
could discover about James Dexter Robinson, particularly whether
he was related to Clarence Robinson and whether he could have
had those keys to let himself in and out of the auditorium. If it
checked out, it was the biggest and best break they could have
hoped for. But it would take time. For today, they had to hold
back. Except for one interesting little game they could play with
Peter Speers III.

De Geurin had never had any illusions about Jim Keeshan. He
had always had a good relationship with him, because he had
played along with the white man's courthouse and sat around
while they all made jokes about niggers. But De Geurin had never
trusted him and he was glad he had been promoted out of the
case. He wondered about Speers. The new District Attorney had
an innocent, maybe even honest, look about him. De Geurin was
toying with the idea of trying to talk to him privately, to appeal
to some decent streak in him and suggest that they should all
work together to save this innocent man. It was only an idea.
Now Don Brown suggested that he would test it, in public. They
agreed on a plan.

The hearing was before Judge Lynn Coker. That, in itself, marked
a small victory for the defence. Judge John Martin had done his
best to take over the case again. After setting the death date he
had continued to act as though he was in charge, ignoring the
recusal which had swept him out of court three years earlier. But
the defence did not want him there. They regarded him as a
ringleader in the attack on Clarence Brandley and believed that
his presence was a guarantee that Brandley would die.

Late one spring afternoon, De Geurin took a copy of the recusal
papers and went to see Martin in his office in the courthouse. Like
Morris and Brown before him, De Geurin had known Martin as
a defence attorney and had previously thought well of him. He
reckoned there was no need to go back to court to recuse him
again. He just walked into his office and told him that he had no
business in the case. Martin did not take it well.

'All right,' he said. 'All right. You can get some other son of a bitch to look him in the eye and tell him he is going to die.'

'Well, you know you have been recused . . .'

'All right. All right. You think I care?'

And with that, Judge Martin grabbed a large box of Brandley papers from the side of his desk and with his arms stretched round it, he started heaving himself out of his office, prising open the door with his toe, and then staggering down the corridor towards the District Clerk's office with it, muttering all the while: 'All right. That's just fine with me. I'm off the case. That's just fine.'

At that moment, Don Brown happened to be passing. All he saw was the judge in his black robe, red in the face with exertion, straining to hold the box of papers, while he kicked helplessly on Peggy Stevens' door, which had, unfortunately for Judge Martin, already been locked for the night.

Now, with Judge Lynn Coker back on the bench, De Geurin prepared. He was not about to telegraph his punch. He played along with the hearing. He raised a new issue about Brandley's trial – the fact that every potential black juror had been excluded by the District Attorney. He argued with Speers, who was complaining that things were moving too slowly and demanding a speedy execution. Then just as Judge Coker was about to close the hearing, De Geurin set his test for Peter Speers.

'One further thing, to keep this from being piecemeal on down the road, I would ask the prosecutor at this point, if there is any other exculpatory evidence which has come to their attention in this death penalty case that they are willing to pass on to me so I can add that also on to the writ of Habeas Corpus?'

Speers shook his head. 'Your Honour, that's not our burden. I don't know of any exculpatory evidence – period – in this particular case.'

De Geurin had got his answer. They were trying to bury Brenda Medina's lead. Peter Speers had just failed the test. He was no different from his predecessor. The judge set a new date for the hearing and told both sides that they should be ready with their witnesses for 17 July. They had exactly one month to find out the truth about James Dexter Robinson and to loosen the noose round Clarence Brandley's neck.

Richard Reyna grew up tough. His father was Italian, his mother a Mexican-American. He was one of nine children who were crammed into a hole-in-the-wall apartment in a crime-riddled housing project in Houston with one stove and one bed for all the children, the girls on one side, the boys on the other, all head to toe. He got an ass-kicking a day. When he was seven his father died, and things got worse.

It was not just his toughness that made Reyna a natural-born law officer. He was also street-wise and smart as a whip. People talked to him because he would keep playing parts and pulling strings and teasing them along until they wanted to tell him every secret they had ever had. And like most law officers he was conservative, an active member of the Republican party, with pictures of presidents on his wall and a basic faith that, if the American way of life could rescue him from the ghetto, it could rescue anyone. He believed that by becoming a law officer he could help people who grew up like he did, and rescue more of them from the ghetto and its crime.

His only problem was that he became a law officer in Montgomery County Sheriff's Department in Conroe. He could handle the racism. As soon as he joined the sheriff's department, his new colleagues started calling him Poncho and Chillibean, so Reyna, who had the build of a small bull, told them in all seriousness that if they did that again, he was going to have to tear their tongues out and stuff them up their asses. No, the problem came through trying to rescue people.

Once, a woman from Montgomery came in and said three of her horses had got out of their field and strayed on to her neighbour's land, and the neighbour had just gone ahead and shot two of them – one in the eye and one in the leg. She had complained to the police in Montgomery but they had done nothing, because the neighbour happened to be the mayor of the town. Reyna called him up and the mayor laughed at him. So Reyna went out and arrested him and locked him up and helped the lady from Montgomery. He made himself no friends in high places by doing so. Another time, he tried to help a woman who had been beaten up by her husband, but her husband was one of the county judges in Conroe and he came and kicked in Reyna's office door and demanded to see the file. Reyna told him to get his fuckin' ass out of his office and again made himself no friends in high places by doing so. Then there was the businessman who was keeping illegal Mexican immigrants in a filthy shed in Conroe and paying them starvation wages. Reyna gave the story to a television reporter in Houston but the businessman complained and his complaint mattered, because he was paying money towards the election campaigns of most of the people in high places in Conroe.

It all came to a head in 1983. Reyna was accused of taking bribes. The sheriff, most of his deputies, the District Attorney, and most of the people in his office all said that Reyna was corrupt. Reyna worked his butt off trying to find out what had happened and when the case finally came up in front of the Grand Jury, he produced his own evidence. The Grand Jury declared that he was innocent and then filed a perjury indictment against the deputy who had pointed the finger at him. But though Reyna was exonerated, Sheriff Joe Corley sacked him because, during his fight to clear his name, Reyna had spoken to the press without permission. Reyna was out of work, aged 37.

That was when he became a private investigator and revived his dream of trying to rescue people, and that was when he became a permanent pain in the butt for all the people in high places in Conroe. Reyna often worked for the attorneys on the courthouse square, serving papers and chasing down information. He had worked for Don Brown, and Brown liked him. They shared a deep contempt for the courthouse and its ways, and neither of them had any patience with the racists in town. With only one month to get to the truth about James Dexter Robinson, Brown, De Geurin and Nugent turned to Richard Reyna for help.

Reyna's first aim was to talk to Brenda Medina, but nobody knew where to find her. Not even her attorney, W. B. Etheridge, had a current address, and the District Attorney's office was not about to help. All anyone could tell Reyna about her was that she was a fat white woman with jet black hair and at least four children. Reyna got in his car and drove east out of Conroe about five miles, towards Cut and Shoot, where just about every trailer and every dusty shack had a fat white woman in it with a pack of children around her ankles.

It was 4 July, and it was hot. Reyna always hated the summer, and this was a bad one. He had only 13 days before the hearing in Conroe. He started knocking on doors, asking for Brenda Medina. He asked in the stores. He drove up into the hills and stopped anyone he saw. He tried the beer joints, the schools, the churches. If a building had a door, he knocked on it. On 5 July, in Midway, about ten miles east of Conroe, some people in a grocery store told him they thought they knew the name and reckoned she lived with a Mexican somewhere close by. Later that day, Reyna knocked on the door of a cramped wood-frame house which had more dust than furniture in it, and Brenda Medina answered it.

She was certainly a big woman – at least 15 stone – and with so many chins that her face seemed to be pushed back at a permanent angle. Two little girls clung to one of her legs like cats on a tree trunk. Reyna always tried to start off calmly with people, so he introduced himself politely and shook her by the hand and was startled when she replied that he was a son of a bitch.

It turned out that Brenda's mother had once complained to the sheriff's department that Brenda was not looking after her children and it was Reyna who had had to go and chew her out. Reyna remembered and immediately tried to turn this to his advantage, reminding her how well they had got on and how he had made sure she was never charged with anything. He started talking to her husband in Spanish and pretty soon, Brenda Medina calmed down and started to tell her story. Reyna turned on his tape recorder and let her talk.

She recalled that it was back in the summer of 1980 and she was living then with James Dexter Robinson and pregnant with their child. He had been out all day and she had gone to bed for the night. 'Let's see, it was about one o'clock, between twelve thirty and one o'clock, I guess, in the morning, and he come in, and he woke me up and he told me that he was going to leave.

'And I said "Well, that's nothing new because you leave all the time", and he told me that he had killed a girl, and I said "Oh baloney" and I turned over and that was the end of it. He told me, he said "No, I'm leaving and I'll tell you, I'll write you, or call you and tell you when I get there where I'm at. If you want to come to be with me, you can." . . .'

Reyna started to nudge her along. Had she asked who he had killed? No. Had Robinson said who it was that he had killed? 'He just said that he killed a girl at the high school and that he hid her well enough so that nobody would find her.'

Had he said where he hid her? 'No, he just said that he hid her well enough so that nobody would find her till he got out of town. The best I can remember, something about that he was gonna take a bus and I remember when I woke up at five o'clock, everything he had was gone.'

Except for one thing. Later that morning, when she had got up, she had found his tennis shoes still in the house, the ones he had been wearing the previous day. She told Reyna how she had found 'little pin-drops of blood' on the top of them at the front.

Reyna was watching her closely. She seemed to be telling the truth, but he needed more. Brenda told him she had not heard from Robinson again for more than a year. Then he had called from Greenville, South Carolina, to ask about his baby son and, during that call, he had asked her if the police had ever found out who killed the girl at the school. She had told him she didn't know; she never read the papers much. She had visited him in South Carolina once, but they had fought, so she had left; and now it was more than two years since she last heard from him.

She said she was scared of Robinson. He had often beaten her and her mother, and he had threatened her with knives. He had a gun, too. 'He was the kinda person that he could look you in the eye and stab you in the back at the same time,' she said. Reyna nodded his encouragement. She told him she had never really known whether to believe Robinson about killing the girl. She thought maybe it was just an excuse to leave, so that he did not have to pay child support for the new baby.

She had forgotten all about it until this May, when she was talking to a neighbour whose daughter was about to go to Conroe High, and the neighbour had said she was afraid to let her daughter go to the school alone because of the girl who had once been killed there. Brenda had told the neighbour she knew all about that killing because her boyfriend had talked about it. Then the neighbour had told her about this black man who was on Death Row for the crime. That was the first she knew of anyone being convicted of the crime, the first time she thought that perhaps she knew something important.

Brenda Medina said she had no use for blacks herself and that they should all be sent back to Africa, but she did not agree with the death penalty, because the Bible says 'Thou Shalt Not Kill.' So, a few weeks later, when she was in court because she had been accused of stealing some money, she told her attorney, W. B. Etheridge, what she knew. He had taken her to the District Attorney's office, where she had been interviewed by Charlie Ray, the DA's investigator. He had tape-recorded their conversation and she had agreed to take a lie detector test. That was about six weeks ago, she said, and she had never heard another word.

Reyna turned off his tape-recorder, arranged to meet her in Conroe during the next week, and drove home. He was not completely sure about her. She could be telling the truth, but she could just be trying to cause trouble for Robinson. He believed he might be beginning to pick at this knot, but it needed more work. He started reading through all the old trial transcripts. There were 12 days to the hearing.

In the meantime, Don Brown had learned that Robinson had a history of violence and that his latest wife, Berdie, was divorcing him and producing witnesses who said he had often beaten her, and had once knocked her out and put her in hospital for several months with injuries which may have damaged her brain. Even more significant, Brown learned that James Dexter Robinson was the son of Clarence Robinson who had taken the missing keys, and that both father and son had worked as janitors at Conroe High School in the summer of 1980. Finally, Brown recalled the blood on the dead girl's socks and how he had believed the girl could have given the killer a nose bleed. Now Brenda Medina was telling them that this Robinson had spots of blood on his tennis shoes.

On 8 July, Reyna met with Brenda Medina in Conroe and persuaded her to take a lie detector test. To his relief, she passed it. Lie tests were not foolproof but Reyna was beginning to feel good about the big woman with the jet black hair. And the more she talked about James Dexter Robinson, the more likely a suspect he became. According to her, he had a history of violence against women. One day she had come home early and found Robinson with a girl, who she guessed was a prostitute, tied to the bed, and Robinson and another man had been in the bed with her. She swore the other man was Gary Acreman. She said she was sure because Acreman had been round to their house several times, when he and Robinson were working together at the high school.

Now Don Brown asked Reyna to pursue a lead that had been nagging at him for nearly six years – old Ed Payne's story of how his son-in-law, Gary Acreman, had come home on the day of the killing quaking with nerves and talking about a dead girl whose clothes were in a school dumpster. Brown had never forgotten how he and Morris had been cheated out of the chance of talking to Payne. Now it was Reyna's turn to try and find out what Acreman really knew. It was 9 July, eight days to the hearing.

When Reyna arrived at the shabby little house in Grangerland, ten miles south-east of Conroe, he thought it was deserted. The place looked like it was still under construction. There was a big hole in the ground, full of water and with ducks swimming in it. There was junk everywhere – disposable nappies, fast-food wrappers, fast food, rotting cars. But when he knocked on the door, a small woman in her 50s answered. It was Ed's wife, Billie. She had nothing good to say about her son-in-law. As she told it, Gary Acreman had abandoned her daughter, Cindy, three years ago and never sent a nickel to support their two children. He was emotionally disturbed, she said, because his mother had been seeing three different men before he was born and Acreman was still trying to figure out who his real father was. Now his mother had died of cancer and one of his brothers was in jail for stabbing another brother to death in some argument. Billie was not sure how to find Acreman, but she had heard he had been seen drunk at Johnny Dalton's club in Conroe just last week.

Reyna kept her talking, hoping that Ed would turn up, but when he finally heard the sound of a car outside it was Acreman's deserted wife, Cindy, who stepped out. Reyna did not like the

look of her. She was a fat, blank-faced girl with long, lank hair
and a clumsy way about her. He had never liked dirty people, not
since he was a little boy in the ghetto, but he forced himself to
shake her hand and treat her warmly. At one point, he even put
his arm around her shoulder and let her greasy hair trail along his
sleeve. He told her she could help him. She could be like an
assistant investigator. He told her he could see she was a good
person, intelligent. He was trying to get to the truth and she could
help him do that. Would she like to do that? He gave her a smile
that twinkled like an engagement ring, and she said she would try.

She told him what she knew. Gary had always insisted that
Brandley was innocent, she said, and that he had told the District
Attorney's office several things that should have cleared Brandley,
but they had never done anything about them. She remembered
something about the girl's clothes being in the dumpster. Her
husband had mentioned it on either the day of the killing or the
following day. One other thing: Acreman was always going on
about a towel and about how Brandley never had a towel that had
anything to do with that dead girl. Then, in her new role as
assistant investigator, Cindy agreed to try and fix it so that Reyna
could interview Ed and also Gary. Reyna thanked her and told
her she would make a good police officer and said he would stay
in touch.

Two days later, on 11 July, Cindy Acreman brought Ed Payne
to see Reyna. They met in a roadside restaurant on the edge of
Conroe. In the five years since he had met Don Brown in the
courthouse, Payne had become even frailer, and had evidently
developed cancer in his throat. He now spoke through a metallic
microphone that he pressed against his voice box. The combination
of the noisy restaurant, Payne's East Texan accent and the microphone, made it impossible to understand what he was saying.
They moved over to W. B. Etheridge's office and there, finally,
five and a half years after his brother John called George Morris
with the story, Ed Payne told his tale to the defence. He confirmed
every word. Gary had come home on the day of the crime, knowing that a girl had been killed and worrying that her clothes were
going to be found in one of the dumpsters at the back of the
school. Gary had claimed that he saw a janitor drop the clothes

in there and he had wanted to borrow old Ed's truck to go back and get them so he could take them to the DA. Ed had refused and told him that if he had nothing to do with it he should stay away, in case the police caught him with the clothes before he had a chance to hand them over, but Gary had kept on.

Cindy agreed with this, and told Reyna that Gary had tried to persuade her to drive him in to the school. He did not want to use his own truck because he was having trouble with it, or maybe because he was afraid it might be seen. Ed Payne said he had lied to Don Brown when they met in the courthouse during Brandley's second trial, because he was scared of the DA and the police. Even now he did not want to talk about what had happened on that Saturday, when Charlie Hayden had come out to see him.

With only five days to the hearing, Reyna spent Saturday 12 July combing through bars in Houston looking for Acreman. He spent hours sitting outside some hole that Acreman was supposed to drink in, but he saw no sign of him. At home that night, he called Cindy. She was still trying to be an investigator and proudly announced that she had been in touch with her husband and fixed to meet him the next day at nine in the morning. Reyna had to be there, she said, and pretend that he had followed her to the meeting. She gave him directions to a roadside store miles away in south-east Montgomery County. Reyna said he would be there. He was glad she was not in the room with him. He might have been tempted to kiss her.

Reyna sat and waited. There was no air-conditioning in his car. He felt like he was beginning to melt. He watched the cars flit past on the road. None stopped. He wondered whether this was Cindy's idea of a joke. Then he saw her over by the store. And he saw Acreman, too, climbing out of an old Cadillac El Dorado.

As Cindy and Acreman talked, Reyna left his car and strode over, took a deep breath and introduced himself. Acreman looked at him as though his soul had just taken leave of his body and started to tremble visibly. Reyna then calmly added that a young man by the name of James Robinson had made an extra-judicial confession to the murder of Cheryl Fergeson and that he needed to talk to him about it. Acreman's fingers were now quivering so violently that he could not get his cigarette pack out of his breast pocket. Reyna nearly offered to help him, but thought better of it.

Reyna explained that he wanted to ask Acreman about some things which his family had been saying about him and turned on his tape-recorder. Acreman, who had managed to juggle a cigarette into his mouth and light it, began to calm down a little. Then he began denying everything that Reyna put to him. He had never said anything to anyone about clothes in any dumpster. He had never asked anyone to take him back to the school. His wife and father-in-law were both lying. He never knew a girl had been killed until the next day when Cindy's mother came home with the paper. 'I remember that like it was yesterday,' he said. Reyna moved up a gear.

'Was James Robinson there that day?'

Acreman looked perplexed. Reyna needed to know. If Acreman confirmed that Robinson was there, then that made Brenda Medina an honest witness, and it made a liar out of Gary Acreman who had never mentioned Robinson's presence in all these years. It would mean he was truly loosening the knot.

Acreman nodded.

'Yes, he was?' asked Reyna, trying to conceal his excitement. 'You saw him at the school?'

Acreman nodded again. 'Yes.'

Reyna paused a moment. He felt as if he held Clarence Brandley's life in his hands. He wanted to be sure that Acreman knew what he was saying. But as he pushed, Acreman started to stumble. He said he did not know whether he knew James Robinson or not. Reyna tried to reassure him that he was not trying to cause him trouble. Acreman said again that he thought he had seen James Robinson at the school.

Reyna changed direction. Did he still say he had not seen anyone throw anything into a dumpster? Acreman said he knew nothing about dumpsters. He had known nothing about the girl until the Sunday. He knew nothing about any of it. Then Cindy, still psyched up and trying to be Reyna's assistant, joined in, reminding her husband that she had been there and she knew he had tried to borrow her father's truck to go back to the school. Acreman frowned at her.

'I don't even remember asking, asking that.'

'You did,' said Cindy. 'I said I wasn't driving.'

Reyna reminded him that Clarence Brandley's life was at stake, and asked him whether he really believed his wife and his father-in-law would lie about him. 'You're telling me here in front of your wife that you didn't ask for the truck to go back to the school and help the District Attorney's office?'

Acreman sighed and changed his story. 'Yeah, I was gonna help the District Attorney's office.'

That made Ed Payne an honest witness, too. But Acreman would give no more. The three of them talked on. Reyna could see Acreman was coming to the end of his patience so he steered the conversation back to the crucial issue – James Dexter Robinson. This time, Acreman said he was sure he knew who Robinson was and finally he made the concession that Reyna was waiting for: 'He was definitely there that day.'

'He was definitely there?' asked Reyna, still trying to double-check. 'You saw him? What time did you see him? Do you remember?'

'I seen him that morning.'

That was good enough for Reyna. He did not believe for one moment that Acreman had told him the whole truth, but he had put James Dexter Robinson in Conroe High School on the morning of 23 August 1980, and that could be enough to slip the knot on the noose around Clarence Brandley's neck.

The trick now was to gather more evidence so that Acreman would not start backsliding and denying the story when they got him into court. It was time to go and see the other janitors. Reyna had four days to the hearing.

If it was possible, John Sessum's home was even dirtier than Cindy Acreman's. It was not even a real house, just a little wooden shack that had once been painted green, off a back road not far from the Acreman place in Grangerland. There was an unmade bed, a chair, a blackened sink and one hell of a mess. The shed smelled strongly of urine and also of wet dog. It had no air-conditioning, and in the July heat, it was Reyna's idea of hell.

He had been tracking Sessum all day, chasing around bars trying to find his address. Finally, he had found someone who said Sessum had got himself a job bicyling round the back roads picking up old tin cans and bottles. So Reyna had driven up and down the back roads south-east of Conroe until finally he had seen a shabbily dressed man hunched over a bicycle, peddling unsteadily down the road. Reyna had stopped him and stood right there by the roadside and told him about James Dexter Robinson's extra-judicial confession.

Sessum had looked at him for a moment. Reyna had been able to smell the beer on his breath and see the grit that lined the creases of his face, his hair matted against his scalp, his skin blistered with sweat and the old bar-room scar over his right eye. Reyna had waited and watched as this ruined face had suddenly collapsed into an expression of the most complete sadness, and John Sessum had slowly drawled: 'I was afeared I should have to take it to my grave.'

Reyna had put the bike in his car and driven him home. Now, sitting in this cesspool of a shack, he was beginning to regret it, when suddenly, as if some almighty hand had reached down to save his sensibilities, Reyna heard footsteps outside. It was Sessum's neighbour, a woman named Mattie Johnson, who had seen Reyna's car and wondered if he would prefer to come up to her house to talk to John. Reyna agreed very quickly. Settled in cleaner and cooler surroundings, Reyna started to question Sessum again on what it was that he did not want to take to his grave. He soon realized that this was not going to be easy. Sessum was confused, his memory fouled by years of alcohol abuse. He was also very nervous. He would not tell Reyna why, but there was no doubt in Reyna's mind that he was worried about something.

He could not or would not say whether James Robinson had been at the school. But he described Gary Acreman doing something that had never come out at any trial. As he told it, Acreman had seen this blonde girl walking down the hallway towards them as they stood outside the cafeteria that morning, and Acreman had said she looked real good and then started talking to her.

Sessum was sure of it: Gary Acreman had been talking to that girl who had died. And something else. Just after he talked to her, Gary Acreman had gone missing for maybe 30 minutes.

Reyna wanted to know why he had never mentioned this before. Had he told the District Attorney? Sessum refused to say. Had he told anyone about this? Sessum nodded slowly and said that he had told the Texas Ranger about Gary Acreman disappearing, and that the Texas Ranger had told him they had already got their man. When he gave evidence at the first trial, Sessum said, he had travelled into Conroe that morning with Gary Acreman and Acreman had threatened that if he mentioned anything about his talking to the girl or disappearing, he would be in trouble. Then the Texas Ranger had told him that he should say that Clarence Brandley had disappeared for 45 minutes and not to mention anything about Acreman disappearing, and that if he said anything different, he could go to jail.

Sessum said he did not like niggers. Nor Mexicans, for that matter. But the truth was the truth, and it was time to tell it.

Reyna pressed him for more of the story. What about James Robinson? What had Acreman said to the girl? Had Acreman touched her at all? Was Robinson there when Acreman spoke to the girl? What had happened to the girl? But Sessum would go no further.

'That's all I know,' he said.

Reyna grinned at him. 'I know damn well that's not all you know, John.'

Sessum suddenly glared at him, and Reyna could see for the first time the kind of drunken temper that had earned him his barroom scar. 'Well, goddam, that's all I'm gonna tell you.'

Reyna thanked him. He could see the lies crumbling, all the twisted strands falling apart. Still, he wanted more. He had three days to the hearing.

Don Brown had one more lead stored away in his internal filing cabinet – Mrs Dolores Martinez. She had been dropping hints for years about her husband Sam, and how he knew more than he was saying about the murder at the school. She seemed to have worked up some romantic feelings for Brandley and she had been writing to him in jail since way back in 1981, and she had started dropping hints about Sam in her letters. But it was hard to make out. She kept on about dreams she had had: in the dreams, Sam was raping the girl and killing her. Brown had never been able to decide whether she was crazy or whether that was just her way of trying to tell them the truth.

The day after he had seen Sessum, Reyna rose early and by 8.30 a.m. he was knocking on Mrs Martinez's door. She was separated from Sam now and living in one of the shacks in Dugan. When she came to the door, Reyna had the rare experience of being lost for words. She was like a black version of Brenda Medina, except that she was probably even bigger. Respectfully, he started asking her if she would talk about the Brandley case. She seemed reluctant. Just like John Sessum, she was worried. Reyna played an angle.

'I'll probably he seeing Clarence soon,' he said. 'You want me to tell him I saw you? You got any message for him?'

Her face lit up. Reyna knew he was all right.

She said Sam had always told her that Brandley was innocent, but he never really explained how he knew that. She had started writing to Brandley to tell him and the next thing she knew, there was an investigator from the DA's office called Charlie Ray at her front door.

The gaol must have told the DA what she was saying in her letters. Charlie Ray said she had to come to the courthouse: she had been very nervous. At the courthouse, she had been taken to see Keeshan and she thought he had a tape recorder in his breast pocket while he talked to her. He had told her not to believe everything she read in the papers and to be very careful of saying things she couldn't prove. Then he had made her go up in front of the Grand Jury. She had been very frightened by it all and had decided not to get involved any more. She said that was all she knew, but if there was anything she could do to help Clarence, she surely would.

Reyna left her and drove back across the railway tracks to Anderson Elementary School, where it took him only a few minutes to find Sam Martinez going about his business as the school janitor. When Reyna told him that someone had made an

extra-judicial confession to the murder, Martinez looked very
scared. Reyna pressed on and told him that a witness had come
forward to say that Acreman had talked to the girl and then
disappeared for 30 or 40 minutes. Martinez started to nod. It was
true, he said.

So why had those facts never been reported? Martinez started
to scuttle away, saying he didn't want to talk any more. Reyna
kept at him. He wanted to know if Acreman had gone across to
the vocational building with the rest of the janitors or had he gone
off alone? Martinez said he was not sure and he had to get on
with his work. He could not talk. What about when Acreman
went off to the Shamrock Station? Had Sam gone with him then?

Martinez cracked a little. 'No, I didn't. He went by himself.'

Reyna knew that was the direct opposite of what Martinez had
said in evidence. Why had he not said all this before? Martinez
said he was sorry. He had to go. He could not talk. He knew
nothing. Reyna must let him go.

It was 15 July. There were less than two days to the hearing.

One of Percy Foreman's most famous cases was in Florida. A
beautiful young woman was accused of murdering her elderly
husband. She admitted firing the gun that killed him. It looked
hopeless, but Foreman, who had enough Golden Rules to start a
small bank, had a Golden Rule for the situation. 'It's not against
the law to kill a sunnuvabitch,' he declared. Foreman spent the
trial talking about the dead man, whom he portrayed as a vicious
bully who had tormented his beautiful young wife beyond endur-
ance. He told the jury that the old man had kept a bullwhip which
he used to snap at his wife's feet to make her dance. To reinforce
the point, Foreman bought and borrowed every bullwhip he could
find, laid them all out on the defence table and constantly played
with them, coiling them through his hands, slapping them on the
table, trailing them on the floor so that by the end of the trial,
the jury were mesmerized by the whips and the image of the bully
who had used them. They voted unanimously to acquit Foreman's
beautiful client.

From experiences like that, Foreman derived his most important
Golden Rule of all. 'Try anyone except your client,' he used to

bark at his partners. Have the jury try the victim or the police or the scientific experts or the press or the client's family or friends, but not your client. This Golden Rule became more than a mere legal manoeuvre. It was Foreman's way of breaking through the flimsy web of rules and rituals which a District Attorney would try to weave around a defendant so that he could get to the moral heart of the case, to all the underlying rights and wrongs, to the real justice that was hidden in the letter of the law.

Mike De Geurin and Paul Nugent had learned this Golden Rule at Foreman's right hand. On 17 July, the eve of the big hearing when they would throw all their new evidence behind their application for a writ of Habeas Corpus, they sat down with Don Brown and reviewed all that Richard Reyna had brought them. They agreed that it was time to stop trying Clarence Brandley. They now knew that James Dexter Robinson had been in the school on the day of the crime and had confessed to a killing. They had Gary Acreman talking to the girl, disappearing without explanation on the day of the crime and then talking about the dead girl and the whereabouts of her clothes long before he should have known either. They had subpoenaed a string of witnesses to testify to all this on oath.

They knew they were still a long way short of the whole truth, but the cumulative case that these two men had some connection with the crime was far stronger than anything that had ever been laid at Brandley's feet. It was time to put Robinson and Acreman on trial.

There was, however, a technical problem with that: exactly the kind of flimsy rule Percy Foreman loved to destroy. According to the Texas Court of Criminal Appeals, anyone who wanted to use new facts to appeal against a conviction had to produce them within thirty days of the end of their trial. After that, new facts were inadmissible and, in effect, the convicted prisoner's innocence was no longer an issue, only the legal correctness of his conviction. All their new information was technically barred by this rule, but they hoped that if they could prove in open court that Robinson and Acreman were guilty, the Court of Criminal Appeals would try to do justice to Clarence Brandley by finding some other reason to release him.

Clarence Brandley had now been in his cell for five and a half years. Nine foot by three foot. Fourteen more men had followed Charlie Brooks through that door. His life had now settled into a steady routine. Nudged along by his mother and by his brother, O. T., he had taken to studying his Bible. That helped him with the bitterness. He still meditated and fasted. He often looked back at his old life. The life in the fast lane. It was impossible to believe that it was his life. He often thought about that Saturday morning and about the craziest thing of all – if he had not been trying so hard to lead a steady life, he would just have forgotten all about going up to the high school and he would just have lain down with Beverley and stayed at home, and then none of this would have ever happened to him.

He tried to keep up with the news, but it was not easy. Once, there had been another guy on his wing who had a newspaper sent into him every day and he used to share it. Then he had gone, and now there was no one on the wing who could afford a paper. There were the televisions but everybody voted on what they wanted to see and the majority ruled. That was just about the only democracy there was on Death Row.

He had thought a lot about the case until it hurt his head. He could not sort it out. Every time anyone came to visit, he would ask them if maybe there was something new. He prayed for God to send him the truth.

One day that summer, Mike De Geurin came to see him and told him all about the big breakthrough. It was the news he had waited for for so long. He told De Geurin that he remembered Robinson, and his father, too. Then De Geurin leaned right forward into the security screen and told Brandley that this was a most important question and that the answer could make a whole lot of difference to their chances in court.

'Clarence, when you were at the high school that day, did you see James Dexter Robinson. In the school? On that day?'

Brandley knew what he could say and how that might help. But the truth was that if Robinson was there that day, it was news to him. So that was what he said.

'OK, Clarence. That's fine. I'm glad you're honest.'

The morning of 17 July 1986, saw a strange scene in the Montgomery County courthouse. All the way from the back of Judge Coker's courtroom to the bar behind the attorneys' tables, the public benches were lined with brown faces, people from Dugan and from the ghettoes of Houston who had ventured into this courthouse to see the truth come out, to see a black man win a battle in Conroe. Reporters from all over Texas squeezed in among them. Deputies huddled by the doors, watchful eyes scanning the crowd. In the empty jury box, a well-dressed woman with brightly coloured fingernails sat stiff and unsmiling. The whole room buzzed with speculation.

Judge Lynn Coker called the court to order and Mike De Geurin began to speak. He outlined the new lines of evidence and their suppression and then he challenged the District Attorney to open up his file on the Brandley case. 'It's time to quit hiding the ball,' he said.

The public benches hummed their support.

Pacing backwards and forwards at the front of the court, his shoulders hunched, one hand clutching his notebook, the other beating the air for emphasis, the blond attorney's voice began to rise. 'There is no reason at this date for the District Attorney to continue hiding the file from us other than to suppress the evidence that might be inconsistent with Mr Brandley's guilt.

'This concealment has been going on for five-and-a-half, six years, and it's still going on. And it's time for this court to step in and say "Open it up, let them see the file, let them see what you have left in the file".'

'Yes, sir,' came the voices from the benches.

Peter Speers hopped to his feet: 'I would like to say for the record that I resent his allegations.'

De Geurin, who was not about to forget how Speers had failed to tell him about Brenda Medina's statement a month earlier, was not impressed. He called her attorney, W. B. Etheridge. But as soon as Etheridge started to tell his story, Speers hopped up again. He volunteered his own version of events, which started with a loud declaration that Brenda Medina was facing criminal charges for stealing money from her employer. De Geurin said he was not interested in Speers's version and continued. A minute later,

Speers was up again, objecting that Etheridge's story was irrelevant. De Geurin persisted. He was damned sure he was going to record the fact that Brenda Medina had made her statement to the DA and it had been suppressed. But as soon as Etheridge tried to explain what Brenda Medina knew, Speers popped up again objecting that he was repeating hearsay, and the judge agreed with him.

De Geurin established that Brenda Medina had made some kind of statement to the DA, but when he turned to the fact that Speers had failed to declare this in court a month ago, Speers jumped up again, objecting that this was hearsay and winning the judge's agreement that it should not be mentioned.

The pattern was set. De Geurin called his witnesses. Speers harried them with procedural objections: this information had been covered by the appeal and should not be mentioned; that information came from the first trial and should not be mentioned; this information concerned the missing exhibits which had been dealt with and should not be mentioned; this was inadmissible, that was speculation, this was hearsay, that was irrelevant, and none of it should be mentioned. Judge Coker frequently agreed with him. On the public benches, there were shaking of heads and mumblings of 'told-you-sos'. Nevertheless, De Geurin followed his lines of evidence through the obstacle course.

Brenda Medina came and told her story of the late-night confession just as she had told it before to the DA's investigator and to Richard Reyna. She added that James Dexter Robinson had a friend called Gary Acreman.

Gary Acreman appeared, and agreed immediately and without argument that he knew James Dexter Robinson and that he clearly remembered him being at the school on the day of the crime and poking his head round the door telling them not to work too hard. That put the cornerstone of the defence case in place.

Don Brown took the stand and tried to build on it. He tried to explain about the tell-tale hairs which had disappeared and which might now have been compared with Robinson's and Acreman's, and about the blood on the dead girl's socks and how that could possibly be linked with the blood on Robinson's tennis shoes, and about how the autopsy report had always suggested that the crime was committed by two people. Point by point, Speers jumped up and said this should not be mentioned and, point by point, Judge Coker agreed with him.

Speers kept on picking at the new evidence about Robinson – attacking Brenda Medina for failing to come forward earlier, challenging Acreman that he did not really remember. ('I remember, I remember,' Acreman insisted.)

He had his investigator, Charlie Ray, reveal that school records showed that Robinson had stopped working at the school on 29 July – nearly four weeks before the crime. Ray then admitted to De Geurin that he had not tried to question Robinson or any other witness to confirm Brenda Medina's story; nor had he tried to establish whether Robinson had a friendship with any of the other janitors.

Ray declared that there could be no significance in any blood spots on Robinson's shoes, since there had been no blood spilled during the crime, and then conceded that he had personally helped to deliver the dead girl's clothes to the DPS laboratory in Austin so that the bloodstains on them could be analysed.

Speers called Jim Keeshan, who said he had never heard of James Dexter Robinson and that it would not have changed the direction of his inquiry if he had.

A tutting and a sighing welled up from the public benches.

De Geurin was satisfied that despite Speers's hailstorm of procedural objections, he had laid out most of the facts about Robinson, and that it must be clear that he was now a prime suspect in the crime and that the District Attorney's office had failed to lift a finger to track him down. At the same time, he followed the line of evidence that led to Gary Acreman.

John Sessum staggered into court, grumbling and cursing that he was losing money by being hauled away from his roadside tins and cans. But he stood by his story and swore that Acreman had spoken to this blonde girl in the hallway and had then disappeared for 30 or 40 minutes. He insisted, too, that the Texas Ranger had told him not to tell the truth and had threatened him with jail if he did. De Geurin tried to get him to tell more of his story.

Sessum was nervous. 'Well, like I said, I've been scared and I'm still scared but I don't know what's going to happen to me.'

De Geurin tried to reassure him that no one was going to jail him for perjury. 'If this judge were to guarantee you that nobody, no law enforcement officer, can punish you for telling the truth in court . . .'

Speers was up again. 'Your Honour, I will object to that. Obviously, if he's admitted to the court he lied at the first trial, I'd ask the court not to promise him such a thing. If it's a charge for aggravated perjury, if that's what he's talking about.'

The judge agreed with Speers. For once, De Geurin was happy to be gagged: Speers had just given a loud and public demonstration of exactly how the courthouse had been frightening John Sessum into concealing the truth all these years.

Sam Martinez came and agreed that Acreman had gone off alone for 30 or 40 minutes, saying he was going to the Shamrock Station. Martinez could not explain why, at Brandley's trials, he had said he had gone with him.

Then Ed Payne limped into court, and in a voice that was twisted out of shape by his butchered throat, he crawled through his story. For the first time he not only publicly described Gary Acreman's behaviour on the day of the crime, but he also recalled some of what happened one Saturday afternoon in January 1981, during Clarence Brandley's second trial, when Charlie Hayden, Montgomery's county constable, paid him a visit.

Charlie Hayden had taken him to an office, he said. The District Attorney had been there with another man who he thought was a police captain, and he had tried to tell them his story. They had started asking him if he believed Gary Acreman was capable of committing this crime. Payne continued in his strange buzzing voice: 'I said no, that he wasn't, that he was scared of everything and everybody. The only way he might commit a crime like this or do something would be with somebody else. Then Mr Charles Hayden jumped up and said "That's an angle we haven't thought about." '

Hayden had gone on to suggest that the crime could have been committed by several white men acting together. But the District Attorney, Jim Keeshan, had not been interested. 'No, I've built my case and we know who did it,' the DA had told them.

And so, Payne said, he had never told his story. 'Keeshan more or less told me to shut up, so that discouraged me in trying to help.'

There was an angry stirring on the public benches.

Don Brown sat silently at the defence table as Payne confirmed his worst suspicions about that agonizing day. He remembered the frustration which he and Morris had felt as Payne was snatched away from them, their bafflement when Payne came to the court-house and denied everything, and then their anger when they had confronted a complacent Keeshan about it. Now they were told that it was Keeshan himself who had got to Payne and put the lid on his story. Brown watched intently as Speers called Jim Keeshan to give his version of events. For once, Keeshan's footwork was clumsy.

He claimed to believe that the defence had already known Ed Payne's story. After all, he said, it was the defence attorneys who had told him about Payne. Brown shook his head in disbelief: they had not told Keeshan anything until after it had all gone wrong. Then Keeshan slipped up. He admitted he had interviewed Payne before Payne came to the courthouse. But Brown knew that he was standing time on its head. When Payne came to the courthouse, he had already been persuaded not to tell his story. So, on Keeshan's own timing, he had spoken to Payne before the defence had. Even after acknowledging in open court that he had personally interviewed Ed Payne about his son-in-law, he publicly declared his blind focus on Clarence Brandley: 'I don't think I ever considered Acreman to be a suspect.'

Once again, De Geurin was happy. Any of these witnesses, particularly John Sessum and Ed Payne, might have succumbed to their fear and refused to tell their stories in public, but they had stood up for themselves and they had stood up to Peter Speers and his objections.

De Geurin swept more quickly through the technical issues. He called Frank Robin from his prison cell to describe how the DA's investigator, Charlie Ray, had come to him back in 1982 complaining that he felt bad because the DA's office was burying infor-mation from a woman who said Icky Peace had tried to assault her. Robin remembered clearly thinking that this was the kind of information that should have been handed over to the defence at the trial. Don Brown recalled how Robin had showed him the woman's statement.

Charlie Ray took the stand and said he had really tried, but he just could not remember this statement he was supposed to have shown Robin: he had looked real hard but he just could not find any record of anything of the kind. The statement, if it ever existed, was now lost and gone forever. Jim Keeshan said the same. So did the Texas Ranger, Wesley Styles, when he was called.

De Geurin put Don Brown back on the witness-stand and tried to get him to explain about the missing photographs and how they could have proved that Brandley was not wearing a belt on the day of the crime. Speers rained down objections and succeeded in drowning their efforts to explain why they believed Brandley wore no belt and how the missing photographs could have helped.

De Geurin raised the exclusion of black people from Conroe juries. Speers immediately persuaded the judge that this should not be mentioned. All De Geurin could do was to make a bill of exception, a legal device to record evidence even though it can have no effect on the outcome of the hearing. Again he called Don Brown, who recalled that in both of Clarence Brandley's trials every single black potential juror had been removed at the request of the DA. He said that in all his years in Conroe he had only once known a black man to be selected for a jury, and that was when the black juror in question was a policeman.

De Geurin asked him if he believed this exclusion was systematic. Speers hopped up to object, and before he had even explained why he was objecting Judge Coker had ruled that this should not be mentioned.

De Geurin and Brown, however, had an answer to that. They called Frank Robin, former assistant DA in the courthouse, back to the stand. De Geurin asked him about the training manuals which were used in the DA's office and about exactly what those manuals had to say about choosing black people for juries. Robin replied: 'On jury selection, the prosecutorial manuals recommend that blacks and other minorities be struck because they tended to be more sympathetic to the defence.'

There were angry gasps from the public benches.

De Geurin said: 'I pass the witness.'

Speers said he had no questions. De Geurin and Brown guessed that must be because he was trained on these same manuals and knew all about them.

After two days of intense work, the hearing paused. It was not quite finished. The defence still had a handful of key witnesses to call, including James Dexter Robinson, who was away in South Carolina. They agreed to stall and resume the hearing on 21 August.

On Wednesday 23 July, Richard Reyna flew to South Carolina. No one on this case was getting paid anything any more, but Percy Foreman had written a cheque for $1,200 of his own money to pay for the trip. All Reyna had was a hired car waiting at the airport and the address of a house in Greenville where, if Brenda Medina was right, he could find James Dexter Robinson. Reyna had no idea what he was going to say to him.

He was still puzzling about it when he found the house. He passed it a couple of times and then just sat and watched for half an hour. It was early evening. Quiet. He believed the guy in the house was a killer. If Brenda Medina was right, he probably had a gun with him. He could not quite see himself just strolling up to the door and calling him a killer to his face. On the other hand he could not just sit there all night. So, before he really knew it, he found himself strolling up to the door and knocking.

The guy who answered the door was short and slightly built, with shaggy black hair and a weird little face, like a pixie or something. He said yes, his name was James Dexter Robinson. He was wearing a dirty T-shirt, and he had a hot dog in his hand.

Reyna started ad libbing like crazy, telling him he was from Conroe, that he worked for Percy Foreman, that he was looking into the murder at the high school, and that some allegations had been made against him.

The little guy just stared at him. 'Yeah?' he said.

'Yeah,' said Reyna, running out of lines. 'Brenda – you remember Brenda? Well, Brenda says you killed that girl.'

The little guy squinted at his feet, and Reyna felt the beginning of an angle to play here. 'It looks like they've got it in for you, James. Because Brenda's not the only one been saying these things about you. I talked to Gary Acreman. You remember Gary? And there's some things been said. You see, James, I think someone is trying to frame you.'

'Yeah?'

Now Reyna had him interested. 'Why did you leave Conroe, James? There's things been said about that.'

'I dunno. Needed the work, I guess.'

'But when did you leave, James?'

'Seven thirty-one,' he said.

'31st July?' said Reyna. 'You sure?'

'I remember it like it was yesterday. And I ain't never been back.'

If that was true, Brenda Medina and Gary Acreman were wrong.

'How did you leave, James?'

'I flew. Yeah, I flew.'

That didn't fit either. According to Brenda Medina, he was supposed to have taken a bus. They were still standing on the doorstep and Robinson was still clutching his hot dog. Reyna asked him if he remembered what airline he flew on.

'No, I don't. You wanna come in? Have a hot dog?'

Reyna thought it looked dirty inside the house and there was no telling where that hot dog had been, so he declined.

'James, I'm just trying to help you out here. I think somebody is trying to frame you.'

'Yeah. It's that goddam Acreman.'

Then Reyna felt it. He felt it in his heart that this little guy knew the truth. He knew just what Gary Acreman knew and he knew that Acreman had the power to blow him away. And Reyna felt he could get him to talk.

'Hey, James, I got an idea here. What about coming back to Conroe, help me clear all this up and sort out that son-of-a-bitch Acreman?'

It took a little negotiation and it involved old Clarence Robinson coming out and saying his piece and then James Robinson repeating that he had left Conroe on 31 July. He kept saying he remembered how they had posted him his last pay-cheque from the high school and how he had cashed it in the store down the road from here. But finally, Reyna won.

Fifteen minutes later, Reyna was driving off in his car looking for a pay phone so that he could call Don Brown and tell him that the little son-of-a-bitch had agreed to come back to Conroe of his own free will.

Brown, who had just started the complicated process of trying to get a court order to bring Robinson to Conroe, could hardly believe it. 'Richard, just get him on a plane. We'll pay for it somehow.'

At five o'clock the next afternoon, Reyna and Robinson flew into Intercontinental Airport, just north of Houston on I-45. It had been a weird flight. Reyna had decided not to push him any more, in case he frightened him off, but Robinson had been doing something very curious.

He kept saying he wanted to be hypnotized and that that was the only way he could get to the truth, because he had black-outs and had been taking a lot of acid, and he did things he could not remember. Reyna, who was already deciding that Robinson was not as stupid as he liked to make out, reckoned he knew for sure what he was playing at – constructing a safety net in case things went wrong in Conroe, so he could plead insanity. This was a little guy with one big guilty conscience.

There were two things that the defence wanted from James Dexter Robinson – a lie detector test and a moment of his time in court to have him placed under a bond to make him come back and testify at the hearing on 21 August.

On Friday 25 July, Reyna collected Robinson from the hotel where he had lodged him overnight, gave him some newspaper clippings from the hearing so that he could see what people were saying about him, and delivered him to the Houston offices of Mr D. Glenn Raney, former military policeman, former Harris County sheriff and now a professional polygraph operator. Robinson was shivering all over.

While Reyna drove anxiously around the block, Glenn Raney invited his subject to talk. Robinson explained how he knew nothing about the murder of Cheryl Fergeson. He did not know Gary Acreman at all. And he had left Brenda Medina just because he thought she had probably been going with another man, and he had never heard of the murder until his father told him about it.

Then Glenn Raney wired him up and read him a series of formal questions. All the while, he watched the needle scratching out its verdict on the answers.

'Is your first name James?'

The needle traced its line, undisturbed.

'Is your last name Robinson?'

'Yes.'

The needle was steady.

'Do you plan to lie to any question on this test?'

'No.'

Still steady.

'Did everything happen like you said it did?'

'Yes.'

The needle skipped a beat. Something in Robinson's mood had changed. Glenn Raney went back to neutral questions.

'Do you live in Greenville?'

'Yes.'

The needle was calm again. Glenn Raney tried another question about the crime.

'Were you actually in South Carolina like you say you were when Cheryl Fergeson was killed at the Conroe High School in August 1980?'

'Yes,' said Robinson.

The needle twitched and jumped.

'Do you know who caused Cheryl Fergeson to die at the Conroe High School in August 1980?'

'No.'

The needle scribbled out a mountain range on Glenn Raney's graph.

'Were you present at the Conroe High School on 23 August 1980 when Cheryl Fergeson died?'

'No.'

The needle calmed down again. Glenn Raney slipped in a neutral question.

'Do you live in South Carolina?'

'Yes.'

Needle steady.

'Did you cause the death of Cheryl Fergeson at the Conroe High School on 23 August 1980?'

'No.'

The needle jumped again, scratching anxiously at the paper. Glenn Raney offered Robinson another neutral question.

'Can you drive a car?'

'Yes.'

The needle was happy again.

'Did you plan with or help anyone cause Cheryl Fergeson's death at the Conroe High School in August 1980?'

'No.'

The needle was steady.

'Did you know that a girl was killed at the Conroe High School before your dad told you?'

'No.'

The needle was still steady.

Glenn Raney double-checked his equipment and told Robinson that the needle suggested he had lied to some of the key questions, although the fact was that the needle seemed unable to make up its mind. He offered him a chance to explain his answers. Robinson started talking. There was one thing that did not happen quite like he said it did, he agreed. But that was just to do with leaving Brenda, he said. She had not really been with another man. So that must be why the needle did not like his answer.

'But why would you tell a lie about that particular thing?' Glenn Raney asked him.

'I don't know. I just did.'

What about whether he knew who caused Cheryl Fergeson's death? Robinson hesitated. 'I was thinking, trying to think about whether or not Gary Acreman told me anything about the murder, or maybe said something while he was driving in Gary's truck to the store, to get a Coke, when we was at the school.'

Glenn Raney reminded him that, according to his version of events, he had left Conroe four weeks before the murder and could not possibly have been with Gary at the school any time after the killing.

'Oh, yeah, that's right,' said Robinson, who then fell silent.

So had he really been in South Carolina when the murder occurred?

'Well, I thought I was. I thought for sure I was. Well, I don't really remember.'

Glenn Raney steered him back to the vital question which, according to the needle, he had lied about. Did he cause this girl's death? Robinson looked at him and hesitated. Glenn Raney waited. And waited. After a while, he started checking his watch, while Robinson shifted and stirred and stared at the floor and still hesitated. When he finally started to speak, by Glenn Raney's reckoning, he had been hesitating for something like four and a half minutes.

'Well, I don't remember,' he said.

'What are you saying?'

Robinson started to ramble. 'I don't know. I'm just not sure. I could have done it and forgot. I don't remember. No, I couldn't have done it. I'm not that kind of person. I'm innocent. I'm not sure. I'm just not sure.'

Had he told Brenda Medina that he did it?

'Well, I don't remember. I could have made those statements to her. I'm just not sure.'

When Glenn Raney's report of the lie test came through, the defence camp could barely suppress their mood of triumph. It was not just that Robinson had failed the lie test. Polygraphs were notoriously unreliable and had no legal standing anyway. It was his whole performance. Any reasonable observer of a man behaving like that would have to conclude that he was guilty.

That afternoon, Don Brown called Judge Coker and the DA's office and told them they had a witness they wanted to bring into court to be placed under bond. Robinson went along like a lamb and signed an undertaking to come back to court on 21 August. As he left the courtroom, two investigators from the District Attorney's office took him by the arm and led him away.

It was shortly before the hearing resumed that Richard Reyna called the phone company. An engineer came round and put a gadget on the line and played with it for a while and then he looked up at Reyna and said: 'Buddy, your phone is tapped.'

It was about a week before the hearing was due to resume. John Sessum was bicycling slowly down a back road somewhere east of Conroe when a car swooped up beside him and two men jumped out. He thought they had sticks. He half jumped, half fell off his bike and ran through the woods as fast as he could go. He could hear the men behind him, running after him. He just kept running and pretty soon the men stopped and shouted some stuff at him and went away. He waited to be sure that they were gone and then crept back out of the woods. He had only seen their faces for a moment. But he knew one of them. He knew Gary Acreman's face all right.

It was three days before the hearing was due to resume, a Monday. Brenda Medina was at home with the children. She heard the car stop outside but thought nothing of it until there was a knock on the door. There were three men outside. She opened the door a little and the men told her they were from the District Attorney's office. They wanted to talk to her about the Brandley case. She let the three men into her house. She soon regretted it. They did not want to hear her story. They wanted her to know that it was an offence to commit perjury. They thought she ought to know that if she went round saying this kind of thing, she could wind up with her ass behind bars. She could wind up having her kids taken away from her.

She said she was only telling the truth. She said she had passed a lie test. The two men said they knew all about lie tests. They could give her another lie test and she wouldn't pass that. She'd wind up in jail. The two men wanted to know why she was saying these things. They said she should tell them who had paid her to say these things. Was it Don Brown? Was it Reyna? Etheridge? Who paid her? How much did they pay her? Did they pay that polygraph operator to say she was telling the truth? She had better tell them everything, or she would wind up with her ass in jail. She could wind up in jail easy if she went round saying what she had been saying. The three men left, their heavy leather boots clumping on the porch, and drove back towards Conroe.

The day before the hearing was due to resume, a Wednesday, Richard Reyna was at Houston Intercontinental Airport, waiting for James Dexter Robinson to fly in from South Carolina. Don Brown had paid for Robinson's ticket and Reyna had come to make sure the little son-of-a-bitch did not change his mind and run off home. They knew they had to watch Robinson. Ever since he had turned up in Conroe, the District Attorney's men had been all over him. Reyna had been doing more work, too.

He reckoned he had found a new witness who could knock a large hole in Robinson's claim to have left Conroe on 31 July. Not even the District Attorney seemed to believe that any more. Peter Speers had told the defence that his investigators had traced Robinson's last pay cheque. It turned out that he had cashed it – not in South Carolina like he claimed – but in Conroe. On 5 August.

Just then, Reyna spotted two of the District Attorney's investigators standing around in the airport concourse. That was no coincidence. Reyna thought there was no point in playing around, so he went up and asked them if they were there to meet Robinson. They said they were, and that Robinson had asked them to be there.

It looked like James Dexter Robinson had changed sides.

On Thursday, 21 August 1986, the courtroom was crowded again. Clarence Brandley and his family, and his friends and supporters and all the press and other bystanders, were there to see one man, James Dexter Robinson.

The defence also wanted to see him. They had arranged and paid for him to come to Conroe, yet they had not seen him since he was whisked through the airport the day before. They had heard from Brenda Medina about the three men who had come to her house and they could only guess at what the DA's office had been telling Robinson since they laid hands on him. They now had no idea what story their star witness might tell. They needed the judge's help.

Their problem was that the law did not allow them to put leading questions to their own witness. If they called Robinson to the stand and he told lies, they would be stuck with them, unless the judge agreed to declare him a hostile witness. Mike De Geurin rose to make the request to Judge Coker, and Speers hopped up. 'They are perfectly aware of what his testimony is going to be and I'm aware of no rule that would permit them to bring some guy in from South Carolina to sit there and cross-examine him about something that they already know. I think that's totally improper.'

'I think so, too,' said Judge Coker. 'I'm not going to permit that.'

With his hands effectively tied behind his back, De Geurin called Robinson to the stand. It was soon apparent that the DA's men had been very busy. Robinson revealed that men from the DA's office had not only collected him from the airport and spent the intervening time with him, but had also previously visited him in South Carolina and warned him that the defence lawyers were 'trying to put a hoodoo on him', trying to have him blamed for the crime.

An angry murmur started on the public benches. Robinson suddenly said he wanted a lawyer. De Geurin asked him exactly what he wanted.

'I'd like to have Mr Speers represent me.'

The public benches burst into jeering and laughter. The judge smashed his hammer down on the bench and the courtroom became quiet enough for De Geurin to explain that the DA was supposed to be an impartial prosecutor. Peter Speers blushed, and Robinson said he would be all right without a lawyer after all.

As Robinson continued his evidence, De Geurin began to understand why this potential murder suspect should want the same District Attorney who would have to prosecute him to represent him. According to Robinson, an investigator from the DA's office named Frank Newton had spent two solid weeks in South Carolina trying to prove that Robinson had been there on the day of the crime. Newton had visited Robinson's employers, looking for evidence that he had started work there before 23 August. He had interviewed his mother, his grandmother, his grandfather, and his friends in search of an alibi witness. He had helped Robinson search through all of his personal papers looking for a bus ticket from Conroe. All that Newton had come up with were some photographs of Robinson at a party which might have been held on 17 August 1980.

Newton had, however, given Robinson an invaluable tip, as De Geurin discovered when he started asking Robinson about his last pay cheque, a line of questioning which should have shown that Robinson's insistent claim to have left Conroe on 31 July was a lie. To De Geurin's surprise, Robinson immediately abandoned his story about receiving and cashing the cheque in South Carolina and admitted that he had still been in Conroe on 5 August and had cashed the cheque not far from the courthouse.

'Now, who told you you had done that?' asked De Geurin.

'Well, it was traced down. Mr Newton told me.'

De Geurin asked him when he had told him.

'I think it was yesterday,' said Robinson.

In one easy move, the DA's investigator had robbed De Geurin of his best chance to prove in open court that Robinson was a liar. But De Geurin was not finished yet. Robinson insisted that he was innocent, but before he left the stand he took two vital steps towards implicating himself in the murder. First, he dropped the pretence he had maintained with Glenn Raney at his lie test and admitted that he knew Gary Acreman. Then, in an admission which had the whole court bubbling with comment, he conceded that he had told Brenda Medina he had killed a girl. He immediately added that this was nothing to do with the high school, and it was months before he had started working there, and he had only said it to frighten Brenda and it was certainly not true.

Having tumbled that far, he tried to stop himself falling the final few feet into the deep hole the defence had prepared for him by insisting, first, that he had never told Glenn Raney that he might have murdered Cheryl Fergeson and, second, that he was certain he had left Conroe on 6 August, the day after he cashed his cheque, and never returned. De Geurin called two witnesses to send him plunging.

First, Glenn Raney came and reeled off his list of law enforcement qualifications. He was not allowed to deliver his needle's verdict on Robinson, but his account of Robinson's performance in his office and of his four and a half minute paralysis about whether he had killed this girl, provoked such a chorus of sighs from the public benches that De Geurin could not see how the ultimate verdict could be in doubt.

An elderly white man named Reggie Slacum, Richard Reyna's new witness, then took the stand. He explained that he had worked at the high school with James Dexter Robinson because he was one of the regular janitors there, one of those who would have been there on the day of the crime except that he had not wanted to work on a Saturday. Slacum recalled that he had owed Robinson $100 and he described how one day James Robinson had come round to his house in Conroe demanding his money, but Slacum had been unable to pay him. A few minutes later, Robinson's father, Clarence, had come to his house and started pushing him round and threatening to use a gun on him.

That night, Slacum remembered, he had woken with a sore mouth and he had had to go to hospital the next day. It turned out that the sore mouth was nothing to do with his scuffle with Clarence Robinson, but that was the reason he could be so sure of the date when the Robinsons had come to his house. He had his hospital records. He had gone to the hospital on 21 August. So Reggie Slacum had no doubt at all that James Robinson had been in Conroe on 20 August, only three days before the murder.

Peter Speers attacked Slacum's memory. Slacum insisted. Speers insisted that Robinson had stopped working at the high school at the end of July. 'Dexter Robinson wasn't working at Conroe High School the month of August, was he?'

'No,' said Slacum, 'but he was coming round.'

That was not what Speers wanted to hear. 'Who told you to say that?' he snapped.

'Nobody,' said Slacum.

As Speers sat down, the public benches rippled with applause. Judge Coker told them to keep quiet or he would clear the court.

Slacum then explained to Mike De Geurin that he remembered clearly that Robinson had been in the school just about every day for weeks after leaving his job, trying to sell cosmetics. So far as the defence camp was concerned, James Dexter Robinson had just been pushed over the edge. He had deserted his first alibi. Now his second alibi was in shreds. Reggie Slacum had put him in Conroe during the week of the crime. Gary Acreman, on oath and despite cross-examination, had put him in the school on the day of the crime. Through his father, he had access to the auditorium keys. Brenda Medina, Richard Reyna and Glenn Raney all said he had made full or partial confessions. Despite all their efforts, the DA's office had been unable to rescue him.

Gary Acreman was not far from the edge. John Sessum and Sam Martinez both now said he had vanished for 30 or 40 minutes on the day of the crime. Sessum swore that Acreman had been talking to the girl. His own father-in-law had pointed the finger at him. The defence knew that there was still a lot of the picture missing but surely, they reasoned, the next logical step would be for the police to interrogate Robinson and Acreman and for Clarence Brandley to be freed or, at the very least, to be given a new trial.

But this was Conroe.

At the end of the hearing, Clarence Brandley was sent back to Death Row. In his brief absence, two more men had been taken away to be killed. Robinson and Acreman walked free.

Mike De Geurin always found it hard to dislike anyone – even this man Robinson, who had, he now firmly believed, not only committed a vicious crime, but also allowed an innocent man to be condemned to death for it. So, as soon as De Geurin spotted Robinson outside the courtroom, he smiled and started making small talk and walked out of the building with him.

On the stand, Robinson had said he would have no objection to supplying a sample of his pubic hair to the defence.

'Did you mean that?' asked De Geurin.

'Sure,' said Robinson, with a smile. 'When do you want it?'

'How about now?'

So the two of them stopped by the courthouse door and while Robinson rummaged down the front of his trousers, De Geurin whipped out his cigarette pack and removed the cellophane wrapper. A few moments later, De Geurin had the prize safely stashed in his jacket pocket.

'Well thank you, James,' he said and shook him by the hand. 'Very kind.'

He drove home to Houston, wondering what Gary Acreman with the sandy-coloured hair knew about that reddish brown hair that had been found on the girl's thigh, and wondering, too, how things might have been if someone in the courthouse had not had the bad luck or the foresight to lose all the hairs that had been found on Cheryl Fergeson's body.

The weeks after the hearing were tense, and riddled with rumours. All of them pictured the defence camp breaking through. The attorneys could smell victory, but insisted it was too soon to celebrate. Judge Coker, they believed, was finally going to stand up for himself. In his cell in Huntsville, Clarence Brandley dared to hope. He had not thought much of Coker. The judge had let Speers have his way most of the time and he had sat up there looking so pleased with himself – like he was having his Sunday lunch, Brandley thought. But now, with all these rumours, he began to believe he could have been wrong.

Immediately after the hearing, both sides had sent written legal arguments to the Court of Criminal Appeals in Austin and the judge had sent his own findings. The defence had been preparing themselves to go up to Austin to argue in front of the judges there, but nothing happened for months. Then, the week before Christmas, word came from the court. There was no need for anyone to go to Austin. The court did not want to hear any arguments. They were throwing the case out now. Brandley had lost everything. Every single argument.

Neither Brandley nor his family nor his attorneys could believe it. They were dazed. De Geurin, normally so amiable, was bitterly angry. But they had only to read Judge Coker's findings of facts to see what had happened. The courthouse's cowardly lion had mauled the defence without mercy.

He dismissed the case against James Dexter Robinson for three reasons: Brenda Medina had not mentioned Robinson's confession for six years; Gary Acreman had not mentioned Robinson's presence at the school for six years; Robinson had stopped working at the school 24 days before the murder.

He dismissed the case against Gary Acreman for four reasons: the defence knew Ed Payne's story before the DA; the defence had failed to call Ed Payne as a witness at Brandley's trial; the Honourable James Keeshan denied trying to influence Ed Payne; the defence had failed to call John Sessum at Brandley's trial.

He also adopted the technical argument, which had been stressed by Peter Speers, that Brandley's innocence was not relevant because of the rule which decreed that new facts must be presented within 30 days after a convicted man's trial. 'Only the legality of the conviction, not the merits, are subject to scrutiny,' he wrote.

With equal ease, he wiped aside Clarence Brandley's other finger-holds on life, rejecting the defence witnesses, repeating the evidence of the Honourable James Keeshan and the legal arguments of Peter Speers.

The Court of Criminal Appeals had simply adopted the findings of the Conroe judge and sent the black man back to the executioner.

8

Fifteen hundred miles away from Houston, in the placid old university town of Princeton, New Jersey, on the first floor of an elegant, wood-beamed house where Woodrow Wilson once lived, a man was sitting at a small desk in a cluttered room. Apart from the desk and a chair, the room contained a bed and a mass of papers, some piled on the bed, some under it, some on the desk, but mostly sprayed across the floor. On the wall over the head of the bed was a crucifix.

The man's name was Jim McCloskey and he had just become famous. Not that he had ever wanted to be. He had abandoned all thought of fame or fortune seven years earlier in the autumn of 1979 when, at the age of 37, he walked out on his well-paid job as a management consultant in Philadelphia. His old boss could barely believe it. After all, McCloskey had a good life – a Lincoln Continental, a nice house in a nice suburb, money in his pocket and more in the bank. But he threw it all away. What good is a 'good life', he asked, if you feel empty inside? But what really made the boss's jaw drop was that McCloskey announced he was leaving to become a minister.

McCloskey set off along the approved route to becoming a Presbytarian minister by enrolling in a seminary in Princeton to study for his three-year Master of Divinity degree. The fame came by accident – or maybe providence – in his second year there, when he was instructed that as part of his studies he should take up a project outside the classroom. He decided to visit the inmates of the New Jersey State Prison in Trenton and there, in the readjustment unit where the hardest of the hard cases were kept, he met a man who was serving a life sentence and who told him he was innocent. McCloskey listened to him and began to believe him, and then he began to be moved by his plight. He felt God had led him to this man.

He took a year off from his studies and threw himself into the man's case. He went back to his old business contacts in Philadelphia and raised money. In Princeton, he made a deal with an 83-year-old woman, who owned the wood-beamed house which once belonged to Woodrow Wilson, that he would go out and get her groceries every Tuesday if she would let him live rent-free in an empty room on the second floor. He hired an attorney and formed a defence committee, but mostly he went out and talked to people. In back alleys and mean streets, where a white man in a suit is usually a cop, people saw the white collar around Jim McCloskey's neck and talked. It took him nearly three years, but he finally succeeded in proving his man's innocence and getting him out of jail. He had found his calling.

So the businessman who set out to become a minister now became a private detective, devoted to releasing the innocent from prison. He set up his own organization, called Centurion Ministries after the Roman soldier who looked at Christ on the cross and said 'Surely this one is innocent', paid himself a meagre $10,000 a year, and set to work.

Now, in the autumn of 1986, the investigator with the clergyman's collar had just engineered the release of his fourth innocent person, a black man named Nate Walker who had been serving life plus 50 years for raping a white woman. McCloskey proved his innocence when he discovered that for 12 years nobody had bothered to test semen swabs taken from the rape victim. He located them, arranged for the FBI to test the blood type of the semen and proved that it could not have come from the imprisoned man. The case made headlines and Jim McCloskey became famous.

The phone had been ringing almost non-stop since the Walker case broke: newspapers looking for stories; sympathizers offering support; but mostly relatives of prisoners begging for help. Now, as McCloskey worked at the little desk in the corner of his room, trying to catch up on the paperwork strewn across the bare boards, the phone rang again. The caller said he had just heard about him on television and he had got his number from the television station. He said his youngest brother was due to be executed for a crime he had not committed. The caller's name was Revd Ozell Brandley, known to his family as O.T..

McCloskey had learned never to say no, no matter how busy he might be. 'Go on,' he said. 'What's the situation, Ozell?'

O. T. Brandley started pouring out his family's agony – the dead girl, all these janitors, racism, missing exhibits, Jim Keeshan, James Robinson. It was all too much for McCloskey to take in at once.

'Well, I'll tell you, Ozell, I'm just about swamped right now. But can you send me something on paper? Some kind of summary of the case?'

O. T. Brandley said he could. A few days later, he posted him Don Brown's brief for the original appeal with its catalogue of pain from Brandley's two trials, and a transcript of the summer's hearing with all the new revelations about Robinson and Acreman.

O. T. Brandley had never stopped working for his youngest brother's freedom. At first, he had concentrated on praying and spreading the word through the Baptist churches where he was a minister. He had tried to interest some of his colleagues at the junior high school in Houston where he taught. None of it seemed to make any difference. One elected politician after another had told him there was nothing they could do. When Judge Coker tore down all his fragile hopes he was near despair. His respect for American justice sank so low that he no longer joined his students when they pledged allegiance to the US flag each morning. Yet he could not give up. At about the same time that he called Jim McCloskey in Princeton in the autumn of 1986, O. T. Brandley also approached the Revd Don Boney.

Revd Boney was well-known in Houston as a man of many images. He was a Baptist minister, like O.T., who shunned alcohol and prayed before any major decision. He was an academic in the mould of his father, who had been Chancellor of the University of Houston and the only black school superintendent in the history of the city. He was a former television producer and radio disc jockey, articulate and charismatic, and he had spent two years on the road with a rock band. But most of all – and this was what caught O.T.'s eye – he was an outspoken radical, a firey protégé

298

of Martin Luther King and Malcolm X, a champion of causes, a manipulator of the media, an organizer of rallies and boycotts and sit-ins, one of the founders of the Black United Front in New York in 1971, and now Houston's pre-eminent civil rights activist.

O.T. showed Revd Boney newspaper clippings and explained the case and the racism that his brother had suffered. Boney said he would look into it. A few weeks later, Boney was in touch again. He had consumed every detail of the case, written his own chronology and summary and prayed about it. Now he told O.T. that he believed that they should organize a major campaign of popular protest to secure his brother's freedom.

On 7 January 1987, the staff of Governor Bill Clements looked out of the window of his mansion overlooking Austin and saw half-a-dozen black people carrying banners and chanting about a man named Brandley. They went on with their work, and the black people eventually went away.

Twelve days later, on 19 January, the anniversary of Martin Luther King's birth, the black people were back. But this time Revd Boney had three dozen supporters with him, carrying banners and chanting. He also had a bucket. Governor Clements thought he had better do something. He did not want these people inside the mansion, so he went out on to the steps to speak to them. He assured them that he would ask the Attorney General to look into the case of this man Brandley. The protesters were not impressed.

They placed a photograph of the Governor on the steps of the mansion and then tipped the contents of Revd Boney's bucket on to it. The bucket contained manure, donated by a cow named Tina who belonged to a farmer friend of Boney's.

'We are burying your career in bullshit,' declared Boney. 'All you have ever given black people is bullshit so now we are giving it back.'

The press liked the story and the campaign got its first publicity.

On 6 February, Boney declared a 'Day of Outrage' for two reasons. It was the birthday of the man who, Boney said, was responsible for the resurgence of racism in America – President Ronald Reagan – and it was also the day when Judge Lynn Coker was due to announce a new execution date for Clarence Brandley.

This time Boney attracted 200 people and they agreed that they would protest, not in Austin, but in Conroe. Black people in the town could not believe it. Blacks protesting in the courthouse square! It had never happened, not even in the 1960s. Not in Conroe. But Boney promised it was going to happen now, on this Day of Outrage.

In the courthouse, they had heard he was coming. All Judge Coker wanted was a quiet hearing. All he wanted to do was to announce when the black janitor was going to die and then carry on with his business. The judge had even suggested that he could do it in a letter to avoid any trouble, but Mike De Geurin had told him that was not good enough. The courthouse came up with another plan.

On the morning of the hearing, Montgomery County deputies searched all black people entering the courtroom. They told some of them, including church ministers, that they could not come in. The judge then called the case early and was finished before most of Don Boney's protesters could even reach the courtroom. It was a stark event.

The judge sat in his black gown and Brandley in his chains. Brandley's mother wept. The judge's teenage son was there to watch. The judge asked the black man if he had anything to say. The black man looked straight back at him.

'Your Honour, I'm innocent,' he said.

The judge looked down at his papers and told Brandley he would die on 26 March – in six weeks and six days. In two minutes, it was over. Without trouble.

But outside the courthouse angry voices gathered strength, murmuring at first, then rising louder in complaint. This might be Conroe, where black people stayed on their side of the tracks, where young men were burned alive or shot and no one dared protest, but today, for once, they were going to make themselves heard. That was all they were going to do – just raise their voices. Nothing illegal. Nothing violent. Yet in Conroe it was an act of outrageous defiance. Don Boney and his supporters from Houston showed them the way. Anger put their fear to flight. They started to parade around the courthouse. They carried a coffin for Governor Clements to bury his career. They chanted 'The people united will never be defeated' and they sang 'Clarence Brandley, Clarence Brandley'. Two men battered drums. Seven times they circled the courthouse, like Joshua in Jericho, their voices rising in volume as they marched. By the time they came to a halt, they were exuberant.

Don Boney stood on the steps and told the crowd, 'This courthouse is defiled. This courthouse no longer represents justice. It represents corruption and hypocrisy. We are not going to tolerate it any more. We are not going to respect it any more.'

They cheered their defiance. Then Boney deposited a birthday present for President Reagan on the courthouse steps. It came from the same cow, Tina. Boney looked around at the white faces peering out of the windows and the deputies shuffling uneasily on the street corners.

'Are you going to arrest us for putting fertilizer on your courthouse?'

Silence. Nobody moved. Victory.

The protestors moved off home, still angry but now determined. Just for once the people of Dugan had found their courage, and they had won. Something had changed in Conroe.

On Friday, 27 February, Jim McCloskey flew into Houston. He had passed through the city two weeks earlier and spoken to the Brandley family and to the attorneys, and had offered to work on the case. He said he did not want to be paid; all he needed was a room to stay in and a car to drive.

That Friday evening, he moved into a room over the garage in the back yard of Paul Nugent's home in a leafy green part of Houston near Rice University. He instantly surrounded himself with piles of paper, the whole six and a half year history of the Brandley case. All through that weekend he hid in his room, reading and writing notes, emerging only occasionally to shoot baskets with Nugent or play with Nugent's children before diving back into the paperwork.

Saturday was another big day in Conroe. The annual Black History Parade, normally a small, downbeat affair built round a beauty queen, had been turned over to the Clarence Brandley case. Revd Boney's campaign was now on a roll. Boney had scheduled regular Clarence Brandley campaign meetings every Tuesday night in Houston and every Thursday night in Conroe, in the black college. By late February, more than 250 people were coming from their shacks in Dugan to join the meetings. There were speeches, prayers and hymns. The black people of Conroe, who had finally sensed their power outside the courthouse on 6 February, were now ready to fight.

They raised funds for press releases, state-wide mailings, T-shirts, posters and bumper stickers to spread the word: 'Free Clarence Brandley', 'Don't let the State of Texas murder an innocent man.' They still had to deal with their fear. A Houston minister told them: 'If you are afraid to put this bumper sticker on your car, then put it on somebody else's.'

On Saturday, more than one thousand protesters marched out of Dugan waving banners and chanting Brandley's name and crossed the railway tracks into a deserted downtown Conroe. Two sheriff's deputies sat quietly in their unmarked car in the shadow of the courthouse, one using a telephoto lens to record the faces, the other scribbling names and car numbers in a notebook. The black people sang: 'Con-roe, Con-roe, have-you-heard? This-is-not-Jo-hannes-burg.'

A delegate from Amnesty International flew in from Atlanta, Georgia to annouce that Amnesty was asking its members all over the world to write to the Governor of Texas to demand Brandley's release. The parade was led by Minnie Ola Brandley.

'My heart is heavy,' she said. 'I'm happy for what the people have done, but my heart is sad, knowing that my son is dying for something someone else did.'

That night, they made all the local television news shows.

By Monday, Jim McCloskey was ready to talk to Clarence Brandley. He left Nugent's house early and set off in the car which the attorneys had found for him. It belonged to Mike De Geurin's mother, a big ugly old 1978 Chevy with red velvet upholstery and miraculously soft suspension, like a bordello on wheels. He turned the radio dial until he found his favourite station, which specialized in 1940s swing music, and to the gentle sound of Tommy Dorsey and Glenn Miller, McCloskey struck out northwards on I-45 for

Huntsville. As usual, McCloskey was running on high-octane enthusiasm. He was itching to see Brandley. He had scribbled out an encyclopaedic list of questions to ask him which he was still rehearsing in his mind as the old Chevy cruised up the long driveway and into the shadow of Death Row. Twenty minutes later, he was sitting down opposite Clarence Brandley, separated only by a thick, glass bullet-proof security screen.

He started with his questions, and two things soon became clear. First, Brandley could not answer most of them: he did not know who had killed the girl or what the other janitors had done or why James Robinson would have been in the school that day or anything else. This man truly had no idea what had hit him. Second, Brandley was not the way McCloskey had imagined. He had expected maybe some salesmanship or, at least, some venom about Acreman and Robinson, but Brandley just looked him straight in the eye – really straight in the eye – and told him what he knew. McCloskey began to feel moved by him.

He had been warned that he would not get long with him. By accident, or maybe providence, he got four hours. When he finally got up to leave, he had almost no answers to his questions, but he had an aching desire to work on this case, to save this innocent man who now had only three and a half weeks left to live.

It was Saturday, 7 March before McCloskey was ready to go on the road, eight days after his arrival in Houston and just 19 days before Brandley was due to die. He had spent more time talking with the attorneys, meeting Don Brown and Richard Reyna, burrowing into the papers, listing facts and witness statements. They all agreed that the white janitors were the key. McCloskey would go back to all of them for the truth. Now, on Saturday morning, he and Richard Reyna sat side by side in the big Chevy, sailing down a back road ten miles south-east of Conroe – Reyna with his cowboy boots, McCloskey with his white collar – looking for John Sessum.

Sessum was hard to find. He was not in his dirty wooden shed, which was a relief to Reyna. His drunken friend, T.D., who lived in an equally dirty trailer in the brush nearby, said he hadn't seen him, but he warned them that Sessum was scared. Gary Acreman and some other guy had run him off the road on his bike and chased him through the woods. It was the first Reyna and McCloskey had heard of it. They thanked T.D. and carried on searching.

It was early evening before they finally spotted him beetling along the road on his bike, hunched over the handlebars with his body sweated up under an old oilskin and a six-pack of beer planted in his bicycle basket. They gave him 20 minutes to get home and then set off after him, swooping up to his house in a swirl of dust as he was climbing off his bike.

Reyna was all smiles and back-slaps as he introduced McCloskey. Sessum hung back like a shy child, squinting at the man in the minister's collar, nodding 'Howdy' and allowing his limp fingers to be shaken before he moved to the back of his bike and peeled a beer out of the six-pack. McCloskey noticed that he had already drunk two of them on his way home.

Standing in the dusk outside the green wooden shed, the two investigators started talking, taking it in turns, playing it by ear. They had to get Sessum over some unseen hurdle, some mental block, before he would tell the rest of his story. They tried to reassure him that Gary Acreman would not lay a finger on him.

'I ain't worried about him.'

'So who are you worried about, John?'

'That sheriff. Gene Reaves. He threatened me that I'd go to jail and all this crap, that I'd get the devil beat out of me.' He said Wesley Styles had threatened him, too. And yet the two investigators sensed that this was not the real block. They kept nudging him along. He gave them a couple of beers and yielded a few small fragments: when Acreman was talking to that girl she seemed scared; he and Sam stayed at the bottom of the staircase drinking from the fountain there; then Acreman and the girl were nowhere to be seen. Later, Acreman disappeared from the vocational building for 40 minutes and returned just before Brandley came across with the keys to let them in; it all troubled him and gave him bad nights.

The two investigators could see there was a gaping blank space in this story. One second, Acreman was talking to the girl. The next, she was gone. Something happened in there. Everything happened in there. And Sessum knew what it was, if they could only get him over this mental hurdle. McCloskey asked him what the girl had said when Acreman was talking to her.

Sessum stared at the ground. 'I remember she said no.'

'Do you remember what Gary said for her to say no?'

Sessum shook his head. He would not look up. 'No,' he said, very quietly.

Reyna tried a new angle, looking for James Dexter Robinson. 'Did you see Gary Acreman talking to anybody that wasn't on the work crew that morning?'

Sessum drank his beer.

'Somebody different?' said Reyna.

Sessum sighed and looked away. 'Oh, boy . . .'

For a moment, Reyna thought he had lost him. Then Sessum started mumbling and sighing. 'He had dirty front teeth . . . I dunno. Might have had no teeth at all . . . Wait, wait, wait a minute . . .'

'Did this guy talk to Gary in the cafeteria?'

'Yeah, but I can't remember when it was.'

McCloskey caught Reyna's eye, and Reyna held up his hand to Sessum – hang on a minute – and strode back to the car.

McCloskey explained. 'If we got a picture of him, would you recognize him?'

Sessum nodded at the ground. 'He had thin hair and I think he had it combed to the left side.'

McCloskey kept talking. What about when Gary and the girl were at the top of the stairs – had the guy with no teeth been there then?

Sessum sighed and started slowly talking: 'He wasn't right there, but he was on the landing down there. When the girl was coming up, he was down by the water fountain. Then he came up too.'

McCloskey could feel his heart beating. For the first time, a witness had put the two prime suspects together with the girl at the moment of her disappearance. They were beginning to fill in the blank.

'Did you ever tell them about the guy with no teeth being there?'

'They didn't ask me.'

McCloskey wanted to know more about this police inquiry

where no one asked the right questions. McCloskey reminded Sessum of the day, one week after the girl's murder, one day after Brandley's arrest, when the Texas Ranger had walked him through the school with Acreman and Martinez. What had they said to him?

'That's when I was threatened. That Wesley Styles – "You tell them what I want you to tell them". He wanted me to tell 'em that Brandley did it. And I still say Brandley didn't do it.' Sessum paused and drained his beer. 'I will tell you this off the record. I believe Gary had something to do with it.'

'How about the guy with no teeth? Did he have something to do with it?'

Reyna rejoined them and showed Sessum the picture of James Dexter Robinson. 'Yeah, that's him. But I can't prove either one did it.'

He was trying to back off again. Had he always believed that Gary did it?

'I knew after he was talking to her. The same day, when Gary was bringing me home, he said "You don't tell any son-of-a-bitch that I was talking to her. 'Cause if you do, your ass is mine." I said "My ass might be yours but if they ask me I'm gonna tell them".'

'Did you ever talk about this to the DA?'

He was looking away again. 'You know how tough this has been with me?'

In his gentlest manner, McCloskey asked him: 'What do you think about when you have a bad night?'

'Like I say, I still think Gary had got something to do with it and every time I have a bad night, he's right in it.'

'In your dream, do you see Gary grabbing the girl?'

'I just see him talking to her and I remember her saying no. Just as loud and clear as we're standing here.'

Had he seen Gary grab the girl and take her off somewhere?

Sessum took a deep breath and slowly blew it out through his yellowed teeth. 'That's still a puzzle,' he said, slowly shaking his head.

He paused and sighed again, a deep, sagging sigh. 'It can put you in . . . It makes you lose a lot of sleep.'

His voice had broken. He was weeping.

They let him recover himself and tear open the final beer can. He seemed to find some new strength.

'I don't give a damn if he is a nigger. I'm not in love with no nigger. Now I want to tell you if he's innocent, I'm gonna fight for him. I guess I'll go back to court.'

McCloskey felt a surge of excitement. Then, without another word from the investigators, Sessum went one step further.

'I guess I'd go back to the school there, show y'all what happened.'

The two investigators could hardly believe their ears. This was far more than they had ever dared to hope for – a witness to the murder offering to reconstruct the crime for them.

McCloskey said: 'Would you have time to do it on Monday?'

'I'll make time.'

Now they were really coming close. They had not yet got over that hurdle – whatever it was that made Sessum weep, whatever it was that had kept him lying all these years. But he wanted to help them. He wanted to tell the truth. They were going to crack this thing.

It was dark by the time they drove away. In Conroe, at the black college on the outskirts of Dugan, they were singing gospel music and selling barbecued chicken to raise more money for the fight.

That Monday afternoon, 9 March, they gathered in the main lobby of the high school to try and reconstruct the day of the crime. Everyone was nervous. John Sessum looked like a dog that had just been kicked in the ribs. Don Brown, who had come along with his internal filing cabinet to check the details of the reconstruction was smoking impatiently, waiting for an assistant principal to bring them the keys they needed. Reyna and McCloskey were trying to look calm, but inside they were desperate to succeed.

Since their visit to Sessum, they had had no luck with other witnesses. They had wasted most of Sunday trailing around the hills outside Cleveland looking for Icky Peace. When they had finally found him, he insisted in his little boy's voice that he was under a gag order and that Conroe High School, where he was working again, would fire him if he talked. With some encouragement from his sister, he had talked a little, describing how he had heard the policeman tell Brandley that he was elected to take the blame, and how Acreman had come over to the vocational building on the day of the crime saying that they should not worry about Brandley because he was having fun with a white girl over there, and there was clothes and chairs scattered all over the place. But Peace was not about to give them any breakthrough, at least not while he thought he was under his supposed gag order.

Ed Payne had been little better. The two investigators had just spent most of the morning with him; they had got him acquainted with McCloskey but had not dug out any new information from him.

And time was moving on. There were now only two and a half weeks until Brandley was due to die. Somehow, they had to get John Sessum to unload his story.

As they all waited outside the administration office, each pacing a different track in the corridor, McCloskey noticed a small round figure with a bucket, polishing his way along the hallway window in their direction, rubbing furiously at the glass, frowning with concentration, trying to pretend he was not at all interested in what they were all doing. It was Icky Peace, keeping abreast of developments.

'Hey, Icky, how are ya?'

At last the assistant principal came with the keys, and led them down to the scene of the crime, to the restrooms at Sesame Street. They could see the tension building in John Sessum. They had brought a friend of Reyna's, Peggy Miller, to act out the part of Cheryl Fergeson, and as she came walking towards them down the empty hallway from the gyms where the blonde girl in the blue jeans had once walked, to the staircase where they stood waiting for her, Sessum froze with fear. He could barely speak to tell them he had nothing to say. He just stood there with his hands buried in his pockets, staring at his mangled old shoes and shaking his head.

After a while, they took him across to the vocational building to see if that would help him. Sessum sat on the steps with his head in his hands. Brown and McCloskey took it in turns to urge him to talk. Sessum finally found words to speak, but all he would say was 'I can't do it. I can't do it.' Finally, they gave up. They could not get him over this unseen hurdle.

Don Brown went back to his office. Peggy Miller drove home. McCloskey and Reyna told Sessum they would drive him back to his bike, which he had left on the edge of Conroe at the depot where he checked in all his bottles and cans. They put him in the old Chevy, told him not to worry, and turned on the Glen Miller music. McCloskey made small talk while Reyna, who was driving, lost himself in thought, trying to cut through all this crap to see what it was that was bugging this guy. Reyna was still turning it over in his mind when they arrived at Sessum's workplace.

McCloskey was talking about the crime again, gently lobbing simple questions at Sessum. Sessum was unlocking his bike, sighing, shaking his head and saying, 'That's 'bout all I know.'

But Reyna was beginning to see something, something that happened by that school staircase all those years before. 'John, you didn't see the murder. But you saw him grab her. Didn't you?'

Reyna was still not sure what he was trying to get at here. Sessum said nothing and straddled his bike. 'I know it,' said Reyna, 'and you know it.'

Sessum was silent. Then Reyna finally saw it – the shame of a derelict alcoholic who wanted to be a brave man. 'You saw him grab her and you got the hell out of there because you didn't want to be involved in it. That's what you've been trying to live with for the last six years.'

Sessum's chin was sunk on his chest, crushed by the weight of his cowardice.

Reyna persisted. 'John? John, am I right?'

Sessum looked up. 'It ain't been easy.'

Now that they could see the hurdle, they started trying to bring him over it. 'John, did he grab her by the throat or by the arms?'

'I ain't . . .' Sessum wiped one dirty hand over the grime on his face. 'I think he caught her by the arm.'

McCloskey pulled him a little further. 'Who was with him when he did it? . . . He needed help . . . Who joined him?'

'The man with no teeth.'

Finally, Sessum's memory was starting to unload its story. It came out like water from a rusty tap, stuttering and choking. He told how he and Sam Martinez had been by the drinking-fountain at the bottom of the stairs, how Gary Acreman had grabbed the girl up by the restroom. That was when she had screamed no. Then the other guy was there, the guy with no teeth, standing next to them by the drinking-fountain, and he had run up the stairs to join Gary. And he had had something in his hands. It was a belt. Every so often, Sessum stopped and cried again, but eventually he got it out.

There were still lots of details missing, but he had told the story – except for one moment he could still not bring himself to recall, the moment his cowardice had been exposed.

McCloskey asked him: 'Did she ask any of you guys to help? Did she look down and say help me. . . ?'

Sessum's eyes were closed, his head sunk. Slowly, he said: 'I can't answer that question.'

'She did, didn't she, John? . . . John? . . . She asked you, didn't she, John?'

'Ask Sam.'

'All right, John. Thank you, John.'

Sessum heaved himself on to his bike and peddled off, wobbling slightly as he hit the road. The two investigators drove back to Conroe.

The only way to get to Sam Martinez was to set up an old-fashioned stake-out. Reyna had never lost the suspicion that Martinez was involved in this thing too, and he had been trying to get him to talk ever since he started his inquiry in July the previous year. He had stayed in touch with Martinez's estranged wife, Dolores, teasing her about her affection for Brandley, trying to use her to somehow persuade Martinez to talk. But he never would.

The next day, Tuesday, McCloskey and Reyna were outside his home in Dugan, slouched in the red velvet upholstery, listening to swing music and talking about anything to pass the time, waiting and waiting until their bones ached. It was hard to stay inspired. In the rearview-mirror, McCloskey saw a young black kid coming bicycling up the road towards them. For want of anything better to do, he watched him peddle past the car and so he saw, as the boy rode off down the road in front of them, the message on the little sticker on the back of his bike. 'Free Clarence Brandley,' it said. McCloskey smiled and felt a little inspiration trickle back. But when Sam Martinez eventually turned up he was adamant. He would not talk. He had nothing to say. They must leave him alone.

They went back to John Sessum. A storm had blown in from the Gulf. The rain was as thick as sea fog, boiling up from the ground in clouds. Sessum invited them to take shelter in his home, and they agreed. It was a mistake. Both men immediately found themselves gagging in the foul stench, wincing and swallowing. Sessum was very tense. Before, he had always been morose and vague. Tonight, he was seething with nervous energy. All the years of guilt and self-reproach were breaking loose in him. He wanted to tell them the truth.

'Y'all wanna beer?' he offered.

The two men accepted and pulled up two metal fold-away chairs from the wall. Sessum perched on the yellow-brown sheets of his bed and started to talk. It was part confessional, part thriller, all of it punctuated by gulps of beer and occasional silent lapses.

He wanted to talk about his guilt. 'I been thinkin' 'bout it. . . . You don't know how it's been with me . . . I been through hell . . . I heard her yell, heard her say "Help" . . . I feel like . . .'

His voice trailed away. He sat slumped with his can of beer between his knees and suddenly his whole body was heaving with sorrow and he was crying with all his heart. 'I feel like I was the one who caused her death.' He was sobbing now. 'If I had gone back, maybe I'd a' had a chance to save her. They still might have done it, but I'd a' been up here, trying . . . That's what's been eating me up . . . And I can still see Acreman, just as plain as day.'

He stopped to suck in air and rub the tears from his face. McCloskey and Reyna told him it was OK and that he was doing the right thing and he would feel better now. Sessum took a deep breath and started to talk some more, still pausing to gulp his beer and to remember. He looked again at the picture of James Dexter

Robinson. 'Yeah. He's got those screetchy-looking eyes. And he's still got that crease down his face . . . If I ain't mistaken, that's the man . . . Yeah, that's the man, because his eyes are still screetchy like that . . . He was going up there and Sam was coming down . . . She hollered for help. I don't know how many times. I started up but Sam stopped me. I couldn't get him out of my way. Sam said "You ain't going up there".'

Determined now to tell his story, Sessum rose from the bed and, using Jim McCloskey as a model, he acted out the grabbing of the girl. Then he talked about Clarence Brandley. Oh yes, Brandley had come walking along the hallway, just like they all said in the trial, but he was not just ten feet behind the girl. He was 10 or 20 minutes behind her. Acreman and Robinson had dragged the girl off long before he got there.

'Did they reappear before Clarence came up?'

'Gary did. About the same time. It was 10 or 20 minutes.'

'Did you hear Gary tell Clarence not to go into the restroom?'

'Yep.'

'Do you think she was dead in the restroom with Robinson at that point?'

'I wouldn't doubt it.'

Now the investigators could see the details beginning to bind together.

First there was the girl, walking innocently up those stairs at Sesame Street; Acreman trying to talk to her, showing off to the others; Robinson joining in; the two men trying to touch her; the girl crying no; and then this casual encounter turning nasty, with each man egged on by the other's presence and the girl being grabbed and dragged into the restroom.

Then, maybe 10 minutes later, Brandley had come down that hallway. Acreman was back on the staircase by now – warned perhaps by Martinez. And the black janitor, completely unaware of the nightmare on the other side of the wall at the top of that staircase, had sent the white janitors over to the vocational building, put his toilet rolls in the boys' restroom and gone off about his work.

On the way out to the vocational building, Acreman must have blocked the outside door open with the rubbish bin, which

Brandley had later found, so that he could go back to clear up the crime. That was why he had gone missing for 30 or 40 minutes, with or without Martinez. He must have gone back to the restroom to help Robinson move the girl's body out of there and into the auditorium, an auditorium that was easily unlocked with the set of keys that Robinson's father had given him. One of them had taken the clothes out to the dumpster. Then Robinson had left the area and Acreman had gone back about his work, already looking for ways to cover his tracks.

That was when he had done something which now appeared crucial – something which, they now saw, was the tiny move that started the avalanche, something that, to a man like Acreman in a place like Montgomery County, was second nature. He had blamed the black man. He had returned to the vocational building and told Icky Peace: 'Don't worry about Clarence. He's got himself a white girl over there. There's clothes and chairs all over the place.' It must have been almost instinctive. Blame the black man. Peace had thought he was just kidding, but he had not known a crime had been committed.

Then when the body was found, it was as if everyone in Conroe had the same instinct, and the teachers and the students and the police and the press and the DA and the judges, and all the ringleaders and all the bystanders had agreed that they should blame the black man and after a while it had stopped mattering how many rules had to be broken or how much evidence had to be lost or how many witnesses had to be threatened. So they had taken Clarence Brandley.

Now, in a way that had nothing to do with the filth in John Sessum's shack, the two investigators felt sick in their hearts. It was ironic that out of all the people who had pointed the finger at the black janitor – all the well-respected officials and all the upstanding townspeople who all agreed that the black man must die – it was a social reject like John Sessum, a walking failure in everything he had ever done, who had finally had the courage to break ranks. Now the important thing was to guard Sessum's new strength and persuade him to put all this into a statement.

McCloskey said: 'Do you know how you can redeem this, and especially bring justice and help her father?'

Sessum lifted an eyebrow and asked why McCloskey did not mention the dead girl's mother.

McCloskey shrugged. 'Her mother died six months before she was killed.'

'Hold on. You just hit something.' Sessum paused and scratched his oily hair. 'Gary did say something . . . Can't remember all the detail . . . He said something about the girl's mother dying, it was just her and her daddy.'

'When did he say that?'

'On the way home that day.'

How could Gary Acreman possibly have known that the girl's mother was dead? Suddenly McCloskey had an image of sheer horror, of the dark restroom and these two animals with the belt, and the little girl on her knees, begging for her life, telling them her mother had died and it was just her and her daddy and how he needed her.

That was maybe the sickest thing of all – this self-righteous mob had been so determined to blame the black man and put him under the ground that they had turned their backs on the real criminals and let these bastards get away with what they had done to that poor girl.

McCloskey explained to Sessum that he must repeat all this to the attorneys. He agreed. The two investigators drove away in silence.

McCloskey and Reyna felt that they had now broken through two vital barriers. They had uncovered what they believed to be the truth; and they had found a witness who was prepared to talk. But they knew it was not enough. Not in Conroe.

The previous year's hearing had taught Reyna that the courthouse would fight tooth and nail to keep Clarence Brandley on Death Row. One witness – one wretched, half-dead alcoholic witness with a bad case of nerves – was not going to be enough to force the courthouse to release its black man. With only two weeks before Brandley was due to die, they started an almost frantic search for more witnesses. They tried to find Gary Acreman, but he was working as a truck driver and was out of the state. They went and asked Ed Payne to get a message to him to tell him to contact them, and Reyna saw Cindy Payne and forced himself to cuddle up to her and ask her to pass on the same message if she got the chance.

They tried Sam Martinez again, but he would not play.

They staked out Icky Peace, and spent hours sitting outside the school watching the day go by. Eventually, they saw him waddle out into the parking lot and drive off. The old Chevy chased off after him and pulled up alongside him at the first set of traffic lights.

McCloskey started waving out of the window. 'Hey, Icky! Fancy seeing you here! How are ya?'

But Peace did not want to stop and talk. He was still convinced that he was under a gag order. The investigators suspected that this was not merely the work of his imagination and that someone at the school really had told him to keep his mouth shut. Somehow, they had to find a break.

On Friday 13 March, Revd Boney officially launched the Coalition to Free Clarence Brandley, an umbrella for 25 different groups in the area, each of whom was now pledged to campaign for Brandley's freedom. Boney called a press conference in a community centre in one of Houston's black wards. It rapidly turned into a rally, with a small crowd of supporters wearing Free Clarence Brandley T-shirts, cheering and chanting.

Boney said they were ready to go to gaol if that was what it took. Texas's only black congressman, US Rep Mickey Leland, announced his support. The President of the local chapter of the National Association for the Advancement of Colored People, Judge Al Green, asked the crowd: 'Would Texas allow a white man to be tried by a black judge and jury, in a town that was predominantly black, for killing a black girl?' The supporters jeered their answer.

The press was beginning to move. Both the big Houston newspapers, the *Chronicle* and the *Post*, ran lengthy features, suggesting Brandley might be the victim of racism. The *Chronicle* interviewed Peter Speers, who announced airily: 'The idea that anybody – even the KKK – would be interested in going and trying to frame someone for the murder just because they are black is totally preposterous.'

Brandley's supporters were not impressed. They agreed they would once again march on the Governor's mansion in Austin in a week's time.

Don Brown opened up a discreet line to the office of the Texas Attorney General, Jim Mattox, who would represent the state of Texas if the case ever reached the federal courts and who had the political clout to help them if he chose to. Brown's contact in the AG's office was a young black attorney named Wayne Johnson, whose father had been a labour leader and an old friend of Brown's. Brown asked Wayne Johnson to speak to the Attorney General to warn him that they were hoping to produce strong new evidence of Brandley's innocence, and to ask if he would issue arrest warrants for the real murderers since the DA's office would never do it. Wayne Johnson said he would do what he could.

Meanwhile, McCloskey and Reyna had persuaded Sessum to make a formal statement to Mike De Geurin and had arranged to pick him up at his house on Sunday morning to take him to Houston. But when they got there, Sessum was nowhere to be seen. They felt a flutter of anxiety. They started driving up and down the all-too-familiar back roads and, after 30 minutes, they spotted him, picking up old cans in the grass. The Chevy glided up alongside him and McCloskey wound down his window.

'Hey, John. Where were you, man?'

Sessum kept on loading cans into his sack without looking up.

'John, you're supposed to be coming into Houston with us. You remember?'

'I ain't going.'

McCloskey felt his heart sink. It was not so much what he said as the voice he said it in, which was not far off a snarl.

'John, you promised you would come with us. You were going to help Clarence. What's happened, man? What's the matter?'

'I ain't going. Get outta here.'

'But John . . .'

'Go on. Get outta here.'

The two investigators shrugged at each other. 'All right, John. Thanks anyway.'

They drove off, cursing. Sessum's shame had risen up and swallowed him again. Now they were in big trouble. There were 11 days until the execution. Without Sessum they could do little more than limp into court and beg for mercy. If they could not get him back, Brandley was a dead man. McCloskey dropped Reyna in Conroe and headed for Mike De Geurin's house to share the bad news. Two hours later, he left with a new plan: De Geurin would come with them the next day to try his famous charm on John Sessum.

As soon as Sessum saw the old Chevy burning up to his shack, he scowled. 'I thought I told you guys I wasn't gonna talk no more.'

They climbed out of the car and introduced De Geurin who never needed to be asked twice to make a new friend and shook Sessum warmly by the hand. Sessum looked stern and growled: 'Y'all wanna come in?'

It was the last thing they wanted to do, but they had to agree. Sessum opened the door of his shack and his dog, which was normally chained up, pounced out snarling, with the hair over its shoulders standing up rigid, and leaped at the nearest available stranger, who happened to be Richard Reyna. It locked its teeth into the top of his left leg.

'Goddamn it,' yelled Reyna. 'Get this son-of-a-bitch off me.'

It hurt Reyna, but it helped their situation. Sessum hauled the dog off and cursed at it, McCloskey and De Geurin started chuckling, Reyna cursed some more, but Sessum ended up apologizing and trying to make amends, and it seemed that the ice was broken.

Inside the shack, Sessum offered them all a beer, turned on an old black-and-white television set over his bed and told them to take a seat. The three men settled down while Sessum turned to the grimy sink where he had some beer cans floating in lukewarm water. Reyna rubbed his leg and checked out the tooth marks in his trousers, and De Geurin started shuffling a notebook out of his briefcase. The next thing they knew, John Sessum was rearing up over them like a nightmare, with a 12-inch butcher's knife flashing in his right fist and his face red and twisted with rage, and he was screaming at them: 'You get the fuck outta here. Get the fuck outta here. Get the fuck outta here.'

The knife was quivering in his fist. All three of them started talking at once. 'Okay, John, okay . . . We're going, man . . . Don't worry about it . . . Stay cool . . . There's no need for that . . .'

As they reached the door, De Geurin, following the habit of a lifetime, turned back into the room, grinned like a pixie and held out his hand. 'Nice to meet you, John.'

Sessum switched the butcher's blade to his left hand and solemnly shook the attorney's hand.

'Jesus Christ,' said Reyna. 'I don't believe this shit.'

But once the shock of the moment had passed, they felt the weight of their failure and drove back to Conroe in despair. They stopped by Don Brown's office, and there Reyna decided to try a different approach. He called up Mattie Johnson, the old lady who lived next door to Sessum and who had saved his sensibilities on his first visit to Sessum's shack. He got her on the phone and explained what was happening and asked her to have a word with Sessum for them.

Half an hour later, the phone rang in Brown's office. It was Mattie Johnson. Reyna took the call, deadpan, then turned round to the others, clapped his hands together and shouted: 'Holy shit! He's gonna do it. She talked him into it. God knows how. But all we got to do is be out there again tomorrow.'

It was St Patrick's Day, Tuesday 17 March. The defence were feeling strong again. That afternoon, thanks to Mattie Johnson, they would try to interview John Sessum once more, and they had arranged to take a video camera so that there would be an indisputable record of his evidence.

In Dallas, the *Times Herald* had splashed the story of the Brandley case across its front page under the black headline, 'Hundreds plead: Don't let State murder innocent man.' The story disclosed that the case had generated more letters of concern to the Governor than any other in the state's history.

By noon, the defence were feeling even stronger: Gary Acreman had walked into Don Brown's office, saying he had heard they wanted to see him. Brown was in court, but Acreman had waited and then left word with Brown's secretary that he was driving up to Corsicana, 150 miles north of Conroe on I-45, and he would call from there.

At three o'clock, McCloskey and Reyna set off from Brown's office with Mike De Geurin and the reporter who had written the Dallas *Times Herald* story that morning, Tom Curtis. Curtis wanted the story of Sessum's revelations, and De Geurin wanted him there as a witness to testify that they were not cheating in any way. Don Brown stayed behind, hoping that Acreman would call.

At four o'clock, John Sessum sat down in front of the video camera and started to talk to Mike De Geurin. He was stumbling and stuttering, he appeared to have been drinking and he said he was scared, but what mattered was that he was talking.

At five minutes past four, Don Brown answered the phone in his office and found himself talking to Gary Acreman in Corsicana. Acreman was curious to find out what the defence were doing and agreed to meet the two investigators. He gave Brown the name and room number of the motel where he was staying for the night. Brown told him to sit tight; Reyna and McCloskey would be there around nine o'clock.

At six o'clock, the defence team left Sessum. They felt triumphant. Sessum had told his whole story on camera, nailing Acreman and Robinson to the crime, right down to admitting that he had failed to do anything to help the girl because, as he put it, 'I guess I had a little rabbit in me'. He had even apologized for attacking them the previous evening. 'I'm a hard-headed baboon,' he said.

By half past six they were in Don Brown's office, preparing to set off for Corsicana and Gary Acreman. Brown was worried that Acreman might be planning some nasty surprise for them. He had no doubt that Reyna could whip his ass in a fair fight, but if Acreman had a gun, the unarmed investigators could be in trouble. Tom Curtis had agreed to travel with them to provide safety in numbers and so, while De Geurin stayed behind to talk tactics with Don Brown, the two investigators and the reporter hurtled northwards to reach Corsicana by nine o'clock.

For McCloskey and Reyna, this was the big prize. Sessum had done well but he was never going to be an ideal witness, and anyway, he knew only part of the story. Acreman was different: if he started to confirm any of their new information, they would surely be strong enough to put the courthouse to flight. He had already started at the previous year's hearing when he had sworn that Robinson was at the high school on the day of the crime, but he had never talked about the attack on the girl. Somehow they had to get him to fill in more of the picture. The big question was why in hell Acreman would do that and book himself a seat on Death Row? The question nagged away at them as the sped north. They had still not found the answer when the old Chevy rolled into the parking lot of the Travellers Inn, Corsicana, soon after nine o'clock. But a few moments after the two investigators knocked on the door of Room 211, the problem was solved for them.

Gary Acreman opened the door, and as soon as they saw his face they knew: this guy was scared shitless. Reyna decided to give him something to be scared about. They took him across the road to the Holiday Inn and settled him into the coffee shop. Curtis sat a few tables away, observing. Acreman and Reyna ordered cups of tea. McCloskey straightened his white collar and ordered a bourbon on the rocks. Reyna went to work.

He threw him off balance from the start by telling him that witnesses were changing their stories, without letting him know what they were now saying. He told Acreman that finally the truth was coming out and watched his eyes flicker nervously round the room. He started playing him off against James Dexter Robinson, urging him not to take the rap for something someone else had done.

Acreman soon started to move. First, he tried to line himself up with what he guessed other witnesses were now saying. 'I'd like to see Brandley get out,' he said. 'I'd like to see him get out because from day one, I didn't think he was the one that done it.'

Reyna resisted a desire to slap him in the face and remind him that he was one of the state's main witnesses against Brandley, and continued to play him off against Robinson. 'Don't protect this guy because he's your buddy.'

'He's not my buddy,' snapped Acreman, moving a little more to distance himself from Robinson.

Acreman started mumbling about the vocational building, and Reyna abruptly told him to forget it. 'We're talking about the period of time the girl was looking for the bathroom. That's what I'm interested in.'

Acreman's eyes were twitching from Reyna's face to the table. Reyna started to let on just how much they now knew: 'Why would they say you went upstairs to talk to her? . . . You talked to her for about three or four minutes . . . The girl said no and she started yelling for help . . . She was grabbed.'

Acreman started to shake. It was like watching a replay of his meeting with Reyna the previous summer. Once again he was wrestling with his fingers, trying to get a cigarette into his mouth, and failing hopelessly. Jim McCloskey quietly reached across the table, took the cigarette from the packet, pointed it into his mouth and lit it for him. Acreman managed to speak. 'I didn't see.'

'Don't protect that asshole,' snarled Reyna. 'Let me ask you this. Would all these people lie when they say that they saw you talk to her and saw you grab her, or that you were talking to her, and Robinson grabbed her.'

'I don't know.'

'Robinson was down there, where the water fountain was, the bottom level. He's already been ID'd as being down there and then coming upstairs with you.'

'Not with me. Not with me.'

'Don't bullshit us. Just help us.'

'I wasn't there with the girl. I left.'

'Was Robinson up there?' Reyna stared relentlessly at Acreman, who was now sitting on one quaking hand and using the other to haul smoke out of his cigarette like it was his dying breath. Reyna jabbed a finger in front of his face. 'You know he was there! Did he go into the restroom?'

'I don't know. We left.'

'You ain't never gonna get it out of your heart until you come forward. You know you saw Robinson do something up there. Don't protect the asshole.'

Then Acreman moved again. 'I saw him go up there. I didn't know he did anything.'

They had broken through. Reyna and McCloskey could see Acreman struggling to tell the story without putting himself into the middle of it. Reyna kept asking him who had grabbed the girl. Acreman kept shaking his head and then finally said: 'Robinson must have put her in the restroom.'

Reyna kept up the pressure. 'You'll be able to sleep better, man. It's been a nightmare.'

'Yeah,' said Acreman. 'And now it'll be another nightmare.'

Reyna reckoned it was time to move on. 'Listen now. What we want to do is this. Very simple. We don't want to bother you any more. We want to get an interview with you. Do it tonight. Take about ten minutes. OK?'

'OK.'

McCloskey kept Acreman talking, Reyna went off to fetch the video camera, Curtis rented a room, and ten minutes later Acreman was settled in an armchair in the room in front of the camera, with a cigarette burning between his fingers. Now he was calmer and more assured. As the camera whirred, he described a scene which confirmed all that John Sessum had told them, with the one exception that in Acreman's version of events it was Robinson alone who attacked the girl while he was merely an innocent bystander like the other janitors, intimidated and powerless to help. But the details were the same – the same scene at the top of the stairs where the girl was stopped, the same cries of no and help as she was dragged into the restroom, the same delay before Brandley arrived on the scene. Sometimes, he paused and sighed deeply. Once or twice they thought he was about to cry. Often, he rested his head on his hand and simply stared in silence. As the interview went on he became more and more outspoken about Robinson's guilt. 'There's no doubt,' he said. He suggested it was no surprise to see Robinson act like that, because he had been round to Robinson's house and seen him fighting violently with Brenda. 'I mean, you'd think they was gonna have a war.'

Towards the end, Jim McCloskey leaned towards him in his

clergyman's clothes and looked him straight in the eye. 'Now, Gary, did you have anything to do with it?'

Acreman shook his head vigorously from side to side. 'No. Nothing. I . . .' He sighed long and deep and ran his hand over his eyes. 'No.' Then his head was back on his palm and he was silent again.

The investigators did not believe him for a minute. They returned to a theme which had been troubling Acreman throughout the interview: he could not explain why he had told the approaching Brandley that there was a girl in the restroom if the truth was – as he now said – that at that moment he knew the girl was in there with someone who was attacking her.

'Did you think she was a dead girl in the restroom?' asked McCloskey.

Acreman sighed. 'I don't know.'

'Why did you say "There's a girl in the restroom"?'

'I don't know that either.'

'Because you knew, you knew that James Robinson was in that room with her at the time, didn't you?'

Acreman nodded. Tom Curtis closed in: 'So you were trying to stop Clarence from going in there and observing that?'

'I guess in a way I was.'

That nailed him. He was never going to tell them he had killed the girl himself, but right there, so far as the investigators were concerned, he had just admitted that he was an accessory to murder.

'Fine,' said Reyna.

They switched off the camera. McCloskey walked Acreman back to his room, reassuring him that he would feel better now that he had got it out of his system. Acreman said he did feel better now and he was glad.

With Acreman out of the way, the two investigators whooped for joy. McCloskey called Mike De Geurin at his home in Houston. It was after midnight now, but De Geurin was still up.

'Mike, we got him. We got him on tape.'

'Holy shit, Jim.'

And De Geurin too had news for the investigators. A reporter had called a little earlier to ask for a comment on the statement from the Texas Attorney General, Jim Mattox. De Geurin had had no idea what he was talking about, so the reporter had explained that the Attorney General had just announced publicly that he believed Clarence Brandley should be given a stay of execution.

McCloskey pointed the old Chevy southwards. 'That's not a bad St Paddy's day,' he said.

In Conroe the next morning, Wednesday 18 March, Don Brown strode across the street to the courthouse and filed a formal request for a hearing before Judge Coker so that the defence could win a stay of execution. He then strode back without disclosing what kind of new evidence the defence had found, leaving a dust cloud of rumour and speculation behind him.

In Houston, Mike De Geurin opened new negotiations with Wayne Johnson in the Texas Attorney General's office. He explained that he did not trust the DA's office in Conroe to handle the vital new evidence which they had now obtained from two witnesses. He wanted the Attorney General to see the evidence personally and to take over the investigation of the crime himself. Wayne Johnson agreed to talk to the Attorney General.

In the community centre in Houston's third ward, Revd Don Boney called for volunteers for a campaign of civil disobedience on behalf of Clarence Brandley, and threw all his energy into the march he was planning on the Governor's mansion in Austin that Friday.

In Huntsville Jail, Clarence Brandley spoke to reporters and said he was hoping and praying for a stay and that he was very happy with the Attorney General's statement. 'It was delightful for me to hear,' he said.

Only Brandley's family knew how desperate he felt. Now only seven days away from his date with the executioner, his face was puffy from lack of sleep, he had lost at least 20 pounds because he was too tense to eat, and he was constantly chewing on the inside of his lower lip.

In Austin, Wayne Johnson went into a huddle with the Attorney General and then called Mike De Geurin to tell him that the

Attorney General would personally meet the defence to review the new evidence within the next 24 hours.

Reyna and McCloskey were still looking for witnesses. With two aces in their hand they figured they might as well go for a third, and so, with Tom Curtis still in tow, they caught a plane for South Carolina.

But the enemy were standing their ground. In the DA's office, Peter Speers was being harried by the press. He assured them that Clarence Brandley was 'the only man on earth capable of committing that murder'. Speers had no idea what the defence had come up with, but he was not worried about any new evidence. Nothing in the state of Texas had changed since the hearing last year: new evidence could not be introduced more than 30 days after the end of the trial. It did not matter how many new facts the defence claimed to come up with, it would all be inadmissible and could not be mentioned. If Peter Speers III had his way, Brandley was going to keep his appointment with the executioner in the early hours of the morning of next Thursday, 26 March. When the *New York Times* called him up and asked if he had any doubts about the execution, Speers confided: 'I wouldn't lose any sleep over it, except maybe to go to bed later than usual to see that it actually happens.'

In the courtroom on the first floor, Judge Lynn Coker agreed to hold a hearing in two days' time, on Friday 20 March.

In the early hours of Thursday morning, outside a textile factory in Greenville, South Carolina, Reyna and McCloskey closed in on James Dexter Robinson. They knew Robinson was in there, working a shift that was supposed to end at three in the morning. It was dark and quiet. They waited in their hired car for Robinson to walk through the gate. Nothing happened. They were tired and tense. In the back seat, Tom Curtis suddenly spoke.

'There's a cop car just pulled up.'

The two investigators whirled round, expecting some kind of trouble. They could see nothing. Then Reyna rolled his eyes up and broke into a long wheezing laugh. There was no car, only a pile of metal pipes by the side of the road, which Curtis in his tiredness had mistaken for the police.

When there was still no sign of Robinson at four in the morning,

McCloskey decided to go into the factory. Wearing his white collar, he walked cautiously through the gate and disappeared. Five minutes later he came strolling back, talking earnestly with a small pixie-faced man whose face Reyna instantly recognized. As they approached the car, Reyna got out and offered his hand.

'Hey,' said Robinson, drawing back, 'You never told me he was with you.'

Reyna and McCloskey gave Robinson their sweetest talk and told him they did not want to question him. They just wanted to show him the videotapes that Acreman had been making so he could see for himself what Acreman was saying about him. Robinson relaxed and said they could come inside with him while he finished his shift, which had another hour to run. Inside the factory, Robinson started scrambling up and down long metal ladders pouring buckets of dye into giant vats. The two investigators scrambled up and down behind him. Robinson told them he would call his uncle to see if they could use his video player to watch the video.

But when Robinson came back from making his call, he spoke to a supervisor who told the two investigators to leave. Back in their car, they saw Robinson walk out of the gate, spot them and retreat inside again. The next thing they knew, a car was speeding past them with a passenger trying to duck down out of sight. They spun their car round and gave chase, lurching over a thick kerbstone and jumping several sets of lights before they saw the futility of it all. Even if they caught up with him he was never going to talk now. They had to let him go.

In Austin that Thursday afternoon, Mike De Geurin sat down with Attorney General Mattox and explained about the black janitor and the circumstantial evidence, and about all the fragments of information which had surfaced pointing to the guilt of the two white men. Then De Geurin played him the videotapes of John Sessum and Gary Acreman – the first eyewitnesses in the history of the case – each describing the helpless struggles of Cheryl Fergeson, and exonerating the black janitor.

De Geurin could see that Mattox was impressed, and asked him to issue warrants for the arrest of Acreman and Robinson and to put his own investigators on the case. De Geurin knew Mattox was a politician and it was common knowledge that he was hoping to make a run for the Governor's mansion, but he was not too worried by that. He hoped that as a lawyer, Mattox would see the strength of Brandley's case and that as a politician, he would see the advantage of playing the hero. Mattox was cautious; he said he would prefer it if the DA in Conroe would invite him to conduct an investigation, but he would see what he could do.

That night, Reyna and McCloskey flew back to Houston from South Carolina. Sitting shoulder to shoulder in the plane, they relaxed for the first time in three days and replayed all that had happened, the setbacks and breakthroughs and now the hope of victory. Before they really knew it, the two of them were crying their eyes out.

Early on Friday morning, before the courthouse was awake, an old bus wheezed through Dugan, over the railway track, and headed west for Austin, 150 miles away. At about the same time, outside a community centre in Houston, three more buses set out in the same direction. Revd Boney's angry army was on the move.

An hour later, the courthouse opened for the day. Throughout the building, there was only one subject of conversation – the newspaper stories which said that two of the white janitors had changed their evidence and now insisted that Brandley was innocent. The District Attorney asked his investigator, Frank Newton, to see what he could find out about that.

Soon after ten o'clock, a rangy guy with reddish-brown hair drove into a parking lot on Route 105 east of Conroe. It was Gary Acreman, keeping a date with Reyna and McCloskey. The two investigators had called him because they wanted to follow up on some of the things he had told them in Corsicana. Now Acreman said he, too, wanted to talk about what he had told them. He had been thinking, he said, that maybe there were a few things he had said the other night that were not quite right, and maybe he should be changing a few things. Reyna and McCloskey could guess what had happened: he had had time to worry about whether his new story was going to fit with all these other witnesses he was hearing about.

Reyna spotted an angle. It was too late to change the video, he said, because it had already been sent up to the Attorney General. 'But, if you really want to straighten out your story, well, Jim and I would be willing to help you make another video. We could do it right now, if you wanted.'

Acreman went for it.

Sitting in front of the camera, Acreman began by repeating without prompting that he had seen James Dexter Robinson grab the girl and drag her screaming into the restroom. No change there. Still, the two investigators were glad he was repeating it: if the DA tried to make out that they had tricked or pressured him into saying any of this in Corsicana, they could now point to the fact that the man had turned up voluntarily and told the same story.

Acreman soon got round to what was bugging him. He recalled how he had gone over to the vocational building and started pacing up and down while they waited for Brandley to come and let them in. 'And in that time that I was pacing, I seen Robinson come out of the side, back at the main building, and go to the dumpster and dump a bag in.'

'OK,' said Reyna. 'Do you know what was in the bag?'

'At the top of it, it looked like it was clothes hanging out of it.'

Acreman went on to describe how Robinson had then collected a large stack of broken ceiling tiles from the school and dumped them on top of the clothes. He then agreed that he had gone home and told his father-in-law that he knew the girl's clothes were in the dumpster. Reyna and McCloskey did not believe this man was necessarily telling them the whole truth. They doubted whether you could even see the dumpster from the spot where Acreman said he was pacing. They doubted even more whether you could identify the contents of a rubbish bag at such a distance. The truth, they suspected, was that Acreman had been very much closer to that rubbish bag as it went into the dumpster and had possibly even carried it himself. But that did not matter right now. What mattered was that he was finally confirming his father-in-law's story and admitting to having vital evidence which he had failed to disclose in court.

There was one more thing that was bugging Acreman. This trip he had made to the Shamrock Station to buy cigarettes and cold drinks with Sam Martinez. He realized now that that had not happened while they were all waiting outside the vocational building. That had been three hours earlier when they had first arrived at the high school, before they even started work for the day.

The two investigators could only guess why he was suddenly shifting his story. It appeared that he was trying to double the strength of his alibi for those missing 30 or 40 minutes: not only had be been with Martinez, who would swear that they had not been moving the girl's body, but also this whole disappearance of his had occurred before the girl was even killed.

Finally, he told them explicitly why he was making these video statements for them. 'Because I don't think Clarence Brandley is guilty,' he said. 'And, well, I know for a fact he isn't.'

The two investigators finished the interview, turned off the camera and thanked him most sincerely for his help.

At noon in Austin, all was quiet outside the towering capitol building that sits on a hill as if in judgement on the city below. The State Assembly was in session. The first that anyone heard of the approaching throng was a soft chant, lapping around the edges of the building. 'Jus-tice! Jus-tice! Jus-tice!' Several hundred voices sang the word. Then there were shouts. 'Stop the racist death penalty . . . Give justice a chance . . . Free Clarence Brandley.'

There must have been 300 of them – nearly ten times as many as the last protest in Austin, two long months earlier. There were children wearing 'Free Clarence Brandley' T-shirts, men and women dressed in their Sunday clothes and waving placards; and, most of all, there were elderly men and women, shuffling slowly arm-in-arm up the hill. The younger ones waved banners and flags and cheered Revd O. T. Brandley and Revd Don Boney when they told them that they would fight until Clarence Brandley was free and the State admitted its corruption. Black assembly-men came out of the capitol building to join the demonstration.

They demanded to see Governor Clements. The staff in the Governor's mansion said the Governor was not available. So the demonstrators decided it was time for some of them to go and get themselves arrested. With the two Baptist ministers, Don Boney and O. T. Brandley at their head, 40 Brandley supporters slowly walked up the steps of the mansion, filed through the door and, softly chanting 'Jus-tice! Jus-tice!', they swarmed into the Governor's empty office.

At about this time, on a back road outside Conroe, John Sessum was busy picking up rusty cans and dusty bottles when a car spun up beside him and two strangers got out, two men with big leather boots. They stood over Sessum and told him they wanted a word. One of them showed him a badge. One of them said his name was Newton.

They started asking questions. Had he made a tape? What had he said in it? Who had the tape? Did he say Brandley was innocent? Sessum told them he didn't want to talk about it. They asked more questions – the day of the crime, the other janitors, the tape. He told them to go and ask Sam Martinez. They said they had. They said Sam told a different story. They said they might have to make him take a lie test. They poked more questions at him. Finally, John Sessum had had enough. He had put up with all this crap from the Texas Ranger and the sheriff once before but he was not going to be pushed around any more. He was not going to listen to that little rabbit in him again. So he told the two men with boots to go away and stop bugging him or he'd have them arrested for harassment. They told him he couldn't do that. And John Sessum said 'We'll see about that' and walked away from them.

Just before two o'clock, three men walked out of a dingy first-floor office in the middle of Conroe, past the blown-up black-and-white photograph of George Morris, down the dusty staircase and out into the deserted street. It was hot. Nothing moved. No one said a word. Don Brown, Mike De Geurin and Paul Nugent could feel the eyes on them as they crossed the street – from the bar in the drugstore, from the offices over the stores, from the windows of the courthouse. The whole town knew who they were and what they had come to do. They strode in silence up the courthouse steps.

Inside the familiar courtroom, the attorneys prepared to present their motion for a stay of execution. For once the court was less than packed. Brandley's family and supporters were all in Austin. Brandley himself was on Death Row. And, curiously, Peter Speers was nowhere to be seen. It appeared to have fallen to his assistant, Rick Stover, to defend the courthouse. For a moment, they could not understand why Speers was not there. They had been told only 15 minutes earlier that he was in the courthouse. Then Rick Stover stood up and insisted that they could not hold this hearing without the DA who, he claimed, was on his way to Florida and would not be back for a week. By which time Brandley would be dead. Don Brown, who reckoned he knew this courthouse pretty well, thought this was just about the dumbest stunt he had ever seen them pull – trying to get a man executed by hiding the District Attorney. Not even Judge Coker was impressed. Rick Stover had to fight on alone.

The three defence attorneys did not envy his position. Not only did they have powerful arguments that ought to persuade any judge to grant a stay, but they also knew that if they lost here, they could go straight to the federal court where the Attorney General would not oppose them. Mike De Geurin launched the attack. He produced his new application for a writ of Habeas Corpus and spelled out six reasons why Clarence Brandley should be given not only a stay of execution, but also a new hearing. The first and most important, he said, was that two eyewitnesses had now established that Clarence Brandley was innocent. Rick Stover objected that innocence was not a legally admissible issue.

De Geurin then complained of a catalogue of past abuse: the secret meetings between the DA and Judge Martin; the plot to conceal the disappearance of all the exhibits; the loss of the most critical evidence, including the semen swabs and the hair found on the girl's body; the blind focus of the investigation, which had opened with the 'election of the nigger' and had then been dedi-cated to proving Brandley's guilt instead of uncovering the truth; and finally, the racist character of the Texan death penalty which was used disproportionately to punish blacks for killing whites.

331

Rick Stover protested that these issues should have been dealt with before, or that they had been dealt with before and dismissed. There was no justification for a stay of execution, and no need for another hearing, he said.

By this time, in Austin, Clarence Brandley's supporters had left the Governor's office and were once again chanting and cheering on the steps of the state capitol. The Governor's staff had agreed that a small group could speak to the Governor about the Brandley case on another occasion. It was not enough, and they said so. They could feel their strength. 'Jus-tice! Jus-tice!' Then, at the top of the steps, a man in a suit appeared. He was a black man, an assistant to the Attorney General. It was Wayne Johnson. He had a note in one hand and now he asked for silence so that he could read it to them.

'At 2.47 today,' he announced, 'Judge Lynn Coker signed a stay of execution for Clarence Brandley.'

Pause. The steps erupted. 'Jus-tice! Jus-tice!' Banners waving. Hats flying. Hands clapping. Everybody grinning and chanting.

Now it was O. T. Brandley's turn to ask for silence.

'Father,' he cried, and the heads on the steps all bowed. 'We thank you for what you have done today.'

'Amen, amen,' they murmured.

'We thank you for what you will do in the future.'

'Amen!' they sang.

'We thank you for making the truth come out – for we know that Clarence Brandley is innocent.'

'Amen! Praise the Lord!'

And then they turned and flowed back down the hill to their buses and rode back to Houston and to Dugan, triumphant.

John Sessum heard about the reprieve, and he felt something like satisfaction. He knew he could never bring back the girl and he could never return to that moment on the staircase and find the courage to stand up and fight for her. But he could stand up now, not just for Brandley but for himself. He could show them that John Sessum from the state of Mississippi was a strong man. He could do what was right. He felt something like relief, too; the nightmares had stopped.

Two days after the reprieve, on Sunday evening, his new courage was tested for the first time. He was trying to clean up his act, shave every morning, keep up a better appearance, and he had cycled down to the washeteria to get the grime out of some of his old clothes. By the time he came out it was dark, so he never saw who hit him.

He had his clean clothes tucked into his bicycle basket, and all he was thinking about was getting home. He had just climbed on to his bike and was peddling off across the car park when some guy – maybe there were two guys – jumped out of a black Ford and knocked him over and started beating him. It shook him up. It gave him a bad pain in his ribs, all down the left side, and in his chest. He never saw who hit him. But he heard what they said. 'Where's that tape?' He heard it loud and clear. And then again. 'Now, will you keep your Goddam mouth shut?'

Then they were gone, leaving him on the ground with his clean clothes scattered.

The defence attorneys guessed it must have been Gary Acreman again or someone from his family, but in the next few weeks there were more incidents, and it began to appear that there were greater forces at work.

Richard Reyna came home to his pin-clean town house on the edge of Conroe and night after night he found his answering machine stacked with messages: 'I'm gonna find you and I'm gonna kill you . . . Pussyhead . . . I'm gonna put your blood on me . . . I'm gonna cut your dick off . . . Man, you are one dead motherfucker . . . You're history. You're dead meat.' Often, it was a woman's voice, shrieking and hissing. After a few weeks, he changed his number and kept the new one secret. The calls started again within 48 hours. Who could uncover an unlisted number so quickly? He never knew, but he could guess. Then his car tyres were slashed and someone put sugar in his petrol tank, fouling the engine and costing him hundreds of dollars. One day, in town, he met a bad cop, a real evil bastard, who asked him 'How's that little daughter of yours, Reyna?' He had to tell his ex-wife that Tiffany had better not visit for a while.

Someone threw eggs at Don Brown's car. The burly attorney was not about to be intimidated. He drove round Conroe for a week with the eggs and their broken shells baked on to his car and parked it each day right outside the courthouse, as if to say 'screw you'.

Mike De Geurin came to Conroe for a hearing, parked his car in the courthouse square and came back to find the petrol tank had been filled with metal filings. Who could look at a car parked in the courthouse square and find out who its owner was? De Geurin never knew for sure.

Bill Srack, however, finally came face-to-face with one of his tormentors. Try as he might, after seven years Srack had never been able to forget the Brandley case. Even though the phone calls at his house had more or less dried up, he still found that nearly every day he would catch himself thinking about that lonely time in the jury room. It was painful but he could not let it go: he collected everything that was written about the case, but he could not bring himself to read any of it. He just piled up the papers and magazines in a corner and left them.

About this time he applied for a new job in Conroe as the purchasing agent for Montgomery County, and sent his details to the committee of judges who had to make the appointment. Since he had experience and unusually good references, he was not surprised to find himself on a short list of three. When he discovered that one of his competitors had admitted lying on his résumé and another no longer wanted the job, his confidence began to build. The interview soon changed that.

He found himself being questioned by three judges, one of whom was the Honourable James Keeshan. Keeshan led the questioning and rapidly turned the subject to the first trial of Clarence Brandley. Why had he held out against the other jurors? Did he realize that 23 other jurors disagreed with him? Did he think he was rational? Did he have trouble getting along with other people? Srack tried to explain, and after 20 minutes of rapid-fire questions about Clarence Brandley he asked what any of this had to do with the post of purchasing agent for Montgomery County. The interview ended. A few weeks later, Keeshan wrote to Srack to tell him that they had decided to fill the post by making an internal promotion.

There were incidents, too, on the other side of the railway tracks, in Dugan. On Avenue E, Minnie Ola Brandley received a letter full of ugly, vicious talk. If she had been less than 72 years old, and if she had not been so weighed down and worn out by Clarence's case, she guessed she might have just torn it up and paid it no attention, but it frightened her. If she had lived in another town, maybe even if she had been down in Houston, she might have felt safe, but this was Conroe and she knew the kind of things that went on, so she packed her belongings and moved out of her home on Avenue E and stayed with relations in Houston until things quietened down again.

One of the first women in Dugan to come out and support Revd Boney's campaign – one of those who had ventured into the courthouse square and shaken her fist in defiance – had her windows shot out by someone. A minister who worked on the campaign was run off the road while he was driving just outside town. A large car swept up alongside him and forced him off the road; as the car sped away, he noticed that it had no licence plate.

Ed Payne did not escape so lightly. He was driving along a deserted road in the dark near his trailer, ten miles south-east of Conroe, when two cars suddenly swooped up behind him. One of them had lights flashing on its roof. The other, a white Chevrolet like the ones driven by Montgomery County sheriffs, sped past him and screeched to a halt across the road, blocking his path. Payne thought he must have done something against the law, so he hauled himself out of the car and started hobbling over to the white Chevrolet, leaning on his walking stick and trying to say 'Howdy' through his voice box. A couple of seconds later he realized he had made a bad mistake.

Some men started running towards him, men without uniforms, men shouting. He turned and started limping as fast as he could back towards his car, but it was too late. One of them was already on him, kicking him in the legs. He swung round and tried to kick him back, standing on his good leg and kicking him with the bad one. Then another guy punched him in the mouth, and split his lip. He was down now, bleeding everywhere, and they were on top of him, and he heard what one of them was shouting at him.

'I want you to keep your Goddam mouth shut.'

Then the men ran back to their cars and whipped out of there.

Brenda Medina suffered, too. She had got up early to drive her husband to work and fallen asleep on the sofa. Her children were still in bed. A sound woke her, and immediately she became frightened.

For several days now, Gary Acreman had been spooking her. She had run into him in a grocery store, and he had stood there staring at her and turning over a knife in the palm of his hand. Then she had seen him hanging around outside her house. She got up from the sofa to have a look. The next thing she knew, he was inside the house and he had her by the throat and the two of them were fighting like cats. She managed to wrench his hand off her throat and he started beating her around the head and chest and clawing at her with his finger-nails. She fought back and tore his hair out in clumps and hit him in the face. At one point, he grabbed hold of her hair and pulled her head down on to the couch and they started shouting at each other, her saying he must have something really bad to hide, him telling her she was a whore and a bitch and the nigger was going to pay and she wasn't going to do anything about it. Then he told her she had better not tell anyone about this or there wouldn't be anything left of her to testify.

'Just leave and leave me alone,' she shouted. Her three-year-old daughter came running in. He left, knocking the girl over as he went.

Revd Boney saw the violence spreading and the danger that fear would smother the new courage of the people in Dugan. At a Thursday-night prayer meeting in Conroe, he urged them to keep fighting, to fight Conroe and the courthouse and, most of all, to fight their fear. They decided that on Saturday 4 April – the anniversary of the death of Martin Luther King – they would march on the courthouse again.

This time, Conroe was ready for them. Inside the fire station, a riot squad from the Department of Public Safety was waiting with batons and tear-gas. Inside the sheriff's department, all leave had been cancelled and every available man was ready to go into action. Inside the police station, every officer in the department had been called up and a ten-man SWAT team, dressed in full riot gear, prowled the hallways. On a table in the back of the building, riot-guns and extra ammunition were stacked in neat piles.

The people of Dugan, some of them so old and infirm that they used walkers, came over the railway tracks and headed for the courthouse. Revd Boney warned them not to give Conroe a pre-text to attack them. Their signs said 'King died so Clarence could live'. As they marched, they sang and chanted, 'We are not afraid.' They felt their strength surge back. They surrounded the court-house, punched their fists into the air and chanted for justice, then fell silent and prayed. As their fear withered, their defiance grew.

There in the courthouse steps, at Conroe's heart, they dared to stage their own act of justice – a People's Court. They put the ringleaders on trial. They made one of their number the judge, made Revd Boney the prosecutor and appointed a defence attorney for the conspirators; he wore a Ronald Reagan mask to fit the role. Then they indicted six of the courthouse's men: the two District Attorneys, Jim Keeshan and Peter Speers; two judges, John Martin and Lynn Coker; the new sheriff, Joe Corley; and the new police chief, Mike Arthurs. They charged them with corruption and conspiracy to murder Clarence Brandley.

They called witnesses, who stood on the steps and told the story of Clarence Brandley and who spoke of racism and fear in the town, and of life with the 'Montgomery County Department of Corruptions'. Then the jury, all 300 of them with their banners and their flags, voted their verdict, roaring 'Guilty' so that the whole town could hear, and sentenced the six guilty men to be stripped of all power and banished to the Caucasus Mountains in Siberia. They deposited one more message from Tina the cow at the bottom of the flag-pole in front of the courthouse and marched back to Dugan, singing and chanting, leaving the riot squads locked behind their closed doors.

That night, they heard, there were men in robes out by the river to the east of town, burning wooden crosses in the dark.

The real fight had started. For the lawyers it was a fight to win the attention of the Court of Criminal Appeals in Austin, to whom Judge Coker had passed the decision as to whether Brandley should have a new hearing. For the courthouse, it was a fight to save their reputation and the political careers of the ringleaders. For Clarence Brandley, it was still a fight for life.

Mike De Geurin landed a public blow to the courthouse when he contacted the FBI and showed them the videotapes, with the result that the Justice Department announced an immediate investigation into civil rights aspects of the case.

The DA's office landed a private blow when they made contact with Gary Acreman. They had spoken to his family and left messages for him to call and, on 23 March, he did. He spoke to the assistant District Attorney, Rick Stover, who tape-recorded the conversation.

Acreman complained that Richard Reyna had scared him into telling a lie. He had never seen Robinson grab that girl at all, he said. There was no truth in it. 'I only seen the man twice that day. The first time, I spoke to him. The second time, he was throwing clothes into the dumpster, throwing something into the dumpster.'

This was the moment. Never before in the seven-year history of the case, so far as anyone knew, had anyone claiming to be an eyewitness directly told a law enforcement officer that he could identify the killer, that he had personally seen the killer disposing of the girl's clothes. And never before, so far as anyone knew, had a central witness in the case approached a law enforcement officer and admitted to withholding evidence that could have changed the course of the trial. This was the moment.

Rick Stover let it pass.

He told Acreman he wanted to stay in touch with him. 'We're going to work with you,' he said.

Four days later, Stover and the DA's investigator, Charlie Ray, flew to Pittsburgh, where Acreman's new job as a truck-driver had taken him. There, they interviewed him on video and recorded his statement that he had never seen Robinson attack the girl. They went on to ask him whether Richard Reyna had tricked and scared him, whether Reyna had tried to buy his testimony, whether Reyna had posed as an attorney, and what Jim McCloskey had done. They never asked him once what he knew about the

338

killer and the dead girl's clothes. And they never asked him at all whether he might have been involved himself.

The defence believed they had landed another blow when the Attorney General announced that he was appointing one of his investigators, Robert 'Duke' Bodisch, to inquire into the case. But the defence began to worry when they heard that the inquiry was being supervised by an assistant AG named David Hess. De Geurin had already spoken to Hess about the case and found him patronizing and hostile.

On the first day of their inquiry, the Attorney General's investigators began their independent inquiry by setting up a base in Conroe – inside the courthouse, in the office of the District Attorney. Television crews and reporters pressed around the office door, jumping on witnesses as they came and went.

From across the street Don Brown watched, and started to rumble with fury. What witness was going to identify the killers in front of a television camera? How were they going to get a confession if the killers were surrounded by people who refused to believe that they were guilty? For God's sake, the DA's office was supposed to be one of the suspects in this inquiry. It was obscene. It was nothing but a media circus. Brown was so angry that he called the Attorney General's office to complain. The next day, the AG's investigators moved upstairs in the courthouse and interviewed witnesses in the Grand Jury room. Brown was not appeased.

Within days, all his fears were confirmed. John Sessum and Icky Peace reported that they had been interviewed by the AG's team who had disputed their evidence and asked them how Mike De Geurin had forced them to change their stories and whether they had been paid for their help. Then it was Gary Acreman's turn to meet the Attorney General's investigators. They interviewed him in front of a video camera. He told them the same story he had told the District Attorney's officers a week earlier. He had never seen Robinson attack the girl, but he had seen Robinson at the school that day.

'I seen either him, or somebody that was dressed like him, drop a bag into the dumpster and then a few minutes later either the same person or somebody else came out with a tile and put it on top of it.'

Here was that moment again. After seven years of circumstantial evidence, after thousands of man-hours of complex investigation, after all the controversy and the chaos, here, at last, on video, on the record, was a live eyewitness, someone who had been on the scene that day, who was prepared to sit down with powerful law enforcement officers and say that with his own eyes he had seen the killer clearing up after the crime. What was more, he believed he could identify the killer. What was even better, he was identifying the same man who had been placed at the scene of the crime by John Sessum, who had spoken to these same investigators just the day before. This was the big breakthrough. Was this man really Robinson? What did he look like? What clothes was he wearing? Where did he come from? For God's sake, what colour was he? For a moment, no one said a word.

Then the investigators who worked for the Attorney General of Texas changed the subject and the moment was gone again.

They took Acreman through the whole of his story and checked back over its most intricate details – all the precise timings and the exact measurements – but they never asked him again about the killer and the dead girl's clothes, nor whether he might even have been involved himself.

All through the rest of April, through May and into June, the fight went on, while the Court of Criminal Appeals in Austin pondered whether to grant Clarence Brandley a new hearing at which all of the evidence could be reviewed.

The defence kept trying to strengthen their case. They made a video with Ed Payne, who repeated the story he had been trying to tell for more than six years. It took Jim McCloskey two months of negotiation to get the video.

Payne had become scared. Since he had given evidence at the hearing in July 1986, Gary Acreman had moved back in with his daughter, Cindy. Payne now had a man who he believed was a killer living on his doorstep, sharing a trailer with his daughter and his two grandchildren. That started to make him scared. Then his family started to take Gary's side against him, telling him to shut up or his grandchildren would have no daddy. But when that gang of men attacked him on the road that night he was pushed over the top. He left home and went into hiding with his sister, Ethel, and agreed with McCloskey that he would not be bullied any more. So he made the video.

The defence made a new video with John Sessum, in which he was clearly sober and also well-groomed and relaxed.

Richard Reyna engaged in a kind of courtship with Sam Martinez, taking him out to dinner, talking to him in Spanish, bringing him home, playing the videos of Sessum and Acreman in the hope that he would finally reveal whether he was a witness or an accessory to the crime. Martinez told him a little. He said it was true that Acreman had spoken to his girl and that he had disappeared, and that Brandley had come along the hallway sometime after the girl had gone. Once, he buried his face in his hands and asked what the penalty for perjury was. But he never cracked completely.

Reyna and McCloskey tried to get to the truth about Jo Ellen Parrish and Pokey Smith, but when Reyna went into the courthouse to read a transcript of Jo Ellen's evidence the District Attorney's office threatened to arrest him. Inside the DA's office, Reyna saw an old magazine cover about a crooked businessman. 'The sleaziest man in Texas,' ran the headline. Underneath it, someone had stuck a photograph of Mike De Geurin.

Revd Boney did all he could to maintain the pressure. He met Revd Jesse Jackson and told him about the case. He flew to Washington DC and spoke to the black Congressional leader John Conyers. He flew to Atlanta and briefed Martin Luther King's widow, Coretta Scott King, and the President of the Southern Christian Leadership Conference, Revd Joe Lowery, who then travelled to Houston to speak at an Agitation Weekend where more than 1,000 Clarence Brandley supporters rallied.

The Press continued to devour the case. The *Courier* sent a reporter to Huntsville to interview the black janitor and then complained on their front page that he had declined to speak to her because he claimed her paper had always been prejudiced against him. The *Houston Post*'s Death Row specialist, Douglas Freelander, wrote a column describing all the men he had met who went to the executioner proclaiming their innocence, and explaining his feeling that they were all liars who were guilty as charged. 'For me, the one exception in this limited arena is Brandley,' he wrote. 'He gives the impression of absolute sincerity.'

The publicity began to worry Conroe. County Judge Al Stahl said Montgomery County was developing such a bad reputation that the state was withholding funds. State representative Keith Valigura said: 'Folks in Austin say "Hey, Valigura, you've got a heck of a county down there, son". Montgomery County is a joke. I wish we could take care of that image problem we have.'

The courthouse tried to protect their image when they discovered that a team from CBS's 60 *Minutes* programme was in town, working on the Brandley case. They locked the team out of the building. Then they relented and let them in, but it did nothing to help their image.

When 60 *Minutes* put out their report in April, millions of Americans learned about Acreman and Robinson and the evidence against them, and about the black man sitting waiting on Death Row, and they saw pictures of Jim McCloskey – the Christian detective – shaking his head sadly and saying that 'unfortunately, in this county, among law enforcement officers, prejudice runs deep.'

The programme brought Jim Mattox, the Attorney General, out of his neutral corner and into the middle of the ring, where he attacked Brandley's attorneys and accused them of 'orchestrating the case for publicity purposes'. He declared that Gary Acreman had passed a lie test, although he had not yet taken one, and challenged Brandley to submit to a lie test himself. The Attorney General's office then conducted a campaign of lie-detector tests. Gary Acreman, James Dexter Robinson and Sam Martinez all swore that the stories they had told at Brandley's trials were the truth. All of them passed their lie tests, and all of the results were leaked to the press. The Attorney General repeatedly challenged Brandley to put his own story to the test.

De Geurin was tempted, until he discovered that the man who was conducting the lie tests, a former Houston deputy called Kelly Hendricks, was boasting that Brandley was 'as guilty as sin'. The head of the American Polygraph Association had to write to

Hendricks to warn him that he was behaving unethically and was too prejudiced to be working on the case.

Reyna and McCloskey spent the first two weeks of June in Louisiana, where McCloskey had been asked to look into the case of a man named Jimmy Wingo who was due to die in the electric chair on 16 June. They found Wingo had been convicted in a one-day trial on nothing but circumstantial evidence and they traced a woman who had implicated Wingo in the crime. She told them she had lied. A deputy had threatened to have her children taken away and she had been so frightened that she had not only lied but agreed to have sex with the deputy. In the 48 hours leading up to the execution date, McCloskey begged Louisiana officials to grant Wingo a stay so that they could re-investigate the case properly. All through the evening of 15 June, McCloskey sat with Wingo as the hour of his execution approached, waiting with him for word of a reprieve. Then McCloskey had to leave while Wingo had his head shaved and was fitted with a nappy for when the electric shock emptied his bowels. McCloskey was still waiting for word from the officials when Wingo was killed in the electric chair. It was McCloskey's darkest hour. In the six years he had now been working as an investigator, he had never before lost an innocent man to the executioner. He returned to Texas, determined that he would fight even harder.

Everyone who has ever seen a cowboy film knows that, when the lynch mob closes in on the small town jailhouse and the prisoner is quaking in his cell, the brave hero steps out in front of the mob, armed with nothing but the best intentions, and tells them to throw down their weapons and go home, because the prisoner is going to have a fair trial and there is going to be justice in this town.

Not in Conroe.

For a moment, back in March, Brandley had hoped the Attorney General might help him. On 22 June, his office produced a summary of their inquiry. They reviewed each of the six issues which Mike De Geurin had raised in Judge Coker's court on 20 March when he won the stay of execution – from the central complaint that Brandley was innocent back through all the history of secret meetings and missing evidence and racial prejudice. The investigators who worked for the Attorney General of Texas concluded that all six defence arguments were entirely worthless and they found no evidence that Brandley was innocent nor that any official involved in the case had ever engaged in any wrongdoing of any kind.

The investigator's findings were not published. The report was marked 'A. G. Sensitive' and each page carried an instruction that 'this report is the property of the Attorney General's office and neither it nor its contents may be disseminated'. All the same, Peter Speers told the press what it said.

By chance, Revd Boney and 40 Brandley supporters were in Austin again on that day. They went to the Supreme Court and crowded into the lobby outside the Attorney General's office. They demanded to see him. They were told he was out of town. At that moment, the doors to the elevator opened and the Attorney General walked out. Revd Boney was on to him in a flash.

'Don't be a politician now,' he said. 'Will you or will you not meet with us?'

'You're meeting with me now,' said Mattox.

'This isn't a meeting. We want to sit down face-to-face and talk about the issues.'

Mattox said he had already talked about the issues, and if they had something to say they should say it now. Then he walked away with the chants of 40 angry people ringing in the lobby behind him.

It all worried the defence. They were the ones who had brought the Attorney General into the Brandley affair. They had truly believed he would set aside good old boy politics, issue arrest warrants and send his investigators into Conroe to uncover the truth.

Not in Clarence Brandley's case.

Now their only hope was that the Court of Criminal Appeals in Austin would reach out a hand to Brandley and grant him a new hearing. The defence could only guess what the odds might be. The judges had already turned down Brandley twice. They had been sent three pages of blistering denials and procedural

objections by the courthouse in Conroe. They would know that
the Attorney General had thrown out all the defence evidence.
But surely some of those judges would want to give them a chance
to develop what they had found, in open court, where both sides
could argue about it and the whole community could judge the
truth. On good days, they persuaded themselves that they had at
least a 50 per cent chance.

When the ruling finally came on 30 June, it was splashed across
the front pages of newspapers across the state.

'Brandley gets a chance at freedom.'

The court had stepped out in front of the mob. Brandley could
have his new hearing.

9

The courthouse was not the same. Paul Nugent felt it as soon as he drove into the square. Maybe it was the early-morning mist hanging in the air, which blurred the edges of the stark white temple and rubbed out the rest of the town and left the whole place eerie and strange. Or else it was that sound, drifting over to him from the steps of the courthouse, the sound of a woman singing an old Negro spiritual, filling the square with echoes. Or maybe it was the sight which emerged through the mist as Nugent came closer, of a hundred black people sitting and lying at the feet of the rearing courthouse, staking out their claim on the building and on justice, holding a vigil which had gone on all night, taking it in turns to sleep and to stand guard, as if their vigilance might keep this town at bay.

Nugent crossed the square to Don Brown's office.

It was 21 September, nearly three months since the court in Austin had stepped in. The new hearing was about to begin. Inside the dimly lit office on the second floor, where Clarence Brandley's brothers had first come looking for help seven long years ago, Nugent sat down with Don Brown and Mike De Geurin. No one on the defence team had been paid anything for about five years – the Brandleys had run out of money long ago – but there was no question of stopping the fight. The sounds of protest floated up to them from the courthouse steps. It was time to consider Percy Foreman's Golden Rule again – 'try anyone except your client'.

For a start, they would try James Dexter Robinson and Gary Acreman again. Since the hearing in July 1986, evidence against the two men had piled up relentlessly and now was the time, the attorneys believed, to go public with everything they knew. But they could go even further. This was no ordinary miscarriage of justice in which well-meaning law officers were confused by circumstances. This was more like an abortion of justice, in which people who were touched by malice and dishonesty and, above all, by racism, deliberately abused the machinery of justice. It was not enough to put Robinson and Acreman on trial. It was time to put the whole courthouse on trial and to expose those who had lied and cheated to take an innocent man's life. Yet the indictment did not stop there.

In any lynching, there were ringleaders and there were bystanders. The people who ran the courthouse were elected by the whole community. Their behaviour was extolled in the pages of the *Courier*. They enjoyed the approval and support of their neighbours. The town rewarded them with power and prestige. They were not alone. They may have been the ones who seized the black man and twisted the facts and threatened the witnesses and broke the rules and packed him off to Death Row, but there were also those who watched and even a few who looked away. The time had come to put Conroe on trial.

Shortly before nine o'clock, the three attorneys crossed the street to the courthouse.

As soon as they entered the courtroom, Nugent felt again how the courthouse had changed. There, on the dais at the end of the room, was a judge who had no connection at all with Conroe. After more than five years, the defence had finally kicked Judge Lynn Coker out of the case. Until now they had left him on the bench, believing that he was at least decent even if he was weak, and calculating that he was better than his more malicious colleagues in the courthouse. But Coker had cut the legs from beneath them in his findings after the July 1986 hearing, and they had abandoned any hope that he would ever rule in Brandley's favour. They had ousted him easily, simply by telling him that they might have to call him as a witness. In his place, the state administrator had appointed this outsider Perry Pickett. He was just about the most senior district judge in Texas. He had spent 30 years on the bench, mostly in Midland, 400 miles away near the border with

New Mexico, where he had also been mayor. Now, he was a
visiting judge who could be pulled out of retirement to handle
particularly sensitive cases. Pickett was an unknown quantity. He
was an elderly man and, so far as the defence could find out, he
had a reputation as a conservative. It worried them that, on the
face of it, he might be a graduate of the same good old boy school
of justice that had produced the Conroe judges.

Their first move now – and the first test of the new judge – was
to try and get this whole hearing moved out of this courthouse
with all its memories of injustice, and out of Conroe with all its
history of intimidation, to another court where their witnesses
would have a chance to speak without fear. They had submitted
a formal motion calling for a change of venue. Today, they had
to call the evidence to prove the point.

As soon as Judge Pickett called the court to order, Nugent felt
the change again. The judge looked down on the ranks of brown
faces in the well of the court and he did not frown, nor did he
tell them to remove their 'Free Clarence Brandley' badges, but he
said: 'Good morning, everyone. We welcome you to the courthouse. We are pleased to have you as our guests.'

Nugent felt it again a few minutes later as the first witness began
to give evidence. Bill Srack had agreed to talk publicly for the first
time about his experiences as a dissenting juror. He was just
beginning to speak when Peter Speers hopped up and objected
that this was all irrelevant.

The judge overruled him.

Srack continued to speak. Speers hopped up again and said that
none of this should be mentioned.

The judge overruled him again.

Clarence Brandley, from his seat in the front of the court,
watched nervously as, for the first time in his seven years of trials
and hearings, his attorneys were allowed to present their evidence.

While Peter Speers sat frowning at his paperwork and Peggy
Stevens stood imperiously at the back of the courtroom, Bill Srack
went on to describe the day a Conroe jury called him a nigger-
lover. He remembered the hail of phone calls which rained down
on his house and the deputy who chose not to prosecute those

who had made them, and then he explained how Judge Keeshan had conducted himself when he interviewed him for a job.

The faces on the public benches were set in grim silence.

Revd John Daviss, the elderly minister from the First Missionary Baptist Church in Dugan, who had been warned by his friends that he was asking for trouble if he gave evidence, then took the witness-stand. In front of the District Attorney and half-a-dozen Montgomery County deputies, he declared openly that prejudice had smothered justice during Clarence Brandley's two trials.

Revd Jerry P. Jones, the towering young minister from Pilgrim Rest Baptist Church, followed him to the stand and told the court he was sure Clarence Brandley could never have a fair hearing in this courthouse. Witnesses felt intimidated here, he said. Blacks in Conroe were supposed to be seen and not heard. The Mayor himself called black people niggers.

There was a stirring on the public benches. Peter Speers challenged the minister to give even one example of how a witness could be intimidated. Revd Jones looked down at Speers from the witness-stand and said: 'One of the things that would be intimidating to them would be you.' Speers protested. The minister insisted. Black people would be afraid to tell the truth, he said, in case they or their children were ever arrested and victimized because of their evidence.

'Reverend Jones, I am offended by your remark. What shred of evidence do you have that I have done anything of the sort in the past?'

The minister leaned forward so that he was looking straight into the District Attorney's face. The whole room was now stiff with concentration. 'I'm very sorry if you're offended by my remarks, but I would like to offend you some more, because I think you are the epitome of everything that is wrong.'

Gasps from the public benches.

Speers protested some more: 'Reverend Jones, you haven't stated a single fact to support that, and you cannot because it's not true.'

Still staring straight into the DA's eyes, the minister replied in a voice that boomed through the court. 'All I can say – and I can state this as a fact – is that this is the most prejudiced, biased, racist city in the whole of America. I am out of Alabama and I know that Alabama ain't never been as bad as this.'

Speers took to his chair. The deputies shifted in their seats. Judge Pickett gazed down on the court without expression. All along the public benches there spread a ripple of pure joy.

The defence had one more witness in their effort to prove that there could be no fair hearing in this courthouse; a witness whose evidence they had deliberately held back for the finale. The prosecutors and the deputies and the woman with the strawberry finger-nails all stiffened as soon as Mike de Geurin rose and said: 'Call Janet Dial.'

Judge Martin's former secretary walked smartly into court with her head raised. The courthouse had frayed at the edges before; bystanders had whispered their secrets to be the defence in dark corners. But this was different. Here, for the first time, was an insider from the courthouse without any stain on her character, standing up publicly to tell what she knew. Cold eyes followed her to the witness-stand. Would she really do it?

Mike De Geurin asked her if it was just his imagination, or was there really an atmosphere of intimidation in the building?

'Well,' she said, and paused before plunging on. 'I think there is an atmosphere that is intimidating to a fair trail and to any witness that would appear.' She paused again and flicked her eyes over to the District Clerk still standing unsmiling at the back of the room. 'One of the things I noticed, for instance, was that Peggy Stevens swore us in. And if I'm correct, Mrs Stevens is to be a witness at some point and, you know, I don't understand why she was allowed to swear us in. It's sort of like she's got some higher status as a witness than possibly the rest of us.'

Peggy Stevens glared into the middle distance. Janet Dial now opened the floodgates and her memories of the Brandley trial came pouring out: 'It seemed to me that it was like we worked for a company and, regardless of the fact that there were people who were to play impartial parts in the judicial system – the judge, members of the District Clerk's office and all that support group – it was like we worked for the same company as the DA's office . . . I didn't feel like I could ask any impartial questions . . .

Even though I worked for the judge, I felt as if I was involved in a project to convict Clarence Brandley.'

Peter Speers did not know Janet Dial very well. If he had, he might have known that she was not the sort of witness who could be steamrollered. As it was, he stood up and defied her to cite even one occasion when a witness had been intimidated.

Janet Dial calmly recalled the day she had sat in a crowded courtroom where Clarence Brandley was being tried and heard an elderly white woman chanting 'kill the nigger'.

Speers shook his head and struggled to bury what he had now uncovered: 'This wasn't an elected official or anybody like that, was it? Or anybody involved with the trial?'

'I don't know that that matters. She was not removed from the courtroom.'

'Did anybody object to her comments?'

'No. Had I been more experienced or been a little bit more competent in my position, I would have brought that to someone's attention. I know that I did tell people who were more experienced and nothing was done about it.'

Speers kept pushing: 'The likelihood is that if anybody who was actually concerned with the trial had heard it, there would have been a remark made and a request that she either be removed or at least zip her lip, don't you think?'

'Peter, it happened. You know, I don't really know exactly what you want from me. It did happen. She was not removed and that was the atmosphere in the courtroom.'

Speers gave up and tried another line, but it soon became clear that he had still not learned his lesson. This time he defied Janet Dial to cite even one reason why anyone from the courthouse would now want to intimidate a witness in the Brandley case.

'Okay, I can answer that question,' came the reply. Speers then had to stand in silence while Janet Dial explained that the courthouse officials were trying to cover up their past behaviour in the case. Speers shook his head and defied her to name even one witness who was actually being intimidated.

Janet Dial calmly told him that the court reporter Mary Johnson, who had been caught up in the scandal over the missing exhibits, had been put under pressure not to give evidence and had also suggested to Janet that she should not testify either. Speers raised his eyebrows.

'Obviously you're not intimidated by testifying to what you believe is the truth?' he asked.

'I'm not easily intimidated, Peter.'

Speers sat down, his lesson learned.

The hearing on the change of venue now rapidly came to a conclusion.

Mike De Geurin summarized the evidence of injustice in both the courthouse and the town. 'You have heard the voice of the community,' he told the judge.

Peter Speers said there was no proof of any of this, and besides, technically, the law permitted only 'trials' to be moved, not hearings like this which had no jury.

Judge Pickett looked down from his dais. The whole courtroom was still, each person weighing their own hopes and fears. Would this white-haired judge breaks ranks and abandon Conroe, or would he go along with all the other judges who had handled this case and give the DA his way?'

'All right,' said the judge in a deep drawl. 'The court makes the following ruling: there exists here a volatile and explosive situation, not conducive to the fair administration of justice. I've read the entire transcription of all the proceedings and there seems to be an atmosphere of fear. The ends of justice dictate that this case be transferred to Galveston County, and it is so ordered. Thank you.'

His last few words were drowned in cheers. The rejoicing spilled out into the street and Minnie Ola Brandley emerged into the courthouse square with tears in her eyes to be greeted as a hero. Soon the chant began again. 'Jus-tice! Jus-tice!' Echoing through the square.

Up on the first floor of the courthouse, in the judge's chambers, Judge Pickett and all the attorneys were looking out of the window at the boiling cauldron of cheering and chanting people below.

Peter Speers was frowning. His assistant, Rick Stover, kept saying that this was intolerable.

Paul Nugent watched the jubilant crowd surging through the

street and nodded. 'There's the constitution of the United States in operation,' he said.

News of Judge Pickett's order burned through the county like a flame on a fuse wire. Before the day was out, it had reached the witnesses whose fears lay at the heart of the judge's decision. It gave them hope. The question for the defence was whether that would be enough. Ever since Brandley's reprieve six months earlier, the attorneys and investigators had been trying to shepherd their witnesses to safety, trying to protect them from physical attack and from official pressure. It had been tough.

All through the summer, Icky Peace was cowed in silence. He was scared, and he admitted it. But the defence still wanted him to talk, not so much about the day of the crime as about the inquiry and the threatening of witnesses.

Four days before the change of venue hearing, on Friday evening, 18 September, Jim McCloskey made one final attempt to persuade the little janitor to find his courage. The old Chevy climbed the hill outside Cleveland, up through the woods to the two trailers where Icky Peace lived alongside his elder sister, Shirley, who had been looking after him since their mother died. McCloskey was at his most polite – almost deferential. Icky Peace, however, was in feisty mood.

He was glad to see McCloskey. He wanted to tell him what had happened to him earlier that week, on Tuesday. He had been called in to the DA's office to talk about this Brandley hearing coming up, and he had been saying to them what he had always been trying to say – that that Texas Ranger choked him with his medical necklace and threatened to kill him if he didn't do as he was told, and that he had gone to Jim Keeshan and told him all about it and he had been told to forget it. But the DA's people had not wanted to hear.

'They told me I was hallucinating,' he complained. 'They said I was imagining things. And I am not. They told me if I said that in public, nobody would believe me and they could sue me and it would be just my word against them 'cos there ain't no records.' And there was another thing, he continued in his fluting voice. That very day, one of his supervisors at the high school had threatened him with the sack if he dared to give evidence for Clarence Brandley. The supervisor had said something like: 'Jobs can get lost, you know. We wait a little time and then you're out of here.' McCloskey had never seen the little janitor angry before. But now he was righteous and indignant. They had pushed him too far, hurt his pride. So, in his own way, he had found his courage. Even so, there was something he still would not say.

'I got a bombshell,' he said, stabbing one stiff index finger at McCloskey. 'I got a bombshell that'll blow this case apart. But there's only one person I'll tell it to. And that's the judge.'

McCloskey was intrigued. He spent the best part of an hour trying to tease this 'bombshell' out of Peace. He uncovered all sorts of other half-familiar stories: the officer saying 'the nigger is elected'; Acreman saying he had seen Brandley having a good time with a white girl; the police on the day of the crime refusing to let him go home until he had signed their statement. Peace recalled how John Sessum had been lying half-asleep outside the vocational building waiting for Brandley and interrupting his nap every so often to ask 'Where's that damned nigger?' But he would not part with his bombshell.

Two days later, on the Sunday night before the change of venue hearing, McCloskey was back. This time he had Mike De Geurin and Richard Reyna in tow. De Geurin needed to hear Peace tell his story for himself so that he could judge how to handle him in the witness-box. And McCloskey thought the attorney might be able to use his famous charm to get a look at the bombshell. It had been raining and the hill roads were slick with mud, but the old Chevy ploughed through it all. As they drove into the clearing in front of Peace's pink trailer, they saw a woman standing outside. It was Icky's sister, Shirley.

The three men gathered round her and started explaining that they needed to see her brother again and that they meant him no harm, and that he had to understand that they just wanted the truth. While they were talking, De Geurin became aware of a strange noise coming from behind him, from the direction of the pink trailer, a wet, squishy sort of noise. He turned round to discover Icky Peace tiptoeing through the mud towards them without his shoes on, his white shocks squelching in the soaking soil.

De Geurin grinned and greeted him like an old friend, and pretended not to notice his feet.

It was soon obvious that Icky Peace did not want to play. The bombshell was his. He would give it to the judge. Not to them. De Geurin pushed, but Peace would have none of it. All through his protests, De Geurin's eyes kept wandering down to the limp ends of Peace's white nylon socks which were now soaking up mud the way new bread soaks up gravy. The sight of it stirred something in De Geurin. One word popped into his mind – Trigger.

'Say, Mr Peace. Look at this way. You got a problem talking about this thing. I understand that. Now, you don't have to talk to me. You don't have to say a word. All I want is the truth. Now, I'm gonna ask you a question. And if the answer to my question is yes, I want you to just move your foot there on the ground one time, just kind of paw the ground one time. And if the answer is no, paw it twice. Understand?'

Peace looked at him, wide-eyed.

'Okay, now. You understand what I'm saying? Now, did the Texas Ranger ever try to threaten you?'

There they stood, all alone in a muddy patch in the middle of the hills: the Tex-Mex investigator and his new partner with the priest's collar; the blond attorney in the $3,000 custom-made cowboy boots; the anxious sister. All standing in a circle staring at this little fat man's socks.

Peace was still staring straight into De Geurin's face. Pause. One sodden white sock flapped once against the mud and fell back into place. Just like Trigger the talking horse.

And so they passed the next half hour with De Geurin asking the questions, Peace silently pawing the mud with his ruined sock, Reyna occasionally stuffing his fist into his mouth and wheezing 'Jesus Christ, I don't believe this shit.' By the time they left, Peace had taken them once again through his story. But even with the aid of his soggy sock, he still would not give up his bombshell. It was as if he had found his courage but was still not sure how to use it.

Peace surfaced once more the next day, as the defence team
headed out of the courthouse and across to Don Brown's office
to relish their triumph at the change of venue hearing. Richard
Reyna found Peace on the pavement, looking lost. 'I can't find
my car,' he was bleating.

'Never mind, man. Come on up to the office. The Reverend's
there. And everyone else. We're having barbecue.'

Peace waddled along beside him up into Brown's office where
he took out his false teeth, launched into a barbecue sandwich and
proceeded to tell his story once more to the entire defence camp.
When he got to the moment a few days earlier when his supervisor
had told him 'Jobs can get lost, you know', Peace waved his bit
of sandwich and said he had told that supervisor that he had been
looking for a job before he got hired there and, if he had to, he'd
go and look for another one now. Then he slapped in his teeth,
told the attorneys and the investigators that he would see them in
Galveston and strode out of the office.

'Jesus Christ,' said Reyna. 'That little guy's ready to kick somebody's ass.'

For Ed Payne, it was a long, bitter summer. When his family
discovered that he had made a videotape for the defence, they
renewed their assault on him.

Payne had made the mistake of moving back home and his wife
Billie, who was afraid for her grandchildren's father, attacked him;
with his bad leg and his skinny frame, he was no match for her.
He complained that she threatened to kill him if he testified for
Brandley and that she kicked him in the ribs and tried to hit him
with an axe. He survived that by starting divorce proceedings, only
to find the investigators who worked for the Attorney General of
Texas on his doorstep.

By the time they finished with him, he had withdrawn his story.
He now said that Acreman could have been nervous on the day
of the crime just because his car had broken down. And he said
Acreman could have told him about the girl's clothes being in the
dumpster after it had been reported that the police had found
them there. Everything he had told the defence on the video was
a lie, he now said. They had tricked him into making the video

and he had only gone along with it to see how they played their tricks. Then Jim McCloskey had made him give false answers and he had made three tapes before they were satisfied with the lies he was telling for them, he now said.

Jim McCloskey stayed in touch with Payne's family, including his brother, John, who had first approached George Morris in January 1981 to disclose old Ed's story. McCloskey was cruising back from Conroe to Houston late one night with Mike De Geurin in the passenger seat and Glenn Miller on the radio, when he decided to stop at John Payne's house to see him and his wife, Marie. As soon as they stepped out of the old Chevy, a snarling dog came swirling out of the darkness at them.

'Don't worry,' said McCloskey. 'It won't bite.'

De Geurin was no fool. 'I'll stay in the car,' he said.

John and Marie Payne gave them both safe passage into the house and then began a conversation which soon degenerated into a sort of parlour game.

Every time McCloskey asked them a question, the Paynes would shuffle off into their kitchen and whisper together for several minutes before returning with their answer. It took a while, but they finally concluded that the story which Ed was supposed to have told the Attorney General's investigators was nonsense. They were sure, for example, that Ed had first told them of Gary's desire to go and fish the clothes out of the dumpster on the day after the murder – 24 hours before the police found them. Ed was scared, they said. He had even made a new will, in which he had told everything he knew, and left instructions that if anything were to happen to him, the will was to be sent to Mike De Geurin. De Geurin immediately saw the significance of that: if the will was hostile to the defence, Payne would hardly want it sent to them. After a final conference in the kitchen, John and Marie Payne confessed that they, too, were a little nervous. Someone had been following them and sitting in a car outside their house watching them.

In the week after the change of venue hearing, McCloskey tried Ed Payne once more. He and Reyna spent a day chasing from one relative to another, only to find that he was back home again with Billie. The two investigators parked the Chevy down the road from his place and talked. There was no telling what was waiting for them in that house: one of the killers lived there. The rest of Payne's family were hostile to them. They would certainly have guns. Reyna was ready to go in, but McCloskey persuaded him that he should go in alone, relying on his white collar for protection.

As he walked slowly up to the house McCloskey noticed a man bent over a car, working on the engine. For a moment he thought it was Acreman, but it was another of Payne's relatives, who nodded him up to the trailer and went back to his engine. As soon as he walked up to the old trailer, he saw Ed Payne standing there, shaking his head vigorously from side to side. 'I can't do it,' he said. 'I won't do it.'

McCloskey put up both hands in a gesture of surrender. 'Ed, I'm sorry but I have to talk to you.' Payne gave him a look of deep disgust and led him inside, where McCloskey found to his relief that Billie was out. They sat down and McCloskey told Ed that he understood the pressure he had been under, that he knew all about the family's problems, that he knew it had been rough with his wife and with the Attorney General's men, and that nobody was going to make him give evidence if he did not want to. In his gentlest bedside manner, he talked to Payne for an hour and a half.

Finally, Payne squeezed an apology out of his voice box and said he was sorry he had gone back on his story. McCloskey coaxed him onwards. 'Ed, you know and I know that Clarence Brandley is innocent. We need you to come and tell what you know. I know it's been hard and I can't say it won't get hard again, but will you do it?' Payne looked up through his thick spectacles, opened his parched old mouth and squeezed two sounds out of his throat. 'OK.'

Mary Johnson was also scared to talk. She refused to meet the defence attorneys. She was afraid of losing her job. She, too, received a visit from the investigators who worked for the Attorney General of Texas and who wanted to know all about the missing exhibits. They tried to tell her she was a liar and suggested she had stolen all the missing exhibits herself. They said she had been dating George Morris and had done it to help him. They gave her a lie test with their regular polygrapher, Kelly Hendricks. He said she was lying and then they read her her rights. She started talking about Jim Keeshan and Judge Martin and whether they had held secret meetings.

'I know Jim Keeshan is real smooth and all that and maybe he . . .'

One of the Attorney General's men cut her off. 'The more important issue,' he said, 'is that the evidence was in your custody and became missing while in your custody.'

By the time they had finished with her, Mary Johnson was completely confused. They had dragged her through the mud. They had not been interested in what Keeshan and Martin had been playing at. They had called her a liar. She was more scared than ever. She begged Don Brown not to make her give evidence.

'I'll be fired,' she said. 'If you make me testify, they'll fire me. Please don't subpoena me.'

But Brown knew that he had to.

Before the hearing resumed in Galveston, the defence studied the thick report which had now been produced by the Attorney General's investigators. Jim McCloskey waded through it, looking for clues. It turned out to be worth the effort. The Attorney General's office defended courthouse witnesses, attacked defence witnesses, and never even bothered to interview most of the ring-leaders. It was clear that the inquiry which had moved into the enemy's camp on its first day had never left. However, they disclosed that they had found a new witness. They had never mentioned it to the defence but the report showed that, some four months earlier, just after *60 Minutes* had broadcast its report on Clarence Brandley, a young woman had contacted the Attorney General's team.

She had been watching the programme, she said, not paying any great attention. Until this photograph of a man's face had been flashed up on the screen. And suddenly she was back at that high school on the day of the crime, back in the gym where she had been playing volleyball, watching these two strange men walking across the room from the direction of the auditorium –

two young white men, one with sandy hair and the other with dark, shaggy hair. And that was him. She was almost sure that was his photograph on the screen. It was James Dexter Robinson. It had given her the chills and so she had called the Attorney General's team to tell them. Her name was Cheryl Bradford. The Attorney General's investigators said they took her back to the school and found that she could not remember the layout of the gym properly. 'She does not attach any particular significance to this event,' they added.

They disclosed, too, that Icky Peace had given them his most powerful version ever of the moment when a police officer elected Brandley as prime suspect. Peace had told the AG's team that the officer's exact words were: 'You're a coloured guy. Conroe don't like coloured people. So, nigger, you're elected.' The AG's team said they were 'unable to verify this'.

The Attorney General's office, however, did something that the defence had never been able to do. They tested the blood of Gary Acreman and James Dexter Robinson. They did not follow it up or even pass any comment on the result. They simply mentioned in passing that both men were Type A. The same as the blood on the dead girl's socks.

On Sunday, 27 September, six days after Judge Pickett's order, Jim McCloskey and Paul Nugent loaded up the old Chevy with legal papers and headed out of Houston southwards on I-45 down to the Gulf of Mexico and over the narrow causeway to Galveston Island.

McCloskey and Nugent could see a great breakthrough at hand – a victory in a little courtroom out here on the edge of the world which would not only free a man but would galvanize the new-found courage of a whole community. They could see, too, the threat of failure – one frightened witness, one twisted piece of evidence, one legal blunder, and they would all plunge off their narrow route into disaster.

The Galveston County courthouse was alive.

Ever since dawn, they had been arriving: the old ladies from Dugan with their flowery hats, the old men with their walking canes, the Brandley family, Revd Boney, scores of young people with banners, a group from Houston with a gigantic card to celebrate Clarence Brandley's 36th birthday, church ministers, civil rights officials, reporters, television crews, attorneys, witnesses, and a phalanx of deputy sheriffs from Montgomery County, who had come to run courtroom security and who now blocked the doorway demanding that anyone who wanted to enter should submit to a metal detector and a manual search. By nine o'clock on this Monday morning, 28 September 1987, 300 people had run the gauntlet of the Montgomery County deputies and filled every space on the public benches in the long rectangular courtroom. In front of them, on the other side of the wooden bar, the spectators could see the jury box running down the left-hand wall, now crammed with reporters; the defence attorneys at their table in front of the jury box, and over to the right the prosecution table. Beyond them was the witness box and then Judge Pickett, an unlit pipe jammed between his teeth, already sitting behind his desk on the raised platform at the far end of the room.

Now, a door at the judge's right-hand side opened, and two burly sheriffs led Clarence Brandley into the room and sat him down next to his attorneys. Judge Pickett welcomed everyone to court, and the case of Clarence Brandley versus the state of Texas began its latest round.

For Brandley and his attorneys this was the day of public reckoning, when all the scraps of information which had been dredged up by Richard Reyna and Jim McCloskey would be displayed for all to see, a day to pitch their evidence not just at the judge, who now held Clarence Brandley's future in the balance, but at the 300 spectators who saw their own lives mirrored in Brandley's fate and at all the unseen spectators in wooden shacks and ghetto dives across the state of Texas who would track his progress. This was the day to put their case across. They believed the press would help them.

The star witness of the day was John Sessum. Reyna had done his best to prepare him for his big moment. He had bought him a new pair of trousers, mended his old spectacles, cleaned him up, cut his hair and kept him sober. Sessum had spent the night in a state of suppressed panic. Right up to the moment that he took the stand, the defence had feared that he might bolt and take refuge in the bottle. But when the time came he prowled slowly into court and took the oath.

He stood there, staring down at his feet, his knees shaking, his voice breaking, occasionally weeping as he told the world that he had seen two men attack a young girl and that he had turned his back and walked away. He admitted he had committed perjury in all of his previous evidence and statements. 'I run from people over this for a long time,' he whispered, 'but you can't run from yourself or your feelings or your own conscience.'

In his faltering voice, he choked out his description of the attack and of the roles of Gary Acreman and James Dexter Robinson. Then he started to peel the skin off the cover-up.

Acreman had not only threatened him as they drove home on the day of the crime, he said, but also when they drove to give their statements to the police two days later. So he had started lying. When the Texas Ranger took him on a walk-through at the school with Acreman and Martinez, the Ranger had threatened him too. He had tried to tell the Ranger about how Gary had grabbed the girl, but the Ranger had told him to do as he was told or he would be arrested. The police had typed up a statement but he had had trouble reading it. 'I ain't good on reading,' he said.

Watching him, Brandley felt a kind of fire-storm in his chest. He was bitter and angry and confused and relieved and frightened and grateful. It was all churning around inside him. All he could do was to sit like a rock, trying somehow to contain it all. Sitting right behind him, McCloskey could see the muscles in his back bunched into tight knots of anxiety.

The attorneys were content. Sessum had launched the attack not only on Acreman and Robinson, but on the courthouse as well.

The defence had felt less worried about Icky Peace who appeared to be ready to stand up for himself, but when he came to the stand, he had only just begun to speak when his courage flickered and failed him. He looked up at Judge Pickett and said, 'Your Honour, I would like to talk to you privately.' The little janitor and the court stenographer followed the judge into his office. The 300 spectators sat and waited, and wondered what was going on. The defence attorneys guessed this was the bombshell that they had all been waiting for. They chewed their finger-nails and hoped to hell that Icky was not going to run out on them now. Eventually, some ten minutes later, the judge, with the air of a patient parent, gently led Icky Peace back into court and told Mike De Geurin to continue.

In a voice that fluttered weakly from the witness-stand, Icky Peace now told his story. The defence attorneys hardly dared to breath. Ignoring the Montgomery County deputies lounging in the courtroom doorway, Peace declared that he had never known what was in the statement he had signed at the Conroe Police Department on the day of the crime, for the simple reason that he could not read: 'I signed a piece of paper that had a bunch of letters on it, a bunch of words. I don't know what it said.'

He said he had told the police he could not read and asked them to bring his sister so she could read the statement to him, but they had refused. They had told him that if he did not sign that piece of paper, he could not leave. So he had signed. Then they had retyped part of it and brought it back to him. So he had signed again. He never realized, he said, that the statement he had signed made no mention of the fact that Gary Acreman disappeared for some time on the day of the crime. Nor did he realize, he said, that it did not mention the fact that Acreman and Martinez appeared to know a girl was missing before anyone came looking for her. Peace then recalled the moment soon after he had signed his statement when the police officer told him about their choice of a prime suspect. 'He told me that I wasn't strong enough or tall enough and that they had a lot of pressure put on them and Mr – well, they called him – Your Honour, can I say what they called him?'

Judge Pickett nodded. 'Yes, sir.'

'They said that the nigger was tall enough and strong enough and he was elected.'

Peter Speers might have felt 300 pairs of eyes staring grimly at the back of his neck.

De Geurin nudged Peace again. 'Now, Mr Peace, did the officer also say to Mr Brandley, "You're a coloured guy, Conroe don't like coloured people"?' This was too much for Speers, who successfully objected that De Geurin was leading his witness.

Peace had not told the story the way he had told it before, but the defence were content that he had done his best to tell it on oath for the first time. He had more. A week after the crime, he said, the Texas Ranger came to see him. 'He got me by the shirt and I don't know if you call it shoving or pushing, but he got me up against the wall and told me that I had killed the girl . . . He had me scared.'

Then the Ranger had threatened to blow his head off.

Peace said he had told all this to the District Attorney, Jim Keeshan, who had assured him he would handle it. Then he had made a second statement without being able to discover its contents and he never realized, he said, that this made no mention of the fact that the Texas Ranger had been threatening him.

'I'm finally telling the truth like I've been trying to tell it,' he said, 'and I'm very glad.'

Jim McCloskey, sitting next to Brandley at the defence table, felt a glow of pride at Peace's courage, a feeling which was soon mixed with profound relief as the judge instructed his stenographer to read out her transcript of the private conversation he had held with Peace. It soon became clear that Peace had been on the verge of desertion, and that there had been no bombshell other than his own fear.

He had told the judge that he felt confused by the defence attorneys because they kept telling him what questions they were going to ask and 'practically what to say, but not coming out telling me to say it', and that he felt worried by the District Attorney who had told him he was hallucinating and there was nothing to back up his story, and that he was still frightened of the Texas Ranger and also that he was afraid he might get fired by the school if he gave evidence. The judge had listened and sympathized and calmed him down. Finally, the two men had agreed that they would go back into court together where Peace would tell the truth without fear.

Richard Reyna had spent the morning in Conroe, where he stopped by the courthouse and found Ed Payne coming out of a hearing on his divorce from Billie. Payne seemed buoyant. He started talking to Reyna about the Brandley case and suddenly announced in his electronic buzz: 'Richard, I'm gonna testify. If you want me to do it, let's do it now.' Reyna put him in his car and headed south for Galveston. Payne was still in high spirits and sat beside him squawking his way through a stream of jokes. Reyna could not understand a word and spent the journey trying to nod intelligently and grinning hopefully every time the old man started coughing up his tinny laugh. An hour after arriving in Galveston, Ed Payne was on the witness-stand.

As soon as Peter Speers saw him, he objected that Payne should not be allowed to give evidence since he had already told his story at the 1986 hearing. Judge Pickett politely overruled him.

Payne then started to tell his story and added a detail which he had never mentioned in 1986 – that his son-in-law Gary Acreman had not only quaked with nerves on the day of the crime and panicked about the dead girl's clothes in the dumpster, but he had also told him that Robinson had been at the school with him. Speers objected that this was mere hearsay. 'Overruled,' said the judge. Payne described how he had been beaten and how his son-in-law had called him a liar. 'I got scars on my hand from his teeth,' he said.

Speers lashed out at the old man, confronting him with the version of events that he had given to the Attorney General's investigators, suggesting that the defence had put words into his mouth and that his whole story was a lie. Payne stood up to him and said that if any of his story was wrong it was because he was repeating what Gary Acreman had told him. 'If I go through life repeating what other people say I'm bound to tell a lie somewhere.'

Finally, Janet Dial strode once more to the witness-stand and swore that Judge John Martin and the old DA Jim Keeshan had been meeting secretly during Clarence Brandley's second trial to fix rulings for each day's hearing. The two men, she said, were leaders of the 'project' to convict Clarence Brandley. The atmosphere had been unsafe and ugly, she recalled.

Jim McCloskey sat at the defence table, glowing with respect for her. He had been in Montgomery County long enough to understand the risk she was taking. She was making powerful enemies by doing this and they were the sort of enemies who would nurture their anger for years. He could imagine the kind of harassment they would deal in: sneers and innuendo and cold shoulders; the kind of job hassles that Bill Srack had suffered; speeding tickets, slashed tyres. Judge Martin had already tried to ban her from the courthouse, despite the fact that it was a public building. McCloskey thought she was wonderful.

On the witness-stand now, she was starting to talk about a letter she had written to the *Courier* in which she had tried to alert the town to what was happening – 'the fact that most of our arresting officers are white, most of our prosecuting attorneys are white and, in fact, in the Brandley case, the jury had been all white, the Judge was white, even the defence attorneys were white. And given the fact that when you go to the grocery store, that there is prejudice, and in the school that there is prejudice, that it was completely unrealistic to think that bigotry could not have taken place, could not have had some influence during the entire Brandley investigation and trial and conviction. And the last thing I said was that a problem is never solved by denial – that as long as everybody was running around saying that each individual that was involved in the case had no shred of prejudice or bigotry, that we couldn't get at the truth.

'It's like we had to acknowledge the fact that this did indeed exist in Conroe, Texas, if we were going to get past that and to the truth.'

She said she believed now that she could never get work again in the courthouse. Peter Speers hopped up and said that was irrelevant. The judge overruled him.

If it had been permitted, McCloskey would have stood up and applauded as she left the stand.

The defence attorneys were elated. They had seen frightened and vulnerable people standing up and risking retribution for the sake of the truth, and they had opened their indictment against the two suspected murderers and against Conroe and its courthouse. The next morning, when the defence attorneys saw the newspapers, they found that the events in the Galveston court had been tele-graphed right across the State. But not in Conroe.

In Galveston, the *Daily News* splashed 'Witness changes story' across the front page and told its readers: 'A former custodian at Conroe High School wiped away tears Monday as he testified that he saw a 16-year-old girl fighting the advances of a school janitor – someone other than Clarence Lee Brandley.'

The other newspapers and the television and radio stations had taken a similar line. But in Conroe the *Courier* told a different story. Under the headline 'Witnesses: force used in Brandley case', the *Courier*'s reporter Carol Williams, told the town: 'Two key defense witnesses gave the indication Monday they had been brow-beaten by defence attorneys into changing their testimony to help Clarence Lee Brandley's case.'

Icky Peace was the first witness she wrote about. She did not mention how he had signed two police statements he could not read, nor how the statements had omitted key evidence, nor how the police officer had elected the black suspect, nor how the Ranger had shoved him against a wall and threatened to blow his head off, nor how the District Attorney had recently told him he was hallucinating. Readers of the *Courier* were informed only that 'Peace, who said he was intimidated by a Texas Ranger, told the judge that the defence had "told me what my testimony was to be, the words". Peace said he was told several times what he was supposed to say.'

Icky Peace had never said that.

Carol Williams then reported that Ed Payne had sat in court and pointed to Mike De Geurin with the words: 'They tried to get me to lie for the Clarence Lee Brandley case. They told me what they told me they wanted to hear. Parts of it was a lie. I was repeating what Gary said. If I go through life repeating what other people say, I'm bound to tell a lie somewhere.'

It was another phoney quote.

In Conroe, some things never changed.

And yet, in Conroe, an unseen tide was turning.

Just as Brenda Medina and John Sessum and Icky Peace and Ed Payne were now telling what they knew after years of silence, so, too, some of the bystanders on the fringe of events began to come forward.

Connie Miller had never said anything to anyone, but she had never forgotten that day when she was in her old office at City Cab and a scruffy young man named Acreman had come in and ended up shouting in her face: 'Clarence Brandley did not kill that girl. I know who did. Clarence didn't do it. But I will never tell.' She had followed the Brandley case in the newspapers the same as anyone else. She never had believed Brandley was guilty. But she had never really considered it her business and so she had never bothered to say anything about it.

But when she read that Gary Acreman was now trying to make out that he knew nothing of the killing, that he was telling the District Attorney that Clarence Brandley was guilty, something in her finally moved. She called up the DA's office and got the name of Brandley's attorney; then she called Don Brown and told him what she knew. Brown wished she had said something seven years earlier, but he was still happy to have her evidence. And she was not alone. The City Cab dispatcher and a man who had been in the office waiting for his grandmother had also heard Acreman's outburst, and they all agreed that the time had come to speak up.

They came to Galveston and told what they knew. Peter Speers's assistant, Rick Stover, attacked them, complaining that they recalled slightly different versions of what Acreman said, ridiculing their delay in coming forward, but all three stood by their stories.

The tide swept forward a woman named Kathy Binford.

She went to Galveston and told the court that Gary Acreman had once been a truck-driver at the place where she worked in Willis, ten miles north of Conroe. In June 1979, more than a year before the murder, he was caught trying to force himself on a young white girl there. She said other girls had also complained about him and so he had been fired.

When she went to court, Kathy Binford was accompanied by her friend Peggy Riggle, the vivacious telemarketing supervisor of the Conroe *Courier*. To her surprise, Peggy Riggle found herself on the witness-stand explaining that she was the one who had persuaded Kathy to speak up. They had been watching television together when the Brandley case came on and they flashed a picture of Gary Acreman up on the screen. As soon as she saw it, Kathy recognized him and told her what she knew.

Apart from taking her friend Kathy to court, Peggy Riggle also took the story to the *Courier* and arranged for them to interview Kathy. Peggy Riggle was upset when the paper never printed a word. After she gave evidence, on the fourth day of the hearing, she stayed in court. She was upset again when she read Carol Williams's report the next day. She thought it was biased and inaccurate. So she went to see the Editor and told him that she had had just about enough of the *Courier* being so prejudiced.

That was on a Friday. The following Monday, the *Courier* fired her.

They said it had nothing to do with her giving evidence for the black janitor and nothing to do with her complaining about the paper's prejudice. It was just that they had decided to eliminate her job, they said. Then they made her sign an agreement not to say anything detrimental about the *Courier*.

Gary Acreman looked as if he was dying. The pits of his eyes were blackened and deep. His whole face had hollowed out and he had a downtrodden, hangdog air about him as he loped into the crowded courtroom. He took his seat beneath the steady gaze of the judge and sat waxen-faced, staring at the floor in front of him. All the attorneys and all the spectators turned to the courtroom VCRs and watched in silent concentration as the image of Acreman's former, fleshier self flickered on to the screens. While he looked away, they saw him as he sat in the motel in Corsicana, smoking and confessing that he had lied and describing how James Dexter Robinson had seized Cheryl Fergeson. Then they saw him again, three days later, sitting in an office in Conroe, still smoking and confessing and explaining that Robinson had not only grabbed the girl but had also thrown her clothes into the dumpster. Finally, he looked up to find Mike De Geurin staring him in the eye.

'Mr Acreman, that was you on the video, was it not?'

'Yes, sir.' Dead-pan face.

'You've lost some weight since then, haven't you?'

'Yes.'

'But there's no doubt in your mind that was you and those were your words?'

'Yes, sir.'

De Geurin paused. There was nothing friendly or affable about him now. 'You know James Dexter Robinson?'

'Yes, sir.'

'How well do you know him?'

'Not that well.'

'By "not that well", do you mean you didn't run around with him?'

'No, I didn't do any running around with him.'

'Never did?'

'No.'

'Drive you to work?'

'Occasionally.'

'Ever go drinking with him?'

'No.'

'Never?'

'No.'

De Geurin hoped the judge would see that for the lie it was. 'Ever have group sex with him?'

'No.'

De Geurin paced back to the defence table, turned and asked Acreman who he had just had lunch with.

'Charlie Ray.'

De Geurin pointed at the DA's investigator sitting with the prosecution. 'The man sitting here at the table?'

'Yes, sir.'

Acreman denied that they had been discussing his evidence. He then admitted that he had made two visits to the DA's office in Conroe in the past week.

'Did you talk about your testimony?'

'I told them what I've been telling them since I talked to y'all.'

'How about telling them what you've been telling them since 1980? Or have you changed some of that?'

'No.'

'Haven't changed a word?'

Acreman shook his head. 'Uh-huh.'

De Geurin moved in close again. 'Did you speak to the girl at the school?'

'Told her where the restroom was.'

'You told her where the restroom was?'

'Yes, sir.'

'Now, you didn't testify about that at trial, did you?'

'Yes, sir, I did.'

De Geurin spun on his heel and started rifling through papers on his table. 'Mr Acreman, you didn't put that in your statement to the police, did you?'

'I can't remember.'

'Are you telling us now you did talk to the girl at the school?'

'Yes, sir. It was in your video, that she wanted to know where the restroom was.'

'You did talk to her then?'

'Yes, sir.'

De Geurin had found what he wanted in the papers. 'Correct me if I'm wrong, Mr Acreman, but didn't you testify at trial that you were 50 feet away from the area where the girl was, that you never saw her face, you only saw her from behind and that you just happened to see her walking down the hallway?'

'No, sir.'

'You didn't say that?'

'No, sir.'

'Well . . .'

'Well, I can't remember what all . . . I can't remember what was said in the trial.'

'But you would have told the truth?'

'Yes, sir.'

Acreman slouched miserably in his seat as the blond attorney paced back and forth before him, now diving for his papers, now striding forward and jabbing the air in front of his face to stress a point. Over and over again, De Geurin tied him to the details of what he had said in the videos and then confronted him with the different versions he had agreed at different times with the

Conroe police and the DA's office. Acreman's answers skidded and slid. He pleaded he could not remember. Whether Robinson had been at the school that day, whether it was Robinson who had thrown away the dead girl's clothes, whether the person who threw away the clothes was black or white, whether he had told any of this to the police in 1980, whether he had seen Robinson grab the girl – he could not remember.

'All right,' said De Geurin. 'Now, when you say on 20 March in the video, that you saw James Dexter Robinson throw the clothes in the dumpster – did you say that?'

'Yes, sir.'

'Sometime since 20th March, you lost your memory?'

'I wasn't sure . . . I wasn't sure about anything really.'

'When you say James Dexter Robinson grabbed her, I believe you made a motion with your hands.' De Geurin's fingers gripped an imaginary neck. 'Grabbing her. Where were you visualizing in your mind that he was grabbing her? What was in your mind? You were going like this . . .'. De Geurin's fingers were clenching the air in front of Acreman's face.

'Nothing.'

'You had your hands like that and you didn't have a picture in your mind?'

'No.'

'Mr Acreman, did you say "I know Clarence Brandley didn't do it"?'

Acreman frowned. 'No. I don't think I ever said he didn't do it.'

De Geurin reminded him of the evidence of Connie Miller and two other witnesses who all recalled his outburst in the City Cab office in August 1980. 'Those people are lying that you said that?'

'Yes, sir.'

De Geurin went back to his papers. 'Then in March 1987, on the video you say "I know Clarence Brandley didn't do it. He's not guilty." '

'I don't think I said in them exact words.'

De Geurin was flicking through piles of paper, while Nugent and Brown leaned across him to join the search. De Geurin looked back at his witness. 'I'll find it in just a moment,' he promised.

'Exact words . . . All right, Mr Acreman, you were asked on 20 March, that's the second video that you did, "Why are you now telling us this?" and you said "Because I don't think Clarence Brandley is guilty of it. And well, I know for a fact he isn't." Now you said that, didn't you, Mr Acreman?'

'Yeah, I guess.'

'Do you want me to show it to you on the video again?'

'No.'

'Do you have any doubts that you said that?'

Acreman scratched his hair and shook his head.

'Any doubts in your mind that on that tape, those thoughts, these words came out of your mind?'

'No.'

De Geurin closed in on him again. 'Mr Acreman, you know, don't you, that Mr Brandley is not guilty?'

With something like desperation in his voice, Acreman told him: 'I don't know. I wasn't there.'

'And you know who did it, too, don't you?'

Acreman shook his head and looked at the floor, as if for refuge. 'No, sir. I don't.'

De Geurin kept jabbing at his conscience. Why had he said that Brandley was innocent? Why had he held back on the truth in his statement to police? 'It still bothers you, doesn't it?'

'No, sir. I don't know of anything I left out.'

'Well, you never said you talked to the girl in your statement, did you?'

Acreman stared morosely at his hands.

'Did you?'

'Yes, sir, that was in one of them.'

De Geurin pounced back to his table, found his statement and thrust it towards Acreman. 'Take your time,' he said with a flick of his hand. 'Read it.'

De Geurin waited. 300 people waited. There was not a sound. 'Have you had an opportunity, Mr Acreman, to read the statement?'

'Yes, sir.'

'Do you say in the statement that you talked to the girl?'

'No, sir.'

De Geurin was not finished yet. He made Acreman confirm that John Sessum had seen him talking to the girl and that Sessum was now telling the truth about it. Acreman tried to fight back and suggested he had just forgotten to mention it to the police. 'That completely slipped my mind,' he said.

De Geurin seized the phrase and, stalking up and down in front of the witness-stand, he started bludgeoning Acreman with it: 'It just slipped your mind that you had talked to the girl a few moments before she was killed? . . . When Ranger Styles was getting your statement after you all walked through the school, it just slipped your mind? . . . And Mr Martinez didn't tell the police . . . And Mr Sessum didn't tell the police . . . All three of you, it slipped your mind? Is that correct?'

'I guess so.'

'Mr Acreman, were you, Sessum, Martinez, afraid you might be implicated in this crime because you talked to that girl?'

'No, sir.'

De Geurin paused and asked, as if it were an afterthought: 'Was she pretty?'

'I don't know. I guess.'

With a look of disdain, De Geurin turned and walked back to his table. 'I'll pass the witness.'

The muffled buzz of comment had dwindled and died by the time Rick Stover, the assistant DA, stood up to try and rescue Gary Acreman.

Stover reminded him he was on oath and asked him: 'Back on the day that Cheryl Fergeson was raped and murdered in the Conroe High School, did you participate in the rape or the murder of her?'

'No, sir.'

'Did you see anyone abduct Cheryl Fergeson prior to her murder?'

'No, sir.'

Now, once again, Gary Acreman sat slouched in his seat staring in front of him while the courtroom was filled with the sound of his voice, first in a recording of his phone call to Rick Stover, complaining that Richard Reyna had scared him into telling lies, and then in a video of his interview in Pittsburgh with Stover and Charlie Ray, insisting that everything he had said at Brandley's trials was still true.

Stover was trying to push a raft out to the drowning witness. All Acreman had to do was to stick to the story he had told at the original trials and dismiss everything else as the voice of his fear, brought on by the terror of dealing with Richard Reyna and Jim McCloskey. In his panic, Acreman kept flailing at the raft and missing.

First, Stover got him to agree that he had told the truth back in 1980 when his memory was fresh: nobody grabbing any girl, no sign of Robinson. Then that he had stood up in the witness-stand in July 1986 and sworn on oath that he had seen James Dexter Robinson at Conroe High on the day of the crime. Now was the time for Acreman to talk about the voice of his fear. Stover set it up for him: 'Now I'm curious why you testified that you had seen James Robinson at the school on the day of the murder when you have told me that you didn't see him there, and you didn't tell the Texas Ranger that, and you didn't tell it on any of the statements, and you didn't tell it in the first two trials that you participated in.'

Acreman shifted in his seat and said: 'I . . . I don't know either. I more or less feel that it being that long a time, I . . . I'm not sure what happened that day and as far as that, you know, some-body saying, saying this, or hearing different things about that would make me wonder . . .'

His voice faded and vanished. Stover made no attempt to conceal his own view of the answer. 'That's your explanation why, after six years, you suddenly decided to say that you saw James Dexter Robinson at the school on the day of the murder?'

Acreman made another grab for the raft. 'Well, not only that. After talking to Reyna the first time, the first couple of times, whatever, when he first came up to me and introduced me who he was, like I said, I don't remember ever seeing ID or anything, credentials or anything, and then he tells me then, that not to take the rap for anything for something somebody else done. Then he starts telling me what, who or telling me who, that somebody had seen Robinson there and that Robinson was there . . .'

Stover could see he needed help and held out a hand. 'When he told you this, did you all of a sudden think "Well, if he says it, it's got to be true, therefore, I'm going to testify to it"?'

Acreman missed the hand completely. 'No,' he said.

Stover winced, abandoned the July 1986 hearing and tried another approach. Slowly, step by step, he brought him up to his meeting in Corsicana with Richard Reyna and Jim McCloskey. He got Acreman to explain that he was nervous in Corsicana because he was waiting to go to court over a road accident he had been involved in where another driver was killed. He got him to recall that Richard Reyna had told him not to take the rap for the killing at the high school.

'How many times did he say that to you?'

'Once, twice, three times.'

'Were you scared?'

'Yes, sir.'

'Were you nervous?'

'Yes.'

Stover was getting closer to the voice of fear. But Acreman still had to explain why he had produced such a vivid account of Robinson attacking the girl if there was no truth in it. Stover inched a little closer. 'What was going through your mind at that time?'

'I don't know. "It ain't me".'

Stover needed more than that. He needed the fear. ' "It ain't me". What do you mean by that statement?'

'I didn't do it.'

'Did you think any further than that?'

'Well, I was, I was sitting there, thinking "Can they make this stick?" I know that I'm innocent and they're coming at me with this.'

He was still not getting there. Acreman started to say that he had gone ahead and made this video because Reyna had insisted.

'Well, Mr Acreman, I could insist that you saw the assassination of President Kennedy, I could say that all day long, but if you didn't see it, that didn't make it true. Is that correct?'

'Yes.'

Stover pushed harder. 'If I told you that enough times, would

I eventually be able to convince you that maybe you were in Dallas on that day and you did see that take place?'

The answer had to be 'No, not unless you frightened me the way Reyna did', but Acreman was lost. 'I don't know.'

'Is it possible?' begged Stover.

'No,' said Acreman, missing the raft again.

The defence attorneys had to admire Stover's stamina. He kept on at Acreman to explain how Reyna had scared him.

Acreman kept groping and grabbing: 'The way he words things, the way he words things to his advantage . . . I don't know, I don't know how to put it . . . He was a, uh, type of person who just take you and put you on the spot . . . Something about him . . .'

Finally Acreman came up with an idea: 'His voice, his tone of voice that he uses.'

The words were no sooner out of his mouth than a look of anxiety swept across his face as he realized that the 300 people who were now looking straight at him had all heard Reyna's voice on the videos.

'The tone of voice that he used,' he added quickly, 'before the video was made.'

Stover was near defeat. 'Mr Acreman, I could use a tone of voice in this courtroom that would scare you right out of that chair, but I don't think it would make you say something that wasn't true, so I don't understand and this judge doesn't understand why you made this video.'

It was no good. Acreman was as exhausted as Stover. When they finally got round to talking about the second video he had made with the defence and Stover asked him why he had sat down in front of another video camera and not mentioned that his first video statement was a lie, Acreman looked at him, looked at the floor, shrugged and said: 'I don't know.'

Rick Stover gave up and returned to the prosecution table, leaving Acreman marooned on the witness-stand with all his words over all the years in mutiny against him.

The turning tide caught Debra Cheney and swept her into court. She lived in a trailer park in Conroe and had once had Brenda

Medina and James Dexter Robinson as neighbours. She came forward to tell the defence that she knew Robinson had been in Conroe during the week of the murder, because she had seen him on that Wednesday with Brenda at the hospital. She knew it was a Wednesday because she had been taking her pregnant sister to the hospital, as she always did on Wednesdays, and she remembered clearly that it was the same week that they heard about the killing at the high school.

She went to Galveston to tell her story. Peter Speers asked why she had not said all this back in July 1986 when Brenda Medina was giving evidence, why she had taken so long to speak out.

She had no answer – no more than anyone else in the town who had looked away.

James Dexter Robinson had his story all assembled. The loose ends that had jumped out of place during the hearing in Conroe in July 1986 were now all neatly tucked away.

He stood in the witness box, his little elfin face twitching with nerves, and told Rick Stover that he now realized that a whole lot of things he had forgotten and which other people were now talking about had really happened to him on 5 August 1980, two and a half weeks before Cheryl Fergeson was killed.

It was on 5 August, he said, that he had cashed his last pay cheque from Conroe High. It was on that day that he had visited the High School for the last time and he was pretty sure he had popped his head round the door and said Hi to the janitors he used to work with. It was on that day, too, he now remembered, that he had gone round to see Reggie Slacum to ask him to repay the $100 he owed him. And it was on that night that he had decided to leave Conroe for good – not because he had killed anyone, but because be believed that Brenda Medina was seeing another man. That was the truth, he said, now that he had had time to think about it.

He explained that he might have said some strange things when the defence arranged for him to take a lie test with Glenn Raney, but that was because Raney had shouted at him and slapped the table in anger and asked him whether he killed Cheryl Fergeson 60 different times. He had not mentioned that at the hearing last year. But now he had had time to think about it. As he told his story, his voice dropped so low that no one in court could hear a word. Judge Pickett leaned forward and made him unhook the microphone from the front of the witness stand and loop the flex around his throat. Paul Nugent wondered at the symbolism of it all as Robinson tightened the noose around his own neck.

Mike De Geurin began to cross-examine him in his gentlest style, persuading him to remind everyone that he had wanted to hire the District Attorney as his lawyer. Then he started to turn the screw. He asked him about his former wife, Berdie. 'Berdie accused you of beating her up. Are you aware of that?'

Robinson shook his head, all innocence. 'No, sir.'

'Now, Mr Robinson, weren't you made aware of the fact that she was put in hospital and claimed that you had repeatedly beaten her?'

'No, sir.'

He smiled. It was a mistake.

De Geurin looked at him in amazement. 'Why are you smiling?'

The smile vanished. 'Because that's a lie.'

'Are you telling me, though, that you never heard that before?'

'No, sir, I've never beat her like you're saying I did.'

'All right. But you have heard that she said that?'

'Yes, sir.'

At last.

'And she's lying?'

'Yes, sir.'

Now De Geurin had Robinson where he wanted him. 'And when Brenda Medina says you beat her up before, she's lying?'

'Yes, sir.'

'Now, Mr Slacum says that you were in Conroe on the 20th and 21st of August 1980. He knows it for a fact, he says, because you and your father had tried to rough him up.'

'No, sir.'

'Okay. Is Mr Slacum a liar?'

'Yes, sir.'

'Now, do you know Debra Cheney?'

'No, sir.'

'Do you remember going with Brenda Medina to a hospital back in 1980?'

'We went in June.'

'Are you saying you didn't go in August?'

'No, sir.'

'Positive about that?'

'Yes, sir.'

'Now, Mrs Cheney says she saw you at the hospital in August, in fact she says it was 20th of August 1980.'

'No, sir.'

'She's lying, too?'

'Yes, sir.'

He was all alone. They were all liars. And Brenda Medina was a liar for saying he had confessed. And John Sessum was a liar for saying he grabbed the girl. And Gary Acreman was a liar for saying the same thing.

De Geurin then made him repeat his claim that he had known nothing of the murder at the high school until several months later, when he was living in South Carolina and had spoken to his father, who was then still living in Texas. 'He called me to ask me how was I doing and everything. That conversation was brought up during our talk.'

'And he told you, asked you if you remembered . . .'

'Clarence Brandley.'

De Geurin stood in front of him, his head cocked to one side. 'Was that the way he referred to him? Is that the way he referred to him?'

'No, sir.'

'How did he refer to him?'

'He said "You remember that black man that was working in the school that was a supervisor?" And I said "Yeah". He said well, he had killed a girl.'

'You're sure that's the way he referred to him?'

'Yes, sir.'

De Geurin darted his hand out to the table and picked up a copy of the statement Robinson had made to the District Attorney about his innocence. 'I'll let you look at your statement, sir. Read the line to yourself. See if it refreshes . . .'

'I don't want to say that part in court.'

'So that's not the way he referred to Clarence Brandley, was it?'

'No, sir.'

'Can you go ahead and tell us how he referred to Clarence?'

Robinson glanced at the sea of brown faces and looked down and mumbled the words he had been happy to say in the District Attorney's office. 'He said "Do you remember the nigger at the school?" '

A shuffle spread along the public benches. Now Robinson, too, was alone and marooned, not only by the words of all those he called liars but also by the words of his own father repeated before 300 strangers.

As the hearing rolled from day to day, its participants developed daily rituals. Each morning, Nugent and McCloskey would go to Gaido's restaurant down by the waterfront to eat breakfast and talk tactics. They were staying in a beach house on the Gulf side of the island which had been given to Percy Foreman as a fee by some former client and was now littered with paperwork from the Brandley case. Most mornings they would be joined by Don Brown who was staying at a motel, and by Richard Renya who had checked into a block of pseudo-Victorian flats. Then they would all travel up to court and find De Geurin, who was staying at the posh Tremont House in the middle of town, pacing up and down outside, smoking nervously with a pad full of notes under one arm and some new idea he needed to unload.

The courthouse foyer was always jammed with people. All the old ladies from Dugan would stand in line for the metal detector, armed now with pillows to soften the long day on the hard court benches. The Montgomery County deputies laboriously searched everyone, including the defence attorneys, and insisted that all the spectators had to leave their little packets of food and drink outside in the foyer.

Every morning, the black people waiting in line watched Peter Speers's wife flounce by without being searched, drinking ostentatiously from a can of Coca-Cola which she was allowed to take with her into court.

Nugent and De Geurin would often slip across the car park to the Galveston County Jail to talk about their plans with Brandley and to reassure him. De Geurin had bought him a white silk shirt with a button-down executive collar and every evening, Brandley would strip it off and send it out to his family, who would bring it back the next day washed and pressed.

Although Brandley was outwardly calm, the two attorneys could see the tension seething inside him. His fingers shook so much that Nugent had to help him knot his tie. All his emotions were running high. He had never been in a jail with young people before and he kept talking about how bad it made him feel to see these young people who thought it was so cool to live in the fast lane. It made him tearful to talk about it.

Every day in court, Nugent played out a minor power struggle with the Montgomery County deputies. He noticed that the prosecuting attorneys had chairs with wheels on the bottom so they could slide effortlessly between their table and the exhibits or the public benches. The deputies slouching at the back of the court had wheels on their chairs, too. But they had given the defence ordinary, immobile ones. On the third day, Nugent decided to do something about this inequity, so while the deputies stood leaning against the wall of the court glaring, Nugent sauntered over and took their chairs and replaced them with ones without wheels. Every morning after that, he would come into court and find that the deputies had been there earlier and taken back the chairs and, every morning, while the deputies stood sullenly watching, Nugent would seize them again for the defence.

Judge Pickett soon became an object of veneration in the court. He would arrive early each morning and take his place on his dais with his pipe clenched between his teeth and quietly watch the goings-on before him. At the beginning of business, he would bid the court good morning and all the old black ladies would chorus him good morning in reply. While the attorneys fought and scrapped, he would sit calmly, endlessly writing his notes, fielding objections, frequently telling the attorneys 'You're probably right, but overruled.' During breaks he would stay seated, still watching, and some of the old ladies would approach him to strike up a conversation.

Slowly, the defence began to trust him. They did a little digging and discovered that, in his own way, he had once had something in common with Clarence Brandley. He, too, had been unjustly imprisoned. During the war, he had been shot down over the Mediterranean and captured by the Germans and had then joined 29 other US officers in breaking out of captivity in the escape from a prison train, which was made famous in cinemas as *Von Ryan's Express*.

Peter Speers's wife soon became an object of contempt. She sat each day in her reserved seat at the front of the court, sipping her Coke, chewing her gum, flicking through *People* magazine during the evidence, sneering derisively at defence witnesses and occasionally lighting up a cigarette.

At the midday break, the defence team would hurry back to De Geurin's room in the Tremont House where the foyer was full of palm trees and piano players and they would sit on his window-sill, eating hamburgers and planning strategy. In the evenings they still stayed together, plotting and planning. One evening, in Candy's Italian restaurant, they were in mid-session when Peter Speers walked in with his assistant, one of the investigators from the Attorney General's office, and Carol Williams from the Conroe *Courier*. They took one look at the defence team, turned on their heels and left.

Every day, the unseen tide brought new witnesses who were now ready to peel more layers of secrecy away from the courthouse and the town of Conroe.

Cheryl Bradford, who was now a sports coach, came forward to tell of the two strange men she had seen in the gym that day. But it was not just what she said about Robinson that caught the attention of the defence. The reason they brought her down to Galveston and had her tell her story to the judge was that on the evening of the crime, less than 24 hours after Cheryl Fergeson's death, this girl had been so concerned by what she had seen that she had contacted the Conroe Police Department and told them all about the two white men, and the Conroe Police Department, who had already elected their suspect, had never bothered to follow it up.

Two black ministers ran the gauntlet of Montgomery County

deputies to recall the trials of Clarence Brandley. Revd C. Anderson Davis, a Houston minister and no relation to Revd John Daviss of Conroe, remembered that in both trials there was 'a racist nigger atmosphere where blacks were supposed to stay in their places and you would never have a fair chance when opposing the opposite race'. The Montgomery County deputies had made it clear that blacks were second-class citizens. The judge had seemed racially hostile. The minister said he had visited trials all over the United States and had only once seen one that was worse, and that was in Chattanooga, Tennessee, where the prosecution openly used the word 'nigger' and said all black people were dishonest and stank. 'Now, other than that trial, I've never seen one more racially hostile than the one in Conroe.'

Another Houston minister, Revd J. J. Roberson, spoke of the anger of white people in the courthouse towards blacks, the cold looks on the faces of the jurors, the surly deputies following black people to the restrooms; but he apologized to the attorneys and the judge: 'You couldn't imagine how I felt because you haven't been black one hour.'

De Geurin asked the elderly minister if he had ever heard of incidents in Conroe's past where black men who had been accused of assaulting white women in the town had been attacked and killed. Peter Speers interrupted the question three times to complain that none of this should be mentioned. The judge overruled him, and De Geurin asked if the atmosphere in the town had changed since then.

'I imagine the attitudes have changed,' the minister replied, 'but the atmosphere is still the same.'

Don Brown stepped forward and took the stand himself to remember the bitterness of the trial: the belief he shared with George Morris that they might well be attacked if the jury acquitted Clarence Brandley; the all-white court; the chill that spread through the room when the schoolboy, Danny Taylor, claimed that Brandley had lusted after white schoolgirls; Sheriff Gene Reaves and the DA Jim Keeshan sitting in Judge Alworth's office and referring to Brandley as 'that little nigger' without a word of rebuke from the judge; the deceit with which Keeshan had tricked

Clarence Brandley into appearing before the grand jury and then
depriving him of his bail.

There was the former assistant DA, Frank Robin, swearing on
oath that Keeshan would have been upset if he had ever allowed
a black person to sit as a juror; a sociologist from the University of
Texas, Sheldon Ekland-Olson, who explained that his exhaustive
research showed that in Texas a black man who was convicted of
raping and killing a white woman was five times more likely to
be sentenced to death than a normal homicide defendant; and
there was Don Brown's law partner, Nat Davis, who swore Don
Brown was right in recalling that both the sheriff and the DA had
called Brandley 'that little nigger'.

Then Mary Johnson, the elegant court reporter, came trembling
to the witness-stand. She was instantly a magnetic sight, with her
huge beauty-queen eyes and white-blonde hair drawn back from
her face. De Geurin needed her to tell all she knew about the
missing exhibits and about the conspiracy in the courthouse to
conceal their disappearance. But he knew that she was struggling
with a dilemma, torn between telling the truth and remaining loyal
to Judge Martin. As De Geurin began his questions, Mary Johnson
started to cry. For a while, the whole room was not so much a
court as a theatre and they were an audience, watching this poign-
ant spectacle of a woman at war with herself.

'I'd like to say to all of these questions that I don't recall,' she
said.

De Geurin grinned his most charming grin. 'I know you would.'

The blond attorney felt the drama of it all himself. He was
confronting her with a moral choice such as she had probably
never had to face in her life. She could tell the truth to save this
man's life, or she could conceal it and save her job and her position
in her community. The fact that she had never met this man and
that a well-to-do white woman in her position was never likely
to meet him only made the choice more difficult – more pure. She
could do right, or she could do wrong.

De Geurin tried to help her by reminding her that he was
himself a close friend of the judge whose behaviour he was now
having to expose. 'It's not easy for either of us, is it?' he said. It
was an instinctive move, but it helped to move her forward.

Slowly, with her handkerchief balled up in her fist, she began to whisper the history of the missing exhibits and all the secrecy surrounding them, rehearsing now in public what she had previously dared to say only in secret.

She explained that there was no way those exhibits could have been thrown out accidentally; that as many as 25 people in the courthouse were told about their disappearance, but that the defence were kept in the dark; and that she had heard how Peggy Stevens showed Don Brown a box of fake exhibits to keep him quiet and then called down to Jim Keeshan's office to warn him that Brown was on the war-path. She had decided she had to tell the defence the truth and contacted them through Janet Dial. In the same way, she had also decided she had to tell them that Judge Martin and the DA had sat down in front of her and rehearsed a scheme to prevent the defence from calling any witnesses and finding out what had really happened to the exhibits.

De Geurin had to coax each line from her but, as she spoke, he felt an admiration for this unlikely heroine. He could only guess how the courthouse in Conroe would treat her once they heard what she had done.

As the layers were slowly peeled away, the defence reached the point where they were finally ready to confront the enemy. One by one, in front of the 300 spectators and all of the unseen spectators across the state of Texas, the ringleaders were called to the stand to explain themselves.

Judge Lynn Coker was called.

De Geurin tried to get him to talk about the time he had ushered George Morris and Don Brown into his office all those years ago to warn them of all the activity over the missing exhibits and how it boggled his imagination. The judge said he could not recall such a conversation. De Geurin felt a flicker of anger at this spineless figure, who was so keen when he had a chance to get someone to like him and so feeble when it came to standing up for an innocent man. He had never cross-examined a judge before, but he started hounding him for the truth. The judge kept pointing to the hole in his memory.

'Well, judge. I'm not going to belabour the point. I want to ask you – are you denying that you told Don Brown and George Morris that the evidence was lost, that Keeshan and Martin were keeping it a secret but you thought they ought to know about it?'

The judge shrugged and smiled. 'Counsel, I'm not denying anything. I do not recall it.'

De Geurin shook his head and turned his back on him. 'I'll pass the witness.'

Dr Jachimczyk, the medical examiner, was called.

The court watched him plead that he could not recall what had happened to the missing swabs he had taken from the dead girl, and he could not recall whether he had given them to the police, and he could not recall whether the Texas Ranger had contacted him, and he could not recall whether he had given the swabs to the Ranger, and he could not recall whether he had destroyed them himself. But he was sure the swabs no longer existed.

As soon as the portly pathologist had left the stand, De Geurin called a Houston police sergeant who said that he had worked on more than 1,000 rape cases and that it was standard procedure to preserve such swabs for comparison with any future suspect, and that he could not think of any scientific reason for them to be thrown away.

Peggy Stevens was called, with her immaculate suit and her manicured nails and her spectacles on the end of her fine gold chain. The District Clerk of Montgomery County, who was elected by the town to serve prosecution and defence without favour, had an explanation for her behaviour over the missing exhibits. She had kept it all secret from the defence, she said, because the DA was conducting a criminal inquiry in to their disappearance, and she had been trained to be discreet about such things. She had certainly not been siding with the prosecution and plotting to deceive the defence.

De Geurin watched her sitting there, like a Siamese cat in the sun. Pacing backwards and forwards, hunched slightly forward, he started to probe her claim to impartiality. He soon discovered that her memory was as fallible as Judge Coker's and the pathologist's. He wanted her to remember how she had shown Don Brown a box full of fake exhibits and then warned Jim Keeshan so that he could hide in his office while Brown waited impotently outside. Did she remember showing Don Brown a box full of fake exhibits?

'I just don't recall it, Mr De Geurin. I'm sorry. I have racked my brains over all those events. I just do not recall that particular instance.'

Had she called Jim Keeshan's office to warn them that Don Brown might know what was happening?

'I just don't recall it. No, sir. I'm sorry.'

'Could it have happened and you just don't remember?'

'It might have. Like I said, I just don't remember one particular incident like that.'

'How about calling Judge Martin and letting him know?'

'No, sir.'

'How about somebody on Judge Martin's staff?'

The reference to Mary Johnson was clear. Peggy Stevens had not been in court to hear her evidence. Her memory revived a little. 'I may have mentioned it but I don't think I ever picked up a phone and called anybody. I'm sure I probably mentioned it in passing.'

It was the beginning of an admission. De Geurin tried to build on it. 'I'm talking about mentioning it in passing, if you will, while Don Brown was walking in the courthouse to go talk to Mr Keeshan, to try to get to the bottom of this problem with the exhibits.'

Mrs Stevens flattened a hand against her chest in shock. 'That I mentioned it while Mr Brown was walking in the courthouse?'

De Geurin persisted. 'Well, you said you may have mentioned it in passing that you think Mr Brown had caught on to the secret . . .'

'Oh,' she said, in a tone that suggested she now understood for the first time what he was asking her.

'And I want to know if you called him and warned him.'

'I do not recall picking up a phone and calling anybody. No, sir.'

De Geurin could see she was not about to fill the gap in her memory.

Still sitting pretty on the witness-stand, she continued to insist it had been her duty to be discreet, and she jabbed at Don Brown, calling him a prime suspect in the disappearance. At the defence table, Brown grit his teeth. De Geurin let her go: he could only leave it to the judge to decide whether she was telling the truth.

Judge John Martin was called. For a moment, De Geurin found it embarrassing. This was not just a judge on the stand. That in itself was strange enough. This was also an old friend, someone he had once liked and respected. For a moment, De Geurin wondered whether he might still be the same man he had been pleased to know, whether he might stand up now and help them peel the layers of lies from the courthouse. De Geurin started gently chipping into his evidence. Was his office on the first floor of the courthouse? 'Yes'. Was the DA's office on the same floor? 'Yes'. Did his secretary routinely note all his callers on a note-pad? 'Yes.' Did he still have the note-pads which his old secretary, Janet Dial, had kept for the period of the second Brandley trial and which would reflect the controversial contacts between himself and the DA? 'No.'

The judge explained that the note-pads had mysteriously disappeared. No other records were missing from his office. Only those note-pads for that period of time. He had no idea where they had gone. They were just lost and gone forever.

De Geurin felt his friendship fade. He chipped deeper. 'Judge, just for the record, were all the jurors in Clarence Brandley's case white?'

Judge Martin hesitated and said: 'Everyone appeared to be white.'

No explanation. No apology. De Geurin started hammering home his questions. The more he hammered, the more the judge fell back on the official courthouse version of events.

He never plotted with the DA to deceive the defence about the missing exhibits. He asked the DA to conduct a criminal inquiry and it had to be discreet. He did not recall Peggy Stevens warning him that Don Brown was on the track of the truth. He never knew the defence attorneys were worried about it. He thought the janitors had thrown away the exhibits. He never held secret meetings with the DA. He only ever wanted to be a fair judge. He had never plotted with the DA to rig the hearing about the missing exhibits. He had only recused himself from the case to help his old friends the defence attorneys. He had never been hostile to black spectators.

The more he denied, the more De Geurin hammered him.

What about Mary Johnson's testimony that he rehearsed with Keeshan how they would prevent the defence from calling witnesses to find out the truth about the missing exhibits?

'That's incorrect.'

'Is the court reporter who testified that that is true, are you saying she's a liar?'

'No. She testified whatever she recalls, counsel. I'm just telling you what I recall. That's all.'

What about the secret inquiry into the missing exhibits? Had it been his idea that the defence attorneys could not be told the truth because they were suspects?

'Everyone, counsel, was a suspect. My court reporter, the defence lawyers, or anyone that – the janitors, the lady that typed for Mary Johnson. Everyone was suspect.'

De Geurin went for the hole in his story. 'Suspects were questioned, weren't they?'

'That's right.'

De Geurin ripped the hole open. 'Of course, they didn't question the defence counsel?'

The judge sighed. 'I don't know. I don't know.'

What about his secret meetings with the DA? Had he met with Jim Keeshan in the mornings before going into court during Brandley's trial?

'Absolutely not.'

'He never came into your office?'

'Oh, he may have come into my outer office and spoken to my secretary, Jan Dial, or something, but I never had an "ex parte" meeting with Judge Keeshan about the case while it was in progress.'

'Are you calling Janet Dial a liar?'

'I'm not, like I say, talking anything about what Jan Dial might have said. I'm just telling you that I have never had an "ex parte" meeting with Jim Keeshan when he was District Attorney during the time of the trial.'

'Then it's your testimony that he never came into your chambers early in the morning or before the trial started, where just you and he were in chambers together during the trial?'

'That's right.'

'Never?'

'Never.'

There was no friendship left now. Only the attorney, bursting with passion, hammering out his questions, and the judge, out of place on the witness-stand, ducking and denying.

There came a point in the verbal brawl when De Geurin started challenging him about why he had never ordered the white janitors from the high school to supply samples of hair for comparison with those found on the dead girl. The judge was saying he could not recall. De Geurin was getting nowhere. Suddenly, somewhere inside the attorney, a dam broke. Words started pouring out of him, his anger gushing over the judge in the witness-stand as he flooded him with the details of the truth he was determined to deny.

Just suppose, he said, his finger jabbing at the judge, that within 30 days of Brandley's conviction, he had learned, as the judge in the case, that an ex-janitor had confessed about the murder to his girlfriend. And just suppose that two people said this ex-janitor was at the school on the day of the murder, that three or four people said he was in town at the time of the murder, that Gary Acreman said he saw this ex-janitor grab the girl and pull her into a bathroom, screaming and yelling for help.

De Geurin was pounding up and down in front of the judge, his hand beating the air for emphasis, all the fragments of fact and all the years of frustration washing through him. 'And let's suppose Acreman further said he lied at the trial that you conducted, and another janitor, that being Icky Peace, testified that he lied at your trial, and another janitor, John Sessum, testified that he lied at your trial and that he saw Gary Acreman grab the girl and pull her into the bathroom, screaming and yelling.

'And let's suppose further that Gary Acreman says "That's true but it wasn't me, it was James Dexter Robinson"; and let's suppose further that James Dexter Robinson and Gary Acreman both are Caucasian and one has sandy blond hair and one has brown hair and that you also learned that a volleyball player had seen two men meeting that general description walking across the top of the boys' gymnasium and out the side-doors during the time that it is perceived and projected the young girl was killed, and that the police never called her back, because her information did not appear to be relevant.'

The judge sat open-mouthed. There was no stopping De Geurin now. And suppose the judge had also heard the evidence of Ed Payne. And the evidence of Ed Payne's brother, John. And John's wife, Marie.

'And let's suppose further that Gary Acreman admits in court that he lied when he said he never talked to the girl at the school, that he lied to the District Attorney, that he lied to Wesley Styles, that he lied to the Conroe Police and that he lied in your trial.

'And let's suppose further that one of the janitors said that Gary Acreman had told him the day of the killing before anybody was supposed to have known the killing had happened "Don't you tell anybody I was talking to that girl". Let's suppose all of that was presented to you . . .'

The judge finally found words to interrupt. 'On a motion for new trial?' he said. 'I'd conduct a hearing.'

'Let me finish,' snapped De Geurin, still pacing the floor. 'Let's suppose those things came to you, not from defence attorneys, but from somebody else, would you think that would be something the defence attorneys should know about?'

'I would conduct a hearing on all of that, Counsel.'

'And if those things were established within the time for a new trial, would you grant a new trial?'

'I would conduct a hearing on all of that.'

Rick Stover tried to interrupt. Judge Pickett told them to proceed. De Geurin's anger was not to be stopped. His voice was rasping now with effort and emotion: 'Would you allow a man to be executed when three of the four janitors that testified at

392

your trial are now being called liars by the District Attorney's office?'

'That's not within my province.'

'Let me ask you personally.' His finger jabbed at the judge. 'Would you allow him to be executed?'

'That's not within my province.'

Rick Stover objected. Judge Pickett said Martin had answered the question.

Now Mike De Geurin stopped square in front of his former friend and looked into his eyes: 'Judge, why don't you just tell Clarence Brandley and these people you're sorry for what happened?'

Judge Martin just gaped. Rick Stover jumped from his chair, objecting. But De Geurin was already walking back to his seat. 'I'll pass the witness.'

On the public benches, some of the old people from Dugan had tears in their eyes.

The Honourable James Keeshan was called.

He was as smooth and self-assured as ever, sitting calm and poised on the stand, paying no heed to the rows of angry faces, marking out his defence in a firm voice as Peter Speers began by leading him through his role in the affair. He claimed to have no gaps in his memory. He did not deal in blunt denials. He simply explained things his way.

Yes, he had ordered Brandley's arrest, but that had nothing to do with race. Yes, he had objected to hair and blood samples being taken from other janitors, but that was because it would have been a 'needless imposition'. Yes, he had agreed to let Brandley have a low bail-bond and then revoked his probation, but that was just standard procedure. Certainly he had later had that bail-bond raised to $75,000 but he was sure he had invited the defence attorneys to a hearing on the subject. At the defence table, Don Brown was tempted to burst into flames at hearing this, but restricted himself to a vigorous shaking of his head.

Keeshan was not afraid to admit the faults of others in the courthouse. He agreed that Sheriff Reaves had called Brandley a nigger, but he was sure he had not done so himself. He then explained that although the sheriff had used that word, he had many friends in the black community in Montgomery County. There was an outburst of derisive laughter from the public benches.

He had noticed no racial tension and no disturbances at either of the trials. He had certainly not held any secret meetings with Judge Martin. It would not have been possible: he was always far too busy preparing his witnesses and, anyway, he could not have anticipated issues that were going to arise, let alone rehearse how they would handle them.

He had helped to replace the missing exhibits with copies, but he had only done that to test the reaction of the defence, who were, he said, the only people with a motive to destroy this material. He had never plotted secretly with Judge Martin to rig the subsequent hearing. It was just that the judge and Mary Johnson had come by his office without being invited and he had suggested that, in order to save any embarrassment to Mary Johnson, he could announce at the coming hearing that he believed the janitors were responsible and it was not Mary's fault.

Peter Speers asked him if he had ever intended to deprive Clarence Brandley of any of his rights. The Honourable James Keeshan replied that his aim was 'only to do my duty to the best of my ability and without the intent to mistreat or abuse anyone.'

Mike De Geurin took him on point by point. Keeshan started to retreat. He admitted that since he had an assistant and an investigator to help him, he would have had time to meet Judge Martin before trial each morning, and he admitted that since this was a second trial, he could have anticipated the issues that would be arising.

He admitted that he had never interviewed anyone from the Brandley defence, even though he claimed they were the only ones with a motive to destroy exhibits. He admitted that Sam Martinez's father worked as a janitor at the courthouse and that he had never interviewed him to see whether he might have destroyed the exhibits for fear that his son was involved in the crime. He admitted that he had never previously claimed that his plan for the hearing about the exhibits was designed to save Mary Johnson from embarrassment. He admitted that Peggy Stevens had warned him that Don Brown was guessing the truth, but he could not explain why Peggy Stevens would deny that in court.

He admitted, when he was confronted with an official transcript, that there had been disturbances at the trial and that he had personally complained to the judge about unruly behaviour and about a black woman who had sat on a white woman's hand, and that he had asked for extra security. He first denied, and then admitted when he was confronted with a transcript, that he had told the Judge that he would speak to the white spectators in the courthouse about their behaviour if the defence attorneys would deal with the blacks.

But on one point he would not move. 'It was, and is my belief that Mr Brandley killed Cheryl Fergeson,' he said.

As he left the stand and walked out of court, he was followed by the wordless stares of 300 people who did not believe him.

The chief investigator for the Attorney General of the State of Texas, Robert 'Duke' Bodisch, was called. He said that as a result of his lengthy inquiry, he believed Gary Acreman could not have seen the dumpster where he claimed to have seen the dead girl's clothes being thrown away, that Cheryl Bradford was mistaken in thinking that the two suspicious white men she had seen had come from the auditorium, that James Dexter Robinson was missing only one front tooth at the time of the crime even though John Sessum called him 'the man with no teeth' and that Robinson had been at a birthday party in South Carolina which, his family said, took place six days before Cheryl Fergeson was killed.

Mike De Geurin then established that in the course of his lengthy inquiry, 'Duke' Bodisch had never interviewed either of the defence investigators who, according to his report, had intimidated witnesses and encouraged perjury. He had never interviewed Peggy Stevens or Judge Martin about the missing exhibits, and although he had spoken to Jim Keeshan, he had never videoed the interview as he did with his other witnesses.

When the prosecution tried to put Bodisch's report into evidence, De Geurin objected that its conclusions were politically motivated, and Judge Pickett sustained his objection.

Finally, the Texas Ranger, Wesley Styles, was called to explain himself.

Wesley Styles walked tall into the court with his stetson hat, his leather boots and his silver badge hammered out of a Mexican five-peso piece glinting in the light. When he spoke, his voice was a ponderous growl. Styles began by telling the assistant DA, Rick Stover, his version of events. He had interviewed all his witnesses in a proper fashion, he said. He believed the white janitors were telling him the truth, he said. He had never threatened any of them and to mark the point, he produced a tape-recording.

On the defence table, all three attorneys immediately started to bristle. What was this? New evidence – seven years after the inquiry? Don Brown suspected this was the tape of Icky Peace being interviewed at Cleveland Police Station, the contents of which had been kept from the jury on the orders of Judge Martin at the second trial. Brown was half right.

De Geurin started by asking why Styles had never produced this tape before. The Ranger explained that he had thought the tape was lost, but he had just happened to find it in his attic a few days before the start of this hearing.

And how had that come about?

'I just happened to think about it,' the Ranger drawled, poker-faced.

On the defence table behind De Geurin, Brown was starting to bubble. There was more than one conversation on this tape. De Geurin asked more questions. The Ranger explained that this was a tape of his first interview with Peace – at Cleveland Police Station late on Saturday evening, the day after Brandley's arrest – but there was also a recording of his conversation with Peace four days later when he walked him through the high school.

Brown shook his head in disbelief – seven years after the inquiry, this came out. They had never before been told that this second tape even existed, never in 47 volumes of testimony. They had to show that this had been deliberately concealed. De Geurin demanded to see the Ranger's report of his investigation. Stover objected. The judge overruled him, and the Ranger gave up his report. The defence attorneys flicked through it: there was no mention anywhere of the existence of this recording of the walk-through, an incident which had been the subject of repeated questions and arguments at both trials, particularly because one of Brandley's former bosses, David Harris, said he had seen the Ranger walking Peace through the school and coaching his evidence.

De Geurin looked at the Ranger in disbelief and pointed at the report. 'You did not put it in there?'

The Ranger shook his head. 'No. I just discovered that a few minutes ago. It's not there.'

De Geurin was wide-eyed. 'You just now discovered that?'

'It was just brought to my attention. I thought it was in there, but it wasn't.'

De Geurin told Judge Pickett: 'Quite frankly, I smell a fish, but I'm having a hard time getting to it.'

He sat down with Nugent and Brown and, while the Ranger told Rick Stover that the tapes showed no evidence of him threatening Icky Peace, the three defence attorneys puzzled over why the prosecution should have concealed this for so long. Before they could find it, Rick Stover pointed them to the answer.

The assistant DA started asking the Ranger whether Icky Peace had said anything on the tape that was not already mentioned in the statement he had given to Conroe police on the day of the crime.

The Ranger said 'Yes'.

The three defence attorneys were all ears.

Stover continued. 'Mr Styles, there is one time during this conversation that Mr Peace makes reference to a statement made by Gary Acreman, where Gary says that he's been over to the building and he's seen Clarence with the girl knocking some chairs around, words to that effect. Do you remember him saying that on the tape?'

'Yes, sir,' growled the Ranger.

So that was it. This was not the first time that the defence had heard of Acreman saying this. The Ranger had briefly mentioned it in his original report. Icky Peace had told the two defence investigators about it and they had seen it as Acreman's first lie, the instinctive moment when he started to cover his tracks by blaming the black man. But by producing the tape, the prosecution were drawing attention to their failure to follow up on Acreman's remark, a failure which, in the light of all they now knew about Acreman, seemed so incompetent as to border on the corrupt. If this had been an honest investigation, the Ranger should have gone straight from his interview with Icky Peace to Gary Acreman and invited him to come to court and say he had personally witnessed this black janitor raping the white school-girl. There would have been no more need to rely on flimsy circumstantial evidence. Acreman would have been an eyewitness to the crime. But the Ranger had ignored it. It was his reasoning which excited the defence attorneys' imagination.

In part, they believed, he might have ignored Acreman's remark because it did not fit the official version of events, which had already been laid out in statements and which held that the white janitors had no idea that a crime was being committed. If Acreman was saying he had seen it taking place, the official version had to be wrong. But, more than that, they believed he had ignored it because it would have led the investigation in a completely different direction. If Acreman had truly seen the black janitor raping Cheryl Fergeson, he would surely have raised the alarm. But he had not done so. Any honest investigator would surely have wanted to nail Acreman and find out why he had failed to cry rape and would, at the very least, have considered the possibility that it was not the black janitor but Acreman himself who was doing the raping and that this was the first move in his cover-up. By ignoring the remark, it seemed to the defence, the Ranger had ignored the truth – and kept the blind focus on the only available black man. It was the closest the defence had ever come to proving the malice that they believed was the fuel of the police investigation.

Stover was still trying to sketch out the prosecution's version of events and was asking the Ranger if Peace had dismissed Acreman's remark as 'bullshitting'.

'That's correct,' came the gravelly reply.

'Did you give this information to the Conroe Police Department?'

'No.' The excitement on the defence table was plain to see. The

Ranger added: 'Since he said that there wasn't anything to it, that he was just more or less joking about it, no, sir, I didn't.'

De Geurin could hardly wait to get to grips with Wesley Styles.

When the Ranger had first walked into court, De Geurin had felt a twinge of uncertainty. This was a real life Texas Ranger. De Geurin was a Texan himself. He had grown up with the idea that a Texas Ranger was truly a special breed of man, someone who brought pride to the state of Texas. He had accepted that idea. The prospect of publicly exposing such a figure had depressed him. But not any more.

As soon as Rick Stover sat down, De Geurin was on his feet, laying out the ground for his attack.

The Ranger told him he had spent 500 hours investigating the murder, and then agreed that Brandley was already in jail accused of that murder before he completed even the first hour of his investigation. The Ranger told him, too, that on the very first day of his inquiry, when he walked three white janitors through the high school, he never warned any of them of their rights because he had already decided that none of them was a suspect.

'Did you let them know, Mr Styles, that you had already made up your mind Clarence Brandley had committed this crime?'

'No, sir. I did not.'

'In other words, you told them they were suspects?'

'No, sir.'

'Of course, it was common knowledge. It was on the front page of the *Courier* the day he was arrested, wasn't it?'

The Ranger straightened in his seat and in his deepest bass assured De Geurin that he had always been ready to charge anyone who had been guilty of this crime.

De Geurin bounced back at him. 'That's the same reason you followed up on this statement that Icky Peace told you Gary Acreman was talking about this girl on the day of the murder before anybody knew she was missing?'

The Ranger conceded he had never asked Gary Acreman about it. He then conceded that he had never asked any of the other janitors about it. Or, indeed, he finally conceded, anyone at all.

De Geurin kept at him. 'You knew at that point that Gary Acreman had left the vocational building twice, at a time when

the girl was supposed to be being killed, or the body hidden –
during the crucial period of time for your investigation? Is that
correct?'

'Yes, sir.'

'And you knew that Gary Acreman had at least gone into the
school himself during that critical period of time?'

'Yes, sir. I do.'

'By himself?'

'By himself, as far as I found out.'

'And you knew he had come back and, according to Icky Peace,
told Peace that there was a girl over there with Brandley and
they're having fun. You knew that?'

'Yes, sir.'

'Are you telling me that because that information came from
Icky Peace, that you just disbelieved it from the beginning?'

The Ranger shook his head. He sighed. Suddenly he looked
old. 'Let's just put it this way. Say I made a mistake and I didn't
check it out.'

He had cracked. De Geurin moved in on him. 'I take it that
450 hours later in your investigation, you still hadn't checked it
out?'

The Ranger nodded. 'That's correct.'

'And that 500 hours of investigation was all dedicated to building a case against Clarence Brandley, wasn't it?'

Styles lifted a wrinkled finger and pointed it at Brandley sitting
below him. 'No evidence whatsoever gathered in this investigation
or this trial pointed to any other person other than Clarence Lee
Brandley.'

De Geurin turned on the Ranger and, in the kind of tone that
mothers use on silly children, told him: 'Well, of course, if Gary
Acreman knew something about a girl over at the school at the
time, it would lead a reasonable person to conclude, I would think,
that maybe you ought to go ask Gary Acreman about that?'

The Ranger's voice was a surly grumble. 'Well, let's say I should
have asked him, but I didn't.'

De Geurin backed off, but he was not finished with him yet.

'Now you learned, didn't you, Mr Styles, that the blood that
was found on the clothing of the girl was Type A blood?'

'Yes, sir.'

'And I take it that you now know that Gary Acreman's blood is Type A blood as well as James Dexter Robinson. Did you know that?'

'If you say so, I'll have to take your word for it.'

'Were you interested at the time, Mr Styles, to see if the other janitors' blood matched the blood that was on the girl's clothing?'

'Let's say I didn't – I didn't have it checked. I didn't check it.'

He had cracked again. De Geurin then challenged him over the hairs that had been found on the dead girl. The Ranger cracked once more and conceded that it would have been a good idea to compare the hairs with samples from the white janitors.

De Geurin asked him: 'Would it surprise you to learn that the District Attorney opposed successfully in court all efforts of the defence to compare the scientific evidence to the other janitors?'

'I don't know anything about that.'

'Are you aware now the hair has been lost?'

'Yes, sir.' The Ranger smiled. It was a mistake.

'Why do you smile?'

'Do what?'

'Why did you smile when you answered that, or did I misinterpret it?'

The Ranger was not smiling any more. 'Well, I think it's what all this controversy is over. That's my thought. And I read it in the newspaper.'

De Geurin shook his head, more in sorrow than in anger. 'Mr Styles, can you for a moment place yourself in the shoes of Mr Brandley – just for a moment?' Rick Stover jumped up and said this was improper. The judge overruled him. De Geurin continued. And the words started gushing through him again.

'Just for a moment, Mr Styles, consider there is a pubic hair, possibly – and most probably – donated by the attacker, and imagine you're accused of being the attacker and that pubic hair is conclusively shown not to be yours and it's Caucasian . . .' While the Ranger sat solemn in his seat, De Geurin laid out all the evidence which had now accumulated against Gary Acreman and reminded him of the DA's refusal to have Acreman's hairs given to the defence and of his own failure to compare Acreman's hairs. 'Now, place yourself in Mr Brandley's shoes just for a moment. And have the man that we thought in charge of the investigation on the stand, and I ask him "Did you learn that the pubic hair had been lost?" – and the man smiled!'

De Geurin's face was a mask of contempt. The Ranger said he resented that. Rick Stover objected that it was not a proper question. The judge told them all to take a ten-minute break.

After the break, Styles admitted that the tape which he had produced to prove that he never threatened Icky Peace covered only 32 minutes of up to six hours of conversation, and that in the course of the recording he had turned it off and then on again no less than 31 times. He said he had not realized that Peace had never read his own statement. He had, however, realized that the Conroe detectives had taken a day's holiday on the Sunday immediately after Cheryl Fergeson's murder and done no work on the investigation for 24 hours. He said he was not proud of that.

Finally, De Geurin brought him back to the central thrust of his questions – the blind focus of the investigation. 'Isn't it true that all of your time was spent building a case against Brandley, a person you had already concluded was guilty?'

Styles raised his wrinkled finger again. 'My investigation was for whoever was responsible, and it pointed to him. All the evidence pointed to Clarence Lee Brandley.'

'And all that evidence was gathered after he was charged by you?'

'Some of it. Yes, sir.'

'Well, all of your work was after he was charged, wasn't it?'

'Yes, sir.'

'And the evidence that you were gathering was all circumstantial, wasn't it?'

'Yes, sir.'

The Ranger then suggested that the scientific evidence also pointed to Brandley. De Geurin recalled Brandley's knife that had no fibres on it, Brandley's belt that had no skin tissue on it, the scene of the crime and the dead girl's clothes that had none of Brandley's fingerprints on them. He reminded the Ranger of the Caucasian hairs on the girl's body that could not have been Brand-

ley's, and of the blood on the girl's shirt that could not have been
Brandley's. 'Now, any other scientific evidence that comes to
mind that convinces you that it was Clarence Brandley?'

The Ranger sighed again. 'No, sir,' he said.

De Geurin let him go.

Peter Speers seemed to have nothing left to fight with. The defence
had waged ten days of pitched battle to seize the ground they
now occupied, but Speers never rejoined the fight. Instead, he
hovered around the edge of the battlefield, moving only to attack
a straggler or turn over some dead issue.

He called two separate witnesses to dispute Icky Peace's claim
that someone at the high school had threatened that he could be
fired if he gave evidence. He called two members of James Dexter
Robinson's family to swear that the birthday party at which he
had been photographed had taken place on 17 August 1980, and
an FBI expert to testify that, so far as he could tell, the photographs could have been taken on that date. He called Kelly Hendricks, the polygrapher who had been criticized for his role in
the Attorney General's investigation, to say that if the defence
polygrapher, Glenn Raney, had really shouted at James Dexter
Robinson and asked him one question 60 times, that would not
be acceptable procedure.

He called Sam Martinez, who swore that he had told the truth
in 1980 in his statements to the police and in his evidence at the
trial. The defence had never made up their minds about Martinez.
It sometimes seemed that he might have been involved in the
crime, that he had watched the rape or stood outside while it was
going on to make sure that Acreman and Robinson were not
discovered. But he had never admitted anything, and neither John
Sessum nor Gary Acreman had ever directly implicated him. One
thing the defence did know about Martinez was that if their
version of events was right, then he must be lying. He must have
seen Acreman talking to the girl and the subsequent scuffle, even
if he then turned and ran away from it all, as John Sessum had.

De Geurin set out to prove that Martinez was a liar. Within
minutes, Martinez confirmed that Gary Acreman had been talking
to the girl in the hallway and then acknowledged that he had never

mentioned this in his statements to police nor in his evidence at trial.

Martinez would go no further and would not admit to seeing the scuffle, but in his anxiety he insisted that he was not up on the landing where the girl was attacked but down at the bottom of the staircase, well away from the action. He went on to describe – just as he had at Brandley's trials – how Clarence Brandley had walked up the stairs, sent them all over to the vocational building and then gone into a janitor's closet at the far end of the landing. But Martinez could not explain how it had been physically possible for him to see Brandley do this from the position in which he had so firmly placed himself.

The two sides were ready to begin their final arguments, but events intervened. Mary Johnson was still in Galveston. The Brandley case was now under her skin. She felt terrified about her job and her court reporter's licence. She had done nothing wrong, but she knew she was going to be punished. And she could not stop thinking about those horrible men from the Attorney General's office who told her she had failed a lie detector test. She could not believe she had failed it. So she went to see Richard Reyna in his flat. Mary Johnson knew Reyna from the courthouse where he was always padding round, checking on cases or looking for documents. She asked him if he could find out whether she really had failed her lie test or whether they had been saying that to frighten her. They started talking.

At first she just talked about the men from the Attorney General's office and how they had treated her like a criminal and tried to humiliate her. Then she talked about everything. Reyna sat, shaking his head in disbelief, as her pride and her resentment at being bullied finally swept away her last loyalty to the courthouse.

As soon as she had finished, Reyna went straight to the phone and called Mike De Geurin. He told him that Mary Johnson had more information and he outlined it for him.

In his room at the Tremont Hotel, De Geurin listened. 'Oh my, oh my,' he said.

This time, the court reporter was in tears before she even took her place on the witness-stand. But she was no longer torn between the courthouse and the truth. It took her less than five minutes to rip away the final layers of secrecy.

In a room that was wreathed in silence, she took the fragile web of recollections that had been so carefully constructed by Peggy Stevens, Judge Martin and Jim Keeshan around the disappearance of the exhibits and swept it away. She had no doubt, she said, about what Peggy Stevens had been up to when Don Brown was trying to get to the truth. It might have slipped the District Clerk's memory, but Mary Johnson remembered clearly that Peggy Stevens had warned both Keeshan and Martin that the defence attorney was on to them. More than that, Peggy Stevens had run down to warn Jim Keeshan in person and then, while Keeshan's secretary stood outside telling the defence attorney that she could not help him, Peggy Stevens and the District Attorney had been hiding inside the office – or even in a closet in the office – giggling together. Mary Johnson said she had no doubt because she had been with Judge Martin a few minutes later when Peggy Stevens had come in laughing to share the fun with them.

Where once Don Brown had felt righteous anger at the way he had been treated that day, he now felt only disgust.

The court reporter turned then to her own predicament. She had always said she would be fired if she testified. Now the court reporter explained why she had always been so sure – because Judge John Martin had been making that plain to her for some time. The judge had told her that some people wanted to blame her for the disappearance of the exhibits and that she might be fired if he did not protect her. Then he had told her how worried he was about the Brandley hearing and how he lay awake at nights and how he would always say there had been no secret meetings with the DA. But he had told her he was not going to worry about it all any more. He was going to leave it in her lap. The court reporter had no doubt what the judge meant. 'He was telling me if I would keep my mouth shut on the witness-stand about what truly happened, that I'd have a job.'

It was already starting to happen. In the few days that had passed since she first gave evidence at this hearing, she said, Judge Martin had sent a message to her attorney that she should not come in to work for two weeks. Judge Martin had plans, too, for

Mike De Geurin. While Peter Speers sang a chorus of objections, the court reporter explained that in the last few days, Judge Martin had come up with a new twist. He was due to pass sentence on a woman who was then being prosecuted by Peter Speers and who was being defended by Mike De Geurin's brother, Dick, also a prominent Houston attorney. Judge Martin had been saying that if Mike De Geurin gave him a bad time on the witness-stand in the Brandley case, he would make sure his brother's client suffered for it: it would make the difference between whether he gave her probation or a prison sentence.

Now it was De Geurin's turn to feel disgust. He and his brother and his father before him had spent their lives working in the courts of Texas. And now this man – a judge, no less – was ready to intimidate witnesses and abuse his power, fouling everything the courts were supposed to stand for, just for the sake of his own petty ambition.

But Mary Johnson had still not finished. She had one more dark secret to share. As she spoke, the silence in the courtroom was finally cracked by shock, a shock that was all the more intense since it was this graceful, beautiful figure, sitting poised in the witness stand, who now disclosed the final ugliness – that Peggy Stevens had arranged with Judge Martin to have the black man killed on her birthday.

Now the disgust spread all along the public benches in a tide of sighs and whispers as the court reporter explained that she had no doubt about this – because her own birthday fell on the same date and they had expected her to join in the celebration.

It was Thursday night, 8 October. After 11 days, the two sides prepared to put their final arguments to Judge Pickett. All through the hearing, a new and calm confidence had been building in the defence camp. Reyna and McCloskey, who had taken a back seat to the attorneys, went out fishing together and agreed they had never felt so proud to belong to a team. For Don Brown, who had once been elected to the State Assembly to fight racism by the people of Galveston, the hearing had become a kind of homecoming, the fulfilment of a lifelong mission.

For Nugent and De Geurin, who had decided to share the

next day's final speeches, there was still tension and the nagging knowledge that they were not yet finished. De Geurin, whose courtroom performances were driven by impulse, found it hard to decide how he and Nugent should divide up the material for their speeches. They turned it over for a while, and De Geurin finally came up with a formula. 'You take the facts,' he said. 'I'll handle the bullshit.'

Nugent went off on his own, pacing for miles along the beach until the small hours of the morning, trying to clear his mind, stripping the saga that had now run for more than seven years down to the skeleton that gave it shape. De Geurin took to his hotel room, paced his way through a pack of cigarettes and filled one of his legal books with scrawled notes.

But when they came to court the next morning, they found Peter Speers had presented them with one more task before they could mount their finale. Judge John Martin was back on the witness stand. The judge, whose face was bruised with fatigue, explained that Mary Johnson was telling lies. There was no truth in anything she had said the previous day. She must want to hurt him, he suggested. Judge Martin seemed particularly insulted by the suggestion that he had ordered Brandley to die so that the courthouse could celebrate the event at a birthday party. He was only doing his duty, he said, in sentencing him to death. All the time the judge was laying out his denial, Mike De Geurin was sitting at the defence table, longing to get at the gaping hole he could see in the middle of the story.

Stover asked the judge if he had realized that the date was Peggy Stevens's birthday. 'Not really. That's a birthday of several people I know, you know. But it wasn't set on anyone's birthday. It was probably the most difficult – one of the most difficult jobs I've ever had as a judge is to sentence a man to death. And that's not an easy job. It's a very difficult, onerous burden, and it's certainly not something that I would do so somebody could have a party or anything.'

Finally, De Geurin got his chance.

First, he pawed the judge into position, inviting him to confirm that he did not enjoy sentencing a man to death. Then he cuffed him a little by persuading him to admit that Peggy Stevens had been in court to see him set the death date, challenging him to recall that Jim Keeshan had stopped his work on another case so that he could be there too. He pawed him once more by inviting him to confirm beyond doubt that the only reason he had set this execution date was because it was his duty.

Then he clawed the Conroe judge without mercy by forcing him to admit that it was not his duty to set the death date at all – that he had been recused from the case long before and that Judge Coker had been in charge of it, and that he was not supposed to take any further part in the proceedings at all, let alone sentence the defendant to die.

Clarence Brandley watched John Martin retreat from the court, his eyes cast down to the ground. He would not look at Brandley. None of them would. It had been different in the courthouse in Conroe when they had been sitting up there, with all their authority. They could look at him then and tell him he was going to die. But these ten days, Brandley had sat here and stared straight into their faces and none of them had dared to look back into his eyes – these people who were supposed to stand for justice.

Brandley wanted nothing more to do with them. He did not even want to think about them. He thought instead about the people who had helped him. Truly, they made him feel humble. Not nigger humble, bowing and scraping. But humble like any man would feel – black or white – who saw people come out and take risks like that for him. His heart went out to Janet Dial and Mary Johnson and Ed Payne and even John Sessum, even though he did still say he was a racist. All he had ever prayed for was that someone would tell the truth. Just tell it like it was. All he prayed for now was that this Judge Pickett would be fair with him.

The courtroom settled down for the final speeches. It was more crowded than ever. All along the back of the court, flanking the Judge like bodyguards, there were Texas Rangers, standing with their legs apart and their arms folded and a pair of pistols on their hips, staring silently at all the brown faces. They said they were there for crowd control. The defence attorneys thought they were there to bolster their beleagured colleague, to show who was really boss.

On his walk along the beach, Paul Nugent had found the skeleton that shaped the case of Clarence Brandley. Now, he tried to lay it out before Judge Pickett and the 300 spectators: the black ministers who felt intimidated by the white courthouse; the officer who elected the nigger suspect; the systematic exclusion of black jurors; the disproportionate use of the death sentence on black defendants; the lone juror who had been hounded as a nigger-lover; the Mayor who said 'nigger'; the Sheriff who said 'nigger'; the District Attorney who said 'nigger'. The skeleton soon became clear to see.

Nugent then fleshed it out: the long trail of lost evidence; the Ranger and his blind focus; the white janitors who now admitted they had lied and who had been tied to their lies by threats; the clues that had never been investigated and the questions that had never been asked; the 23 jurors in two trials who had joined the project to convict Clarence Brandley. The young attorney sat down to an angry silence.

Peter Speers began his speech by oiling the wheels of justice. 'Judge Pickett, I'd like to preface my remarks by saying I've appreciated your patience and tolerance during this rather arduous ordeal over the last two weeks. I think it can fairly be said that Clarence Brandley got a full and fair hearing.' Then he fought back with the letter of the law and accused the defence of dragging up all kinds of evidence which should not have been mentioned. If they wanted to claim the death penalty was used in a racist fashion, they should have done that back at the original trial and it was not correct procedure to raise it now. Bill Srack's experience was irrelevant because he was a juror in the first trial, whereas this hearing was concerned with the conviction which arose from the second trial. The loss of the exhibits was no longer a debatable issue since it had already been dealt with by the court in Austin, as had the allegation that there was a conspiracy to conceal their loss – although, he added, the word 'conspiracy' might not have been used. The only evidence that Judge Martin and Jim Keeshan had held secret meetings was hearsay, he complained. The evidence that Brandley was innocent was unbelievable and, anyway, even if everything the defence said was true, it made no difference because, according to the law, new facts were not relevant to the courts more than 30 days after a conviction.

At some point during Peter Speers's speech, Mike De Geurin's blood started to boil. He had seen DAs doing this before – trying to use the law to obstruct justice. He loathed it. As soon as the District Attorney had finished, he jumped forward, glanced once at his pad full of notes, shoved them under his left arm and never consulted them again. How could all this be irrelevant, he asked. What about Janet Dial and her courage? What about Mary Johnson and her tears? At what personal cost had these people dared to tell the truth?

'Apparently, Mr Speers has never done such a thing or he would know how difficult it is and what a terrible price a person pays for telling the truth in Montgomery County when it's embarrassing to the officials. Where is Mary Johnson tomorrow? Where is Janet Dial? What do they have to gain from testifying the way they did?

'William Srack. What had he had to endure because he did his duty and when he found that the evidence was insufficient, he so voted and didn't go along with the pack?

'Is it irrelevant to prove the "project" atmosphere, the chilling effect, the judge that tells his court reporter "Keep your mouth shut or you lose your job"?'

And what about the secret meetings between Judge Martin and the DA? Were they irrelevant? What about the secret meeting between an earlier judge, Judge Alworth, and the DA, when they raised Brandley's bail-bond without telling the defence?

'The only legal argument we learned about in that hearing is the Sheriff didn't want the little nigger on the street.'

What about Don Brown and George Morris – 'struggling along in Conroe, fighting for this man's liberty, going along with the Rules of Evidence and law, like they're supposed to?

'And then let's skip from there to after the trial, what we can prove beyond doubt . . .'

De Geurin suddenly abandoned the sentence and turned on Peter Speers. 'And, by the way, Mr Speers, you questioned whether or not I used the word "conspiracy". If I have not used it, I'll use it now. They conspired against Clarence Brandley. They conspired to trick Don Brown and they conspired to trick George Morris.

'Not only did they try to keep secret that all of the evidence was lost in the case, but much more, much worse than that. In addition to that, in keeping it secret, they made fake exhibits and entered fake exhibits into official records hoping that Don Brown wouldn't find out about it. And not only that, but they thought it was funny . . .

'Now, that's not irrelevant. If it is, then I have missed the boat, Your Honour, all the way through.'

He finally paused and turned back towards the defence table. Paul Nugent saw his eyes were brimming with tears.

Then his words rushed on again, over the missing exhibits, and the District Clerk's birthday, and the blind focus of the investigation and all the evidence that had now emerged about Brandley's innocence.

He turned to Judge Perry Pickett. 'You put all that together, judge. What you have is this county sucking the oxygen out of the courtroom until you suffocate. And I ask for a new trial for Clarence Brandley – breathe some fresh air back into the justice system.'

From his bench, Judge Pickett looked solemnly down on the attorneys gazing up, and at the reporters with their pens poised, and at Clarence Brandley still sitting solid as a rock at the defence table, and at all the rows of spectators with their hopes written across their faces and he put down his pipe and he began to speak.

'This is the 200th anniversary of our Constitution. One of the basic rights of this noble document is equal justice under the law and the inherent dignity of mankind.

'For the past ten days, I have presided over an evidentiary hearing, tried to determine if equal justice under the law has been self-evident from all the evidence adduced under oath.

'The litany of events so graphically described by the witnesses – some of it chilling and shocking – leads me to the conclusion that the pervasive shadow of darkness has obscured the light of fundamental decency and human rights. I can only sadly state that justice has been on trial here, but of more significance, injustice has been on trial.

'My statement of facts and conclusions of law to the Court of Criminal Appeals will be conclusive and unequivocal.

'I shall recommend a new trial for the defendant and, if granted, recommend the trial be removed from Montgomery County.'

10

Judge Pickett had hardly finished speaking before pandemonium seized the courtroom. Don Brown was hugging Brandley. Reyna and McCloskey were swaying in each other's arms. Nugent and De Geurin were shaking hands and smiling their thanks all over the court. The reporters were shouting and shoving. Revd Boney was leading a victory chant, and all the old ladies were standing up clapping and cooing and praising the Lord.

As the jubilation flooded around Clarence Brandley, the mask of self-control which had concealed him through the hearing finally broke, and he began to weep.

Peter Speers swept up his papers and scuttled swiftly through the crowd towards a waiting car, pressing through the howling pack of newspaper and television reporters with their babble of questions, pausing only briefly as he ducked into his car to mumble a hasty 'No comment'.

The people of Dugan bubbled out of the courthouse, past the scowling Montgomery County deputies and the sour-faced Texas Rangers, hugging and kissing the attorneys and the investigators, singing and chanting 'Jus-tice! Jus-tice!'

For a while, the defence camp were tempted to believe that all would be well. They had only to wait for justice to take its course: Judge Pickett would produce his detailed findings of fact; the Court of Criminal Appeals in Austin would agree that Brandley should have a new trial; Peter Speers would have to acknowledge that there could be no trial since all the evidence had been either thrown away or discredited. Brandley, the defence believed, would be free by Christmas.

On 19 November, the wheels of justice began to turn. Judge

Pickett produced his findings – 47 pages of unyielding analysis. The judge's opening words set the tone for what followed. 'After ten days of trial,' he wrote, 'the court became convinced that Clarence Lee Brandley did not receive a fair trial, was denied the most basic fundamental rights of due process of law, and did not commit the crime for which he now resides on Death Row.'

The judge went on to give the defence a clean sweep of the case. He found that the evidence showed not only that Clarence Brandley was innocent, but that 'Gary Acreman and James Dexter Robinson are prime suspects and probably were responsible for the death of Cheryl Dee Fergeson'. Both Acreman and Robinson, he said, had lied at the Galveston hearing.

He moved through the Conroe courthouse like vengeance.

Judge John Martin, he said, was a liar. 'The court finds that Judge Martin's testimony, perhaps tempered by a motive for self-preservation, was simply not credible.' Judge Martin, he concluded, had held secret meetings with the DA during the trial as well as after the disappearance of the exhibits, and he had been hostile to Brandley and to any other black people who came into court.

The former District Attorney, now The Honourable Judge James Keeshan, he found, was a liar. Specifically, Pickett ruled that, despite his denials, Keeshan had held secret meetings with Judge Alworth at which the amount of Brandley's bail-bond was raised; that he had also held secret meetings with Judge Martin at which they had rehearsed key rulings in Brandley's second trial; that he had referred to Brandley as 'this little nigger'; that he had intended to cover up the disappearance of the exhibits and tried to deceive the defence with fakes; that he had deliberately and wrongly concealed other evidence from the defence, and that he had showed a 'personal white versus black posture'.

Peggy Stevens, he said, was a liar. She was 'not a credible witness and her testimony was untruthful'. In particular, he found that, despite her denials, she had asked Judge Martin to arrange for Brandley to die on her birthday and that she had hidden with Jim Keeshan and laughed while Don Brown stood outside trying to find the missing exhibits. This was, he said, 'a sordid instance where the "project-like" mentality overbore any sense of justice and decency at the courthouse'.

The Texas Ranger, Wesley Styles, was also a liar. The judge found that the Ranger had threatened John Sessum; that he had roughed up Icky Peace and threatened to blow out his brains; that he had deliberately concealed the tape-recording of his conversation with Peace and then lied about it in court, and that he had consistently kept a blind focus on Clarence Brandley. 'Styles failed to conduct a proper investigation in that the Ranger operated with the state of mind that he had already gotten his man, and that he was not going to investigate any leads that might prove his preconception wrong.'

Judge Pickett even jabbed at Peter Speers whose behaviour had never been formally examined by the court, and recorded his failure to tell the defence of evidence which tended to show Brandley's innocence: first when he buried Brenda Medina's statement and then when he failed to disclose that Ranger Styles had found his tape-recording of Icky Peace ten days before the Galveston hearing began.

Judge Pickett left no doubt about why, in his view, the courthouse had conspired to put Clarence Brandley to death for Cheryl Fergeson's murder. 'The court unequivocally concludes,' he wrote, 'that the colour of Clarence Brandley's skin was a substantial factor which pervaded all aspects of the state's capital prosecution against him, and was an impermissible factor which significantly influenced the investigation, trial and post-trial proceedings. The tone of the courtroom, as fostered by the District Attorney's office, the judge and the District Clerk's office, was white against black.'

Once the black janitor had been elected as the prime suspect, Judge Pickett wrote, the courthouse set out to convict him, regardless of the facts. 'The authorities wholly ignored any evidence, or leads to evidence, which might prove inconsistent with their premature conclusion that Brandley had committed the crime. The conclusion is inescapable that the investigation was conducted not to solve the crime, but to convict Brandley.'

By the time he reached the last page of his findings, Judge Pickett, this conservative veteran of the Texan bench, had made ruins out of all the pillars which supported the reputation of Conroe and its courthouse. 'In the thirty years this court has presided over matters in the judicial system, no case has presented a more shocking scenario of the effects of racial prejudice, perjured testimony, witness intimidation, an investigation the outcome of which was predetermined, and public officials who for whatever motives lost sight of what is right and just.

'The continued incarceration of Clarence Lee Brandley under these circumstances is an affront to the basic notions of fairness and justice.'

All those who had been put on trial by the defence – Acreman, Robinson, Conroe and its courthouse – had been found guilty. And Clarence Lee Brandley had been declared innocent. The victory was total.

Shortly after Judge Pickett published his findings, John Henry Faulk found himself once again by the riverside north of Conroe with his fishing rod and his old friend, and once again, just as they had on the day after Cheryl Fergeson's murder, they fell to talking about these sad events and about the judgement of Perry Pickett. After all these years, Faulk had learned to live with his friend's opinions about black people. Underneath it all, he knew his friend was intelligent and well-informed in his way. So Faulk was pleased to hear him admit that it looked like Clarence Brandley might be innocent.

The two men waited a while, watching the water, and then his friend spoke again. 'Yep,' he sighed, and scratched his chin. 'Ah reckon it must a bin some other nigger done it.'

Conroe is the kind of town where a stranger might never notice the truth. It all seems clean and efficient, traffic-lights blinking on and off, a smiling policewoman handing out parking tickets, ordinary people going about their business. No one stands in the courthouse square denouncing black people. There are no signs on the edge of town as there used to be in old redneck towns, warning 'Nigger, don't let the sun set on you here'. It is part of the change which has taken place since the civil rights movement that the *Courier* now reports the Miss Black Conroe Pageant and

the conviction and years after the appeal was refused – years after. How long are they supposed to keep it? Keeshan and Speers are just politicians like the rest of them but I don't see how they've mishandled this case. That judge down in Galveston was strictly out of line. How in hell can a judge say Brandley is innocent when a jury says he is guilty? Under law he is guilty. Nobody has proved he is innocent. I am sure that if somebody came up and proved that he is innocent then the people of Conroe would applaud and get him out of there, but nobody has proved it. No, sir. All they have is Brandley's word for it.'

Faye Cryar was the same. An elderly white lady with pearl earrings and a grandmotherly smile, she said she had definitely heard that Brandley was guilty because he was the only one who could have got in that auditorium. She was sure of that and, she continued in her gentle voice, she had lived in Conroe most of her life and she had never had anything against coloured folk. To illustrate her point, she recalled the time of integration which she said was never needed in Conroe.

At that time, in the 1960s, she belonged to a Home Demonstration Club which was a product originally of the Land Grant College. Faye and the other women in the club would teach people how to sew and how to prepare food. But when integration came, the college sent a woman to say they had to integrate with the coloured women, who had their own group. 'Well, we didn't want to do that. Why should we? We didn't know the coloured women and the coloured women didn't know us.' So Faye and her friends all resigned and formed their own club, nothing to do with the Land Grant College. They called it The Lamplighters because it was shedding light. They had their own by-laws. You couldn't join unless you were invited and then you had to be voted in. Faye said the coloured women didn't mind. 'They had their own club and you know how coloured people stick together. White people have their friends and coloured people have theirs. Coloured people have different customs. They wouldn't want to be in a club for white people.' Just the same as Faye's church, which has 3,000 members, and there's only two or three coloured people that ever go to the church. 'Coloured people are different'.

As a matter of fact, Faye said, there was more opposition to integration from the blacks in Conroe than from the whites. 'They wanted to keep things the way they were because they felt secure in their own group. They were afraid of being shunned.' Faye and her friends helped them all the same because, as she said, she has never had anything against coloured folk.

This was not the legendary racism of the old south, red in tooth and claw. There was no venom, no scorn and certainly no guilt. This was a deeper, subtler, more mysterious approach which took heed of the new climate in which the brazen simplicities of the old days were no longer acceptable. This was racism with a smiling face – the easy assumptions of white people who had always lived with black underdogs. The Mayor and people like Art Rohnser and Faye Cryar took it for granted that black people lived in shinny shacks while white people lived in brick-built homes with garages and central air-conditioning. It was not an issue, simply a fact of life. And if black people were too poor to eat in the white restaurants and spent their time instead in their dirty juke joints, then that too was just the way things were. White children played in sandpits; black children played in the dust. In their eyes, black people not only naturally lived in these conditions, but liked it. There was no hint that people in Dugan ever feared their white neighbours or resented their poverty or mourned the dead-end prospects of their young. In the same way, the white people took it for granted that black people were different – lazy or stupid, like the black people in the old jokes column the *Courier* used to run. There had always been good niggers and bad niggers and, even though the Chamber of Commerce might now refer to them as 'ethnics', the myths about black people had not changed. The myths made it easy to accept their living conditions and to explain their separateness.

In the months after Judge Pickett's ruling, the most senior black law officer in the town, Sgt Leonard Taylor, complained of racism in the sheriff's department. He said the department was run on 'a good ole boy system'. One of the incidents he complained about was the posting of a notice which announced 'Open season on porch monkeys, also known as Negro, Nigger, Burrheads, House Apes, Jungle Bunnies and Saucerlips. This season has no relation to the porch monkey breeding season which is year round.' When he complained, he was fired. No one in the town came to his defence. Around the same time, a group of 50 black parents formed a committee to protest about racism in Conroe schools. They said there was an 'unwritten code' which worked against their children. They were allowed into the sports teams, but they were excluded from cheerleading. They were not encouraged to lead or to do well in class. There was a shortage of black teachers and guest speakers. But the schools superintendent, Dr Richard Griffin, said he had taught in towns where they had problems but Conroe really never had suffered that way. 'I just don't see it,' he said.

Much of this new, gentle racism was passive – failing to notice that their town was still physically segregated, failing to be shocked at black inequality. The active, positive racism which Judge Pickett had seen in the Brandley case flowed directly from these blithe assumptions. In spite of all that had been revealed at Galveston, these people still truly believed that Brandley should die, and they had gathered little twisted scraps of fact to prove it. There might have been those in the courthouse who were well enough aware of the true facts to know beyond doubt that Brandley was innocent; their racism consisted of their belief that they could sacrifice a worthless black life for their pride and their careers. But in the town, they were still happy to believe that Brandley was guilty. It was easy. It required no bad conscience, nor any wrestling with the facts. Their racism was so natural it was almost benign. They simply took it for granted that a black man would commit a crime like that.

A sheriff's deputy confided that Brandley not only killed that girl at the high school but had also raped his own mother. Lucy Proctor, one of the reporters who had covered the Brandley case for the *Courier*, declared: 'There is no way Brandley is innocent. I wouldn't believe him if he told me there was oxygen in the air.'

There were a few whites who admitted that Brandley was innocent and that there was racism in Conroe, but even they seemed unable to see the racism in themselves. In his office by the courthouse square, the veteran attorney W. B. Etheridge, who had a reputation as a decent man and had helped the Brandley defence, recalled the day when as a child he had seen Joe Winters burned to death in the square outside the window where he now sat. 'It's mob violence,' he said. 'You get carried away with things like that and then later on you wonder why in the world did you ever do a thing like that. But I think the blacks took the attitude that he got what was coming to him. At that time, we had some of the best black folk that ever were in Conroe – they weren't unruly, they didn't give any problems at all. Fact of the matter is, blacks haven't had that much to complain about. They are just a different kind of creature. We have some blacks who are intelligent, but most of them . . .' Etheridge waved his hand in the air, as if to dismiss the thought of them, then he continued. 'Anytime the blacks move into a place, it goes down hill. One or two blacks go into a neighbourhood, land values drop, all the trash everywhere, the don't-care attitude – "why should we work?" Crime everywhere. There are always exceptions. Some blacks are intelligent, but most of them . . .' Etheridge went on to describe the day that Bob White was shot dead in a Conroe courtroom, referring to White throughout his story as 'the nigger'.

The town's bad ways were plain to see for Peggy Riggle, the Bette Midler lookalike who had lost her job in the *Courier*'s telemarketing department after testifying for Brandley at Galveston. 'I'm not going to say there's no racism in Conroe,' she said, 'because there is. Tell the truth, Conroe is one bigoted little town. You just don't see blacks hanging out with whites. The more you go out into the country, the worse it gets and out in east county, well the mentality there – no one ever taught them about charity. Montgomery County is just one hypocritical county, if you want to know the truth.'

But Peggy Riggle insisted that each generation got a little better. Six generations back, her family had owned slaves but her own father wouldn't stand for any racism. There was one Sunday, she recalled, when he took the family to a restaurant in Hillsboro' and two black couples came in who were very well dressed and nice, but the restaurant refused them service. Her father got all the family up and made them leave. 'If you won't serve them, you won't serve me,' he said. Of course, Peggy Riggle added, her father and mother never would have let a black person visit their house – never would have dreamed of it. They didn't even know any black people. But each generation got better, she believed.

'I've had black friends,' she said. 'Sure I have. Not boyfriends, you understand. I'd never do that because right, wrong or indifferent, I can't help the way I feel. It just wouldn't be right. One of my kids now, they might go out with blacks and they might say "I'm in love with this black girl and she is decent" but of course my first question would be "Well, how decent?"'

As Conroe came to terms with Judge Pickett's findings, Clarence Brandley waited for his freedom. His hope that he would be released by Christmas soon faded as the nine judges of the Court of Criminal Appeals in Austin relapsed into silence, some of them evidently distracted by the election primaries they had to fight the coming March, none of them willing to speak out on Brandley's behalf. Twice before, this court had failed him. Despite all the joy of the victory at Galveston, Brandley now began to wonder whether his life was safe, whether these nine white judges had the political courage to stand up for him.

He saw the backlash against Judge Pickett gather strength in Conroe. Peter Speers publicly denounced the Judge, telling the press that he was illogical and irrational and 'totally lacking in any attempt at objectivity'. The *Courier* ran a front-page report detailing some of the conclusions of the Attorney General's investigators. Soon after Christmas, Judge John Martin fired his court reporter, Mary Johnson. Since the day she had tearfully put her fears behind her and testified at Galveston, Mary Johnson had never been allowed back to work. She had been suspended immediately after the hearing. No one from the courthouse would have anything to do with her. She had tried to work as a freelance, hiring herself out as a court reporter, but all the judges and the attorneys shied away from her. Some of the defence attorneys told her they were sorry but they could not jeopardize their clients' chances by being seen with her. She no longer felt safe going into town and drove miles in the opposite direction to do her shopping. Someone called her up and warned her to get out of Montgomery County. Someone went to her little office in The Woodlands, south of Conroe, and painted an obscenity on her window. Now she had been formally fired, just as she had always said she would be, for daring to tell the truth.

In Houston, Revd Don Boney was arrested. The police said they had found a small amount of cocaine in his pocket. Boney, a Baptist minister, furiously denied the charge. He said he was 'completely against drug use' and that the police had searched him twice before claiming to find anything. He suggested that the law was being abused to punish him for his role in the campaign for Clarence Brandley.

Finally, in March 1988, after a delay of more than four months and after the election primaries were over, the judges in Austin announced that both sides in the Brandley case would have to submit written briefs to them before they could make a decision. In the meantime – despite Judge Pickett's declaration that it was an affront to the basic notions of fairness and justice – the incarceration of Clarence Brandley continued.

Jim McDougal sat at his kitchen table, his body hunched forward, pools of sweat filling the armpits of his shirt, his right hand shoved across the table fingering his heavy, black pistol. 'I'll kill 'em,' he said. 'I'm not kidding. If they come for me, I'll kill 'em.'

McDougal had never thought he would hear himself talk that way about anyone, and certainly not about law enforcement officers. Now, after all that had happened, he admitted he had been pretty damned innocent in the past, but he had truly believed that law officers were basically honest, and that had had a lot to do with why he had become one himself. Now it was all over: after twelve years service he had been fired by Joe Corley, the Sheriff of Montgomery County, and his former colleagues were threatening his life. His offence had been simple.

Working on traffic duty, he had kept coming across cases where drivers who were involved in one-car accidents were not having their blood tested for alcohol. He knew that was bullshit. How else were you going to know if the man had been drinking? Then there were cases of driving while intoxicated which he would bring in, only to find later he was told to drop the charges. It did not take him too long to find out what was going on. These drivers were paying bribes to some of the senior deputies to have evidence destroyed or to get the paperwork fixed. McDougal started taking his own blood samples and then he tape-recorded some conversations in the sheriff's department. The next time he discovered a driver bribing his way out of trouble, he went and complained to his bosses and told them that law enforcement in Montgomery County was a joke. That was when they fired him.

Since then he had been fighting and looking over his shoulder. He had taken his evidence to the DA's office and, just in case they got any ideas about covering it up, he had taken it to the press, too. Already, three senior deputies had been forced to resign, and Jim McDougal was still gathering evidence – about illegal phone tapping, about the reason why no cocaine dealers had been busted in Montgomery County, and about the hit squad of deputies which settled scores with people who dared to cross the courthouse. That was what worried him. Just the other day, his neighbour had seen a car going by real slowly, stopping right by McDougal's driveway. The neighbour had taken the number and McDougal had traced it. Sure enough, it belonged to a detective from the Hit Squad. 'I went straight into the sheriff's department and I told them to get their people away from me or there's gonna be trouble. And I told 'em I'm not kidding.'

Jim McDougal's allegations were only part of an avalanche of complaints which tumbled down on Conroe as the Clarence Brandley case came to a head. In a way, it was like the summer when the Brandley case had begun, back in August 1980, when the land had been poisoned by the sun and every living thing was withered and brown and wild fire had broken out every day in some different corner of the country, and the firemen had raced from one outbreak to another trying to keep control. Only now, it was not fire but some kind of rotteness in the town that kept breaking out, as if all the corruption and greed could no longer be contained. Peter Speers was in the middle of it all, rushing from one crisis to another.

There was a wrecker driver, Vernon Cowan, who said he had been pushed out of business by Sheriff Joe Corley because he refused to pay him money. Since then, Cowan said, he had been shot at, beaten and robbed by a deputy, had his house burned to the ground by deputies, had three cars and two trucks torched, seen police cars prowling round his house and been the victim of a failed attempt to plant stolen goods in his truck. One of Cowan's sons, John, said he had been beaten by deputies until he had agreed to make a statement against his father. Another son, Jay, said deputies brutalized him and threatened him with homosexual rape until he agreed to make a similar statement. A Houston journalist who started to investigate had his windows shot out, and Cowan's attorney, a former FBI agent named Phil Swisher, said that deputies had tried to plant cocaine in his car and that someone had fired shots into his home.

A federal jury found that Sheriff Corley had been routinely beating up prisoners in his custody. The jury ordered the county to pay $40,000 damages, but the sheriff lodged an appeal. A former chief deputy, Steve Graeter, told the federal jury how Sheriff Corley had strapped a prisoner into a barber's chair and punched him until he was exhausted and how he had been victimized for trying to expose the incident. A prisoner who complained that the sheriff broke his nose and jaw said he had been shot at, hit by a speeding car, and arrested by deputies who carried machine-guns and who ordered him to crawl through the dirt and tried to force him to drop his complaint.

A group of ex-prisoners joined the wrecker driver's family in suing Montgomery County Sheriff's Department under the RICO statute. As far as they knew, it was the first time that the anti-Mafia law had ever been used against a law enforcement agency.

A scandal rocked the county's Republican party, which had ridden to power in Conroe on Ronald Reagan's coat-tails, ending decades of Democratic supremacy, and which now numbered numerous former Democrats including Jim Keeshan and Peter Speers among its members. One of the party's biggest wheels, County Commissioner Weldon Locke, was arrested and charged with swindling $220,000 out of county funds. A Justice of the Peace had been helping him in the swindle. A local couple, Kaye and Joe McCoy who helped to unearth the evidence of his corruption, complained that the DA's office had tried to persuade them that Locke had committed no offence and that a Conroe judge had issued an unlawful gagging order against them, forbidding them to say anything which might embarrass Locke. On the day he was due to appear in the courthouse to be arraigned, Locke was run down by a cement truck on I-45. Some people in the town said he had been murdered to stop him exposing corruption by other big wheels in the Republican party. But the Houston medical examiner, Dr Joseph Jachimczyk, looked into it and said it was certainly suicide.

Another county commissioner, 'Bo' Calfee, admitted accepting $9,000 from a businessman. In separate incidents, five different Justices of the Peace were caught embezzling public money. A 76-year-old municipal judge admitted soliciting sexual favours from a 21-year-old woman who was trying to pay an overdue traffic ticket. An official in the county tax collector's office was charged with stealing nearly $3,000 from public funds. A county constable admitted forging records to conceal the disappearance of money from his office. Three jailers were sacked for taking a prisoner on a two-day shopping spree. Eight Conroe officials admitted they had received illegal campaign contributions. The minister of the First Methodist Church was gaoled for ten years after failing to pay $89,000 restitution to two elderly spinsters he swindled in a crooked land deal. Two employees of the school district were investigated, one for embezzling $25,000, the other for molesting young children. A deputy, who had been fired from two previous law enforcement jobs for sexually assaulting young women, was fired again after a 17-year-old Californian girl complained that she had been forced to have oral sex with him. A new hearing for a convicted murderer, Glenn Earl Martin, was delayed because key evidence had gone missing from the courthouse.

Yet just as the white people of Conroe overlooked the truth about black people in their town, so they appeared to accept the corruption of officials as if it were part of their way of life. There was no campaign in the *Courier* to clean up the courthouse. There was no outcry from the city council or the county commissioners. Corruption had become so common that it was no longer controversial. For generations, the courthouse had respected the law in the morning and ignored it in the afternoon. If the rules were in the way, they were simply set aside as an inconvenience. It had been that way in the old days, and it had not changed. Corruption had become a habit. And the people of Conroe continued to tolerate it as if, by denying that their leaders were corrupt, they could excuse themselves for having elected them.

In the autumn of 1988, there were elections in Conroe. The townspeople had a chance to register their feelings about some of the officials who had run the Brandley case and who had been hit by the avalanche of new complaints. Peter Speers and Judge John Martin were the only officials from the Brandley case who had to stand that year. Both had been condemned by Judge Pickett, both had played key roles in pursuing a man who had now been declared innocent; yet the people of Conroe voted both of them back into office for new four-year terms. Sheriff Joe Corley also had to stand. A federal jury had condemned him for beating prisoners, and he, too, was given the support of his town.

By the autumn of 1988, Clarence Brandley had seen 27 men led through the door at the end of Death Row to be killed in Huntsville. Every time it happened it was tough. Inside that place, you got close to people. You had to if you were going to survive. So when another man was taken away, everybody felt it. After Galveston, it had all been different. The other guys could hardly believe the things that had come out at that hearing. Then he had won. And when he won, they all won. They all scored a point against the system and, more than that, if he finally ended up raising some big legal issue, there were guys in there whose lives might also be saved because of it. Then as the months passed and the judges in Austin still showed no sign of interest in Judge Pickett's urgent demand for justice, they relapsed into pessimism and hopelessness.

Brandley became increasingly afraid that the judges were more interested in pleasing their white voters than in seeing justice done. They had waited for the primaries to be out of the way before they decided that they needed written briefs from the attorneys. They had had the briefs since June and yet they had said nothing.

In July of 1988, in Princeton, in an elegant house where Woodrow Wilson once lived, a man with a white collar around his neck and a crucifix on the wall heard that the nine judges had gone off for their summer vacations without a word about Clarence Brandley. 'Those sons of bitches,' he said.

Brandley believed that the judges were now holding out for the November election. Sure enough, no sooner had the judges been re-elected to their jobs than they announced that they would hold a hearing to consider Brandley's case. They made their announcement one year and eleven days after Judge Pickett ruled that his incarceration was an affront to justice.

Brandley's brother, O. T., told the press: 'I guess this is progress, but it takes longer for a black person to get justice than it takes for a white person.' The hearing was set for 18 January.

The day before the hearing, Mike de Geurin flew into Austin from Houston, holding a legal notepad on which he had written four words. They were the heart of the message he was going to try to present to the nine judges the next day. He had written: 'Bumblebee on a billboard'.

It was something his father, who had been an attorney and then a judge, had once told him: that you must never get so close to the fragmented detail and dry legalities of a case that the big picture is lost the way the message on a billboard is hidden from a bumble bee in the middle of it.

De Geurin was trying hard to feel confident, but it was not easy. If these judges had wanted to see the big picture – that Brandley was innocent and had to be released – then they would have opened the door of his cell months ago, back when the case was fresh after the hearing in Galveston. Instead, it seemed, they had crawled over the meat of the case like so many fat-bellied flies and dropped little seeds of doubt all over it which were now hatching out into a squirming mass of tiny questions, eating into the case, completely obscuring its true shape.

In purely legal terms, Clarence Brandley's claim on freedom had come down to seven 'grounds for relief', yet the court had now asked the attorneys to address them on only three of them. That suggested that the judges had already made up their minds on the other four. And surely, De Geurin believed, if they had made up their minds in favour of the defence on even one of those four points, they would have declared that there was a reason for Brandley to have a new trial. Their silence suggested that the defence had already lost four of the seven grounds.

Those four points covered all the evidence of secret meetings between Jim Keeshan and the Conroe judges; the whole story of the cover-up of the missing exhibits; the suppression of the Ranger's recording of his conversation with Icky Peace; and, most important of all, the central contention that Clarence Brandley was an innocent man.

In De Geurin's mind, the only way that the court could possibly have rejected all that evidence, complete with Judge Pickett's conclusion that it was credible and true, was if they had allowed it to be eaten away by legal technicalities – that the evidence should not have been admitted at Galveston, or that the complaints had already been rejected at previous hearings, or that the issues should have been raised earlier. Or – worst of all – that innocence was irrelevant if it could be proved only with facts which were introduced more than 30 days after the original conviction.

The big picture was being lost. Still, De Geurin believed there was great power in the three remaining points. The first was the blind focus of the investigation into Cheryl Fergeson's murder – the intimidation of witnesses and the suppression of any clue that led anywhere other than the black janitor. The second – and linked – argument was about racism and the history of a black man accused of a crime in a white town. Their third point was that Brandley had been denied due process by the loss of crucial evidence such as the semen swabs and the hairs found on the dead girl's body.

Even though there was power in the remaining arguments, De Geurin was still troubled – by the judges themselves. Only two of them had been elected as liberals. Several of the others were notoriously conservative. There was a chance that the defence were dealing with a built-in majority which had already secured a 15-month delay and demolished four of their arguments, and which would shy away from the political consequences of accepting that Conroe and its courthouse were corrupt. The defence had left Galveston with a total victory. Now they were fighting for survival again, with their chances of winning perhaps as low as two out of nine.

The possibility that Brandley could yet be cheated of his life was now more galling than ever: as the weeks dragged by, new evidence to confirm all their theories about the case kept dropping into their lap. Two of the members of the original Grand Jury which had indicted Brandley in September 1980 separately approached Don Brown – nervously and secretly – to confide that Jim Keeshan had done something highly irregular at the end of the hearing. Despite Keeshan's ferocious questioning of the black janitor, fewer than the required nine members of the Grand Jury had wanted to indict him. Keeshan, according to both Grand Jurors, finally swung the vote only by telling the Grand Jury that he had more evidence against Brandley – evidence which would prove beyond any doubt that he was guilty, but which he was unable to put before them at that moment. The DA's claim had swung the Grand Jury, according to Brown's informants, even though it now appeared that the claim had been dishonest.

Then there was a woman who approached the defence – again nervously and secretly – to say that at the time of Brandley's trials, there had been a janitor from the high school lodging in her house. She was not saying he was involved with the murder. It was a smaller – but revealing – point. This janitor had keys to doors all over the school. She had seen them in her house, so she knew that Brandley was telling the truth when he said he was not the only one with keys. She thought it was important, and back in 1980 she had called the District Attorney's office to tell them. According to the rules, the DA should have passed on her information to the defence. But he had not.

The most tantalizing new information surfaced in early January, as the attorneys prepared for their hearing in Austin. A woman called up Don Brown and said that Gary Acreman had confessed to her that he had killed Cheryl Fergeson.

Her story was that Acreman had been working for her as a security guard and had wanted to be licensed to carry a gun. Looking into his background, she had come across his connection with the Brandley case and had started talking to him about it. Acreman had told her first that he had been a witness in the case, then that he had been present at the school on the day of the killing, then that he knew who had really committed the crime. Finally, he had told her: 'I was one of them that done it, but the nigger's gonna swing for it.'

That was not all. The woman said that she had immediately fired Acreman and had then contacted the Montgomery County sheriff's department to tell them what he had said. And they had told her not to say anything to anyone about it.

The difficulty was knowing how to use all this information. Reyna and McCloskey wanted to hold a press conference, so that the court in Austin would be forcefully reminded of the big picture. But the three attorneys were not so sure. They saw a risk of alienating the court, which might complain that the defence was trying to put improper pressure on them. There was also the risk – closer to a certainty – that the courthouse in Conroe would start twisting and turning the new information: investigators in big boots would go round and tell the woman she was a liar; Gary Acreman would say he had never said any such thing; Peter Speers would tell the *Courier* that this was all illogical and offensive; the whole issue would soon become lost in lies. The defence decided to hold on to their affidavit and try and trust the nine judges to do their job.

The hearing was due to start at 1.30 p.m. on that Wednesday, 18 January 1989. All through the morning, knots of people started to gather beneath the heavy stone memorials to confederate heroes around the pink granite capitol building in the centre of Austin. It was a cool, grey day. Revd Boney was there. Since Galveston, he had been organizing sporadic raids to keep the Brandley case alive: rallying outside Huntsville Jail; burning the Confederate flag outside the State Capitol; filling a section of the Astrodome during a Houston Astros game with people wearing 'Free Clarence Brandley' T-shirts; running a 'bike ride for Brandley' and a rolling hunger strike, in which supporters took it in turns day by day to fast for 24 hours in solidarity with Brandley. That morning, he and 30 other supporters had visited the State Commission on Judicial Conduct to file a formal complaint against Judge James Keeshan and Judge John Martin, calling for their immediate removal from office because of their 'heinous and reprehensible judicial misconduct'.

As more supporters arrived by car and bus from Dugan and Houston – some after journeys that had started before sunrise –

the lobby outside the Court of Criminal Appeals filled to capacity and then kept filling, first scores and then hundreds of people swarming and pushing round the door to the court, which was closed.

Brandley's mother and father were there, leaning on each others' arms, united despite their long divorce by fear for their son. Richard Reyna was there with Mike De Geurin's wife and elderly mother and Paul Nugent's wife. Jim Keeshan's father was there, holding the front of the line, with Peter Speers's wife and Carol Williams of the *Courier*. Gwynn Fergeson, sister-in-law of the dead girl, was there, too. Almost the whole cast of characters from the long saga of Clarence Brandley was there for this legal climax, not merely because it was a climax but because, despite all the certainties of Galveston, its outcome was now in doubt. The one figure who was conspicuously absent was the central character who had not been allowed to come to court to be a spectator of his own fate.

Revd Boney appealed for calm and reminded Brandley's supporters that they must neither cheer nor jeer. A minister called for a moment's silent prayer. There were scuffles at the front of the line as reporters and supporters clashed. Then they opened the doors and Clarence Brandley's supporters flooded in. Paul Nugent's wife, Mary, a Texan with the looks of a Californian and the politics of a Massachusetts liberal, immediately spotted something which started her blood boiling. Peter Speers's wife had seized a seat in the front row and, despite the milling crowd, she had reserved an empty seat next to her. Mary Nugent had learned to dislike Mrs Speers at Galveston and she could see no reason why she should be reserving seats while others were standing and waiting outside, so she went and sat right down in it. Mrs Speers protested. Mary Nugent held her ground. The two women then sat, elbow to elbow, stealing hostile glances at each other.

Just after 1.30 p.m., when the nine judges paraded on to their raised platform at the end of the room to take their places in the arc of high-backed green chairs, they looked down on rows of seats which normally stood empty but which were now filled from front to back with strangers and which were surrounded on all sides, on every spare space of carpet, by more spectators, many of them spilling out of the doors and into the lobby, all of them gazing anxiously up at them. The judges looked nervous. A detective game began.

Everyone was looking for clues. The three defence attorneys – Brown, De Geurin and Nugent – the two Conroe prosecutors – Peter Speers and Rick Stover – seated at their tables at the feet of the judges, the spectators and the supporters and the relatives and the friends were all looking for clues, all hanging on every hint of a movement from any of the judges that might betray the way they were thinking.

Mike De Geurin watched them as he stepped forward from his table to take the podium. 'It's been a long journey to get here,' he began, 'and there's a lot to be said. So much to be said and so little time.' It was a gentle dig at the judges who had waited 15 months to hear the case and who had now ordered each side to restrict its submission to a total of 20 minutes. To make room for Paul Nugent's submission and for any argument that might develop, De Geurin had to try to concentrate all his thoughts into exactly six minutes. The judges leaned into the high backs of their chairs, impassively ignoring the dig.

De Geurin struck at the heart of the matter. 'There is one inescapable fact and that is that a truly innocent man has been condemned to death. How did this happen? What can be done about it? It's not realistic and probably impossible to point to any one minute fact that caused this tragic thing to happen. My fear and concern is that we might – at the urging of the prosecution – dissect this tragedy into such minute particles that we will lose sight of the big picture – much like a bumblebee on a billboard. Too close to read the message.'

De Geurin scanned the faces on the platform. Not a flicker of a smile, not even a hint of irritation. He pushed the same point again, harder. 'On behalf of Clarence Lee Brandley, on behalf of his family and on behalf of the people of Texas, I beg this court not to lose sight of the illness while it studies the germ.'

Still no reaction. But if the judges were determined to remain unmoved, something was nevertheless stirring in the rest of the courtroom. There was no cheering or jeering, not even any whispering or sighing. It was nothing that was said, only an intense concentration, a silence so deliberate that it screamed, as one by one the faces in the seats settled into a mould of subdued resistance, a glowering resentment. The more De Geurin spoke, the more tangible it became. By the time he had finished his whirlwind legal argument, a kind of dignity had descended on the silent spectators, like mourners at a funeral whose pain is so deep that they choose not to share it.

Now, Paul Nugent came to the podium and spoke directly to the heart of their pain, recalling the now-familiar incidents of racism in the case, trying to compel the judges to react. 'As much as we would like to say it didn't happen, as much as we would like to say "This is the 1980s and we are not in the 1930s or 40s", as much as we would like to close our eyes to reality, the fact is that the colour of Clarence Brandley's skin was a factor in this case.'

The pain belonged not only to Clarence Brandley. The nigger who was elected to take the blame might just as easily have been any other black man in Conroe. The nigger who was not allowed to get bail might just as easily have been any other black man or woman trapped in a white courthouse. The black man who had been dispatched to Death Row by white prosecutors and a white jury serviced by white officials and supervised by a white judge could just as easily have been any one of these black spectators sitting here now – before nine white judges, five white attorneys, six white security men and a scattering of white court officials. Black people only came to court as victims. Clarence Brandley's pain belonged to all those in the court and to all those beyond the court who shared the colour of his skin, to all of them.

At the podium, Nugent was remembering the white woman who sat in a crowded courtroom chanting 'kill the nigger'; the sheriff who said Brandley was a little nigger, and the DA who said Brandley was a little nigger and who spoke for whites and not for blacks. 'As much as we would like to say that this does not happen in 1980 or 1981, that that was part of our past, the record shows that it did happen. The jury would have to have been deaf, dumb and blind not to be influenced by what happened in that courtroom.'

Nugent went back to his seat. Perhaps now, the tide of emotion which had risen in the court was beginning to lap around the feet of the judges. As Peter Speers stepped up to the podium, the judges were still frozen in silence. But as he spoke, they began to break out. Finally, there were some clues to their thinking. Speers was trying to put technical arguments. This idea that the trial was infected by racism, he complained, had never been spelled out in the defence's original writ. 'From a legal point of view,' he said, 'that issue is not even before the court.' Speers agreed that a police officer had said that 'the nigger is elected' and explained that the officer had only said this because he thought Peace was too small to have hauled the dead girl up into the props loft.

One of the judges leaned forward. 'How does that diminish the racial overtone?' he asked.

'If he used a racial epithet,' said Speers, 'that's not to be tolerated or condoned, but it was not his race, it was his stature and build that he was making reference to.'

The judge leaned back again and listened while Speers explained that although the sheriff had called Brandley a nigger, that was just because old-time East Texan sheriffs spoke that way. Anyway, the defence had never mentioned this story in any previous appeal or writ so that, technically, it was not an issue for this court. The judge stared at him grimly.

A moment later, Speers launched into an attack on Judge Pickett, and another judge leaned forward. 'If there is evidence to support a trial judge's findings of fact, then this court will defer to that finding,' he said.

Speers protested. 'You are free to reject them,' he said.

Another judge joined in. 'Has this court ever rejected findings of fact that were supported by the record?'

Speers stammered and the judge repeated his question, which was beginning to sound more like a challenge.

'Right off the top of my head, I can't remember a case,' said Speers, anxiously pinching one thumb with his fingers. 'But if I find such a thing I will absolutely make the court aware of it.'

As the judges started sniping at Peter Speers, Mary Nugent watched the DA's wife beside her starting to pick nervously at the polystyrene cup she was holding. By the time Speers had finished his submission, four different judges had thrown hostile questions at him and the polystyrene cup was in shreds.

Then the time was up. The nine judges stood up and paraded out of the court. The attorneys and the spectators turned and swarmed into the lobby, everybody adding up the clues and exchanging guesswork.

No one could be sure what those judges were thinking. It appeared that at least four of them were on Brandley's side. That included both the known liberals and none of the hardline conservatives. They would need five judges to win a new trial. They were still stuck on the politics of the court. Minnie Ola Brandley spoke for everyone who had come from Dugan and from Houston to support her son. 'I don't know,' she said, 'but I feel better.'

In the cell, nine foot by three foot, Clarence Brandley waited and waited and shaped his life around the court in Austin.

He had been told that the nine judges would announce their decision on a Wednesday. To begin with, after the Austin hearing, he would wait all week until Wednesday morning came around and build up his anticipation to nine o'clock – which was the first moment he reckoned he could hear if the judges had left a decision about him on the table outside their court. Then he would sit by his radio to listen for news.

But there was none and he soon decided that he was cutting it too fine, so he started spending all of Wednesday listening to the radio on the hour every hour in case the news came through later in the day. But there was still none, and he thought that maybe he was still not covering all the options, so he developed a routine where every hour on the hour from Monday through Friday he would turn on his radio to try and find out if the judges had decided to spare him. He took Saturday and Sunday off and then started again on Monday. He found it gave him something to look forward to.

Death Row had changed him. He had grown up and had been awakened to all kinds of things. A bit like when someone loses their sight and develops much sharper hearing to make up for it. He had lost his life out there in the world, so he had developed a life inside his mind to make up for it. He read black history and politics and good novels as well as the Bible. He talked, he thought, he wrote down his thoughts, he still meditated. People who had always known him could hardly believe the change. He had once been shy with people – unless he was out drinking – and he had been bad at putting his ideas into words. But now he seemed to have become more intelligent. He was more articulate and reasoned than he had ever been, and he believed he understood a whole lot of things he never had before.

He had no illusions any more. It seemed crazy now, but for a long time he had thought he was the victim of nothing worse than bad luck, that he was just in the wrong place at the wrong time and that if only he had stayed in bed with Beverley, he would have been free. It was only now, after Galveston and after all his thinking, that he saw the truth. The truth hurt. What hurt the most was that he had never seen it. The truth – which was now as clear as the sun in the sky – was that he had been the victim of racism, not bad luck. If everything that day at the school had been the same, except that he was white, he would never have been arrested. Those dumb cops would have railroaded Icky Peace instead. His skin had shadowed him through every step in that courthouse; it was still shadowing him now. Looking back it was clear; yet he had not seen it. He hadn't seen it all his life. Now he could see how the white people in Conroe had been conditioned, all going to the same schools and then to the same churches and the same social functions. They were all in this white man's union. And he saw how the black people had been living in fear. Ever since he was a child in Dugan he had been conditioned to be frightened – his grandmother warning him about going downtown, his father telling how Putt had died, the old people who remembered what happened to Joe Winters and Bob White, and then Greg Steele. Every day, he had lived with that fear. It had become part of him, like skin. Now, at last, he could see it. He knew things had changed. Sure enough, just 20 or 30 years ago, he would have been dead by now. If a mob hadn't got to him, the old white courts would have finished the job by now. Things had changed just that much. But his skin had not and he was still trapped in it.

It was not only the people of Dugan who knew about Joe Winters and Bob White and Greg Steele. The white people in town remembered, too, but they remembered them a different way. They wrapped up their deaths in the same bundle of discarded history as slavery and the Jim Crow laws. They were all in the past, part of a time when the whole south was like that, nothing to do with Conroe, nothing to do with today. Anyway, hadn't Winters and White been rapists? Greg Steele might not have died so long ago, but hadn't the officer who shot him been tried and acquitted in a court of law? Didn't that prove the killing was just?

But there was something else, something which had vanished entirely from the white people's history of their town. Even the old people in Dugan could hardly grasp it. Their memories were fogged with fear and confusion, but they knew there was more. It was the stuff of legend and rumour, hardly there as memory any more, more like a stain at the back of their minds, something they knew only vaguely and something they knew that they did not really want to know.

Nevertheless, the truth which had been swept aside by the fear of the black people and the self-delusion of the whites did survive – not in living memory, but in yellowed old bundles of newspapers in dusty archives. The truth survived there in all its grim detail – a hidden history of the seeds of violence which had produced the story of Clarence Brandley. For the truth was that, in their short history, the white people of Montgomery County had repeatedly indulged in the public murder of black people. Joe Winters and Bob White and Greg Steele were just three names from a much longer list. These people had killed at least eight other young black men in collective acts of racial hatred: lynchings. Clarence Brandley was the latest in their roll-call of victims.

Andrew McGehee was shot to death in his cell by a mob of white men in Willis, ten miles north of Conroe, on 15 May 1887. He had been accused of attacking a wealthy young white man and was being held for trial, but when the mob arrived, Marshall Goss walked away and let them break in and empty their guns into McGehee where he lay curled up in chains on the floor.

Clem Scott was hanged on 27 February 1908 from the old elm tree outside the courthouse where the people of Conroe used to shelter from the sun. A group of white men said he had been prowling outside a white woman's house, intending to attack her. Sheriff Maben Anderson and his men did nothing to save Clem Scott as the white men bound him tight, slipped a noose over his head and slowly heaved him into the tree, squeezing the breath out of his neck as his feet danced wildly above them. The next day, a Justice of the Peace, C.T. Darby, investigated the death and concluded that he had died 'in the hands of unknown parties'. Darby later became mayor of Conroe.

In one week in March 1908, three men were killed by Montgomery County mobs. On Monday 17 March, James Kinder and Alf Riley were shot to death by an angry crowd in Magnolia, 15 miles south-west of Conroe because, it was said, they had tried to assault a white girl. On Sunday 23 March, in Conroe, an anonymous black man was accused of prowling near a white woman's house, and was shot through the head.

Warren Lewis died on 23 June 1922, only a month after Joe Winters. Lewis was mentally retarded and made the mistake of walking up to a white woman's house in Dacus, 15 miles north of Conroe, to ask for water. She screamed and Lewis ran. A group of white men went to his house where a crowd of 300 watched as the tearful 18-year-old was pushed up on to the back of a horse, had a rope hooked under his chin and was sent choking into the air. His death was reported on the front page of the *Courier* underneath an advertisement welcoming the citizens of Conroe to the Conroe Methodist Episcopal Church.

Tom Payne was hauled out of a patrol car on North Frazier Street on 2 February 1927, and hanged. He had been arrested earlier that day for robbing and wounding a white lumber millworker named Jack Rogers. The mob was led by Doc Medley, a friend of Rogers and a famous Conroe figure. He weighed some 400 pounds, wore a bushy beard and had a belly like a barrel. The officers in the patrol car, however, said they were unable to identify any of the men who abducted and killed their prisoner.

All this could not be disposed of as unwanted history. No matter what the whites might say, this was part of Conroe today. The sheer number of killings in itself made Brandley's ordeal seem almost inevitable, like the recurrence of an unstoppable pattern.

Despite all the years that separated these other victims from the time of Clarence Brandley, frail threads linked their ordeals to his. Like Brandley, each of them was black and each had been accused of attacking a white person – almost always a white woman – and, like him, they had been condemned by the whole community without hope of defending themselves, while law officers turned a blind eye. There was one victim in particular whose short life was full of potent symbolism for Brandley's supporters – Bennett Jackson, a young farm labourer who died a few days before Christmas 1885, aged only 19, the first of Montgomery County's victims.

Jackson was born the son of emancipated slaves in 1866, the first year of his parents' freedom, the child of a new generation, growing up like Brandley a hundred years later with the promise of liberty. He lived in a lumber town called Mink Prairie, a mean, dusty little place which once stood about 15 miles south-west of Conroe, near where Magnolia stands today.

No one knows too much about why he died. They said he had attacked a white woman and her children. Maybe he did; maybe not. Maybe he was insane. Maybe he committed cold-blooded murder. No one knows, because he was never put on trial, except by 'Judge Lynch', in whose court the regular rules of law meant nothing.

Bennett Jackson's life was as good as over the moment that a Mink Prairie farmer named John Smith came home and found his wife and two children beaten and bloody on the floor of their house. John Smith was one of the most prominent white men in Mink Prairie and, as news of the crime spread, the whole town rose up to find the attacker. Within the day, they had arrested Bennett Jackson. At first, they were content to send him up to Montgomery, which was then the county seat, for him to be tried and dealt with by old Judge Masterson. Then came word that one of John Smith's children had died from injuries inflicted in the attack. Now the whole community rose again.

There was never any doubt about what was going to happen. In Houston, the *Post* of Saturday 19 December 1885, declared in its headline 'Judge Lynch Will Preside In Montgomery Today'. The *Post* explained that Judge Masterson had tried to send Jackson to Houston for safe-keeping but that 'the people in the majesty of their might would not permit it'. The town had planned to kill Jackson on Friday but then, out of respect for Judge Masterson who was still holding court in Montgomery, 'the lynching picnic was postponed until Saturday'.

The *Post* understood the way the town felt: 'No man in this county feels that his wife and children are safe from outrage and murder as long as so fearful a demon lives . . . A thrilling time is expected here. If he is lynched, however, it will be openly and boldly done without disguise or any attempt at secrecy. It will be the act of the people . . . Every good citizen approves of the lynching as the negro outrages are too frequent in this section.'

In the small hours of Saturday morning, a crowd of white men took Bennett Jackson from his prison cell and led him into the woods. History does not record what they did to him there, but Jackson was still alive at noon when he was dragged into the middle of Montgomery. The whole town had gathered in front of the courthouse to see the spectacle. Men, women and children filled the square. According to the Houston *Post*, it was 'the leading citizens of the county' who then bundled Bennett Jackson on to the back of a horse, ran a rope over the branch of a stout tree, looped the noose around the young man's neck, and jerked the horse away. Bennett Jackson was soon dead.

The story of Clarence Brandley rang with echoes of Bennett Jackson's ordeal: the rules of law that had been abandoned; the Judge who had fallen in with the mob; the press that had relished his fate; the 'leading citizens of the county' who had committed the crime; the bodyguard of new civil rights which had turned and deserted him; the whole town that had stood by and let it happen. And that was the loudest echo of all.

The whole town had been tangled in the death of Bennett Jackson. There were those who held the rope and those who held the man and those who hurled the rope over the limb of a stout tree and those who sent his body wriggling into the air, and then there were also all those who watched and even a few who looked away, but all of them – the ringleaders and the bystanders – were involved in Bennett Jackson's death.

That was how it was in Conroe as Clarence Brandley waited for his freedom. The whole town knew what their ringleaders in the courthouse had been doing. They knew what Judge Pickett had found and they knew about the cloud of corruption swirling round their courthouse, and yet they did nothing. The link with the past was more than mere symbolism. This history of public murder went to the heart of the treatment of Clarence Brandley.

It was part of the corruption which had become their way of life. They had always got away with taking the law into their own hands. After Joe Winters was burned to death, reporters from outside east Texas came to Conroe to find out what had happened. One of them asked Sheriff Hicks why he had not intervened to save the man. The sheriff shrugged him off, saying: 'I just looked away for a moment and when I looked back, the Negro was tied to a burning stake'. The law in Conroe had always looked away. That was why Dude Cochran had been able to walk free after killing Bob White in front of a courtroom full of witnesses. Killing black men was easy.

Not only had they always got away with it, they had also always been able to justify it. Killing one black man was a means of disciplining the whole of his community. Just as a secret police-force tries to quell the courage of a whole people by arresting its figure-heads; just as terrorists try to frighten a whole society by throwing fear into the lives of each of its members, so the white people of Montgomery County had for years ruled black people with fear by picking off their young men. Murder was disguised as a necessary social task. If it was true, as the myths and the jokes pretended, that all niggers were lazy and dishonest rapists, then it was essential for whites to teach them a lesson, to keep them in line. They were always open and sincere about it. In March 1908, when the people of Montgomery County murdered three young black men in one week, the Houston *Post* reported an incident in Palestine, north of Conroe, outside the county, in which a black hack driver had been attacked for complaining about the way one of his friends had been abused. The *Post* reported: 'A band of determined men took him in hand and when they finished their work, the Negro's hide would not hold shucks. There is an element of lawless Negroes in Palestine who become very insolent just before an election. The people, however, because of several recent trying situations, have become of one mind, and that is to suppress this element, and the Saturday affair is but an indicator of what will happen if this element persists in lawlessness.'

In Conroe, in 1989, the ringleaders of the attack on Clarence Brandley were still getting away with everything they had done, still proudly justifying themselves.

Behind his large, wooden desk in the DA's office, Peter Speers was full of boyish enthusiasm for the cause. Brandley was a vicious killer who deserved to die, he said, and Brandley's defenders were all crooked. 'I'm convinced that a large part of what the defence has been doing is literally for publicity – not because they think it is legally valid in any way. De Geurin and those attorneys are not working for free. Do you think McCloskey and Reyna are working for free? The more sensational they can make this case in the news media, the more money they can raise for themselves. That's what this is all about.' And Judge Pickett? He was crooked, too. 'All this crap about the Constitution. I categorically deny that any injustice was done to Clarence Brandley. Pickett gives off all this mumbo-jumbo. It's outrageous. I have been told that Judge Pickett is an old personal friend of Percy Foreman, which might explain why he was so totally biased.'

Jim Keeshan was just as confident. Revd Boney might have reported him and John Martin to the State Commission on Judicial Conduct. A veteran judge might have ruled that he had lied on oath and perverted the course of justice, but he was unmoved. 'I'm proud of my efforts in the Brandley case,' he said. 'I'm proud of how I carried out my duties the best way I know how. I don't have anything I should feel ashamed about regarding that prosecution.'

If any doubt remained that the killing of unruly young black men was still an acceptable necessity in East Texas, it was soon dispelled when the roll-call of victims gathered two more names.

Loyal Garner died in the county jail in Hemphill, about 100 miles north-east of Conroe on 27 December 1987. He had never been in trouble in his life and was, in the words of a white friend, 'the finest man I ever met in my life, white or black'. He was stopped by a group of white policemen, who accused him of drunken driving and locked him up without allowing him to call his wife to tell her and his six children what had happened. According to two friends who were arrested with him, the police lost their tempers when Garner beat on his cell door demanding to be released. Several officers took him away, beat him unconscious and then left him lying unattended on his cell floor all night, breathing unsteadily through his bloody mouth. He died the next day without regaining consciousness. According to the police, they hit Garner only once after he attacked them in a drunken rage. They suggested he might have hurt himself by falling over a chair and they claimed he was a drug trafficker. A Hemphill jury cleared the police of all wrongdoing.

Hambone Simpson had been in trouble all his life. He was found dead in a cell in Cleveland Police Station (where Icky Peace was questioned by Wes Styles) after being 'subdued' by 11 officers on 16 March 1988. The man in the next cell said he had heard Simpson pleading for his life. An autopsy found that pressure had been applied to his neck and a Justice of the Peace said his neck was bruised with finger-marks. The Texas Rangers were called in to investigate. The police explained that they had had to subdue him because they had found him smoking marijuana, which had not been detected in any search. One officer claimed that he had tape-recorded the whole incident and that the tape proved that Simpson was still alive when they left his cell. The assistant Attorney General for Texas, David Hess (who supervised the inquiry into the Brandley case) announced that Simpson had probably died from 'positional asphyxia' – a condition in which someone lying in an awkward position may block their windpipe with their own body-weight. Hess conceded that this was a rare cause of death but added that it had been found to occur in police cells. The Texas Rangers concluded that no officer should be prosecuted for any offence and a Cleveland Grand Jury agreed.

Hemphill. Cleveland. Conroe. They are all the kind of towns that strangers never notice because they are all the same. They all have the railway tracks that split the whites from the blacks, and split the power and the wealth the same way. They are all peaceful and plump and content to remain obscure. The civil rights laws hit the racism in these towns like a knife stabbing the wind. The laws might have changed them more if the racism was part of a criminal conspiracy, but towns like Conroe do not work that way. Jim Keeshan and his judges might have put their heads together to plot Brandley's fall, but for the rest there was no need for conspiracy among the smiling racists. Keeshan did not have to go to the Conroe *Courier* and persuade them to prejudice Brandley's trial or, later, to misreport the Galveston hearing. No one had to bribe or bully 23 jurors into finding Brandley guilty. No one had to organize the phone calls that rained down on Bill Srack's head. Mayor Barton did not have to race round the town telling his citizens to deny there had ever been racial problems in Conroe. No one had to persuade the white people of Conroe to insist on Brandley's guilt. There was no need for conspiracy, because each of them in their own right agreed with what was happening. The bystanders not only stood by but welcomed events, just as they always had.

The project to convict Clarence Brandley was never a guilt-riddled conspiracy. It was a popular event, just like the public lynching of Bennett Jackson a hundred years earlier. It was exactly as the *Post* had recorded at the time: 'If he is lynched, it will be openly and boldly done without disguise or any attempt at secrecy ... Every good citizen approves of the lynching as the Negro outrages are too frequent in this section.' It was truly, as the *Post* had said, 'an act of the people'.

On 13 December 1989, more than two years after Judge Pickett called for Clarence Brandley's immediate release, the nine judges in Austin finally published their decision. By six votes to three, they supported all of Perry Pickett's findings of fact, ruled that there had been a blind focus on Clarence Brandley and overturned his conviction. His treatment, they said, had been blatantly unfair and 'a subversion of justice'.

On Death Row in Huntsville, Clarence Brandley met reporters and cried with relief. His family and supporters prayed and celebrated and prepared for his release.

But the ringleaders in the courthouse still would not yield in their righteous mission to kill the black man. Jim Keeshan went on radio stations in Houston to denounce Brandley as a killer. Peter Speers attacked the Austin judges, demanded a second hearing, claimed he would go to the Supreme Court, called press conferences and declared that this was 'the biggest miscarriage of justice I've ever seen'. For a month, they succeeded in stalling Brandley's release. Then, on 22 January, the court in Austin spoke again and formally rejected Speers's request for another hearing. Conroe might still be anchored safely in its history, the 'good ole boys' might still be standing proud, but there was a new wave of courage sweeping by them. The truth was not their property any more. Things had changed just that much.

Peter Speers still insisted that he would go all the way to the Supreme Court in Washington, but Mike De Geurin flew to Austin and told the judges that it was over. Peter Speers could do what he liked but it was time for the victim to be released. The judges agreed and gave him bail.

And so, on Tuesday 23 January 1990, just after noon – nine years, four months and 25 days after he was first put in chains – Clarence Lee Brandley walked through the heavy gates of Death Row and out into the sunlight. There were photographers and film crews, a whole lot of cheering and crying and general confusion; but the final fact was clear as day. He was free at last.

Epilogue

Because this is a true story, it does not have the tidy, convenient ending that a piece of fiction might. Despite numerous investigations, there are still little mysteries lurking in the background. It is impossible, for example, to be sure what really happened to the exhibits which went missing from the courthouse in Conroe in January 1982. The same is true of all the disappearing evidence: the swabs from the post-mortem, the photographs which would have shown that Brandley was not wearing a belt on the day of the crime, the original statement made by Jo Ellen Parrish. In the context of all that is now known about the case, it is reasonable to guess that one or more malevolent figures in the courthouse were responsible for the disappearance of all this material. But it can only be a guess, and so I have held back from giving any definitive conclusion.

The story is unfinished, too, in the sense that justice is still catching up with its various characters. Some of the minor players have already been caught. The police officer who killed Greg Steele has been gaoled for robbing a bank. Jo Ellen Parrish, the prostitute whose claim that she had been raped by Clarence Brandley helped Jim Keeshan have him sentenced to death, has been charged with possession of cocaine. Duke Bodisch has been sacked from the Attorney General's office for exploiting his position there to try and write a book about the Brandley case.

At the other end of the moral scale, Jim McCloskey has now won the freedom of eight innocent men and women who had been wrongly jailed, and Richard Reyna has become a regular partner in his investigations. Don Brown is still tussling with the courthouse in Conroe and has succeeded in running a campaign to have a woman Democrat elected Mayor instead of Carl Barton. Percy

Foreman died in the summer of 1988, but Mike De Geurin and Paul Nugent are still fighting the good fight in the courtrooms of East Texas and telling Percy Foreman stories. Revd Don Boney launched a new campaign for black workers in Houston and was cleared of possessing cocaine. Clarence Brandley spent the first 9 months of his freedom under a cloud, while Peter Speers petitioned the Supreme Court in Washington, D. C. to send him back to Death Row. Finally, on October 1 1990, the court threw out Speers's application and the District Attorney conceded defeat. Brandley became a Baptist minister in Houston, trained to work as an electrician, and got married. He never set foot in Conroe again.

Yet there are others for whom justice is still waiting in the wings. More than three years after Judge Perry Pickett found that they had perverted the course of justice and lied on oath, Jim Keeshan and John Martin still sit in judgement in the Conroe courthouse, and the Texas Commission on Judicial Conduct has still not seen fit to take action against them. The various law officers who conspired to send Brandley to Death Row have all kept their jobs or retired peacefully. Gary Acreman and James Dexter Robinson have never been arrested and questioned.

The ordeal which Clarence Brandley suffered was effectively a legal lynching. It was the law and not an old rope which was twisted into a deadly weapon, but the intention of those who attacked him was to kill him just as surely as their predecessors had killed young black men in the past. His supporters were strong enough to rescue him and save his life. Their strength derived from their own inner resources and also from the past victories of others like them who had fought in the civil rights movement, but still there was a limit to what they could do. As a result, the lynch mob is still free, and in that very important respect, this story still has no ending.